ROGER STEVENSON
MAY, 1996

WHAT AMERICAN LEADERS SAY ABOUT
FACING UP

"*Facing Up* is an impressive book about an issue of tremendous consequence to all of us. Peter Peterson's insights provide us with a balanced and sensible way to reduce the deficit, restore economic growth, respond to the challenge of global competition, and ensure an equitable future for succeeding generations of Americans."
   —DAVID ROCKEFELLER, *former Chairman, Chase Manhattan Bank*

"Pete Peterson's *Facing Up* is the best up-to-date analysis of the nation's budget deficit problem. He shows us why the Clinton budget won't do the job and offers the kinds of practical deficit-cutting options that will be needed to revive the economy's long-term economic growth."
   —DR. MARTIN FELDSTEIN, *President of the National Bureau of Economic Research and former Chairman of the Council of Economic Advisers*

"*Facing Up* is the culmination of a decade of Peterson's intense study of the budget, combining his unique business, financial, and government experience. It provides the definitive program for resolving America's premier economic problem. It is the benchmark against which Clinton and all others should be judged."
   —C. FRED BERGSTEN, *Director, Institute for International Economics*

"*Facing Up* is a frank and compelling account of how government debt threatens our financial future. Peterson tells hard truths about our condition, and proposes strong medicine to deal with it. There is much in this book with which to agree and disagree. But *Facing Up* is certain to spark controversy and promote a long overdue debate on what we need to do to put our financial house in order."
   —WILLIAM E. SIMON, *former Secretary of the Treasury*

"This superb book comes to us from America's most articulate and persistent voice on the price the next generation will have to pay for our profligacy. All of us who care about the nation's future should read *Facing Up* and then share it with a friend under thirty-five . . . ideally an adult child of our own!"
   —JAMES E. BURKE, *Chairman, Partnership for a Drug-Free America, former Chairman and CEO of Johnson & Johnson*

FACING UP

How to Rescue the Economy from Crushing Debt and Restore the American Dream

by Peter G. Peterson

Foreword by
Senators Warren B. Rudman and Paul E. Tsongas

SIMON & SCHUSTER

New York   London   Toronto   Sydney   Tokyo   Singapore

SIMON & SCHUSTER
Rockefeller Center
1230 Avenue of the Americas
New York, New York 10020

Designed by Irving Perkins Associates
Manufactured in the United States of America

1   3   5   7   9   10   8   6   4   2

Library of Congress Cataloging-in-Publication Data
Peterson, Peter G.
Facing up : how to rescue the economy from crushing debt and
restore the American dream / by Peter G. Peterson.
p.   cm.
1. United States—Economic policy—1981-1993. 2. United States—
Economic conditions—1981-   3. Debts, Public—United States.
I. Title.
HC106.8.P458   1993
338.973′009′048—dc20   93-30838
CIP
ISBN: 0-671-79642-9

*for my grandchildren, Alexandra, Peter Cary, and Steven,
and all the other children of their generation*

Table of Contents

PART II
The Choices We Must Make

Acknowledgments

A great many people have helped me in bringing this book from the idea stage to the printed page. As a self-styled vicar of the need for Americans to take responsibility and make tough choices, let me stipulate that the responsibility for the argument in this volume—and therefore any flaws in it—rests squarely with me. However, I also want to express my appreciation for the help that others have given me throughout the process. I cannot hope to mention all of them here, but I would like to acknowledge the vital contributions of a number of them.

First of all, I want to thank two great American patriots, Senators Warren B. Rudman and Paul E. Tsongas, not only for supplying the foreword to this book but, more important, for their great contributions as cofounding chairmen of The Concord Coalition. I'm also very grateful to Ross Perot for his help in paving the way for getting the message of *Facing Up* to the American people.

The development of the substantive content of this book was greatly aided by the efforts of a talented team of researchers and advisors. Neil Howe should come first on this list by any reasonable standard. He and I have worked together for ten years on virtually every subject in this book—competitiveness, productivity, deficits, and, certainly, entitlements, on which he is an acknowledged world-class expert. Happily, in more recent times, he has also brought along his able colleague and a genuine expert in health care, Richard Jackson. When I asked another fine contributor, Martha Phillips, executive director of The Concord Coalition, who could provide me with the best data on the income and tax effects of our various proposals, she instantly said Pete Davis, and she was right. Jim Sebenius and I have been long-time collaborators in business and public policy, and he has helped me in particularly material ways in thinking through what national security means these days. Finally, there is Dan Burstein, whose idea culminated in this book. He was there for me every step of the way.

Other wise friends have, over the years, tried to teach me, with only some success, some of the important lessons of economics and political life: Fred Bergsten, Harold Brown, Jim Burke, Jason Epstein, Marty Feldstein, Larry Kotlikoff, Peggy Noonan, Fred Plum, David Rockefeller, David Sawyer, Diane Sawyer, George Shultz, Bill Simon, Tony Solomon, David Stockman, Phil Verleger, Paul Volcker, John White, Dan Yankelovich. Nor should I neglect Tom Bayard, Richard Beattie, Michael Brockman, Ty Cobb, Bob Gaskin, Les Gelb, Bill Hoehn, Charles Iceland, Jim Smallhout, Susan Tanaka, Jerry Traum, and Carolyn Weiner, who always responded helpfully to my usually unreasonable requests in connection with this book.

The Atlantic Monthly and *The New York Review of Books* opened their pages to extensive articles based on the ideas in this book. For their support and encouragement I would like to thank Jack Beatty, Bill Whitworth, and Mort Zuckerman at the *Atlantic* as well as Bob Silvers and Barbara Epstein at the *New York Review.*

I must also mention the tireless support, long hours put in, and supreme organizational skills of my assistants, Linda Vitulano and Patricia Wilkinson; the word-processing assistance I received from Paul Tepperman; and help on every logistical front from Frank Pena. I would also like to thank Peter Bradford, who designed the charts that appear in this book, for his efforts in helping the reader visualize the issues I discuss.

On the publishing front, a special debt of gratitude is owed to Frederic W. Hills, my editor at Simon & Schuster, who believed in the importance of this book from the first outline he saw of it and shepherded it through an arduous and uncertain publishing process. I would also like to thank Carolyn Reidy, Wendy Nicholson, and the many people at Simon & Schuster who nurtured this book, and supported it, and labored over its many drafts, changes, and updates.

I also thank my Blackstone partners for their understanding and support.

Finally, I must express my deepest appreciation to my family and, in particular, to my wife, Joan Ganz Cooney, who has probably put up with more preoccupied weekends than any spouse in America.

To these, and many more, I say thank you.

Peter G. Peterson

Foreword

by Senators Warren B. Rudman and Paul E. Tsongas

We come from different parties in a political system that has made disagreement and confrontation a way of life in Washington. Many issues continue to divide us, our former Senate colleagues, and our parties. Yet on the most fundamental question facing us as Americans—our long-term economic predicament—we have found a remarkable expanse of common ground.

Today, with a new President in office and a spirit of hope in the air, the challenge is clear. We see a nation whose economy is plainly failing to meet the needs and aspirations of its people. Staggering deficits choke off critical public and private investments. The quality of our educational system erodes as our once-dazzling infrastructure buckles. Our nation is becoming two polarized Americas, one privileged, one poor. Our productivity grows meagerly compared to our competitors'; our savings and investment rates are a fraction of theirs. The general interest and the future are drowned out by the strident claims of today's special interests. Even at a time when the electorate has made it clear it wants change, many elected officials dare not speak the truth.

Son of poor Greek immigrants, Pete Peterson exemplifies the power of the American Dream for his generation, having risen to the presidency of a major corporation, served as a cabinet officer, and founded a successful investment bank of which he is now chairman. In Pete's view, as in ours, the American Dream—the promise of steady improvement in private and public life and parents' conviction that their children's lives would be better than their own—is now at risk of extinction for many citizens and may survive for future generations as but a wisp of historical memory.

Pete's concerns about these issues have transcended partisanship. He has always made it clear that no progress can be made if the focus is on narrow partisan blame. The only solutions to America's economic problems are nonpartisan solutions—a point he emphasized when he encouraged us to come together to head The Concord Coalition.

This coalition is a nonpartisan grass-roots organization of American citizens dedicated to telling the truth about our economic predicament, to working with our fellow citizens to shape the hard choices we must face as a nation, to debating those choices with the national interest and future generations uppermost in mind, to empowering citizens who want honesty and real change but do not know where to turn, and to empowering political leaders who need the force and support of public opinion to act as they must to solve our problems. Our goal is formulating and building support for a realistic long-term program that will pull America out of economic stagnation and enable a stronger, richer, and fairer nation to emerge.

The Concord Coalition has no orthodoxy, no programmatic litmus test for membership. Yet it passionately stands behind four principles: telling *hard truths, investing* in America's future rather than consuming it, acting *fairly,* and insisting on the obligation of citizens to inform themselves and to work for the *common good.* Pete's book, *Facing Up,* embodies these principles and represents the culmination of over a decade of one man's analyses and writings aimed at solving America's most pressing problems.

In the words of Robert Louis Stevenson, "Everybody, sooner or later, sits down to a banquet of consequences." As this book makes painfully clear, our generation is enjoying the banquet, and future generations will get the consequences. Our children (and their parents) should read this book to learn what kind of country they will inherit if the debts and deficits of our consumption addiction keep growing at their present rate. They should know about deficits rising to 21 percent of our economy, about forecasts that 32 percent of federal expenditures may go to nothing but servicing the debt, about Social Security and Medicare taxes going from today's 15 percent to as much as 40 percent or more of their payroll, as well as about the equivalent of a $140,000 mortgage each family is leaving to its children in unfunded entitlement benefit liabilities. We and our children should soberly appraise the real risk that these projections—all unsustainable and unthinkable—pose of an ugly generational war as we move into the early decades of the next century.

As Pete points out in these pages, compared with our historical record and with our global competitors, we have become the world champions at borrowing and consuming rather than saving and investing. Once among the world's highest, our net savings rate has fallen to the *bottom* of the industrial world. Since 1980, our cumulative deficits have *quadrupled* the entire national debt run up over the past two centuries. The health and future of our factories, our laboratories, our infrastructure, and the minds of our students have all been placed at unconscionable risk by our failure to invest in them. Somehow we seem to have forgotten that a high-productivity, high-growth, high-wage economy depends on high savings and investments—publicly and privately, in minds and in machines. In the long run, such an economy brings not only a higher private standard of living but also enormous social, public, and environmental improvements.

Pete sets forth a program of broadly shared sacrifice and investment in our collective future that would transform today's fears and pessimism into a bright, sustainable twenty-first century for our generation, our children, and our children's children. But his program is not utopian. Indeed, he is among the few public voices who has chosen to face up to the *politically toxic question of paying for this investment agenda.* The only way to do this is to temporarily restrain the growth of consumption in both the public and private sectors. The surest way to provide the needed resources is to tackle the federal deficit, a pernicious form of negative savings that now devours between half and two-thirds of all private savings.

To cut the deficit, we must debate and enact concrete reforms in our trillion-dollar system of federal entitlements from Social Security, Medicare, and civil service and military pensions to farm supports and to the employer-paid health-care exclusion. We must direct our reform efforts to where these programs provide windfalls to those who don't really need them. We must also enact judicious cuts in defense spending so we are truly prepared for tomorrow's threats, not those of yesterday. We must change our tax policies to favor investment and savings over borrowing and consumption (a prime candidate for such change is our wasteful, inefficient, and environmentally dangerous use of energy). Further, we must drastically overhaul our medical care system to stanch the bleeding not only of public budgets, but of private ones as well. This book offers a fair and comprehensive blueprint for shifting from a consumption-based to a savings- and investment-based economy.

There will be some pain—discomfort, really—as we, the world's leading consumers and borrowers, overcome this consumption and borrowing addiction so we can grow again on a sustained basis. Politicians as usual will pander to this and that special interest group to gain votes. But we are committed to coalescing behind programs on behalf of the general interest, the common good, our future, and our children's future.

As we grow older, the overriding importance of our children becomes even clearer. It is not simply economically destructive to bequeath them an inheritance of diminished investment, productivity, and competitiveness—along with the debts for our past consumption. It is immoral.

As Pete reminds us all in *Facing Up*, our parents and grandparents and many in our generation pulled a country out of depression. They won a World War and later a Cold War. They acted for the future peace of the world by rallying around the Marshall Plan and they bettered their own future by supporting massive outlays to young veterans for housing and education. When there was a need to invest in classrooms and in vaccines and in highways, they rose to the occasion. When spending did rise, few said it was better to borrow than to tax. All the while, they managed a net savings rate twice today's.

In substance and in spirit, this is the legacy left to America's children over the years. Tragically, we seem to have abandoned that tradition. Once again, it must become our legacy. This book is a courageous effort to chart the path and lead the way.

WARREN B. RUDMAN

PAUL E. TSONGAS

August 1993

Introduction:
Facing Up
to the Harsh Realities
of the Nineties

In the interest of full disclosure, I should say at the outset that I have been a registered Republican for over forty years. I was Secretary of Commerce in Richard Nixon's White House and also served as assistant to the President for international economic affairs. I was CEO of a major industrial company (Bell and Howell) in the 1960s. I was CEO of one of Wall Street's most venerable and profitable financial houses (Lehman Brothers) in the 1970s and early 1980s. In 1985, I cofounded The Blackstone Group, a New York investment bank of which I am chairman. I suppose I fit any reasonable definition of a "Republican fat cat."

I happen to believe in a lot of things that are considered—or at least used to be considered—Republican values. Beginning with my education at that bastion of free market theory, the University of Chicago, and continuing through a lifetime in the business world, I developed and have maintained an abiding belief in the virtues of a free marketplace. As readers of this book will come to see, quintessentially "Republican" buzzwords like "savings," "investment," "productivity," and "economic growth" are my mantras.

But I also believe in other things that evidently make me part of a vanishing breed of Republicans. As a "social moderate" (working with Martin Luther King, Jr., in the turbulent, riot-filled late 1960s is still fresh in my memory), I found that the 1992 Republican convention was clearly not my place. Yet what makes my personal political philos-

ophy such an anomaly among Republicans today is not only my views
on civil rights and social policy, but my insistence on what it used to
mean to be a fiscal conservative.

A REPUBLICAN IN EXILE

During the Reagan-Bush years, I felt increasingly like a Republican
abandoned by his party. Republicans may have been in power, but as
I quickly discovered, the Reagan Revolution was disconnecting itself
from the old-fashioned Republican ideas that Ronald Reagan had campaigned on. Our savings rate was going down, our capital investment
was disappearing, our productivity was stagnant. To the degree we
were achieving economic growth it was coming at the expense of the
future—in the form of the most massively un-Republican bloating of
government expenditures, deficits, and debt in American history. What
is more, a Republican administration that was otherwise focused so
intently on national security seemed to me to turn a blind eye to new
types of security threats that could prove to be as great as any posed by
the Russians—namely our decline in economic standing relative to
other countries and our massive borrowing of foreign capital.

Turning sixty, becoming a grandfather, and starting a new investment banking business in the midst of the Roaring Eighties on Wall
Street all caused me to focus more than I ever had before on our
economic future. And I did not like what I saw. As I studied the
numbers and the trends, I was shocked at what was happening to the
living standards of the average American, and to his and her American Dream—even while the Reaganomic band played on and the
stock market soared. I couldn't contain myself. I began to write articles, give speeches, and organize bipartisan budget appeals. These
efforts were all directed at pointing out the ruinous long-term course
we were on as the deficits mounted, core strengths of the American
economy were sapped, and our global competitiveness eroded. That
I had the temerity to point out the great and growing chasm between
the stated beliefs and goals of Reaganomics and the tragically opposite and unintended results made me persona non grata at the Republican White House.

The mad, drunken bash was on in Washington and the debt party
grew more careless and frenzied with each passing day. I was seen as
the ultimate party pooper—a voluble critic, taking every opportunity
to castigate those in charge for their excesses and irresponsibilities and
never missing a chance to warn (as I did in a cover story for *The Atlantic
Monthly* in October 1987, which the editors titled "The Morning After") that when the Reaganomic party was over, we would wake up to

a country that had "let its infrastructure crumble, its productivity dwindle, its savings evaporate, and its budget and borrowing burgeon."

The October 1987 stock market crash lent a measure of frightening, if entirely unintended, credibility to that prediction. The crash itself was the result of a confluence of technical, mechanical, and short-term factors. Nevertheless, it had the effect of focusing attention on some of the long-term trends I had been writing about. Despite the talk of "Morning in America" and the proliferation of new economic theories suggesting that razor-thin savings rates and ballooning foreign debt didn't matter—indeed, that they were a great vote of confidence in Reaganomic policy—the signs were there for those who cared to read them that America was obviously on a wrongheaded, economically dangerous course.

I spent the Bush years continuing to worry publicly (my friends would say the operative word was not "worry" but "obsess") about mounting U.S. deficits, dwindling savings and investment, and slow productivity growth—as well as the huge bill for our present consumption we were leaving to our children and grandchildren. As the Cold War ended and the Desert Storm triumph glowed, I suggested that it was not too late for Bush to seize the moment, capitalize on the unique change of circumstances, and boldly turn the platform of presidential leadership to the cause of marshaling the country's resources to renew the economy on a sound basis. I wrote an article and spoke frequently on the need to redefine "national security" as a field that linked and integrated *economic* security—particularly our *domestic* economic agenda—with traditional concerns about military and foreign policy.

But George Bush wasn't listening to my kind of Republican any more than he was listening to the American people.

Finally, during the recession of 1990–91, the voting public began to break away from the "Don't worry, be happy," "All we need is one more tax cut" spell that dominated the 1980s. And, with the votes they cast in the 1992 election, they delivered the message of worry and fear about the future that many of us had been trying to express to the White House ever since the first Reagan administration.

After a decade of denial of our national economic predicament by those in power, the election of Bill Clinton on a platform of renewed commitment to building our future was like the pause that refreshes. Although I may still cling to my Republicanism as a nostalgic identifier of my basic political beliefs, I lost no sleep over the possibility that a Democrat would be the one to bring an end to the politics of denial and to address the nation boldly, honestly, and forthrightly from the bully pulpit of the presidency. My decade in Republican exile had frayed any lingering partisan feelings; my study of the cancers afflicting the American economy told me that the only possible treatment had to be *bipartisan*—or better still, *nonpartisan*.

THE DAWNING OF THE CLINTON ERA

Like the rest of the nation on inauguration day 1993, I listened with renewed hope to Bill Clinton as he spoke of the need for change. "We have heard the trumpets. We have changed the guard," Bill Clinton proclaimed. "And now . . . we must answer the call." Yes, I thought to myself: These are the right words.

In his first State of the Union address, and in the text of his economic manifesto, *A Vision of Change for America*, released the same night, Bill Clinton went on to tell the American people some hard truths. We were preparing poorly for our future, he said. Our nation was failing to make the crucial investments in people, technology, business plant and equipment, and infrastructure on which tomorrow's prosperity depends. Our skewed priorities were already visible in stagnant living standards at home and flagging competitiveness abroad. He warned that for the first time in American history, our children's generation may "do worse than their parents"—unless we change our course.

Bill Clinton was also refreshingly forthright about the key role the federal deficit plays in clouding our economic future. That was a subject George Bush had found worthy of mention only once in his five-thousand-word State of the Union address the year before. The borrowing that Washington must do to cover our huge deficits, our new President stressed, threatens our future because it siphons off our already shallow pool of national savings into present government consumption instead of long-term private investment. "Rising fiscal deficits as far as the eye can see," the President said, also mean rising interest payments on a growing national debt—and this crowds investment priorities out of the federal budget itself.

When it came to writing his first budget, the President actually used relatively realistic assumptions—"real numbers," as the Clinton people put it—about economic growth and interest rates! Gone were the days when ridiculously rosy forecasts were routinely employed by the White House to predict deficits far smaller than they would inevitably become.

The President's budget also shattered some paralyzing dogmas of the Reagan-Bush years. The nonsense that we could put our fiscal house in order without raising new taxes was finally laid to rest. He dared to use both the "S" word (sacrifice) and the long politically incorrect "T" word (taxes). It may seem odd for a "fat cat Republican," but I had no problem with Bill Clinton's asking that the rich pay higher income taxes. This was only fair, fiscally necessary, and politically essential—especially in view of the massive tax cuts we enjoyed in the Reagan-Bush years. Another commendable step was the President's opening the door to energy taxes, which not only have the potential to increase revenues, but also represent a means to curb a particularly toxic kind of consumption.

Then there was the acknowledgment that we would have to do something about the spiraling costs of our middle- and upper-class entitlement programs—the single most important cause of burgeoning budget deficits. By establishing a Task Force on National Health Care Reform as one of his first acts in office, the President signaled his seriousness about tackling one of the fundamental drivers of our entitlements explosion: runaway medical bills. By proposing to tax more of the Social Security benefits of well-to-do seniors, the President even put our great-granddaddy of all sacred cows on the budget-cutting table . . . if only at the table's edge.

All of this talk was welcome—even intoxicating—to us deficit hawks. Clearly, Clintonomics was to be preferred to what had come before.

But as the weeks and months wore on, it became clear that once again we were face-to-face with a widening gap between announced intentions and actual results. As more budget and policy details surfaced, and as the White House began to dance with a Congress that was Democratic but not docile, it soon became obvious that the President was about to squander a great opportunity.

NO TRIP TO CHINA

Many who were concerned about America's long-term economic future had hoped that President Clinton was going to give us the domestic equivalent of Nixon's trip to China. The President, after all, had declared himself a "New Democrat," ready to reject the failed policies of left and right alike. Perhaps, it seemed to me, America would be willing to trust Bill Clinton and his party to make the kinds of tough but absolutely essential choices about spending and taxing and broadly shared sacrifice that they would not—or could not—trust Republicans to make. Above all, we needed him to be as bold in deed as in word and squarely attack the root causes of our pervasive consumption ethos—especially the spiraling growth in federal entitlement programs.

But we did not get a trip to China. The new taxes on the "rich" turned out to spare almost entirely a much enlarged but fiscally misnamed middle class that excluded all but the top 1 percent of U.S. tax filers. Despite all the cries of draconian sacrifice, the President's proposed energy tax was far too small to make a substantial contribution toward deficit reduction—much less toward curbing our dangerous dependence on foreign oil or improving the environment.

As for entitlements, the thing that mattered most, the President barely managed to crimp their growth. From 1993 to 2004, federal benefit spending under the original Clinton plan, which in its handling of entitlements and its overall budget savings differs only in detail from what Congress approved, would have soared by some $730 billion—compared with $790 billion under the Congressional Budget Office's business-as-usual baseline scenario. And that doesn't count likely entitlement spending increases due to the President's proposed new health-care benefits.

Early on in his campaign, Bill Clinton spoke about the need for Americans to pull together and "sacrifice." But in the end, the actual sacrifice called for under the Clinton plan is so mild and selective that it can hardly be said to address our long-term economic challenges. According to economist Benjamin Friedman, 74 percent of the burden of what deficit reduction the Clinton plan does achieve through higher taxes or benefit cuts will be borne by the small share of U.S. families earning more than $100,000. Without much broader sacrifice—and a presidential vision that truly explains its purpose and inspires us to consume less today for a better tomorrow—we will never cure America's economic cancers.

What is the bottom line? The Clinton plan doesn't come close to balancing the budget, even in the near term. According to the numbers developed by the White House itself, if the President's entire original budget package had been passed and implemented, by 1997 the federal deficit would have declined by only $140 billion from what it otherwise would have been. That will put it at $206 billion, or 2.7 percent of GDP—just a smidgen under where it was (3 percent of GDP) in 1989 before the recession began. If 2.7 percent of GDP doesn't seem like a lot, consider that in 1992 a deficit that size would have soaked up about half of U.S. net private savings. And consider also that about three-quarters of the spending cuts that the President has proposed for 1994 to 1998—modest as they are—are only to take place after the 1996 election, which, of course, raises the risk that they will not happen. (Quite a risk, it seems to me, given our politics of procrastination—or what I have called the "not now" syndrome.)

After 1997, the federal deficit will once again begin to rise rapidly. Under the impact of continued growth in entitlement spending, by 2004 it will have climbed to about $465 billion, or 4.6 percent of GDP. Yet that is only the ante. As the Baby Boom generation begins to reach retirement age in the years that follow, a General Accounting Office study indicates, the deficit could then spin off the charts—climbing to an unthinkable 21 percent of GNP by the year 2020, when today's toddlers are starting their own families.

Inevitably, Clinton's deficit path will mean a much larger public debt. Economists disagree on many things, but almost none would disagree about the importance of *not* letting our public debt grow faster than the economy. Yet under the Clinton plan public debt is on track to grow *far faster* than the economy. Today, public debt is already at a higher level—55 percent of GDP—than at any time since the mid-1950s, an era when we were still paying off the costs of World War II. Because the Clinton budget plan leaves on the table a full two-thirds of deficits previously projected for 1993 to 2004, public debt will grow to a whopping 65 percent of GDP by the end of that period. And along with the debt, needless to say, federal interest costs will soar.

The President's original budget plan, it is true, would have given us a bit more near-term deficit reduction if some of its savings weren't slated to fund his new public investment agenda. I agree—in theory, anyway—with the President's proposal to boost public investment. Unlike some of my Republican friends in the Senate—and even some conservative Democrats—I have no objection to the idea of investing publicly in our collective future on things from high-speed trains to Head Start, even at this time when deficit reduction is so important.

The problem is that much of what the Clinton budget labels "investment" isn't any such thing. Housing subsidies? Food stamps? Enforcing antidiscrimination laws? These may be worthy social goals, but they are not "investments" in a meaningful economic sense: They can't yield positive economic returns over time. Other "investments" favored by the President have been appropriately excoriated in Congress as little more than pork barreling and political patronage to favored cities, mayors, congressional districts, unions, and trade associations. All told, about half of Bill Clinton's proposed "investment" budget represented relabeled present consumption, not future-oriented investment. We need more *real* investment. The best way to find the funds to pay for this is to cut our budget deficit deeply and permanently.

Considering how ravenously large deficits consume national savings—and Clinton seems to understand as much about this as any president in my memory—and how important the availability of savings is to making the future-oriented investments Clinton says he wants (and America surely needs), how can we possibly justify short-term tweaking of the deficit in lieu of radical surgery to balance the budget?

I have asked the Clinton people this question. One answer they offer is that the volcanic eruption of red ink projected for after 1997 will never occur owing to steps they are going to take to control that most intractable force driving our deficits—exploding health-care costs.

The President is right to go after health care. This is where much of deficit reduction *must* indeed occur. But as to whether Bill Clinton will find all his hoped-for health-care savings, I am more than a bit skeptical.

As Charles Schultze, a former chairman of the White House Council of Economic Advisers, put it, "God couldn't design a program" that will achieve net savings in health care in the near term. The President, after all, is proposing to spend *more* on health care. According to some experts, the new benefits debated by Hillary Rodham Clinton's Task Force could carry an annual price tag of up to $100 billion to $150 billion in new public and private spending. In the longer term, achieving real savings elsewhere in health care will require real sacrifices—including, ultimately, selective "rationing" of high-cost, low-benefit medical technologies and services. But the administration isn't preparing the American people for such sacrifices. Until it does, it won't be able to come up with enough offsetting health-care savings to cover the benefit expansions it is now talking about, much less contribute to overall deficit reduction.

Bill Clinton warned of an economic Armageddon if we fail to change course—but then all he was able to give us to cure our economy's ills were a few teaspoons of syrupy medicine.

What happened? The President, according to senior aides, kept asking: "What is politically feasible? I do not want this to be another budget that is D.O.A." In the end his political advisors told him he couldn't ask for sacrifice where he had to—from the great American middle class. Let me now speak the unpopular truths I am sure the President knows but believes are too politically dangerous to act upon. Let me dare, here at the beginning of my book, to offend many among my readership.

Let me turn to the problem of the great American middle class—and the absolutely essential role it must play in shared national sacrifice if we are to reclaim our future.

THE MIDDLE CLASS: THE REAL THIRD RAIL OF AMERICAN POLITICS

I can't remember who it was who first said that you could take all the economists in the world, lay them end to end—and still not reach a conclusion. But if you listen carefully to most economists and policy experts today, there is actually a great deal of consensus about the magnitude of America's economic challenges and what sorts of reforms will be necessary to overcome them.

In particular, most would agree to the following: (1) To get American living standards rising again, we must increase productivity.

(2) To boost productivity we must invest more—much, much more—not just in machines, but in R&D, in infrastructure, and in people. Many, myself included, think that *at least $400 billion a year in new investments are needed*. (3) This in turn means we must save much, much more—*$400 billion a year more*. (4) The surest and fastest way to increase our savings is to reduce and eventually eliminate the federal deficit, which is really just a form of "negative" public savings. (5) To reduce the deficit and keep it down we must make major cuts in consumption spending, and in particular in entitlements. But this, alas, requires us to confront a brute question: If we are to save more by consuming less, *whose* consumption growth do we propose to cut?

It's at this point that agreement on what needs to be done—while not exactly breaking down—comes face-to-face with a truth that remains politically inexpressible. That truth is that the problem is all of us. *Most Americans—emphatically including the middle class—will have to give something up, at least temporarily, to get back our American Dream.*

We all remember Bill Clinton's damning campaign slogan: "It's the economy, stupid." Well, when it comes to the budget the watchword ought to be "It's entitlements, stupid." From Social Security and Medicare to our vast tax favors for home mortgage interest and employer-paid health insurance (policy wonks call these benefitlike subsidies in our tax code "tax expenditures"), consumption-oriented spending dominates the budget today. And the explosive growth of these entitlements will continue to rob our future. The budget arithmetic is inescapable: We just can't get the spending cuts we need from anywhere but entitlements. (See the two charts on entitlements and the budget on pages 26 and 27.) As big as it is, even defense spending isn't big enough. We could shut down the Pentagon tomorrow and still not balance the budget. Nor can we count on saving much on our huge interest bill unless we first reduce other types of spending. Interest on the national debt is something that we must pay to avoid a devastating financial panic—and it keeps growing as our national debt grows, just as it would fall if we began to attack the deficit. The rest of what government does represents just pennies out of the overall budget dollar.

But if entitlements are at the heart of our budget problem, it's the middle class that's at the heart of our entitlements problem—and hence must also be at the heart of any realistic plan for balancing the budget. Consider the numbers in the two charts on direct entitlements and tax expenditures on pages 28 and 29. Taken together, the major benefit programs for which we have income data on recipients—spending roughly 80 percent of total federal benefit dollars, and including everything from Social Security and Medicare to AFDC and food stamps—deliver 99 percent of their benefits ($529 billion in

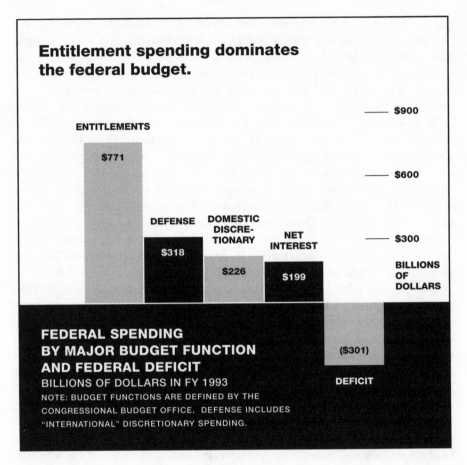

Entitlement spending dominates the federal budget.

ENTITLEMENTS

—— $900

$771

—— $600

DEFENSE   DOMESTIC
          DISCRE-
          TIONARY   NET
$318   INTEREST   —— $300

          $226 $199
                                   BILLIONS
                                   OF
                                   DOLLARS

**FEDERAL SPENDING
BY MAJOR BUDGET FUNCTION
AND FEDERAL DEFICIT**   ($301)
BILLIONS OF DOLLARS IN FY 1993
NOTE: BUDGET FUNCTIONS ARE DEFINED BY THE   DEFICIT
CONGRESSIONAL BUDGET OFFICE. DEFENSE INCLUDES
"INTERNATIONAL" DISCRETIONARY SPENDING.

1991) to the 99 percent of U.S. households with incomes under $200,000. This is the upper boundary of what President Clinton has for political convenience defined as the "middle class." (The President's proposed income tax increases begin at $140,000 of taxable income, the number usually quoted. But that's really equivalent to about $200,000 of adjusted gross income from all sources.)

Yet 43 percent of such benefit dollars—or $227 billion in 1991—go to households that cannot possibly be considered "poor": those with incomes between $30,000 and $200,000. And note that this absolute dollar figure surely understates the total since it reflects only 80 percent of all benefit dollars. What about the remaining 20 percent? We cannot be sure. Some of it flows through programs such as Medicaid, which mostly benefit lower-income households; some too flows through programs such as student loans, farm aid, and veterans' health care, which disproportionately benefit upper-income households. All told, it would be safe to assume that total federal benefit outlays reach-

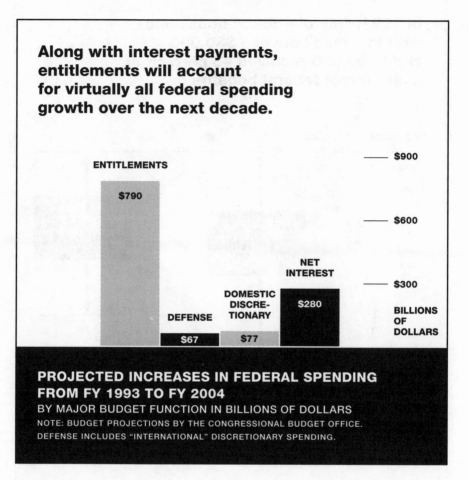

Along with interest payments, entitlements will account for virtually all federal spending growth over the next decade.

ENTITLEMENTS

$790

NET INTEREST

DOMESTIC DISCRE-TIONARY

DEFENSE

$280

$67

$77

—— $900

—— $600

—— $300

BILLIONS OF DOLLARS

PROJECTED INCREASES IN FEDERAL SPENDING FROM FY 1993 TO FY 2004
BY MAJOR BUDGET FUNCTION IN BILLIONS OF DOLLARS
NOTE: BUDGET PROJECTIONS BY THE CONGRESSIONAL BUDGET OFFICE.
DEFENSE INCLUDES "INTERNATIONAL" DISCRETIONARY SPENDING.

ing the $30,000 to $200,000 income bracket amounted to at least $265 billion in 1991.

And what about our ocean of so-called tax expenditures—the subtle subsidies that help Americans borrow huge sums for home mortgages and that underwrite gold-plated employer health plans? Over two-thirds go to tax filers with incomes between $30,000 and $200,000. Just 7 percent go to the Americans whom the President calls "rich."

The top-earning 1 percent of Americans, it's true, receive 13 percent of all income in the United States. But it does not require any arcane knowledge of fiscal arithmetic to see that, even with the substantial tax increases proposed by the Clinton administration, trying to balance the budget is quite literally impossible on such a narrow stretch of income territory. In fact, to meet this goal by the year 2000 by taxing the "rich," we would need to tax away *all* the taxable income of *everyone* with more than $175,000 of adjusted gross income. Or, if we would

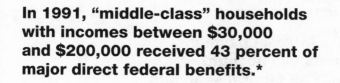

In 1991, "middle-class" households with incomes between $30,000 and $200,000 received 43 percent of major direct federal benefits.*

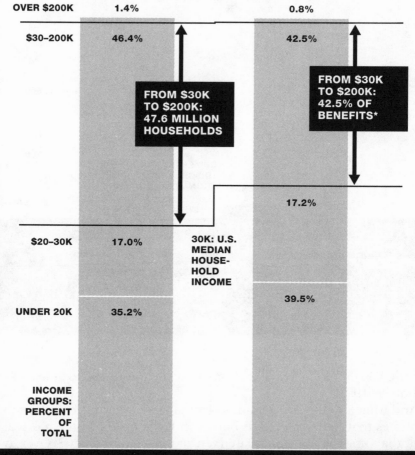

	NUMBER OF HOUSEHOLDS	BENEFITS
OVER $200K	1.4%	0.8%
$30–200K	46.4%	42.5%
$20–30K	17.0%	17.2%
UNDER 20K	35.2%	39.5%

FROM $30K TO $200K: 47.6 MILLION HOUSEHOLDS

FROM $30K TO $200K: 42.5% OF BENEFITS*

30K: U.S. MEDIAN HOUSEHOLD INCOME

INCOME GROUPS: PERCENT OF TOTAL

DISTRIBUTION OF ALL HOUSEHOLDS AND MAJOR FEDERAL BENEFIT DOLLARS
BY HOUSEHOLD INCOME, CALENDAR YEAR 1991

*NOTE: MAJOR FEDERAL BENEFITS INCLUDE OUTLAYS THROUGH SOCIAL SECURITY, MEDICARE (HI AND SMI), CIVILIAN AND MILITARY PENSIONS, FOODSTAMPS, AFDC, SSI, VETERANS' PENSIONS, UNEMPLOYMENT COMPENSATION, AND EITC REFUNDS. THESE CONSTITUTED ROUGHLY 80% OF TOTAL FEDERAL BENEFIT OUTLAYS IN CY 1991, AND INCLUDE ALL FEDERAL BENEFITS THAT CAN BE ALLOCATED BY INCOME OF RECIPIENT. HOUSEHOLD INCOME IS CENSUS-DEFINED CASH INCOME PLUS CERTAIN SMALL ADJUSTMENTS SUCH AS CAPITAL GAINS.

In addition to direct federal benefits, "middle-class" households in 1991 received 67 percent of the benefit-like tax subsidies known as tax expenditures.

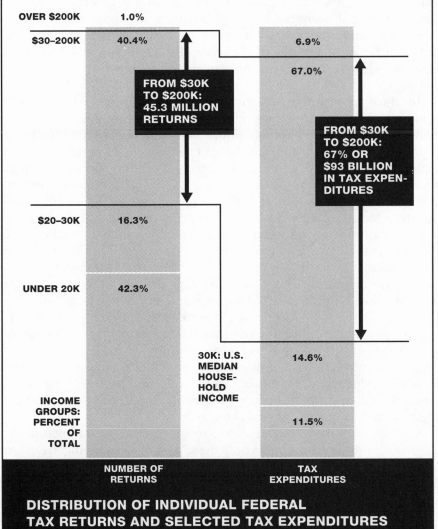

	NUMBER OF RETURNS		TAX EXPENDITURES
OVER $200K	1.0%		
$30–200K	40.4%		6.9%
			67.0%
	FROM $30K TO $200K: 45.3 MILLION RETURNS		FROM $30K TO $200K: 67% OR $93 BILLION IN TAX EXPEN-DITURES
$20–30K	16.3%		
UNDER 20K	42.3%		
		30K: U.S. MEDIAN HOUSE-HOLD INCOME	14.6%
INCOME GROUPS: PERCENT OF TOTAL			11.5%

DISTRIBUTION OF INDIVIDUAL FEDERAL TAX RETURNS AND SELECTED TAX EXPENDITURES
BY INCOME BRACKET, CALENDAR YEAR 1991
NOTE: TAX EXPENDITURES INCLUDE DEDUCTION FOR HOME MORTGAGE INTEREST, EXCLUSION FOR EMPLOYER-PAID HEALTH CARE, EXCLUSION FOR MEDICARE AND SOCIAL SECURITY BENEFITS, CHILD CARE CREDIT, THE EITC, AND DEDUCTION FOR THE ELDERLY AND DISABLED. INCOME BRACKETS DEFINED IN TERMS OF "ADJUSTED GROSS INCOME PLUS"—WHICH IS THE CONVENTIONAL AGI PLUS SEVERAL ADDITIONS, SUCH AS NONTAXABLE GOVERNMENT AND EMPLOYER BENEFITS, NONTAXABLE INTEREST, AND INSIDE LIFE INSURANCE BUILD UP.

prefer a less draconian approach, we could merely *double* the income taxes of "affluent" tax filers—but we would need to include everyone down to about $50,000 of income. Even this kinder and gentler approach would amount to something more like expropriation—hardly the kind of policy consistent with either free markets or democracy.

As for direct entitlement benefits, here too not much help is available from the rich. The maximum entitlement savings obtainable from the 1 percent of households enjoying incomes of more than $200,000 is unfortunately limited to the benefits that go to them—about $5 billion if we took away *all* of their benefits (something that even Bill Clinton, with his laser beam on the rich, has never dreamed of suggesting).

But if we are willing to ask for even modest sacrifices from all Americans with incomes above about $30,000, the picture changes entirely. Suddenly we're talking about a whopping 73 percent of national household income. We're also talking about a stunning 74 percent of all tax expenditures and 43 percent of major federal entitlement benefits, which, taken together—and including our estimate for all benefits—amounted to $372 billion in 1991. That's a sum that we simply cannot ignore if we are at all serious about putting our fiscal house in order.

Let's pause for a moment to ask ourselves, what in reality is the "middle class"? Ask any American if he or she is "middle class," and the answer will almost always be "yes!" The truly poor will admit to being "lower middle class" and the rich will go along with "upper middle class," but few will forthrightly call themselves "poor" or "rich." This is a characteristically American self-perception, and it reflects our desire to live in a basically egalitarian society. But in recent years it has also been used to convince nonpoor Americans that they deserve universal federal entitlements—much of them windfalls—such as Social Security and Medicare, which are often disingenuously called "insurance," and which people mistakenly think of as the payback on their contributions to "their accounts."

Next, ask any group of Americans to specify the annual income that defines "middle class" and you'll hear responses ranging from, say, $20,000 all the way up to $200,000—if we include the Clinton administration's definition. But there are more precise and realistic definitions. If you include nontaxable entitlement benefits and other tax-exempt income along with adjusted gross income reported to the IRS, the *median* family in the United States had a total adjusted gross income of $31,700 in 1993. If you then narrowly define middle class to comprise one-half of all American families, equally distributed around that $31,700 family, the statistical middle-class income turns out to range from $14,040 to $55,880.

This exposition regularly startles those who are new to it. A family with $60,000 of income invariably thinks of itself as "just getting by," but it actually stands in the top quarter of families. A two-earner family with an income totaling $120,000 may think of itself as just middle class. In fact, that two-earner family stands in the top 5 percent of American families. By the time we reach those with incomes in excess of $200,000—the only households targeted for significant sacrifices by the Clinton administration's proposals—we are left with a mere statistical sliver of the population: roughly 1 percent.

Middle-class Americans today, it seems, suffer from what might be called a "reverse Lake Wobegon" syndrome. As Garrison Keillor fans know, Lake Wobegon is a wonderful fictional place where all the children are *above* average. When it comes to incomes, however, most middle-class Americans, trying hard to make ends meet, assume they must be *below* average.

The broad middle class likes to think that because they aren't genuinely rich, they can't possibly be part of the solution to America's economic problems, and that because they aren't truly poor (aren't a dysfunctional family on welfare, for example), they can't possibly be part of the problem itself. Both lines of reasoning are fallacious. As the accompanying charts show, a huge share of the escalating budget for federal benefit programs is not spent on welfare for the poor, as is commonly thought, but on subsidizing the broad middle class. The truth is that middle-income Americans, just like all other Americans, are on the dole—the entitlement dole. But few realize it. Facing up means facing the fact that we are *all* on welfare of one kind or another.

When middle-class benefits come in the form of Social Security and Medicare payments, or military and civil service pensions, they don't seem like *subsidies* in the sense that welfare checks to the poor are. "I've worked hard all my life; I'm just getting what I am entitled to," middle-class retirees say. And there's exactly the problem! As we shall see throughout this book, *all of us* have decided that we are *entitled* to much more than our society can afford to pay for—especially if we want to find the means to invest in our children and our collective future.

Twelve years ago, when Ronald Reagan ascended to the White House, I hoped that his politically candid talk about cutting the budget deficit would lead to politically courageous action. But instead we found a convenient scapegoat. The "poor," we learned, were bankrupting America. Just eliminate the "waste, fraud, and abuse" in our welfare system—all those mink-wearing welfare queens driving Cadillacs and buying vodka at taxpayer expense—and a balanced budget would be within reach. The premise, of course, was wrong from the beginning. Despite cuts in programs for the poorest Americans during the Reagan years, the deficit kept exploding.

When Bill Clinton ascended to the White House, I was once again hopeful that the President would seize the moment and make the tough choices needed to cut the deficit and boost savings and investment. But we seem to be caught up in another form of scapegoating. This time it's not the poor who are to blame. It's the rich who are not paying their way.

Going after the rich to help balance the budget is fine—as far as it goes. Unlike some of my Wall Street colleagues, I see absolutely nothing wrong with imposing higher tax burdens on the wealthiest in our society. And this would be true even if the richest Americans hadn't enjoyed huge windfall tax cuts in the 1980s—becoming the greatest beneficiaries of the very Reaganomic policies that have produced such deep fiscal dysfunctionality in the United States.

I am entirely unmoved by the old supply-side argument that a few percentage points of higher tax rates—imposed on top of today's relatively low tax levels—will somehow deny sufficient incentive to entrepreneurs to invest, start companies, and create jobs. Let's recall Ronald Reagan's claim back in 1981 that if we only could get the maximum income tax rate *down* to 50 percent (from the 70 percent that then prevailed), we would release an unprecedented burst of work, saving, and innovation. With the Clinton plan calling for a top marginal income tax rate that will still be ten percentage points *lower* than Reagan's dream rate of 1981, I am not fearful that the rich will go on strike because their taxes are too high.

I am somewhat more concerned that, faced with higher marginal tax rates, the wealthy will use their high-paid accountants to find ways to shelter their income. Many will shift more of their compensation into nontaxable forms, move more capital into tax-free municipal bonds, and take advantage of a huge and much-widened differential between income tax and capital gains rates to reignite the reviled tax shelter game. This may mean that the President gets less new tax revenue than his number crunchers now forecast. But some revenue there will be.

In many ways, I go further than the Clinton administration when it comes to what responsibility should be borne by the wealthiest in our society. Not only do I favor higher tax rates for the rich, as readers will see I advocate stringent "affluence testing" of welfare for the well-off—whether it is in the form of direct entitlement benefits or in the guise of tax subsidies. There is no earthly reason that the Pete Petersons of America should receive Social Security and Medicare windfalls far in excess of their contributions, tax-free employer medical insurance, or subsidized luxury housing—as is the case under our current entitlement system. If I am to make a credible appeal to average-income Americans to sacrifice more for the good of their country, how could I possibly justify continuing such public favors for the wealthy?

But in the end, there is a fundamental problem with the Clinton plan's "tax the rich" approach. It's the "Willie Sutton factor." When Sutton, a notorious bank robber, was asked why he robbed banks, he is said to have replied, "Because that's where the money is."

If you want to go where the real money is in the United States, you have to begin to ask for sacrifices from the broad middle class. Facing up to the harsh realities of the nineties requires not only a new understanding of why the middle class feels so hard-pressed, but also a realistic view of just how extensive the benefits are that the middle class now receives.

George Bernard Shaw once characterized middle-class morality as the attitude that "I have to live for others and not for myself."

Times have truly changed since Shaw uttered that Victorian truism. Back then, everyone assumed that the middle class was supposed to set an example of altruism, prudence, and farsightedness for rich and poor alike. Today, almost no one makes that assumption. Instead, we talk of the meltdown of the middle class. The popular view is that, like Michael Douglas in the film *Falling Down,* average Americans are as likely as not to crack under the pressures of daily life. Rare is the politician who suggests anymore that the middle class should do anything for others. Instead, politicians all seem to agree that others should be doing more for the middle class—which is precisely why candidate Bill Clinton proposed a fiscally unwise middle-class tax cut.

Middle-class Americans today feel hard-pressed and beleaguered—and they are. No one could possibly argue that even a well-above-the median $50,000 a year in household income will put one on easy street. It's hard to make it on a typical middle-class income today—when paychecks barely keep up with the cost of homes, of college educations, and even of necessities.

Working hard and trying to follow the rules, middle-class Americans have adopted a kind of siege mentality in the face of evaporating expectations about future income growth. The middle class is already making a de facto and unplanned sacrifice in terms of the loss of upward mobility. But an organized, planned, and temporary additional sacrifice can reverse that trend. Only if we all give up something to reinvest in our future will we be able to rekindle the rise in U.S. living standards. If we all just hunker down to protect what we feel we're entitled to, we will condemn ourselves to a future that grows bleaker each year. Evaporating and diminished expectations are not what America is about. The willingness of middle-class citizens to sacrifice a little today for a better tomorrow is, however, exactly what America *used* to be about and ought to be about once again.

In spite of the recent stagnation of its living standards, the American middle class is still the world's richest middle class, consuming far more than any of its counterparts in Europe or Japan—and paying far lower taxes than most. Indeed, Americans may think themselves over-taxed, but we pay some 10 to 20 percent less of our GDP in taxes than do the citizens of most other industrialized countries. The actual economic room for sacrifice exists; what we are missing is the public understanding and the political will to recognize such sacrifices as being in our long-term best interests.

We can't, of course, call on the middle class alone to sacrifice. The rich must pay their fuller and fairer share. Many of the same people who argue that the middle class is too beleaguered to contribute to solving our economic problems stand by silently as the $30,000-a-year middle-class worker pays ever-increasing payroll taxes (which, in many cases, come to more than his or her income taxes) to subsidize the entitlement benefits of retirees who are getting ten times their contributions in Medicare payments (tax-free) and who may be earning $100,000 or more a year in retirement. This is unconscionable.

We must also reexamine our welfare programs to see how they can work best. The "sacrifices" we call on the poor to make won't be material, but changes in today's "culture of poverty" are also central to reclaiming the kind of future that is worth preparing for.

Yet one thing is certain. We can't do it without the middle class.

One of my mentors at the University of Chicago was W. Lloyd Warner, the influential sociologist and author of *Social Class in America* and *American Life: Dream and Reality*. He was perhaps best known for calling attention to the social and economic distinctions within what we sometimes think of as homogeneous class groupings.

In the Warner tradition, let me make some distinctions here. Except the poor and near poor, everybody must be part of the solution to America's economic problems. But as we move through the various strata of the "middle middle class," "upper-middle middle class," and on into the "upper middle class," the sacrifices called for in the form of higher taxes or curtailed entitlement benefits should get much larger. By the time we reach the genuine "upper class" we should have increased the tax bite significantly from present levels, cut deeply into tax subsidies—especially the home mortgage deduction and the health-care tax exemption—and entirely cut off *all windfall* entitlement benefits, such as payments beyond contributions to Social Security and Medicare.

"Aha!" many of my old-time critics who have read this far will no doubt chortle with glee, thinking they've found my political weak spot. We thought Peterson was a "granny basher," but now he's a "middle-class basher!"

To the crime of daring to suggest the politically unpalatable idea that the middle class should pay its fair share, I plead guilty—with the extenuating circumstance that I am also insistent on the rich paying their fair (and *much* fuller) share as well.

But to the crime of being a "middle-class basher," I plead innocent. There is nothing I advocate in this book that inflicts unbearable hardship on individual middle-class families. This is because the huge size of America's middle class is a powerful asset in trying to eliminate the deficit, just as ignoring the huge middle class is a crippling liability. Under the budget plan I propose in Chapter 10, individual middle-class families do not have to sacrifice too much, because there are numerically such immense numbers of them that the sacrifice can be well diffused. And, as I emphasized above, whatever they are asked to sacrifice will rise along with their incomes so that those toward the upper reaches of the middle class contribute much more than those in the true middle.

Let me give an example of what I mean. My plan includes a steeply progressive "affluence test" that uses a sliding scale to withhold entitlement benefits from families with incomes above the U.S. median—generously assumed to be $35,000 by 1995, when the test's phase-in begins. (Naturally, all the income thresholds at which the test applies will be indexed for inflation.) Families earning $30,000 to $40,000 (and who are receiving benefits and have high enough incomes to be subject to the test) would, as a group, lose just 1 percent of their benefits. Families earning $40,000 to $50,000 would lose 5 percent of their benefits—and so on up the income scale until we reach families with incomes of $200,000 and over, who would lose 72 percent of their benefits. And what about poor families—those earning less than $10,000 a year? Other targeted benefit expansions I propose would *increase* their incomes, on average, by about one quarter!

Perhaps I am naive. But I believe that the majority of Americans would be willing to make these sacrifices if they believed, as Ross Perot has so often put it, that in return they were "getting their country back"—in other words, recovering the possibility of a bright future for themselves and their children. First, however, they must understand these simple basics: The "poor" have not caused the deficit. Those of us in the broad middle class have. The poor have suffered grievously from "fiscal austerity"; the rest of us continue to benefit from untrammeled public largess. If the middle class doesn't accept this, the job of balancing the budget won't get done.

In short, as former CEA chairman Herbert Stein so wonderfully put it, the American public "will have to make it safe for politicians to do the right thing." No matter how resolutely our leaders promise to attack our fiscal maladies, the fear of middle-class retribution at the voting booth always sends them searching for a scapegoat instead.

BILL CLINTON'S POLICY TRAP

How exactly did Bill Clinton fall into this trap? Perhaps, to coin a phrase, "It's politics, stupid." My reading of events suggests that the origin of the problem lies in the extremely unwise promise candidate Clinton made to provide a middle-class tax cut. In the heat of the 1992 presidential campaign, Bill Clinton was trying to find favor with voters against a then-surging candidacy of Senator Paul Tsongas. With Tsongas offering a program of fiscal responsibility that included a gasoline tax and an entitlement cap, it seemed expedient to suddenly propose a middle-class tax cut. When it came time to govern instead of campaign, however, Bill Clinton realized that a tax cut was absolutely out of the question if he wanted to prevent a surging tidal wave of red ink from drowning his first years in office. Yet knowing how George Bush had suffered politically from breaking his infamous "Read my lips, no new taxes" pledge, he did not want to make a similar error. During the public's early honeymoon with him, his advisors believed he could get away with shelving a tax cut. But to *raise* taxes on the middle class would be rubbing salt in the wound. His advisors no doubt spelled out for him what the campaign commercials would look like in 1996 if he raised income taxes on the majority of middle-class voters just months after having promised to reduce them.

We can imagine the President asking his advisors what they thought *was* politically feasible. The answer would have been that he should leave both the income taxes and entitlement benefits of the middle class—including the upper middle class—largely untouched and focus on raising revenue from the rich. After all, the voting numbers of the wealthy are small to begin with, and one can almost hear the advisors reminding him that the rich are not his constituency—raising their taxes is not political heavy-lifting, to use the administration's phrase—but the middle class is the core Clinton constituency, and will continue to be. Doubtless at that point Bill Clinton concluded that a politically "feasible" program was a program with no arithmetic hope of balancing the budget—or even coming close. At that point it became crystal clear that the middle class was the true third rail of American politics. At that point the politics of change became the politics of the status quo. At that point the "New Democratic" candidate began to look more like an old-style Democratic president—the conventional tax and spend kind that soaks the rich and leaves entitlements alone.

To be sure, President Clinton will get further with his scapegoat than President Reagan did with his. The rich man can contribute much, much more than the poor ever could or should have. But both ways of dodging tough choices veer away from the heart of the problem. We are all implicated in our budget deficits, our entitlement ethos, and the overall consumption bias in our economy. *All of us* are the "enemy," not "someone else." And *all of us,* most particularly the broad middle class that is the backbone of America, must now be part of the solution.

Having said all of this, let me add that I believe Bill Clinton erred in what he judged politically feasible. I want to expand briefly on that notion, because it gets to the heart of where we go from here.

Presidents by definition are politicians—not kamikaze pilots—and are therefore concerned not with the ideal world but with the politically feasible one. The positions taken by a good political leader should be somewhat ahead of the public at large, but the president cannot afford to appear to be too far out in front. Still, there is considerable room for a courageous president to maneuver, as Harry Truman did in the late 1940s. He took a nation that was smug about its wartime victory and leaning toward neo-isolationism and convinced America that it was now our responsibility to win the peace. The vast majority of Americans at the time were skeptical of or outright opposed to the Marshall Plan and similar global leadership initiatives. But President Truman reached out to Republican leaders—notably Senator Arthur Vandenberg—and built a bipartisan consensus behind a global leadership role for the United States. Ultimately, Truman convinced us not only of the value to all of us of heroic efforts like the Marshall Plan, but of the need for American taxpayers to pick up the bill.

Alas, there are all too few Harry Trumans. Although his mantle was claimed by Democrats and Republicans alike in the presidential campaign of 1992, neither party has demonstrated much in the way of Trumanesque leadership in recent years.

On the question of America's long-term economic agenda, Bill Clinton may actually have had less convincing to do than Truman did with the Marshall Plan. To judge by the 1992 election campaign—including the surge of public support for Ross Perot and Bill Clinton's own ultimate election victory—most Americans were ready for a change of direction. People were telling the pollsters that they were prepared to make sacrifices for a better future. After the Clinton plan came out, constituents told their representatives they wanted *more* spending cuts in the package, while at the same time there was little public support for some of the President's spending increases. Most people may not have been aware what decisive change would really entail, but most Americans nonetheless believed that decisive change was essential.

I thus think President Clinton missed an important opportunity. I believe his initial economic program could have been tougher than it was and could have gone further than it did in proposing the reductions in entitlement spending needed to achieve a balanced budget. In his no-punches-pulled "infomercials," Ross Perot had already paved the way by bringing the entitlement and deficit issues directly to the American people. Had Clinton's plan more closely approximated Perot's, I believe he would have gained necessary public support and confidence, rather than watching it erode as quickly as it has. In the name of "good politics," Clinton forsook good economics. And his was not an ordinary opportunity lost. It was an *extraordinary* opportunity—one that may not be repeated. If not at that moment in early 1993, when? It was then that Clinton had his maximum political capital and public support. He had what may be his only chance to put a grand plan on the table—to pose the goal of a balanced budget as a kind of 1990s version of putting a man on the moon—and to rally Congress and the public behind the cause.

As Congressional Budget Office director Robert Reischauer observed at a symposium sponsored by The Concord Coalition in 1993:

> The notion of balance is important primarily because it provides us with a clear and definable destination for our deficit reduction journey. One can't underestimate . . . the importance of having a clear destination when one embarks on a major public sector undertaking. If you think back to the 1960s, I doubt if the space program would have gone too far if President Kennedy had simply asked for the ability to develop the capacity to send a man 239,000 miles into space and then have him return. We needed the moon. We needed something out there to go to. Similarly, Columbus probably wouldn't have gotten funding from Isabel and Ferdinand if he had said "I want to sail west and see what's out there," as opposed to saying "I want to go and find India and India has all the riches."

But so far, Bill Clinton has failed to rally the nation around an economic moonshot. The goal he proposes is an amorphous one that will get us only halfway there—maybe—by the end of his first term, and could leave us even further away than we are today by the end of a second. What is more, without a firm, understandable presidential target for deficit reduction—and without credible enforcement mechanisms for even the limited goal he has set—we may lose a crucial tool for easing the pain of what sacrifice we do make: the cooperation of the financial markets in keeping interest rates low.

The response of the financial markets to a specific, enforceable presidential plan for balancing the budget by the year 2000 would almost certainly be a lower-than-expected future path for interest rates that would drive down the cost of mortgages, other interest-rate-sensitive consumer debt, and investment projects to a degree that would significantly offset the impact of new taxes or entitlement reductions. We saw the beginning of this tendency after Bill Clinton's election, when his economic plan looked better than the markets had expected. DRI, the prestigious economic forecasting firm, has estimated that enactment of a credible long-term budget-balancing plan, even if the ultimate balancing date were set well in the future, would, over the remainder of the 1990s, cause long-term interest rates to fall by a stunning 2.5 to 3 percentage points beneath what we can otherwise expect in a business-as-usual scenario.

Bad economics may end up being bad politics as well. For one thing, Clinton is attracting sniper fire from Ross Perot's army, instead of capitalizing on the possibility of a real alliance to attack what ails the economy. The President has, in effect, ceded leadership on balancing the budget to whoever wishes to claim that mantle in 1996.

Even as I write this, Ross Perot continues to call the nation's attention to the dire nature of our debt problem in a way intended to make Clinton look all the weaker and more timid by comparison:

> Today we have a $4 trillion debt. By 2000 we could have an $8 trillion debt. Today, all the income taxes collected from the states west of the Mississippi go to pay the interest. By 2000 we will have to add to that all the income tax revenues from Ohio, Pennsylvania, Virginia, North Carolina, New York and six other states to pay the interest on the $8 trillion.

As more and more people come to view our compounding debt nightmare in these stark terms, President Clinton's decision to work only at the margin of the problem may boomerang at the ballot box. As 1996 approaches, not only will he inevitably face a second major budget-cutting exercise, he runs the distinct risk of being tagged the Biggest Borrowing President in history—and he won't even have the excuse of having presided over a divided government. It's easy to imagine a 1996 Republican campaign advertisement along these lines: "Bill Clinton raised your taxes, still borrowed a billion dollars a day, built a bunch of bridges to nowhere—and this time you know who to blame."

Granted, avoiding excessively rapid spending cuts or large tax increases in the midst of a creeping recovery was an understandable concern—though for all too many years it has never been the right moment in the business cycle or the political-election cycle for decisive action on the long-term economic predicament that by now also harms our short-term economic prospects. Any responsible budget plan must be phased in gradually, if we are to avoid too bumpy a ride. But I believe that a clear goal of budget balance—and a commitment to meeting it by the end of the decade—would ultimately play better with both the markets and the public than the course Clinton has chosen.

Indeed, if one accepts Richard Nixon's dictum that the economy that matters most is the one that prevails three months before the next

election, the President's current approach is a dangerous one. By
not asking the public to swallow the bitter pills at the outset, Clinton
risks being forced to ask the public—and especially the middle
class—to swallow them later, closer to the 1996 election. In so doing,
he runs the risk of another boomerang effect. He has denied the
middle class its promised tax cut—and indeed, has created the impression that Americans are already making the needed sacrifices when
they're not. The public therefore may wonder at the need for further
sacrifice when the time comes to really get the job done. That's the
problem with crying wolf: People stop believing.

Moreover, the lift given to the bond market in 1993 by the early
promise of deficit reduction may, by 1996, have reversed itself. With
health-care and other entitlements still spiraling out of sight, and with
private credit demands likely rising as we and the rest of the world fully
emerge from recession, the United States could once again see soaring
interest rates right about election time. Interest rates are not the only
yardstick the market and the public use to gauge our short-term economic situation, but they are crucial to investor and consumer psychology. Henry Kaufman, perhaps the best-known of bond market
watchers, warns that in 1995 and 1996, when continued high deficits
meet a surging demand for credit, the impact on interest rates won't
be pretty.

INTRODUCING THE CONCORD COALITION

Despite the apparent readiness of the public for change, there's no
denying that going all the way on the deficit would have been a real
gamble for President Clinton. When Americans sense that our country
is on the wrong path, we turn to leaders who speak to our long-term
hopes and aspirations. In 1980, it was the Republicans who promised
us long-term religion. In 1992, it was the Democrats. But because we
aren't quite ready to face up to the tough sacrifices that real change
will demand, once our leaders are in power we encourage them to
backpedal and indeed to lie to us about what really needs to be done.
Then, when they fail to deliver what they promised, we send them
packing.

A lot of politicians are now acutely aware that the "expert" consensus about what changing course will really entail is currently way out in
front of the public's perception. They know we have run out of incremental, piecemeal solutions—that we can't any longer debate over a
few nicks and cuts, make a few compromises, and then go home. Many
in Washington are beginning to realize that the necessary steps must
be quantum leaps in policymaking. We can no longer get by with a
lowest common denominator kind of package, a "pragmatic hodge-

podge," as former CBO director Rudolf Penner puts it. We can't simply, in Senator Bob Kerrey's words, keep on "splitting the difference" and "doing the same old thing we have done in the past."

True, the public is furious at Washington and today expresses unprecedented contempt for the legitimacy and efficacy of government. But the fury is diffuse, unfocused. It could turn on any target at any time. No one wants to stand out and be the bearer of bad news. No one wants to play the sacrificial martyr. Many officeholders suspect that something must happen—perhaps some dramatic signal of imminent national crisis that galvanizes public opinion and makes action possible (the Pearl Harbor syndrome)—before they risk their careers. Until then, they hope the other guy goes out, gets killed first, and thereby paves the way.

What we need to counter this dynamic is an honest dialogue between policymakers and the public. That's where The Concord Coalition comes in. It's a nonpartisan, grass-roots coalition aimed at breaking today's political gridlock with a message that is pro-investment, pro–general interest, and pro-future. Such an effort requires principled leaders who know how to communicate with public audiences and who understand how Washington works—and how it doesn't work.

I have kept my eyes open for such rare specimens. One night in 1992, just after Warren Rudman announced his retirement from the Senate, I saw him on the *MacNeil/Lehrer Newshour*. I was watching the show with a very Democratic friend who has never met a Republican politician he liked. Now this Democrat started listening intensely to Warren. He'd heard me talk about a coalition. He leaped out of his chair and said, "Now, there's the leader you need for the Republican side of your bipartisan coalition. He's a series of oxymorons." I asked, "What do you mean by that?" "Well," he said, "he's a passionate Republican. He's a compassionate Republican. By God, I've never heard of one of these, he's a fair-minded Republican. I can't believe it." Fortunately, Warren Rudman agreed to be one of Concord's two founding cochairmen.

I found another sterling public citizen to serve as our other cochair in Paul Tsongas. He had certainly gotten my attention and that of many other Republicans in the presidential primaries. For many years, my parents had told me "sensible Democrat" was also a kind of oxymoron. I listened carefully to Senator Tsongas. Was I hearing him accurately? We should cap entitlements above some income level? We should enact a significant gasoline tax? I liked what I heard. As a result, I did something in the 1992 campaign that didn't come at all naturally to me. I contributed $1,000 to Paul Tsongas's presidential campaign. But I rather limped it, I'm embarrassed to say. I waited until after he withdrew, so that I would have a rationale, just in case some Republican asked me to explain it. But that was where my heart was.

One day Warren Rudman and I were free-associating about why we have such affection and respect for Paul Tsongas. Warren said, "You know, he is one of the few Greek Wasps I have ever met in my life." What I think Warren meant was that Paul combines the warm passion of his Greek ancestors with the moral compass of his New England ancestors. When he speaks of moral connection to the children, I haven't any doubt that he means it. When he speaks of courage, all you have to do is look at him. He lives it.

These two senators had known and respected each other and had previously talked about working together. They quickly agreed to co-found and cochair The Concord Coalition. Neither is affluent, yet both will donate perhaps half their time to this effort. They know we need to explain the economic truth to the American people so that it becomes safer for Bill Clinton and Congress to do the right thing. We need to elaborate a program and argue the case for it in such a way that when Bill Clinton next turns to his advisors, they will recognize that a real plan for deficit reduction is both economically necessary *and* politically feasible.

That is the core purpose of The Concord Coalition. And that, we presume, is at least one of the purposes of the Ross Perot army, United We Stand. Show the way. Educate the American people. Organize the young whose future we have jeopardized. Plow the early ground. Absorb the first blows. Provide political cover to the President and Congress.

At the heart of our mission will be getting the American middle class to take responsibility for America's future again. It is still the world's greatest, most productive, most inventive middle class. My origins are there, and chances are yours are too. But our notions of middle-class entitlement and middle-class victimization, I'd argue, have badly hurt the middle class and the country along with it. We are rapidly forgetting not only what the middle class is, but what the middle class is all about. It does tremendous damage to the social and economic legitimacy of the middle class when its self-appointed spokesmen insist on portraying it solely as a victim, with many rights and no duties.

To say that the middle class must make some sacrifices is simply to be an advocate of its own interests—which is to say America's. And the hard truth is that middle-class Americans *are* going to have to make sacrifices in the years to come. The question is whether those will be relatively modest, planned, fair-share sacrifices made soon as part of a let's-pull-together national effort, or much more painful and arbitrary sacrifices imposed later by the social and economic dynamics of an increasingly chaotic, dangerous, and bankrupt America.

I may seem relentlessly negative in this book—a modern-day Jeremiah. If so, it is with a purpose. I want my readers to understand the dangers we face and to be able to help choose the brighter, more positive future of a restored American Dream. I believe Americans are still capable of making good choices when they understand what's at stake. I still remember the America I knew in my formative years, during World War II, when all Americans knew we were all in the war effort together, and when they saw their individual sacrifices pay off concretely for the greater good. I don't believe we've changed so much since then. Americans will endure the short-term pain if they believe it will produce long-term gain. They just don't believe that now. If our nation's political environment gives Bill Clinton a fighting chance of success, I still believe he can make the honest, courageous choices.

Dominating our political environment, of course, is our Congress. Today's Congress is torn between hoping for a leader who does right by the nation's future and preferring a leader who doesn't do so because effective action might require every member of Congress to commit political suicide come the next election.

It is the task of The Concord Coalition, among other groups, to help bring that hope and that preference into alignment. For far too long they have been viewed as mutually exclusive. To those who say the challenge ahead is too hard, I suggest the deep wisdom of an aphorism coined by a professor of mine at the University of Chicago long ago: "If you have no alternative, you have no problem." I believe we have no choice but to try to reverse the trends before us. The "alternative"—an American future without an American Dream—is so unthinkable as to be no alternative at all.

WHERE HAVE YOU GONE, THOMAS JEFFERSON?

More than two centuries ago, Thomas Jefferson wrote a letter to James Madison in which he warned of the utter inappropriateness in a democracy of a value system that allows the debts of one generation to burden the next. The earth, he wrote, should by all rights belong to the generation alive at any given time. He observed that if one generation could leave its debts to encumber the next, "then the earth would belong to the dead and not to the living generation."

Contemplating the issue of national debt, Jefferson urged nascent democracies to "declare in the constitution they are forming, that neither the legislature nor the nation itself can validly contract more debt than they can pay within their own age."

Jefferson would be shocked, saddened, and ashamed to see the $4 trillion noose of national debt we have put around the necks of our progeny—not to mention the many trillions more in unfunded federal benefit liabilities we are passing on to future workers.

We seem to have forgotten what Jefferson understood so clearly at the dawn of democracy in the modern world: To encumber the next generation with debt is to deny them the full measure of their freedom. To place the weight of these trillions upon trillions of dollars upon unborn children is to rob them of what Jefferson and the founding fathers promised us: life, liberty, and the pursuit of happiness.

This book is not really about deficits, entitlements, and consumption. Nor is it really about savings, investment, and productivity. Ultimately, it is about our freedom and our future.

PART I

Learning How to
Choose Again

My father, George Petropoulos (at right behind the counter), in 1923, getting ready to greet customers in the Central Cafe in Kearney, Nebraska, the twenty-four-hour-a-day, 365-day-a-year restaurant he opened with his savings from working on the railroad. The long hours and hard work meant little to him. He was building the American Dream.

1

What My Father Knew About Economics

I am the firstborn son of Greek immigrants. In today's world of fragile and failing role models, their example is as indelible as it is inspiring.

My father, George Petropoulos, and my mother, Venetia Pavlopoulos, each single and alone, came to America in their teens with nothing more than third-grade educations from schools in remote Greek farm villages. They were fearful, but opportunities in their homeland were meager and the promise of America filled them with hope and confidence. After all, the United States of America was the land of limitless frontiers, the land where dreams came true.

MY FATHER'S AMERICAN DREAM

Like many other young men, George Petropoulos headed west soon after his arrival in 1912. And like so many immigrants, then and now, he took whatever work a recent immigrant speaking a foreign tongue could find. He made his way to Nebraska, where he joined his older brother Nick, who was working for the Union Pacific Railroad. Because the foreman had trouble pronouncing the family name, Nick changed "Petropoulos" (which means son of Peter) to "Peterson." My father also took the new name, so I was born a Peterson. Years later, he was to tell me he was sorry he had changed our name. In his always clear but often broken English, here is how he put it: "I wouldn't want anyone to think we weren't proud of 'our race.' "

He worked long, sweltering hours at a menial job no one else wanted—washing dishes in a steaming caboose kitchen. Although he didn't earn much, he saved most of what he earned. He borrowed as little as possible—and even then, only to invest in a better future for his family. "My son," he used to say, "if we spend a little less and save a little more today, we will all have a lot more tomorrow." To him, the term "big spender" was the ultimate pejorative. And borrowing to consume was unforgivable. My father's third-grade education did not include economics, but he certainly grasped its essential principles. His common sense told him that a better future requires investment. But to invest, one must save. And to save, one must temporarily consume less. His commitment to the future made him a genuine "supply-sider" decades before the term was invented and disingenuously applied to policies that would have appalled him.

Slowly but steadily, my father's savings accumulated and before long were transmuted into the inevitable Greek diner, the Central Cafe in Kearney, Nebraska. It was an establishment distinguished not for its cuisine but for the fact that for a full quarter century it stayed open twenty-four hours a day, seven days a week, 365 days a year. And for many—too many—of those hours, days, weeks, and years, my father was on his feet in that restaurant, varicose veins and all.

As a child during the Great Depression, I recall watching with a mixture of pride and edginess as my father offered food (often in return for simple chores) to any jobless, out-of-luck soul who approached the back door of the Central Cafe. In his best year, my father never made more than $20,000, yet throughout his working life he shared what fortune he had with his family and with the rural community he left behind in Greece. He bought homes for sisters and brothers still living there and paid for so many municipal improvements in Vahlia that the village's main street is now called Petropoulos Street. In 1963, King Paul awarded him the First Gold Medal in recognition of his philanthropy.

True to his Mediterranean heritage, my father was an emotional man. "God Bless America," the only American song he could sing, never failed to produce patriotic tears. His America was about an exuberant confidence in the future that withstood even the economic collapse and fearful headlines of the 1930s. His America was also about faith in our freedoms and in equality of opportunity. It was a faith that withstood even the Ku Klux Klan when it picketed his restaurant with signs saying "Don't eat with the Greek." "Those aren't the real Americans," he told me. After all, *he* was a proud member of the Elks. His Sunday poker game at the Elks Club—the highlight of his week—sealed his acceptance by the community and demonstrated that, in those days, much of what fell into the American melting pot actually melted.

Many years later, when I informed him that President Nixon had invited me to join the White House, my father did not hesitate for a second. "You have no choice," he said. "It is your duty to serve *our* country." Before long, he was known to greet newcomers with an unusual salutation: "Good morning. My son is the first and only Greek cabinet officer in the United States government." No doubt I would have winced had I been present, and no doubt he would not have cared. My father's pride in any and all of the achievements of his family was irrepressible. No other pleasure was comparable.

Indeed, his passionate feelings about future and family were inseparable. What prompted him to save so energetically was not so much a concern for his own retirement (what economists today call the life-cycle motive) as a concern for the family he would someday leave behind (what economists today call the endowment motive). It is a sign of our own times that "the lifecycle hypothesis" has, in today's universities, become the dominant explanation of savings. My father never would have grasped it.

At his funeral in 1986, as I gazed upon his prosperous (and perhaps overindulged) children and grandchildren, I found myself wishing that he might have lived life a bit differently—that he might have enjoyed the present tense a bit more and worried about the future tense a bit less. Yet the task of burying a parent also concentrates the mind on the horizon of one's own life. The event prompted me to reflect on what I was doing personally—and what my generation was doing collectively—to pass on this remarkable heritage. The fact that we are the very "posterity" our parents and grandparents once fussed over with such love and dedication made me think hard about what we are doing for our own posterity, and what that posterity will someday say about us.

My father's life embodied not just an endowment motive but an endowment *ethic*. His was a consciously perceived obligation to choose the future over the present. He gained more satisfaction from giving than from receiving. And had he not done all in his power to ensure that his children "did better" than he had done, he would have considered himself an abject failure. Like many others in his survivalist generation, my father's definition of "doing better" was highly—perhaps excessively—focused on material yardsticks. It did not give much weight, for example, to emotional self-discovery, aesthetic sensibilities, self-esteem, and the like. On the other hand, the concrete results of his generation's approach proved to be spectacular. And the unprecedented rise in living standards that was their legacy gave later-born Americans the leisure to enjoy the "higher" things in life.

At the core of my father's notion of "doing better"—his understanding of the American Dream—were four principles. The first was a better education for his children. He never asked what kind of education he could afford for my brother and me. Instead, he asked "what was the best education money could buy." As he saw it, education was an investment that no financial misfortune could ever take away. It took obvious precedence over any sort of frivolous spending on the here and now.

The second was attaining a higher living standard, measured either by household income or by household net worth. "How much was your raise?" my father used to ask me. "What are you worth now?" My monthly paycheck was a subject of his relentless interest.

The third principle was that primal dream of most American families—buying the better home. I had not successfully lived up to his expectations until he visited my own first home in the Chicago suburbs. For months thereafter, his fellow Elks heard exaggerated stories about the number and size of bedrooms and bathrooms. Though he seldom talked about it, he also valued the quality of home life and struggled to try to spend some of his rare free moments (for instance, on Sunday mornings) with his children. Striking a balance between work and family was always difficult for him. Late in life he confessed to me his greatest regret was that he could not share more of his time with us.

Finally, my father wanted a better life not just for his own children, but for his children's children. An essential component of "doing better," in other words, was sustainability *over time*—ensuring that the same promise of rising living standards came true for future generations. To this end, doing the best he knew how, he took great delight in giving his grandchildren his most successful investment, stock in a local onion products factory. He used to tell them that Nebraska was "Apache Country," a fact I remembered when I later learned that the Apache language uses the same word for grandfather and grandson. My father would have appreciated the symbolism, reflecting the endless link between generations.

AMERICA'S FORTUNATE GENERATION LOOKS BACK

"How are we doing, big shots?" This was my father's favorite greeting to his dishwasher sons, whose sudsy hands must have reminded him of his own early work experience. Ever since, I have often heard this question echo in the back of my mind. Not just how am *I* doing, or how are *you* doing, but "how are *we* doing?" Perhaps the plural pronoun has something to do with my lifelong interest in America's economic future.

How, collectively, is my generation doing? And where, collectively, is my generation leading the country? For most of us who came of age in the years immediately following World War II, the answer to how we are doing is clearly: "Just fine, thank you." After all, ours was the era of the "American High," an era of surging investment and prosperity on practically every front. From 1947 to 1967, U.S. hourly productivity grew by 92 percent; college enrollment grew by about 175 percent; homeownership grew from less than half to nearly two-thirds of all households; the share of Americans in poverty cascaded from 40 to 14 percent; and inflation-adjusted median family incomes grew by 69 percent—with the incomes of younger families shooting up by over 80 percent.

Demographers and economists have rightly called my generation of Americans "the fortunate ones." Unlike our parents, we did not have to defer our adult ambitions. Born between the mid-1920s and early 1940s, even the oldest of us came of age after the great crises of depression and world war had passed—and thus could step directly from high school and college onto a fast-rising escalator of affluence. And unlike our children, we did not have to start careers and families at a time of stagflation and soaring mortgage rates. Even the youngest of us were already well launched into adult life by the late 1960s, when the post–World War II momentum of progress and prosperity began to falter. When I think of the rapid ascent enjoyed by so many in my generation, I am reminded of a Woody Allen line: "Eighty percent of life is just showing up."

Yet today, as our generation begins to enter elderhood, many of us feel mixed emotions about our good fortune. Yes, our parents did very well by us. But on our watch, as heads of families, firms, and government institutions, have we done as well by our own children? At best, the verdict is deeply troubling. As objective evidence, one can cite colossal federal deficits, razor-thin savings rates, stagnating household incomes, feeble economic productivity, failing schools, and resurgent poverty. As subjective evidence, one can point to opinion surveys indicating that an unprecedented share of young Americans doubt that they will live better than their parents.

From today's vantage point, I can look back with a new appreciation of my father's passionate attachment to the future. His generation may have loved the future too much. But surely my generation has taken the future for granted—at immeasurable cost.

I must confess that I did not always see it that way. In my youth, I often seethed at my father's iron-clad rules of thrift and work. They struck me as irrational if not downright masochistic. In those days, the purchase of a new car was a transcendent symbol of middle-class arrival. Marketers urged every paterfamilias to trade in his car when it was only three years old. But they were wasting their time on George Petropoulos. He had no use for such "excessive" consumption. As our

DeSoto approached its fifth year, my brother and I pored over new car ads hoping that some innovation could seduce my father into buying a new car. Perhaps the Air-Flo DeSoto? No. A few years later, we hoped the Oldsmobile Hydramatic, with its pathbreaking automatic transmission, might do the job. No again. As the aging DeSoto rattled into relic status, our disappointment turned into a mix of desperation and embarrassment.

My father did believe in the occasional vacation: a ten-day family trip to Colorado every two years. Once more, my brother and I tried unsuccessfully to get him to consume a bit more luxuriously. We wanted to take the train. A trip on Union Pacific's City of Denver streamliner was that era's equivalent to a child's first trip to Disneyland today. But according to my father, the newfangled comfort of air-conditioning was a singularly unpersuasive reason to buy expensive tickets. We even appealed to his sense of history. The tracks on which the City of Denver raced were, after all, the very tracks he and the Union Pacific crew had built years earlier. But all to no avail. Instead, on the hot, dry, 110-degree plains of Nebraska, seven of us—assorted relatives included—would pile into the DeSoto for the twelve-hour rattling crawl to Colorado. To George Petropoulos, this was the "sensible" way to travel.

Only years later did I understand what my father was seeing as he drove along that desert highway. He was looking ahead to a future in which his family would do better—and to the savings that would make it possible. So, when it came time for college, he had the money for "the best education that money could buy"—even at those "fancy eastern colleges." And because my father was so "sensible," my mother lived out her eighty-nine years comfortably in the same home in Kearney, Nebraska—enjoying the rental income from three modest retail store buildings he was able to buy with his hard-earned savings. My parents' generation understood that, sooner or later, the welfare of those they leave behind necessitates something both unpleasant and unpopular—real choices, real tradeoffs, and real sacrifices.

Today, we Americans are having trouble relearning this concept. We know we've been on the wrong track for some time now, but can't face up to what it will take to get back on the right one. So we bank on rosy GNP scenarios; we procrastinate; we await miraculous new technologies; we push liabilities off the books or into the next accounting year; we cut taxes and pray; we implement buck-passing "budget processes" that trumpet our good intentions. But we rarely prove how much tomorrow means to us by actually giving up something important today. We don't say: This year the DeSoto and not the Denver streamliner.

Where my own generation seems to leave the future to Providence, my father's took just the opposite tack—making sure of the future and assuming that today they would somehow get by. But it's not just the future that my parents sacrificed for. They also understood that American-style social and economic progress at times means putting the needs of the community ahead of your own individual needs. They looked out for those broader interests at the back door of my father's restaurant—as well as in their ancestral village back in Greece. And, most definitely, my parents knew that along with rights always come duties.

What I'm talking about, of course, is really a matter of balance and priorities—of knowing where to make the tradeoffs. Always opting for future, for community, and for duty would be tantamount to totalitarianism. By never satisfying the present, you betray the future; by founding a community that prohibits individualism, you end up with no community at all; and by banishing "rights" you mock the very concept of "duty." But the other extreme is, if anything, more dangerous. A society that always opts for the present, for the individual, and for rights is not long for this world. To an extent that would have deeply shocked my parents, America has become just such a society.

It's not that there aren't millions of Americans like my parents today. Every time I stop by a Korean market or a Vietnamese restaurant I see people just like them, working together and saving for a better future. And it's not just recent immigrants, of course. Most Americans still care deeply about the kind of future they give their children. As families, they struggle to do the best they can. But somehow fewer of the decisions we make represent clear choices on behalf of the future. Somehow less is deferred and more is consumed. Over time, and in the aggregate, there is no mistaking the sea change in generational behavior—in the types of choices we make, whether privately or publicly. As a book about America's collective future, this is also naturally a book about averages and majorities.

Nor is it that as a people we're no longer absorbed in polarizing debates over matters that address issues of principle. Sometimes it seems that Americans show more heated moralism over more issues today than in almost any epoch in our history. There's art-porn, abortion, school prayer, censorship, Murphy Brown, gun control, flag burning, animal rights, and the private lives of our politicians, to name but a few. The difficulty is that we are no longer able to muster the same moral fervor when it comes to the *economic choices* on which our success and survival as a nation depend. Or if we do manage to muster something of that fervor outwardly, we don't follow through by making even the modest but genuine sacrifices that might tangibly benefit the long-term future.

"It's the economy, stupid," may now have become the mantra of those in power. But we have yet to really face up to the hard economic choices and shared sacrifices restoring my father's American Dream will entail. As our national debt grows and our borrowing binge continues unabated, we are *told* that America's increasing indebtedness poses a *choice* between those who want high spending and those who want low taxes. The principled left claims to be incensed because they supposedly can't spend more, and the principled right because they cannot tax less. But, as has been the case in so many dimensions of our public life, *both* sides have had it their way: high spending *and* low taxes. The politicians fool and the voters want to be fooled. Neither side balks at an outcome that evades choice by funding today's spending though massive borrowing against the future—which is to say, from our children. It brings to mind the biblical story of Solomon where he sat in judgment of two women, each claiming to be the true mother of a child. A modern version might end differently—with *both* claimants merely shrugging their shoulders while Solomon brings down his sword.

THE POLITICS OF GRIDLOCK

I recently had an experience that illustrates just how difficult it can be to get even those most expert on the issues to face up to the hard choices before us. I was in Washington to present the report of the Competitiveness Policy Council's (or CPC's) Subcouncil on Capital Formation to the full body. The CPC is a congressionally chartered body that brings together government officials, business and labor leaders, economists, and other academic experts—all with the aim of developing specific proposals for boosting U.S. economic performance and competitiveness. Every member of the CPC has a long and sterling record of outspoken concern about tough issues facing the American economy.

Over the preceding months, we had seen the reports from other subcouncils. In these meetings, it had been relatively easy to achieve general agreement on the pressing need to invest more in order to boost productivity. Everybody spoke about putting more resources into infrastructure, R&D, plant and equipment, and education and training. As chairman of the Subcouncil on Capital Formation, my job was to present a plan for how the American economy could *pay* for these badly needed investments. It was a given that any plan I presented had to show how we could eliminate the federal budget deficit that so ravenously consumes our private-sector savings and prevents us from keeping up with our competitors in making productive long-term investments.

The plans I presented were quite specific. They would have enabled us to make the investments we most urgently needed while eliminating the budget deficit over an eight-year period. But as soon as I had finished, this august body, which had been in such agreement when we were discussing the merits of new investments, suddenly broke down into contentiousness over how to pay for them. A business lobbyist frowned on the notion that we might have to raise marginal income tax rates to 40 percent. A labor leader vehemently opposed any taxes on or reduction in benefits to the middle class—in other words, he wanted to exempt almost all of us from any sacrifice. An economist seconded that by insisting that American households with incomes under $100,000 were all "pushed to the wall" and couldn't possibly tolerate even the smallest reduction in their consumption. Another labor leader even said he couldn't endorse a program that proposed ending taxpayer subsidies of junk mail sent out by nonprofit organizations! Apparently his union's role as a thriving part of our great American democracy depended on that subsidy.

Sadly, American politics and culture have come to be so dominated by special interests and by self-interest that even when good, serious people are brought together around a shared commitment to make a better future for all of us, the consensus that exists in theory about the need to consume and borrow less and save and invest more breaks down the moment you start talking about *whose* ox will have to be gored.

LOOKING FORWARD TO A TROUBLED FUTURE

The mystery for those of us past age fifty is why our parents were never tempted to look for ways to escape their collective responsibility for the nation's future. They were, on average, much less affluent than we are today. Yet from 1940 to 1955, they pulled America out of the Depression, fought and won a world war against fascism, led another war against communism in Korea, gave prodigious sums of foreign aid to Europe, supported massive outlays to young veterans for housing and education, and (if we except the total war years of 1942 to 1945) still managed a level of net national savings more than double what *we* have managed since 1980. Many opposed big government spending, but when they saw a national investment challenge—in highways or vaccines or rockets—they did not turn away. And when spending rose, few advocated borrowing instead of taxing. Many were sympathetic to the construction of a safety net to support the poor and disadvantaged, but no one suggested making public benefits rise "automatically" without regard to individual need or the ability of the rest of us to pay. Certainly no one justified current cash windfalls for himself by slipping his own children a huge, hidden bill that promised away a third or more of future payrolls as we're now doing with our Social Security and Medicare programs. A vast majority disliked the Marshall Plan. But, in what was perhaps our finest hour, the nation ultimately rallied around this investment in world peace that cost over $50 billion in today's dollars and consumed 16 percent of the federal budget. Even the opponents of the Marshall Plan would be astonished that now we cannot spare one-fiftieth that amount to help Eastern Europe on its road to democracy.

Today we thank our parents for the many sacrifices they made. Because they cared for the future so much, my generation enjoyed decades of national and economic security.

Someday, our own children will look back on us. When they weigh our material affluence against the challenges that *we* faced, they will surely take a dim view of how few sacrifices we deemed worth making for their benefit—of how we sleepwalked, choicelessly, through critical years, and of how we denied, mortgaged, and cheated the future. If they judge us by our deeds rather than our words, they may conclude that what we really wanted most was to protect ourselves at their expense.

That we are failing our children is a serious charge. But let's return to my father's question, "How are we doing, big shots?" and direct it not at my generation but at my generation's children—those who have mostly entered the workforce since the early 1970s. This time the answer would have to be, "Not well at all, thank you." Recall again the four components of my father's American Dream: education, income and net worth, homeownership, and sustainable upward mobility. In each case, the trends are disturbing, if not grim.

First, take education. Over the last decade, innumerable private and public commissions have all come to a near-unanimous verdict: Today's teens and twenty-somethings may be the first generation in our history to come of age worse educated than their parents. "If a hostile power had attempted to give America the bad education it has today," the National Commission on Excellence in Education declared in 1983, "we would have viewed it as an act of war." The symptoms of our failure include, of course, such academic catastrophes as the plunge in Scholastic Achievement Test scores between the 1960s and the 1980s. But they also encompass the multiple social and emotional pathologies today's youths bring with them into the schoolroom—from drugs and teenage pregnancy to street violence and suicide. Here are just two statistics for posterity to judge us by: Among teenagers, the suicide rate and the homicide rate have both tripled since 1960.

Then consider incomes and net worth. From the Great Depression until the early 1970s, the real median income of American households rose steadily among all age groups. Since 1973, it has continued to climb for those of us who are older—by 6.1 percent for Americans aged fifty-five to sixty-four and by a huge 28.4 percent for the elderly. But among younger households, real income has actually fallen since 1973—by 9.7 percent for Americans aged twenty-five to thirty-four and by 15.3 percent for Americans aged fifteen to twenty-four. If a flood of working wives had not helped out, the trend for younger households, of course, would have been much worse. Since 1973, the real median income of men under age thirty-five has fallen by 25 percent. This steadily widening income gap between the young and the old is a trend that inevitably also manifests itself in most measures of household wealth. According to economist Frank Levy, Americans aged thirty-five to forty-four are now only half as wealthy as their parents were at the same age.

Now let's look at the third element in my father's American Dream— the better home. The quantitative indicators reveal the same generational difference as the trends in household income and wealth. From the Great Depression until the late 1970s, the rate of homeownership in America rose briskly for nearly all age groups. It continues to rise for Americans over age sixty-five, but has stagnated for Americans aged forty-five through sixty-four—and has dropped sharply for still younger Americans.

For the "underclass" huddled in the basement of our economy, the American Dream has turned into an out-and-out nightmare. Nearly half of our inner-city young men are unemployed (and some would say unemployable). Nearly *half* of our black children are poor. About two out of three are born to an unmarried mother. (As an indication of the desultory direction of things, that number was not much more than one out of three as recently as 1970.) Today, the average black male child is more likely to go to prison than to college. Indeed, in a number of our major cities, we already see the numbing statistic that half of young black males are either behind bars, on parole or probation, out on bond, or being sought on an arrest warrant. With violent death a daily occurence, mothers are sufficiently worried that their children may be shot that "child murder" insurance to cover the cost of their burial is a new "growth product." We have seeded a poverty-stricken and violent Third World within our First World. Without families, skills, education, or hope, today's inner-city kids are sometimes collectively referred to as a "lost generation."

These problems, of course, are not simply economic or political. Their roots are also cultural, moral, and even spiritual. What's more, though we like to comfort ourselves by thinking otherwise, the shadow they cast over the American Dream reaches well beyond the underclass. Consider a few overall statistics from a melancholy study released by William Bennett, the former secretary of education and former drug czar. Divorces are up 200 percent over the past three decades; illegitimate births up 420 percent; violent crime up 560 percent.

America has become a society of deep divisions and contradictions. We are the world's richest nation but have the highest poverty rate among industrial nations.* We pioneered in universal education but now trail the rest of the industrial world on math and science achievement tests and lead in rates of functional illiteracy (one-fifth to one-third of our young people are functionally illiterate on entering the workforce). We are the world's peacekeeper, but we can't seem to keep the peace at home.

In the future, the health of our economy, the glue of our society, and the quality of our lives will be greatly affected by how we deal with these divisions and contradictions. I don't pretend to have all the answers. But I do know what two necessary—if not sufficient—parts of the solution must be. We must get our overall economic act together, boost America's rates of savings and investment, and get living standards growing again. We must also find new public resources to make investments in the human capital we are squandering—investments like the Committee for Economic Development program to help improve the health and education of underclass kids that I recommend in Chapter 10. What will achieving both of these goals require? Reexamining our priorities and spending less on consumption today, both publicly and privately, in order to invest more in the future, both publicly and privately. In other words, we will have to make tough choices.

By way of comparison, take a look at other major industrial countries, where the birthrate among teenage girls is two-fifths what it is in America, the murder rate among children is one-fifth, and the rate of imprisonment is one-sixth. Can anyone doubt that differences like these will not only further undermine our ability to compete in a global economy but also threaten our sense of national community? Will we be able to keep the lid on our urban pressure cooker? Could it be, as some suggest, that America's melting pot is in danger of a meltdown?

Any reasonable assessment of how young people are doing must also include the liabilities on our nation's collective balance sheet. It was

---

* See Chart 1–9 in Part III, entitled "Social Indicators: International Comparison," for an overview of how the United States compares with other major industrial nations on a wide variety of social indicators. Also, for a revealing picture of the broad impact of the breakdown in family structure on some of America's most pressing social problems—poverty, crime, and declining school performance—I would suggest the article "Dan Quayle Was Right," in the April 1993 issue of *The Atlantic Monthly*.

Herbert Hoover (my only predecessor who ever made it anywhere after serving as secretary of commerce) who used to say: "Blessed are the young for they shall inherit the debt." But he never could have imagined the size of the debt tomorrow's workforce will confront. We seem to have adopted the dictum attributed to Donald Trump: "The way to get rich is to borrow." Rather than invest so that tomorrow's workers can *earn* more, our deficit-intoxicated government keeps handing out consumption promises so that tomorrow's workers will *pay* more. Some of these promises consist of future interest on the national debt; others consist of future benefits under such entitlement programs as Social Security, Medicare, and civil service and military pensions. The sum total of these federal liabilities is staggering. It exceeds, by $15 trillion, the value of all federally owned assets, tangible or financial, plus all future payroll taxes payable by today's adults. This mind-numbing bill—equivalent to about $150,000 per household—is supposed to be paid by our kids. There are three basic ways they can pay it: through higher taxes, through higher inflation (a kind of hidden tax), or both. Some choice! But then again, our children *will* have a real choice. When they understand the size of the bad check we are passing them, they could, amid ugly intergenerational conflict, simply decide not to honor it at all.

In sum, the hard truth is that *full disclosure and honest accounting would show that today's generation of workforce entrants is the first in American history to be bankrupt.* A good indication of how bad they're doing is how well a certain firm called Crane and Company is doing. That's the firm that makes the paper on which U.S. currency and other financial instruments like Treasury bonds are printed. It has been reporting record sales.

My generation's grandchildren—like my Alexandra, age seven, Peter Cary, age three, and Steven, born just last summer—are the true proxy for our long-term future. We should also ask, "How are those little big shots doing?" now and how will they be doing when they become adults. What are we investing in *them*? If the bottom-line progress for my generation's children is starkly different from mine, the prospect for our grandchildren is, simply, *stark.*

A quarter-century ago, funding for programs aimed at improving the lives and prospects of children was at the top of the public agenda. The poverty rate among Americans under age six was lower than that among Americans over age sixty-five. Today, including as income the value of noncash benefits such as food stamps and health insurance, the overall poverty rate among Americans under age six is nearly three times the rate among Americans over age sixty-five. Half of these poor children are not even immunized against major diseases. Meanwhile, the elderly have shown the largest relative income gains of any age group—and, of course, have universal Medicare. Imagine the public outcry if it were not the young but the elderly whose poverty rate was hitting its worst level in more than a generation!

This replacement of our traditional "endowment ethic," which is all about investment in the future, with an "entitlement ethic," which is all about consumption, especially by those of us who are older, is all too evident in one more statistic my father would have found unthinkable. The federal government spends eleven times more per capita on old people who are approaching the end of life than it invests in children at the beginning of life.

On moral grounds alone, I would have hoped that we would have heeded Dietrich Bonhoeffer's powerful message that "The ultimate test of a moral society is the kind of world it leaves to its children." My father, and most of his generation, never heard of Dietrich Bonhoeffer. Yet I am certain they understood his message. Even during the reviled tax-and-spend days of the 1960s and 1970s, Americans still remembered it, if imperfectly. Whatever one thinks of the wisdom of the policies, at least they had a certain moral virtue: Society paid for virtually all of the current spending through higher taxes then and there. Our recent borrow-and-spend policies have no such redeeming virtue. We receive the benefits of the spending; our children and grandchildren pay the costs.

A DIMINISHED AMERICAN DREAM

The American Dream has always been about optimism. The current "middle-class meltdown" has diminished even our children's view of the American Dream. When a recent survey of middle-class children posed the question, "Which would be worse, to be poor or to be blind?" the majority of the children chose "poor" and explained their answer in a most moving way: "You could do something about being blind, but you couldn't do anything about being poor."

In particular, Americans have always been optimistic about the long-term future. This is the optimism that fueled our confidence to save and invest. How do the American people currently view our long-term future? By stunning margins, Americans now seem to feel that while we won the Cold War, we are rapidly losing our economic war—and, in many cases, may not even be on the economic battlefield. The public's view is that the world economy has changed profoundly but that the United States has failed to change with it. Rapidly overtaking us in income and wealth, Japan has become the metaphor for our deepening anxieties. By an extraordinary margin—77 percent to 14 percent—Americans say they believe Japan's economy is *already* stronger than ours! This perception is wrong. Our GNP is still about 80 percent bigger than Japan's; per-worker output in the United States is still higher as well, though not by nearly so much. But the American public senses the direction of things and has adopted one of Yogi Berra's dicta: "The future ain't what it used to be."

In their bones, the American people know the melancholy fact is that our nation has been suffering from a long-term, silent, and progressive disease rather like arteriosclerosis. We've been on a consumption binge, piling up debt in our economic system just as eager eaters pile up fat in their arteries. It takes many years of careless living to develop arteriosclerosis, and it may take many years of careful "dieting" and "exercise" to cure our economic maladies.

The common denominator of America's various economic ills, it seems to me, is the difficulty Americans have in making explicit choices about allocating national resources and determining a national direction. The relevant question is not why the politicians obsessed with getting re-elected want to fool us, but why we apparently want to be fooled. Why have we been so ready to believe panglossian projections about the future? Why have we swallowed the preposterous fantasy that we can deny the existence of free lunches at the same time we're eating them? Why are we paralyzed in the face of such tasks as cutting the deficit, improving education, rebuilding our infrastructure, and reversing the spread of poverty and social dysfunction in our underclass— problems that are universally described as "compelling" and for which action is said to be "imperative"? Why do we tolerate so many things we say are "intolerable"? Why was my father's generation thrifty and why is mine profligate? How can we regain our former habits of thrift and industry? Why, in short, have we become the "Choiceless Society"—one in which we and our politicians above all dread the day that events will force us to confront *real* choices and *real* tradeoffs?

FROM THRIFT ETHIC TO ENTITLEMENT ETHIC

Let me focus for a moment on one central manifestation of our choicelessness: our seeming inability to save enough. Finding ways to replenish America's reservoir of savings is, I believe, the single most important thing we can do to improve our nation's long-term economic health. Yet all one hears are misleading excuses for doing nothing. Even many of those who fully agree that our savings rate is low by international standards argue that it has always been low. Americans are just lucky and plucky and have always gotten along just fine without much thought for tomorrow. In this view, self-denial and savings are the traditional Old World poisons; self-indulgence—consumption—is the liberating New World elixir.

But this kind of argument is historical nonsense. When America entered this century, roughly the era my father immigrated, we were tied with Germany for the world's highest saving rate—and tied with no one for the world's swiftest productivity growth. True, we borrowed from abroad. But we did so only to expand our already-massive pool of home-grown savings. When we took out loans from the French, we invested nearly all of what we borrowed in capital goods such as steel plants, locomotives, and even the rails of the Union Pacific trunk line my father and uncle helped build. In that era, those added investments so increased our productivity that we were easily able to pay back our foreign debt. It was only in the late 1970s, by which time we were consuming 93 percent of our GDP, that America's savings rate became the lowest among all major industrial countries. By the 1980s, the only record we could beat was our own. And that we did—consuming an incredible 97 percent of our economy's production. As for our foreign borrowing, much of it didn't go into investment at all. In effect, what the Japanese lent us enabled us to buy ever more autos and VCRs. When those wear out, all we'll have left to show for our borrowing is the debt.

The flip side of our failure to save is our addiction to entitlements, that fathomless river of federal benefits, which, including both direct outlays and benefitlike tax subsidies, now amounts to about 16 percent of our GDP. From 1965 to today, just the *growth* in direct federal entitlements as a share of GDP has been about 50 percent greater than the share of our economy we have devoted, on average, to *total* net investment in business plant and equipment *and* public infrastructure since the mid-1980s.

Few political leaders like to talk about entitlements as a reverse or "negative" endowment to the young. Yet the evidence is clear that they crowd investment outlays out of public-sector budgets, crowd savings out of private-sector financial markets, and generate trillions of dollars of unfunded liabilities that we are passing on to our children. This frightening reality is greeted with embarrassed silence—or else we paper over our choicelessness with unrealistic projections and "off-budget" accounting tricks.

Yet no such reticence prevents us from talking about what we will receive as opposed to what we will give. It appears that everyone today, rich or poor, is "entitled" to something—from the elderly, who are entitled to windfall Social Security checks and more health care than they need, regardless of income; to veterans, who are entitled to free health care whether or not their disabilities are service-related; to homeowners, who are invited to finance even million-dollar homes through borrowing at the taxpayer's expense; to hog ranchers (in return for the hogs they don't raise); to corn farmers (in return for corn they don't grow for the hogs that aren't raised); to ranchers generally, who in good times or bad are entitled to cash payments, cheap water and electricity, and free grazing rights; to government employees, some of whom are entitled to more income in retirement than they ever earned in government service; and—yes, you guessed it—to Peter G. Peterson, whose simple citizenship entitles him to a panoply of tax-sheltered public benefits upon retirement, regardless of his financial need or whether he has paid for them.

Having crossed the threshold into official senior citizen ranks, each day brings me news of my own public- and private-sector entitlements. Experts tell me that my various federal entitlements will net me, of all people, at least $100,000 in benefits above and beyond my lifetime contributions plus interest. And much of this will be tax-free. As to my private-sector entitlements, I have recently enjoyed handsome senior citizen discounts at retail shops, the movies, and of all places, the liquor store! Welfare for the well-off elderly has become the most sacrosanct, most costly, and fastest-growing of our entitlements. Our public old-age benefit programs are now so embedded in our political economy that we can, with a straight face, say it is "impossible" to do anything about reforming them at the very same time that we say programs for our poor children are "unaffordable." At some point, we will have to relearn the true meanings of "impossibility" and "unaffordability."

In the meantime, we'll have to continue to borrow to pay our way— adding to the mountains of debt we've already accumulated. During the 1980s, a single president could congratulate himself on having sold twice as much federal debt to the public as all the cumulative paper issued by Presidents George Washington through Jimmy Carter over the course of two centuries. By themselves, debts and deficits are neither good nor bad. They are *means* to an end, which may or may not be constructive. Alas, our public debt is largely used to finance extra consumption, not extra investment. Indeed, even as the federal deficit has been rising, public investment has been declining—until, by 1992, barely five cents out of each federal dollar flowed to nondefense outlays for any form of research or equipment or structure that remained standing after the fiscal year was over. The current federal budget is all—or virtually all—about consumption. America's future agenda is—or should be—all about investment.

The road leading up to our 1980s debt binge was long and broad and wide. For many years everyone had been helping us get there. And for many years to come everyone will be paying the price. Literally. Since 1979, interest costs have been far and away the fastest-growing item in the federal budget. They soared by 376 percent, compared with 148 percent for defense, where most people assume the major growth

occurred. All told, our cumulative public debt is now adding an extra
$200 billion to the budget each year—just to pay the net interest! To
borrow a line from The Concord Coalition, if there is a real line item
in the budget we could label "waste, fraud, and abuse," that's it: the
cost of our past profligacy. What does this extra burden of $200 billion
mean in the context of the federal budget? It is over fifteen times more
than the federal government spends on the "war on drugs"; about ten
times more than it spends on education; seven and one-half times
more than the federal government spends on nondefense R&D; and
four times more than it spends on means-tested cash benefits for the
poor.

The recession separating the 1980s from the 1990s—with its credit
contractions and wrenching balance-sheet adjustments—has made the
country suddenly willing to face the possibility that every component of
the American Dream is in danger, sustainability most of all. From a
decade of false hope, we have entered one of sobered expectations.

The presidential campaign of 1992 made clear that there is a growing desire for change. First, there was the early success of Paul Tsongas's truth-telling campaign. Then came the groundswell of support
for H. Ross Perot when he entered the race with the message of getting
serious about tackling America's long-term economic problems. Finally, there was Bill Clinton. He ran and won his whole campaign on
the theme of change—especially economic change. If the constituency
for a shift in national direction is not yet a majority of Americans, it is
manifestly not a silent minority, either. What we—and the leadership
we elected—have yet to face up to is the magnitude and types of
changes we must make to get our future back.

AN AMERICAN "BUSINESS PLAN"

I readily confess that I do not understand all that ails America, nor do
I know how to cure all the ailments. From my perspective as a businessman raised in Kearney, Nebraska, I simply find the direction of our
current public policies very troubling. When I look at government as a
business—a business entrusted with the security, prosperity, and social
welfare of our people—I am shocked by the poor use of resources,
poor management, and poor results.

Any long-term "turnaround" of the U.S. economy must begin with
a much more businesslike approach to government. Indeed, we should
start with something roughly akin to a *business plan*. Why does government need a business plan? Not because business managers know
more about the ends of government than anyone else. (Obviously they
don't.) Nor because the challenge of fiscal discipline can be reduced

to uncovering some fraudulent act of accounting or some gross act of mismanagement. (Though these may contribute to the problem.) Rather, government needs a business plan because such a plan forces us to make rational, responsible, long-term choices about how to allocate our limited public resources among potentially limitless public objectives. The goal of a government business plan would be easy enough to state: By freeing up resources for private investment and by increasing what we invest publicly, we want to make America the most competitive, productive, and affluent economy in the world of the twenty-first century. Everyone would agree with that goal. Yet all the tough questions in such a business plan would still remain unanswered: How much more must we invest and in what to achieve our productivity growth goals? And what are we willing to sacrifice or trade off to make those investment resources available? Alas, you don't raise productivity by declaring your desire to do it. You need to save for it. You need to commit resources of all kinds—financial, intellectual, and political.

Let me give an example of what I mean by sacrifices and tradeoffs. Consider prenatal medical care for low-income mothers as a potential investment. First we must ask what are the long-term social costs of premature or low-birth-weight infants. If the costs are large (as most experts agree they are), then how certain are we that resources spent on such a program will reduce the costs? And, if we are certain, how much should we spend? Where should we make the tradeoff between the current consumption of today's taxpayers and an investment whose full return (on each infant who will not later require extra government-paid health care and special education) will not show up for years?

Finally, we come to the hardest choices. *How do we pay for it? What else do we forgo?* Providing prenatal health care to every low-income pregnant mother might cost, say, an extra $2 billion per year. That's roughly equivalent to the cost of maintaining twelve thousand American troops in Europe. Do we forgo those troops? Or to 20 percent of one year's automatic COLA raise in Social Security benefits. Do we forgo that COLA? Or to a two-cents-per-gallon gasoline tax. Do we pay that tax? We need to say: If you want to make this investment, you can. But—as any businessman knows but our government has forgotten—you *must* choose a way to fund it. You cannot claim to be a courageous children's advocate by demanding that child benefits be funded through additional debt. That's tantamount to asking children to pay for their own care. We can no longer tolerate the mentality that says, "Yes, we insist on it; but no, we don't want to pay for it."

Some will deride what I propose as the "Peterson Sacrifice Test" for American political leaders. That's okay. It's the right test. Under the Peterson Sacrifice Test, the public always needs to know what the costs and the tradeoffs are now and in the future. Then they will need to make a choice: If we decide we really need this program, what are we willing to give up, either in benefits forgone or in new taxes raised? It's that simple.

REMEMBERING OUR PARENTS

Unless a nation pays the dues for economic progress, its politics become a harsh and illiberal contest over scarce resources. With each passing day the losers are more likely to be the poor and the weak, our children and grandchildren.

My father's definition of the American Dream, though unambiguously economic and "materialistic," is in fact closely tied to most qualitative measures of national progress. History clearly teaches us that societies that choose economic progress also tend to achieve most of the other goals of a liberal and advancing civilization—from a cleaner environment, better health, and better education to social mobility, equal opportunity, and a greater sense of national community. In short, the connection between economic and noneconomic quality of life is not neutral. It is either a virtuous circle or a vicious circle.

As I have given voice to my concerns about the future in articles and at dinner parties and business meetings over the last few years, critics have called me a "Cadillac Cassandra," the worst kind of Cassandra. Friends have said, "What's with you, Peterson? Don't you know that we've won the global battle with communism, and now the rest of the world is striving to emulate *our* kind of democracy and *our* free markets? Don't you, of all people, a son of poor immigrants, realize you're a beneficiary of this greatest, richest, and freest country in the world, which you are so bent on criticizing?" Invariably, I answer them: "Yes, I certainly do, and in the decades to come I want to *keep it that way*. I want America to remain as great and rich and free for my children and grandchildren as it was for my parents and as it has been for me." The real question, of course, is not whether we complain about our problems, but what we do about them. I agree with Ben Franklin, who after a personal, public attack said this in 1775: "Grievances cannot be redressed unless they are known; and they cannot be known but through complaints. . . . If these are deemed affronts, and the messengers punished as offenders, who will henceforth send petitions? . . . Where complaining is a crime, hope becomes despair."

The challenges ahead are indeed daunting. To face up to them, it may help to look back to my father and his generation for inspiration. When George Petropoulos arrived in America and found out how hard it was to deal with life in a foreign country with a foreign culture and a foreign language, he resisted all temptation to look backward and simply pressed on. When my mother and father found out how much a new home cost, or how much they would have to save to put their kids through college, they did not shudder at the numbers. Rather, they and millions like them rolled up their sleeves and went to work.

We would do well to see ourselves as new immigrants and pioneers of a kind, attempting to clear the new American wilderness of debts and excess entitlements in order to create a new future. When I look at my grandchildren, Alexandra, Peter Cary, and Steven, I hear my father's voice telling me that we must do whatever it takes to allow their generation and their America to "do better."

2

How We Became the Choiceless Society

To govern is to choose.
—PIERRE MENDES-FRANCE

Since World War II, this country has gone through some fundamental transformations.

- From the world's biggest saver to the world's biggest consumer
- From the world's largest creditor to the world's largest debtor
- From a country that sometimes borrowed from abroad mainly to fund investment to one that consistently borrows much larger amounts, mainly for consumption
- From a country with rates of investment and productivity growth that were among the highest of all industrial nations to a country with rates of investment and productivity growth that are among the lowest
- From a "bank-vault" government that saved for our common future to a "vending-machine" government that doles out consumption to entitled interest groups, each one an entrepreneur for its own private advancement
- From a country that invested in its children to one that borrows from its children

- From a country that we knew was astride history to one in which we feel that history is astride us
- From a country with the built-in discipline of a political system that was reluctant to say "yes" to public expenditures that might be deficit-inducing to the undiscipline of a system that seems incapable of saying "no" to added spending, even in the face of deficits that would have terrified the parents and grandparents of today's leaders

HAVING IT ALL

Even now that the 1980s boom is over and everyone speaks of waking up to the 1990s, one still sees everywhere the distressing symptoms of the new American motto: "We can have it all—now." As a firstborn son of a Greek mother, I was born to be an eager eater. Food is a chosen instrument for communication and connectedness in Greek families. *The New York Times* food section is thus a must-read. Recently, I couldn't stop reading about a new invention: the "mix-in cuisine" prepared so that you "don't have to choose" and "you don't have to worry about what you are missing. You can have it all." Ice cream with candy mixed in. Cookies with ice cream sandwiched between. The culinary equivalent of high spending and low taxes. No decision required. No consequences mentioned. We even make a virtue of being choiceless.

Sometime over the past few decades, Americans leaped to an incredible conclusion: Because we could do seemingly anything—invent atomic bombs, eradicate polio, yes, even fly to the moon—we apparently decided we could do *everything*. We lost the capacity to separate the essential from the desirable. But one doesn't lose something without first losing sight of its importance. So we have to explain how we lost the ability to think, talk about, and then act on the choices that really matter, by which I mean those choices that directly affect our economic future—and thus indirectly affect every other aspect of our future.

I do not believe that the American people made a deliberate choice for deficits and slow growth—or indeed against the future. The process of losing our way economically has been largely uncritical, undeliberate, and inadvertent. The choices were never framed honestly and seriously. The American people were never provided with realistic assessments of the costs and benefits of different courses of action. In the special-interest, single-interest, self-interest, vending-machine political economy we gradually acquired, who stocked the machine and how we ensured that it would not run out of goods were questions whose importance was forgotten in the scramble to pull the levers.

Because the progress of our economic disease is silent and gradual, there is no noisy crash. The house isn't falling down. To use the familiar phrase, it's more like having termites. As Charles Schultze has put it, "The crisis is there is no crisis."

Unfortunately, national consensus is usually the product of historic crises. Germans support sound money because they remember that in the 1920s their parents and grandparents had to carry around deutsche marks in wheelbarrows. The Japanese display an extraordinary unity behind policies favoring savings and investment because they recall a period when their nation's entire capital stock lay decimated by war. For Americans, the only remotely parallel economic crisis was the Great Depression, and the lessons learned—that "excessive savings" can stall economic growth, that at all costs consumer demand should never be allowed to collapse, and that the government can stimulate the economy out of any predicament—have little application to the low-savings economy America has acquired over the course of the postwar era. Yet these lessons engendered a long-standing fiscal infatuation with a crude version of Keynesian theory (the much-maligned English economist would be shocked to learn we now run deficits during periods of economic expansion and contraction alike) that continues to divert our attention from the fundamental savings and investment inputs on which future living standards ultimately depend.

It is hard to have a collective view of our future without a collective view of our past. We must gain such a view, or our silent, gradual, noncrisis disease will eventually put our society in the intensive care unit. Along the way, we will have to answer some uncomfortable questions. Why did we, particularly my generation, stand by and let it happen? How, when, and why did the future and the young and the poor and the general interest become so under-represented? Why is there so little connection between our short-term personal cravings and long-term national needs? How did we manage in a few short decades of hubris to forget that fundamental lesson of two centuries of American history: To bequeath a better future to those who come after us, we must be willing to give up something today? In short, how did we become the "Choiceless Society"?

By "choiceless," do I mean we have no choices? Of course not. Even the decision not to choose is a choice of a kind. Indeed, to continue the status quo is one of the most profound choices of all. What I mean is we are *not* making *real* choices—the *tough* economic choices that confront us directly with tradeoffs between today's consumption and tomorrow's higher living standards for ourselves and our children.

When we ostensibly focus on economic "choices," it's often just demagoguery and diversionary tactics. The American people, for instance, have been led to believe—and apparently do believe—that "waste, fraud, and abuse" account for most federal spending. All we have to do is get rid of congressional and executive perquisites or perhaps clean up the post office mess in the House and, eureka, the deficit will be slashed. On matters fiscal, that kind of "it's not us but them" scapegoat-conspiracy theory is about all we seem able to agree on when it comes to "choosing."

Other so-called economic choices we engage in are better described as *rhetorical* posturing—left, right, and center. We hear that we must invest more in our children, or invest in solving the problems of our underclass, or invest in infrastructure, or invest in R&D, or invest in advanced manufacturing technologies like robotics—we must invest, invest, invest. We also hear we must not only invest more but save more, because it is downright dangerous, not to mention impoverishing, to borrow the investment capital abroad—especially given rapidly changing priorities in Western Europe and Japan.

But, if we are really serious about saving and investing more, we must *temporarily* consume less. Alas, this does require *temporary* sacrifice. And in our politics of pleasure the "S" word (for sacrifice) has been more politically toxic than the "L" word (for liberal). I'm reminded of what the ancient historian Livy said in summing up the decadence of his time: "The citizens of Rome can neither bear their ills nor their cures."

LOSING OUR WAY—AND OUR WILL

Somewhere along the way we lost our way and we lost our will. George Bush was fond of saying, "We have the will but not the wallet." That's backward. In an investment agenda I will outline in Chapter 8, an additional $400 billion a year could do the job of spurring productivity growth and reigniting the rise in U.S. living standards. In a $6 trillion economy—still the world's richest and largest—it is absurd to say we don't have the wallet. It is the will that we lack.

Not being an economist bothers me not at all. But not being a historian, or social scientist, or political scientist does. It is to those disciplines that one must ultimately look to understand where, when, how, and why America became the Choiceless Society.

But this layman can at least ask some questions. What happened to weaken our commitment to posterity? What collective decisions and what national character traits helped us toward this fall from grace, this course into the wrong future? Professionals from many disciplines, and we the people, must probe deeper. We must assess the new cultural currents since the 1960s that have gradually undermined principles of public responsibility and replaced them with relativistic ethics and the therapeutic language of personal victimization. We must assess changes in our political institutions that have severed an ever-growing number of individuals from any sense of reciprocal ties to the national community. We must assess how the loss of another unifying element within our national psyche and between America and its competitor nations— the loss of fear of the Soviet Union—further unravels the conviction that we have vital common interests. We must assess how weakened families, increased geographical mobility, and frequent job changes have made it more difficult for individuals to develop habits of group or community sacrifice. We must ponder the impact of generational change: how the aging of the generation of World War II veterans, with their boundless faith in community, social discipline, and public progress, has left a vacuum in American life that younger, more in-dulged, less civic-minded generations cannot fill. We must explain why these elders have themselves subtly transformed their own ethos of collective duty into an ethos of collective reward.

Surely, the causes are many and dauntingly complex. Yet surfacing again and again in the story of America's postwar journey are certain economic and fiscal themes that go right to the heart of what this book is about. Allow this layman to sketch a few of the steps in that story as he has witnessed and understood them.

As I look back, it seems the road leading to our current debacle was traveled by many in both parties. Although it is the failed policies of the 1980s that have finally pushed our economy up against the fundamental equation linking long-term economic outputs with long-term economic inputs, we should recall that the prospects for the American Dream were grim even before Ronald Reagan took office. The "Morning in America" Republicans have no monopoly on blame. Long before the Reagan revolution, it was Democratic opinion leaders who had originally persuaded the public to regard the budget and tax code as the means to cost-free consumption. But in the end, neither the rise of the "litigation liberal" nor the rise of the "supply-side conserva-tive"—though I have been voluble in my criticism of both—offers a full explanation for the advent of choicelessness in America.

A NEW LOOK AT POSTWAR HISTORY

Our tilt toward choicelessness started soon after World War II. America's industrial plant was undamaged. If anything, its output had been greatly spurred by the innovations, investments, and incentives of our extraordinary wartime effort. I vividly recall FDR's fireside chats spur-ring us on to one almighty production goal after another—fifty thou-sand planes one day, one hundred thousand tanks another. We always seemed to reach, and even exceed, his goals.

With our typical American hubris, small wonder that we concluded *we* had won the war. Some years later, I was to find others had a very different view of how that war had been won. In 1972, while I was representing our government in its negotiations with the Soviet Union on trade and Lend-Lease payments, Secretary General Leonid Brezhnev took me aside for a rare one-on-one exchange. As the two of us looked over the terrace of his very capitalistic Black Sea resort home, Olympic-size indoor-outdoor swimming pool and all, he grasped my arm, looked me squarely in the eye, and with voice shaking said: "Does not your President understand that while you ask for cold cash interest payments on Lend-Lease, we already have paid far, far more, with the blood of twenty-one million human Russian lives?" That's seventy times the number of Americans who lost their lives in battle in World War II!

But whatever history's ultimate verdict, we indeed felt *we* had won the war. And the sole possession of the world's only atomic weapons did nothing to diminish that view, or our hubris. With our world-dominating industrial plant capacity intact and our technological leadership in virtually every field, economic competitiveness was not something we had to strive for. It was a given.

This postwar economic hubris lived side by side with our terror of the "lessons" of the Great Depression. Everybody, economists and the business establishment alike, was reading from the same prayer book—authored, they thought, by Lord John Maynard Keynes. The problem, it seemed, was that the private economy tended inexorably toward "excessive savings." That may indeed have been a problem for the world in which Keynes was writing during the 1930s—and for an America that, during the Great Depression, suffered from a variety of policy-induced maladies, such as tariff mania and monetary contraction, not to mention a catastrophic implosion of business and household demand. Yet it has hardly been a problem over most of the postwar era, when our once world-leading savings rate has lagged far behind those of faster-growing economies in Europe and Japan.

The countries we perceive as our main "competitors" today took a far different course—180 degrees different. Japan's rise to superpower status as the ultimate supply-side economy was aided by the common view of its people that it was a humble little island that had little food, few resources, and even fewer friends. The Japanese knew they had no alternative but to rebuild their capital stock the old-fashioned way: They would have to earn it. In other words, they would have to invest a lot, and to invest a lot they would have to save a lot. This Japanese sense of national self, enhanced by such incentives as zero taxes on personal savings up to substantial levels, spawned what has become the world's highest-saving, highest-investment economy.

Then there's Germany. Like Japan's, its industrial plant was devastated. Like Japan, it was fearful—especially fearful of its *own* economic and political history. Germany's postwar leaders were determined never again to allow the conditions that helped give rise to Nazi triumphs. Condition number one, at least in the minds of those who lived through that era, was runaway inflation. From the summer of 1922 through the end of 1923, prices in Germany rose over *one trillion* percent! A loaf of bread came to 450 billion marks, up from less than one-third of one mark during the pre–World War I period.

I remember listening to former West German chancellor Willy Brandt as he described how, as a child, he had to pack his family's lifetime savings of deutsche marks into bags and take them to the local orphanage. There they were used to start a fire so the children would be kept warm. "You Americans simply have never experienced the hell that can take place in a country if it doesn't get inflation under control," Brandt said. "It is what brought us Adolf Hitler. It's what transformed, in a hideous way, our entire values and society." Thus, post–World War II Germany became inflation-phobic—and a deep believer in high savings, high investment, high productivity, and low interest rates.

So there we have it. Japan and Germany, two very different countries, from their own separate and deeply painful political experience, forged their own brand of future-friendly, supply-side, producer economy. Both of them did it the old-fashioned way. We Americans, however, rewrote our own historical experience. We began to forget our two centuries of endowment ethic history. We set out to build a consumption ethic and a demand-side economy. We succeeded—all too well. Too much of our Yankee ingenuity began to turn away from new ways to produce wealth. Too much turned instead toward imaginative ways of consuming it.

We encouraged borrowing and consumption in virtually every way possible. We didn't just glorify consumption, we implicitly declared savings to be bad by penalizing savers. We gave tax breaks for debt. We made housing cheap through government-guaranteed mortgages and unlimited tax deductibility for mortgage interest. In America, we're proud that home buyers may only have to put down a nickel on the dollar as equity. In Japan, a nation of savers, consumers often put one-third to one-half down! Until recently in America, the interest on consumer borrowing for practically everything was fully tax deductible—a provision of tax laws unheard of in the rest of the industrial world. We even called income from savings and investment "unearned income," much to the astonishment of our trading partners. During my official days at Commerce, I recall the question asked more than once by the Japanese minister of finance: "Mr. Secretary, please explain putting the highest taxes on what you call unearned income. We have always assumed that income from savings was the most earned of all. It is hard work to save, don't you think?" Why are we surprised that Japan became the producer society even as we became the consumer society?

Our consumption tilt was not due to tax incentives alone. It was regularly reinforced by our media and in our schools. American children were offered unlimited television and called on to do minimal schoolwork, while children in our competitor nations were permitted only limited television and were required to do much heavier schoolwork. My wife, Joan Ganz Cooney, cofounder of the Children's Television Workshop and originator of *Sesame Street*, has always been appalled by our laissez-faire attitude toward the television fare offered up to our children. "The United States," she tells me, was "the only country in the world that permitted the available VHF channels to be dedicated 100 percent to commercial interests, with virtually no regulation of the networks and very weak, very loose, very minor, intermittent regulation of local stations or of the number of commercials aimed at children." The continual message of most commercial television is a glorification of instant gratification—unbalanced by any call for long-term thinking or for making any difficult tradeoffs between what you have now and what you can have later. My own children's Saturday morning television fare was one endless stream of cartoons and commercials with at least sixty-seven varieties of a simple message: "Buy now."

The fast pace of economic growth lubricated the shift to consumption and choicelessness. During the 1950s and 1960s, real take-home pay increased at a yearly rate of 2.5 percent, while our productivity growth averaged 2.3 percent per year. In the span of twenty years, real GNP doubled and real per capita GNP rose by 50 percent. By the mid-1960s, the expectation that seemingly effortless economic growth would continue indefinitely had become an unspoken article of national faith.

As for our economists, their rhetoric certainly helped to ignite the spirit of limitless expectations. In the late 1960s, Congress heard testimony from one eminent economist suggesting that accelerating affluence would, by 1985, translate into a twenty-two-hour work week or, alternatively, retirement at age thirty-eight. David Riesman declared that "the problem of production had been solved" and that now we were "moving into the frontiers of consumption." Stuart Chase advised us to "cash in on the triumph of our thrift." William Baumol wrote that "in our economy, by and large, the future can be left to take care of itself." John Kenneth Galbraith, in his best-seller *The Affluent Society*, assured us that we had entered an era of guaranteed plenty and that the consumption and distribution of wealth, not its creation, had become our main economic challenge. Affluence, in a word, was our manifest destiny.

The buoyant mood of these times is summed up in a now-classic *Newsweek* column by economist Paul Samuelson, who cheerfully predicted in 1967 that Social Security could pay generation after generation of retirees huge returns above and beyond their contributions. Samuelson wrote:

> The beauty about social insurance is that it is *actuarially* unsound. Everyone who reaches retirement age is given benefit privileges that far exceed anything that he has paid in. And exceed his payments by more than ten times as much (or five times, counting in employer payments)!
> How is this possible? It stems from the fact that the national product is growing at compound interest and can be expected to do so as far ahead as the eye cannot see. Always there are more youths than old folks in a growing population. More important, with real incomes growing at some 3 percent per year, the taxable base upon which benefits rest in any period are [sic] much greater than the taxes paid historically by the generation now retired. . . .
> Social security is squarely based on what has been called the eighth wonder of the world—compound interest. A growing nation is the greatest Ponzi game ever contrived. And that is a fact, not a paradox.

Over the next five years after Samuelson wrote his *Newsweek* column, Congress persuaded itself to enact massive and permanent benefit-level increases to all Social Security recipients, rich and poor alike, without any regard to whether they had "earned" the increases through prior contributions or (in retrospect) any realistic assessment of how younger Americans would be able to pay for them. During those boom years, in short, Americans gradually came to assume that Yankee ingenuity had invented the perpetual prosperity machine, that any combination of national goals could be achieved without straining our economy, that our resources were limitless, and that success would be effortless.

BOTH GUNS AND BUTTER

John F. Kennedy's inaugural address memorably embodies the spirit of the 1960s with all its limitless expectations: "Let every nation know, whether it wishes us well or ill, that we shall pay any price, bear any burden, meet any hardship, support any friend, oppose any foe to assure the survival and the success of liberty." And Kennedy meant it. Soon American forces were plunging into conflicts in remote corners of the world. We did not ask if U.S. involvement in Laos or Vietnam or Cuba was worth the cost. It was an irrelevant question in a country whose President had declared we could afford "any price." Any price? Any burden? Fitting slogans, perhaps, for a nation engaged in total war—but a dangerous siren song for a nation already longing to release itself from the need to make realistic resource tradeoffs. Listening to this we-can-do-everything message, perhaps a few Americans felt premonitions of trouble to come. But once the business cycle began revving up late in Kennedy's presidency, we put our worries behind us. The stodgy Ike years were over. A nation taking "longer strides" (as Kennedy put it)—ready to police the world, guarantee affluence, cure poverty, build monorails, and fly to the moon—was about to get moving again.

When Lyndon Baines Johnson assumed office, U.S. GNP was projected to soar to such unimaginable heights by the end of the century that it seemed practically *immoral* not to force much wealthier future generations to share some of their inevitable riches with those of us living in the (comparatively impoverished) present. Richard Nixon later confided to me that far more than morality was involved. According to Nixon, LBJ was so obsessed with the sophisticated Ivy League, Brahmanlike Kennedyites that he was going to out-Kennedy the Kennedys when it came to liberal innovations in domestic policy.

How did LBJ intend to finance two wars at the same time, one against the communists in Southeast Asia and the other against poverty in the United States? Some of his economic advisors, fearful of the inflationary effects of military expenditures rising at nearly 20 percent per year, proposed a surtax. But LBJ had no intention of risking his popularity that way. A proposal to hike taxes, he knew, would force Congress and the public to make a choice between raising the military stakes in Vietnam on the one hand and going ahead full bore with the Great Society on the other. With the help of some hasty accounting changes*—and inflation—LBJ was determined to pursue both courses simultaneously. "Guns and butter." We were on our way to a new answer to the question: Which? The answer now was: Both.

Once again, America's leading academics came to the political rescue. For several years, the team of "New Economists" that Kennedy had brought with him to the White House had been advocating deliberate budget deficits as a cure for recession. But the message propounded by these academics did not sit well with public opinion. Unreasonably—or so it seemed to the academics—most Americans retained an instinctive distrust of government debt in any form. (Back then, believe it or not, many business groups actually opposed Kennedy's investment tax credit because they deemed it fiscally irre-

---

* Among other things, LBJ pushed through a change in the budget law moving Social Security "on-budget." The change itself was sensible. Like any other spending program, Social Security consumes tax dollars that might instead be spent on other public purposes. It most definitely should be counted as part of our "unified" or "consolidated" budget. But the timing of the change was political. It allowed LBJ to cover up a deficit with a Social Security surplus in FY 1969—the last time we ever balanced the budget.

sponsible.) In response, the New Economists organized an educational campaign aimed at ridding the public of its irrational "Puritan Ethic." By the time LBJ was in the White House, and our 1960s boom well under way, their new gospel had won America over. Good-bye, Puritan Ethic. Hello, Go-Go Sixties.

By the end of the decade, vast new initiatives—some stillborn and others ultimately enacted—rose up in spectacular variety: Model Cities, Volunteers in Service to America (VISTA), Community Action, the Comprehensive Employment and Training Act (CETA), the Older Americans Act, and Medicare were some of the more memorable. We believed that *without any significant rise in taxes* or any other means of moderating the growth in private consumption, we could still afford to fight a major war in Asia, rebuild our cities, cure age-old diseases, fly to the moon, and—most fatefully in terms of cost—reallocate wealth through public benefits, whether of old New Deal or new Great Society vintage.

Wilbur Cohen, Secretary of Health, Education and Welfare, tells of coming to LBJ with a proposal for a 10 percent across-the-board hike in Social Security benefits. Johnson's reaction, according to Cohen, was to tell him it was too little—"Come on, Wilbur, you can do better than that!" But the greatest of all bound-to-balloon entitlement expansions was Medicare. When President Johnson signed the Medicare act in 1965, he defended the program by saying that an extra $500 million (that's right, "million," not "billion") of new spending would present "no problem" for the federal government. Today—twenty-nine years later—the size of Medicare is three hundred times that original estimate. Its cost is about $150 *billion*—and is now growing by over $15 *billion* each year.

In retrospect, Medicare was a prime example of choicelessness. When an overwhelmingly Democratic Congress debated the pros and cons of various elderly health-benefit proposals in the spring and summer of 1965, the idea of financing such a program on any basis other than open-ended fee-for-service reimbursement was never even seriously considered. Why not? One reason, to be sure, was that few legislators at the time had the slightest inkling what Medicare would cost a couple of decades down the road. But there was certainly another reason: the implacable hostility of the American Medical Association and the American Hospital Association to any program that impinged on the "freedom" of their members to treat any beneficiary or to charge for services in their customary manner. The proponents of guaranteed health care for the elderly worried that the AMA might rally enough support to block Medicare—or that health-care providers might turn it into a fiasco by organized resistance (such as a boycott of beneficiaries).

Medicare's reimbursement policy was thus the product of what critics have called a great "bribe." Legislators got what they wanted: acceptance of Medicare by the medical profession. And doctors and hospitals got what they wanted: freedom to practice medicine in return for public money just as they had always practiced it in return for private money.

THE ENTITLEMENT REVOLUTION

Meanwhile, America was also witness to the beginning of a sad social and political transformation. Recall how three presidencies were destroyed in a row: those of Kennedy, Johnson, and Nixon. The John Kennedy, Bobby Kennedy, and Martin Luther King assassinations plus Watergate might alone have caused the American people to lose faith in public institutions. But, in my view, the Vietnam tragedy did the most damage. It did not escape the attention of many, and certainly not America's disadvantaged, that the affluent could avoid the draft and the death of their children, while the poor and minorities could not.*

In any event, the multiple cultural and social shocks of this era seemed to sever our common bonds of citizenship, our "sense of the platoon." Throughout American society, the breakdown of trust in our public institutions helped catalyze the unleashing of an unbridled quest for individual consumption. Our attitude seems to have become "Don't be a sucker. Don't produce it. Grab it. There's plenty, and besides you deserve it." The general interest and the national interest that had long animated this country gave way before the demands of a numbing array of special-interest organizations, PACs, and the like.

Our political system began to push pluralism to extremes. Though American politics is typically centrist, and avoids the ideologies of the left and the right, the "center" was steadily losing its intellectual coherence on its way to becoming merely a collection of intensely parochial and self-interested groups. In step with the declining capacity of political parties to mediate among diverse interests and forge unified coalitions, every group became an entrepreneur for its own private advancement. Political energies in America coursed through ever narrower channels. Deep loyalties often developed around single social issues—clean air, women's rights, abortion, the nuclear freeze, food labeling, school prayer, and "save the porpoises," to name but a few. The special interests found common ground in using the federal budget to expand today's consumption at the expense of investment in tomorrow's prosperity. The future, unrepresented, would be sacrificed.

---

* In looking back on this troubled era, we often forget to give praise where praise is due. To his credit, President Nixon gave us an *all*-volunteer army.

Out of this evolving political culture came our "entitlement revolution." Everybody seemed to acquire a grievance-oriented conviction that their own organized group—farmers, textile companies, auto unions, weapons contractors, civil servants, military pensioners, S&L depositors, Social Security retirees—possesses a "right" to some prearranged award, regardless of what the economy can afford. The budget and the tax system became little more than means of paying benefits to those groups most successful at voicing their grievances and claims. Production was taken for granted, even though productivity was beginning to slow and foreign competition was rearing its head. Ensuring one's share of the consumption pie became the central political concern.

That was perhaps the beginning of what Robert Hughes has recently called our "Culture of Complaint" and Arthur Schlesinger has dubbed the "Disuniting of America"—a balkanization of society so extreme that the notions of victimization and redress have come to replace the idea of the common good as our defining link of citizenship. It's not, of course, that many of the new rights Americans have asserted since the 1960s—above all, civil rights—did not address real and painful wrongs that had for too long festered in our society. The problem is that all too often in our entitlement revolution those with grievances to redress were concerned not with asserting constitutional or political rights, but with staking out claims to "their" share in today's consumption pie. And as for those who made the claims, they were not just—or even primarily—the disadvantaged, but the broadest possible spectrum of America's middle class. We thus ended up with an entirely nonsensical notion: universal entitlements. If we are all victims, the unspoken reasoning goes, we all deserve to be on welfare. But if everybody is on the bandwagon, who will be left to pull it?

Once under way, our entitlement revolution swiftly entrenched itself. Each of our benefit programs acquired and nurtured its own "iron triangle," a public, bureaucratic, and congressional constituency. This iron triangle, in turn, protected the program and assured its continuous expansion with a kind of "what's next" mentality. Between 1965 and 1981, the number of publicly paid staffers per U.S. senator climbed from 16 to 36, the number per U.S. representative from 9 to 17. In 1971, only 5 state governments had D.C. offices. By 1982, 34 did. From 1973 to 1993, the number of trade and professional associations with offices in the Washington, D.C., area more than doubled—from 1,128 to 2,325. Meanwhile, the number of lawyers at work in the nation's capital soared from 15,501 (in 1970) to 32,114 (in 1988).

Thus, over the course of the past quarter century, each of our non-poverty benefit programs acquired a voter constituency, which, with the aid of its corresponding bureaucratic and congressional constituencies (not to mention the battalions of special-interest lawyers) worked to ensure and protect its expansion. Inevitably, those who

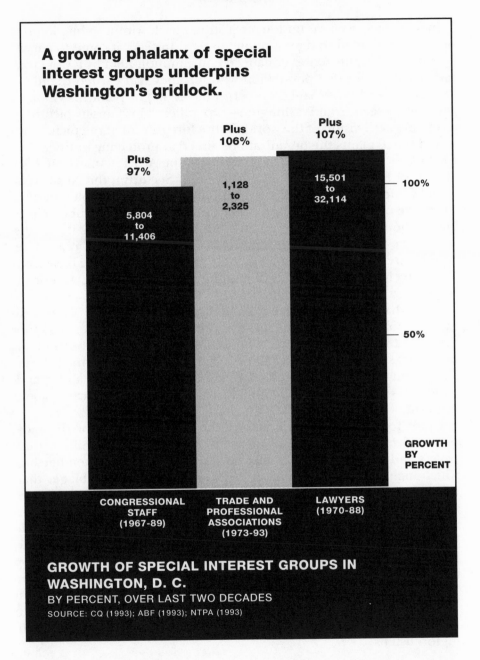

A growing phalanx of special interest groups underpins Washington's gridlock.

Plus 97%

5,804 to 11,406

Plus 106%

1,128 to 2,325

Plus 107%

15,501 to 32,114

100%

50%

GROWTH BY PERCENT

CONGRESSIONAL STAFF (1967-89)

TRADE AND PROFESSIONAL ASSOCIATIONS (1973-93)

LAWYERS (1970-88)

GROWTH OF SPECIAL INTEREST GROUPS IN WASHINGTON, D. C.
BY PERCENT, OVER LAST TWO DECADES
SOURCE: CQ (1993); ABF (1993); NTPA (1993)

needed the public help the most—especially the poor and the young—were not so adept at pushing to the front of the line. And since those who wanted something concrete from government now were well organized and talked loudly, while those who would have benefited from future-looking public policies were a vast and silent majority, the interests of posterity were ignored.

Increasingly, welfare no longer justified itself with a public interest or even pretended to have a public design. Instead, it came to consist of individual rights to debt-financed consumption held by a vast cross-section of an entitled population who felt they had earned them.

I once asked artist Saul Steinberg how he might paint his vision of America as seen from Washington—a parallel to his famous picture of a New Yorker's vision of the world. In the foreground of the picture, we would see as giants the organizations aimed at protecting entitlements for today's retired and elderly Americans: the AARP (American Association of Retired Persons), SOS (Save Our Security), the NCSC (National Council of Senior Citizens), and the Gray Panthers, plus another thirty-five-odd pressure groups that claim a combined membership of 100 million. Still quite prominent—but just a little further in the distance—we would find the hundreds of other agricultural, real-estate, health-care, labor, industrial, and Wall Street lobbies whose business it also is to champion the rights of middle- and upper-income Americans to publicly subsidized consumption.

And what about the backdrop of Steinberg's picture? There, diminutive in size, we would find the young working families who foot the bills for our public entitlements. Along with them, but only as tiny specks of dust on the map of our approach to governing America, we might also catch a glimpse of America's children and grandchildren—the most compelling reason we have to care about posterity.

Pause for a moment to consider the awesome clout of the most powerful of these interest groups: the AARP. With 33 million dues payers and more than 3,600 state and local chapters, its membership, which includes one in every four registered U.S. voters, is bigger than that of any other organization in America aside from the Catholic Church. It is more than twice the size of the AFL-CIO. With an operating budget of over $300 million, AARP is also the largest single business entity in the Washington, D.C., area. Its annual cash flow, about $5 billion according to a 1988 estimate, would put it near the top of the Fortune 500 if it were a public corporation. Its magazine, *Modern Maturity*, has a circulation second only to *TV Guide*. Its mailroom even has its own ZIP code. When AARP speaks, it speaks loud and clear. In my deficit-fighting battles in the 1980s, I learned just how much Washington listens.

OF COLAS AND LOBBIES

America's mindless sleepwalk from an endowment ethic to an entitlement ethic was nowhere more evident than in the story behind the adoption of 100 percent cost-of-living adjustments (COLAs) in the early 1970s. As a new member of the White House staff and Richard Nixon's assistant for international economic affairs, I was at the time trying to persuade the foreign policy establishment that we really did have a global competitiveness problem.* Nonetheless, I had a front-row seat at our domestic COLA drama. No one then looked at adding automatic COLAs to our entitlement programs as an immensely important fiscal decision. Yet over the last decade alone, these 100 percent COLAs—virtually unheard of in the private sector—have added $111 billion to our annual budget and $444 billion in cumulative federal spending.

The estimable Wilbur Mills was then the eminently sensible and enormously influential chairman of the Ways and Means Committee. He was always a man to be taken seriously around the White House, but particularly when he announced his candidacy for president. When Wilbur Mills spoke, particularly on Social Security and tax matters, all of Washington listened. It was Mills who was the key player in Congress's 1972 decision to enact both a 20 percent across-the-board hike in Social Security benefits and automatic COLAs—a role, it seems to me, that just goes to show what presidential ambitions can do to otherwise sensible people. As far as I could tell, the White House reaction to these extravagant benefit proposals was entirely political. I do not recall any of our domestic economic staff talking of fiscal costs or future tax increases. I *do* recall Richard Nixon's chief of staff, Bob Haldeman, walking into a morning staff meeting with a yellow legal pad of notes from his regular meeting with the President. For starters, he asked what we would think of putting the American flag on the generous new benefit checks. (The American flag was then the code symbol of the Republican party.) He then wanted to know what we thought about the President sending out personally signed notices with all the checks, which were to be mailed just after the 20 percent benefit hike and before the 1972 election.

As it turns out, the Democratic Congress swiftly passed a resolution barring such notices. But the benefit liberalizations themselves were enacted into law. Indeed, after a rushed debate during the summer of 1972, the vote in favor of a 20 percent benefit hike *plus* automatic COLAs was close to unanimous (302 to 35 in the House, 82 to 4 in the

---

* At the historic August 15, 1971, Camp David Economic Conference, I did venture into the realm of domestic economic strategy long enough to suggest to the President that he might consider a theme of *sacrifice* as a way of funding what I considered to be desperately needed increases in R&D and investment. In characteristic Nixon style, he was to give a friend, but not me, his unvarnished—and unfavorable—view of my suggestion. Any sacrifice by this richest of all nations and the world's only economic superpower was entirely unnecessary . . . and, in any event, very bad politics.

Senate).* The conservatives rationalized their vote on COLAs on the
grounds that they would *restrict* future Social Security increases to the
level of inflation. The liberals said they would assure that future benefits were *at least* the level of inflation.

Once again, *both* sides got their way.

And why not? For federal civilian and military retirees, after all, we
had already decided in the early 1960s to institute 100 percent COLA
indexing. And then we sweetened the pot still further in 1965 and
again in 1969 by offering them twice-a-year indexing plus an entirely
gratuitous "1 percent kicker" to their annual benefits. When a few
lonely critics pointed out that this treatment was vastly more generous
than any private pension plan, Congress sanctimoniously declared that
the federal government should be a "model employer"—as if marble
bathrooms in Senate office buildings ought to shame all Americans
into fixing up their own in similar style. Since we found it easy to be so
generous with federal employees—with virtually no discussion of the
liabilities to be borne by future taxpayers—why not up the ante with
Social Security as well? So, with fulsome pronouncements about the
"courage" of Congress, the 1972 Social Security amendments were
signed into law by lopsided majorities.

Only months afterward, the Social Security actuaries woke up and
realized that their complex new indexing formula would overload and
short-circuit in the presence of higher inflation rates—that they had,
in their confusion, "double-indexed" payments to new retirees. But
five years passed before Congress would enact a remedy (even then, in
1977, it took the threat of Social Security's immediate insolvency), and
then five more years passed before the remedy was fully implemented.
To appreciate how badly the system had gone awry, consider the trend
in new retirement benefits at age sixty-five as a percent of earnings in
the year prior to retirement. This so-called replacement ratio leapt
from 38 percent in 1974 to 45 percent in 1979 and 51 percent in
1981—the best year ever to retire on Social Security. Why was nothing
done for so long? The excuse was that these formula errors were not
the fault of the beneficiaries and that therefore they should not "suffer." Yes, we made a choice. A very soft choice.

What's most significant is that the 1977 Social Security "rescue act"
prompted little discussion of how we allowed such excess to happen.
Instead, it impelled hundreds of thousands of newly retired Americans

---

* It is a little-appreciated fact that the budgetary savings that appeared when we abandoned the Vietnam conflict—which every president from Kennedy to Nixon had
insisted, rightly or wrongly, was being fought for future generations—were quietly
transferred over to the 1972 explosion of Social Security outlays. In other words, we
went from "guns and butter" to "butter and butter." Two decades later, we are now
witnessing another peace dividend—our Cold War dividend—go to fund the continued explosive growth in our federal retirement and health-care entitlements.

born just too late to enjoy the windfalls—the so-called Notch Babies (born 1917–1921)—to organize into a vociferous and well-funded lobby demanding that they get just as good a deal as their next-elders. Few phenomena better reflect the gathering power of our principle of personal entitlement. It made no difference that "the Notch" was still receiving benefit levels superior to those of anyone who retired before the mid-1970s—and at least equal to anyone born after them. It only mattered that they were getting less than those born just before 1917 (a group that Robert Myers, former chief actuary of the Social Security Administration, has dubbed the "Bonanza Babies").

Years later, Richard Nixon was to tell me that the COLA decision was probably his most serious economic and fiscal mistake. I believe he was correct.

Indeed, the timing of our passage of automatic indexing in 1972 and the huge increases in Social Security benefits it generated was one of the great fiscal tragedies of American history. The COLAs, after all, were enacted only months before a sequence of events—an oil import embargo, accelerating inflation, a devastating recession, and a slowdown in productivity growth—that would certainly have moderated our decision had we waited just a bit longer. The most obvious consequence of this tragedy was the explosion of entitlement spending as a share of our GNP. But there was a political consequence as well. By sheltering retirees from the sinking trend in family income experienced by most younger age groups over the past two decades, we effectively insulated our most active age bracket of voters—the elderly—from the economic realities of post-1973 America.

Until the 1970s, most federal spending was discretionary and unindexed, and Congress still functioned under the very strong presumption that dollars spent should be paid for out of revenue. Large deficits were therefore difficult to achieve, because so many corrective options were available, both in spending and in taxing. We eliminated the spending rule in the early 1970s with our decision to make most nonpoverty benefit programs "nondiscretionary"—in other words automatic, inflation-proof entitlements. The taxing rule was then eliminated in the early 1980s by the jihad prayers of supply-side economists.

Our federal deficit thus became no one's responsibility. It is still subject to "projection," but we can now claim with a straight face that it is no longer subject to control.

COOKING THE BOOKS

Another great fiscal tragedy of that era was the invention of unusually reckless means of cooking the books—ways of moving vast unfunded entitlement liabilities out of our budgets and off our balance sheets.

During the 1970s, perversely enough, Congress passed ERISA (the Employee Retirement Income Security Act) to ensure that private pension plans were fully funded. Thanks in large part to ERISA, the financial status of the U.S. private pension system improved dramatically. Although a minority of plans (mostly concentrated in rust-belt industries) remain seriously underfunded, by most accounts the system as a whole has enjoyed a comfortable surplus in recent years. Compare that record to the estimated $14 trillion in unfunded liabilities that we are passing on to the future for our federal social insurance and pension programs. If the federal government had to conform to the ERISA legislation it enforces for private business, it would be required to amortize these unfunded liabilities over thirty years. Amortizing them all would add a mind-boggling $1.1 trillion to each year's deficit; just amortizing the unfunded liabilities of civil service and military pensions would add over $80 billion. By the standards of ERISA, quite simply, most of Congress and the executive branch could be sued and convicted.

On the subject of civil service pensions, I speak with some experience. In 1975, I served as chairman of President Ford's Quadrennial Commission on Executive, Legislative, and Judicial Pay, charged with reviewing the appropriateness of civil service compensation. Again, the question of honest accounting raised its head. All of the federal witnesses we interviewed were only too happy to compare the "take-home pay" of federal and private-sector workers—since this was the principal cash outlay that showed up in the annual budget and was also (they thought) the area where federal pay looked worst relative to private-sector pay. But as soon as I inquired about the rest of the federal worker compensation package—the generous vacation and sick pay, the comprehensive health benefits, the very lenient disability policy (one in four federal pensioners is "disabled"), and especially the extravagant retirement age and other pension benefit provisions—the witnesses hedged. Well, they said, it wasn't "customary" to compare such things. Several years later, the Grace Commission was to find that all of these nonpay fringes, taken together, cost four times more as a share of payroll in the federal government than in a large, private-sector corporation. Yet nowhere does the federal budget account for what this *total* compensation package will cost future taxpayers.

FROM "TAX AND SPEND" TO "BORROW AND SPEND"

Jimmy Carter then campaigned to add his contributions to an even greater society—including universal national health insurance and the federal government's assumption of one-third of the vast local education bill. But in this case, external events, in the form of exploding energy prices, soaring interest rates, and inflationary fears, made the choice for us. When he entered office, Carter inherited a $74 billion deficit triggered by the worst recession thus far in the postwar era. In 1980, the year he was defeated in his bid for re-election, he was saddled with another $74 billion deficit, another recession, and a terrifying new bout of inflation. I recall one meeting with Carter and congressional Democrats at which everyone seemed anguished at the prospect of such large deficits. Clearly, they had not yet learned the motto of the 1980s: Don't Worry. Be Happy.

After a decade of shattered expectations during the 1970s, America seemed ready for radical political change and a program of national renewal. Anyone over the age of thirty can easily recall the desperate state of the U.S. economy as the 1970s drew to a close: stagnant real wages, plunging rates of savings and investment, inflation in double digits, and the prime rate hurtling past 20 percent. It is no exaggeration to say that by 1980 our national spirit was sagging into bewilderment. Along with millions of others who voted for Ronald Reagan in 1980, I too cast my ballot, or so I thought, for policies that would give us a high-savings, high-investment, high-productivity economy, with reduced government spending and budget and trade surpluses.

But instead we got a redoubled consumption boom financed by foreign borrowing and cuts in private investment, with debt-financed hikes in public spending and huge balance-of-payments deficits. Those of us who were "entitled" kept grabbing the goodies as fast as ever, all the while being told that government was nowhere in sight, that free lunches had vanished, and that a self-reliant private sector was responsible for our comfort.

By replacing the reviled "tax and spend" motto of the 1970s with a new "borrow and spend" creed, we managed to create a make-believe 1960s—a decade of "feeling good" and "having it all"—without the bother of producing a real one.

When the supply-siders launched their Kemp-Roth tax-cut missile it was intended to be a single warhead that would lower federal revenues by about $1 trillion over the next decade. But by the time it landed on President Reagan's desk, the single warhead had MIRVed. Splintering in midair, it rained down on Washington in the form of so many bright and shiny Christmas tree ornaments that it took professional accounting firms to keep track of all the tax favors. They included much-liberalized investment depreciation, tax-free savings certificates, special writeoffs for trucking companies suffering the trauma of deregulation, bigger pension plan writeoffs for the upper income brackets (Keoghs), tax benefits to farmers, tax breaks for mass transit systems, tax exemptions for citizens living overseas, major exemptions of estates from federal inheritance taxes, and Employee Stock Ownership Plans (ESOPs). Some of the tax favors may have been legitimate savings and investment incentives; others were just sops to special interests. But whatever their nature, in the frenzy to hand out the goodies any distinction was lost.

What gave rise to this episode of wild logrolling that simply burst out of control? According to my colleague David Stockman—who, as director of the Office of Management and Budget, was present at the creation—the supply-side doctrine had the unintended effect of starting a bidding war. "And once the war started," writes Stockman, "we became ensnared in its logic. If it was logic, it was that of the alcoholic: One more couldn't hurt, given all that had gone down already." Stockman then goes on to describe how "everyone was accusing everyone else of greed, and in the same breath shouting 'What's in it for me?' " At a White House strategy meeting, Minority Whip Trent Lott summed up the mood: "Everybody else is getting theirs, it's time we got ours."

Few could do better than Stockman did in his memoir, *The Triumph of Politics,* in relating what happened next. By the time Washington had finished its tax-cutting orgy, "nearly a trillion dollars in tax revenue had to be spent on the business coalition plan and the congressional ornaments in order to pass a supply-side tax reduction for individuals costing almost an equal amount." On the conservative side, writers like Irving Kristol were adamant in their message to Republicans. Stockman summed up its jist this way: "Don't cut spending, it's bad politics. Don't raise taxes, its bad politics. Don't worry, $200 billion deficits are nothing to fear because they'll go away on their own." As for the other side of the aisle, one disgruntled liberal congressman, David Obey, observed that "it would probably be cheaper if we gave everybody in the country three wishes."

Stockman bottom-lines this "poker game of calling and raising," as House Majority Leader Jim Wright called it, in one devastating statistical table. "The smoking gun is on line *six*. It shows that had taxes not been raised after the 1981 tax cut, this year [1986] we would be collecting only *16.9 percent* of GNP in taxes. Built-in spending amounts to about 24 percent of GNP. What kind of crackpot theory says the federal government can issue new bonds in the amount of 7 percent of GNP each and every year and not ruin the economy?" And what about all the rhetoric about the American Dream, the future, and the like? Stockman again perfectly captures the mood that settled over the White House: There didn't seem to be much point squandering "a lot of political capital solving some other guy's problem in 2010."

Yes, it's true that during the Ford and Carter presidencies we added $450 billion to the gross federal debt and lost sight of the vital tradeoffs connecting our present with our future. But under Reagan and Bush we added another $3.5 trillion. Clearly, our choicelessness in the 1980s went off the rails into the stratosphere.

Opportunities to come down to earth were either blown or seen as politically suicidal. One such opportunity arose in May 1985 after the previous year's "Morning in America" re-election campaign, a campaign based on three premises that, taken together, were irreconcilable with sustainable economic growth: not touching defense, not touching taxes, and not touching middle- or upper-income entitlements. After that, many in the old guard GOP leadership on Capitol Hill became convinced that the time had come to get serious about the deficit. Perhaps they remembered the old Wall Street maxim: "If it sounds too good to be true, it probably is." In what David Stockman has dubbed the "Ping-Pong" strategy, rank-and-file Senate Republicans were first cajoled into passing a budget replete with politically toxic spending cuts—including a COLA cap. The idea was then to short-circuit the opposition of the Democratic House to entitlement cuts by offering Republican acceptance of equally toxic tax increases as the quid pro quo. It almost worked. But when, in the eleventh hour, President Reagan suddenly withdrew his support for the COLA cap, the grand compromise fell apart. Senate Republicans felt totally exposed and politically vulnerable—apparently with reason. In the next election, the Republicans lost eight Senate seats and their Senate majority along with them. Blaming this loss on Reagan's COLA reversal, many developed a persistent allergy to future COLA reform. Thereafter, budget negotiations on Capitol Hill wore down to nickel-and-dime skirmishes on a very narrow field of action. U.S. fiscal policy was in gridlock.

By way of contrast, it is instructive to see what happened in other countries—Japan, for example—in the mid-1980s. New demographic projections unexpectedly revealed to the Japanese people that the costs of their main public retirement system would become a severe economic burden early in the next century. In response, the nation acted decisively. After some serious discussion, a public commission recommended—and the Japanese government implemented—a major reform of the system that will gradually reduce average future benefit levels by about one-fifth. After the decision was announced, there was hardly a murmur of protest. After all, as the Ministry of Health and Welfare explained in a statement that cited "social solidarity," "equity between the generations," and economic "stability over the long term," the need for such cutbacks was self-evident. What society could afford to give its retirees had to be carefully weighed against the future "living standards and liabilities of the working generation supporting the system."

Recently, I had occasion to praise former Japanese prime minister Nakasone for achieving this kind of fundamental entitlement reform so promptly. "Mr. Peterson," he said, "you may not have been told it

took two sessions of our parliament." In this country, we can't even
raise the subject.

Just how different we are from the Japanese in this respect was again
brought home to me several years ago when I visited the office of Texas
congressman Kent Hance. A Democratic fiscal conservative (a so-called
boll weevil), Hance had supported the indexing of the income tax to
stop inflation-driven tax increases and put a cap on federal revenues.
He had opposed symmetrical reform on the spending side, and especially opposed cutting my personal bête noire, the automatic 100 percent COLA. The congressman and I talked about the threat that
runaway entitlement spending poses to the living standards of tomorrow's workers—and in particular the role that 100 percent COLAs play
in inflating the cost of such benefits as Social Security and federal
pensions. As we were wrapping up our discussion, Congressman Hance
turned to his aide and asked her to bring in any communications from
constituents who opposed even the most trivial modification of COLA
indexing. "You mean all of them?" the aide gasped, and proceeded to
bring in a huge stack of letters and telegrams. The congressman then
said, "I wonder if you could now bring in to Mr. Peterson the letters
and wires that favor the kind of cutbacks he is proposing." "But Congressman," the aide exclaimed, "we don't ever get any letters like
that."

Little has changed since then. As soon as Clinton administration
cabinet members and White House advisors even mentioned the possibility of COLA reform, an avalanche of protest mail from America's
huge and well-organized consumption lobbies began flooding in. President Clinton is now learning the awesome power wielded by these
lobbies—just as I did when I saw how easily they sabotaged the November 1987 budget summit that followed that year's stock market
crash.

During the early stages of the summit, which was called to thrash out
a compromise that would at least begin to scale down the size of our
federal deficit, the latest advertisement of the Bipartisan Budget Appeal was posted prominently in the conferees' working chambers. A
lobby for the future I had organized in 1982 along with five former
secretaries of the treasury, the Budget Appeal had taken out newspaper ads, cajoled Congress, sponsored press conferences and forums,
and beaten on administration doors, all to one purpose: to announce
loudly and clearly that the economy was in long-term trouble, and the
trouble would get markedly worse unless we moved quickly to reduce
our deficits and to control our entitlement programs. But as the deliberations were winding to a close, *The Washington Post* reported that
the budget summiteers received a videocassette from Congressman
Claude Pepper, that indefatigable champion of the elderly, in which

he warned of a roll-call vote that would identify anyone in Congress who supported entitlement reform—and intimated that they would be punished by millions of "gray lobby" voters come the 1988 elections. When the tape was over, the Budget Appeal's advertisement was taken down. "Thereafter," one of the participants later reported, "it was back to politics as usual."

Looking back over the 1980s, there's no doubt that the "happy-time" Republicans of the so-called New Right were to blame for much of what happened. As the bill for our debt party comes due, they, with Ronald Reagan chief among them, may well be consigned to obloquy alongside Herbert Hoover. By mid-decade, as public spending ballooned toward record highs and net savings plummeted to record lows, it should have been obvious to everyone that all the talk of a supply-side revolution aside, we were on a consumption borrowing binge. I recall how Senator Pete Domenici raised the ominous deficit issue to the President and his advisors. He pleaded with them to scale back the defense increases and to kill the third year of the tax cut. They told him to "get on the team." As the author of "Morning in America" and the host of the debt party, Ronald Reagan should also have led the cleanup party. But he ended his days in office as the leading demand-side Keynesian in American history.

In what now would seem to be another era, if not another country, the contrasting example of Harry Truman is instructive. He once defined leadership as "getting people to do what they don't want to do and getting them to like it"—in other words, making the unpopular popular. Harry Truman did not confuse popularity with leadership. When he launched the Marshall Plan, only 14 percent of Americans supported him. Yet a determined Truman got the bipartisan support of Congress and an energized American business and intellectual elite, and ultimately persuaded the public to pay for it—to devote nearly a sixth of an enlarged but balanced federal budget to aiding countries emerging from the wreckage of war. Along with the creation of other global institutions (such as the UN, World Bank, IMF, and GATT), the Marshall Plan was an investment that opened the door to a half century of relative peace and economic growth. If Harry Truman, the Kansas City haberdasher, could successfully lead the charge on behalf of the unpopular Marshall Plan, certainly Ronald Reagan, Hollywood's "great communicator," could have led the charge on redemptive fiscal reform. Instead, he simply put the Good Housekeeping Seal of Approval on our collective choicelessness. He was there to sell us popular tax cuts at party time. He was there to teach us the easy lesson of how to prime the pump and drink the water. But when the time came to turn down the music and turn on the lights, if Americans looked to the White House for leadership, they looked in vain.

The economics of the New Right has been the politics of pleasure and consumption—the "we can always grow out of it," or "deficits don't matter," or "not in a recession," or "not in an election year" cant that finally severed any link between the interests of the present and the future in how our nation forges its public policies. It was not just the absurd, "Laffer Curve" promise of their across-the-board tax cuts. There was also the pseudosacrificial chopping away at the means-tested and investment corners of the federal budget; the silent approval of the vast increase in "middle-class" entitlements; and, above all, the unwillingness to take the ominous deficit issue directly to the public.

What is perhaps most astonishing about the 1980s is how we lied to ourselves for so long. Even today, unreformed supply-side gurus scribbling on *The Wall Street Journal*'s op-ed page continue to do logical somersaults in order to paint the past decade's economic failures as shining successes. All went well, we are typically told, until President Bush betrayed the Reagan revolution by reneging on his no-new-taxes pledge. But the truth of the matter is that the betrayal was of a very different sort and occurred much, much earlier. Indeed, when Ronald Reagan's first term was hardly under way the signs were already clear for those who cared to read them that something had gone seriously awry—that the interests of the future that had loomed so large in his campaign rhetoric were rapidly vanishing from view.

I recall that the initial occasion for my own disillusionment came in the spring of 1981 when I was asked by the Women's Economic Round Table to speak on the new Reagan budget. As I did my homework, I first grew perplexed, then deeply troubled. Although I had enthusiastically voted for Reagan just months before, I had to tell the audience about my concern—much to the consternation of some of my business friends, who accused me of carping. In my opinion the numbers simply didn't compute. There was no way on earth that we could cure inflation, slash taxes, feed defense, balance the budget—and at the same time plan for a decade of rising savings and investment. We could not repeal the law that the sum of the various components of our Gross National Product cannot exceed 100 percent. Soon afterward, I was informed by the unofficial spokespeople for the new administration—*The Wall Street Journal* editorial board—that my thinking was linear and limited and uncreative and wrong, that I did not understand the psychological power of "expectations" about economic growth to bootstrap dreams into reality. I replied that the new program could only shortchange our future if it was actually carried out, but it was so top-heavy with consumption and debt that it would hardly avoid self-destructing within a short time. As it turned out, I was right about the bottom line but wrong about the timing. Something unexpected intervened—the something that allowed us to create a make-believe 1960s.

That something was debt, and in particular the huge free ride of foreign debt—mountains of debt created with an abandon that has no precedent in our nation's history. All told, the paper liabilities of all sectors of our economy have tripled since the 1970s, from $3.6 trillion in 1979 to $11.2 trillion in 1991—an explosion that far outstripped economic growth. Over most of the twentieth century until 1983, the ratio of total debt to GNP was remarkably stable in the United States (never much more than 140 percent). Since then, the tidal wave of borrowing has pushed that ratio to about 200 percent. Virtually every sector of the economy—the federal government, business, and consumers—took part in the binge.

And what did the debt party buy us? A simultaneous boost in private and public consumption that our economy would otherwise have been unable to afford. The setbacks of the 1970s suddenly seemed a thing of the past. From vacations on plastic to no-money-down homes, from imported luxury autos to refloated missile-armed battleships, from Day-Glo Keds that cost $100 a pair to redundant CAT scans that cost $1,000 a minute—Americans once again became convinced we could "have it all" and have it now.

To be sure, supercharging the economy did bring some real advantages. Most important, it allowed the Fed to clamp down hard on inflation—the only policy during the Reagan era that seriously tested our threshold of pain—without triggering a recession even worse than what we actually experienced in 1982 and 1983. Indirectly, Reaganomics also helped spur a revival of productivity in manufacturing—the one sector of the economy where productivity rose above the no-growth norm of the 1980s. Scourged by a soaring dollar fed by historically high real interest rates, starved by rising capital costs, forced to fire managerial as well as production workers in droves, U.S. manufacturers producing anything that could be shipped in a box, from machine tools to perfume, were pushed to the brink. Some went over. But many have come back alive—and not just alive, but leaner and meaner, more efficient and more competitive.

There are other things to be thankful for. The Reagan White House deserves credit for helping renew the popularity of markets and entrepreneurial risk, both here and abroad, and for persuading us to abandon the worst vices of regulation in industries like airlines, banking, and energy. Its legacy has also forced politicians of both parties to think twice about again turning to such counterproductive policies as national planning. All of this has brought economic benefits.

THE MORNING AFTER

Yet if there were some notable gains, the long-term costs have been grievous. Even as debt stimulus allowed us to enjoy the longest peacetime expansion in our postwar history, the fundamental economic inputs on which our future living standards depend all continued to deteriorate.

The initial objectives of the Reagan revolution had all been focused on improving those inputs. Yet suddenly we started hearing that such short-term indicators as today's GNP growth were the proper measure of our long-term economic fortunes—no matter that this growth was largely driven by demographically led increases in employment (in fact, the "Great American Job Machine" had produced more new jobs in the 1970s than in the 1980s),* not productivity gains. Or else we learned that the downward trends in the long-term inputs to our economy were themselves something to brag about. Low savings rates were a sign of confident prosperity, we were told. They simply meant that Americans realized they were wealthy and would soon become still wealthier. The same logic was applied to our mountains of foreign debt. Forget the future bills. It was a sign of a robust economy that foreigners were eager to invest here.

And what about the American people as a whole? Why did we become so adept at lying to ourselves? Perhaps the reason, quite simply, is that the 1980s seemingly gave us what we wished so much to believe it was possible to have: cost-free prosperity with no tough choices.

So in our hubris we did to our economy in the 1980s what we had done to our cultural and social institutions in the 1960s and 1970s: We let it "all hang out" without a thought for tomorrow. After all, if self-actualization was the key to happiness in our private lives, then maybe the same was true in our public lives. Why deprive ourselves? Why not enjoy another tax cut?

But now the debt party is over—and as we painfully sober up, those smiley-face buttons have all but disappeared. Morning in America has turned into the Morning After. You see the signs everywhere. Ex-yuppies snipping up their credit cards and staying home for dinner. Department store ads touting austere euphemisms like "extra value" and "back to the simple life." Born-again Democratic budget-cutters suddenly pinching pennies. A new rush of personal bankruptcies and delinquent mortgages. Uneasy supply-siders using the past tense to defend the ten most recent years of economic policymaking—in which

---

* This assertion is sometimes met with skepticism. Yet from 1969 to 1979, civilian employment in the United States grew by an average of 2.1 million annually; from 1979 to 1989, it grew by 1.9 million annually.

the real household income of most Americans under age forty-five actually declined.

It's all telling us that the world's greatest-ever experiment in debt-financed economic stimulus is coming to an end—or at least has been put temporarily on hold.

Finally we find ourselves boxed into a corner from which there are no pleasant exits.

We have lost our innocence.

3

A Trillion Dollars of
Entitlements for Everyone

When it comes to entitlements, I have staked out such a strong position over such a long period that even my friends have been known to drift quickly away when the subject comes up. One such friend, Ted Sorensen, best known as JFK's talented chief speech writer, tells a joke that makes the point. "Pete Peterson and I were on an airplane to the Middle East. Shortly before we landed, two terrorists with machine guns leaped up and rushed over to where we were sitting. One says, 'We're going to assassinate the two of you on a bipartisan basis: a Democrat and a Republican. But before doing so, we want each of you to have your last wish.' The terrorists turn to Peterson, who says, 'My last wish is to give one more speech on entitlement spending in America and its relationship to the federal deficit.' Then they turn to me to ask what my last wish is. I said, 'In view of what you just heard from Peter Peterson, my last wish is to be shot first.' "

But being characterized as a bore is perhaps preferable to another recent experience. An alarmed assistant rushed into my office saying, "Mr. Peterson, an elderly listener to a radio call-in show has just called you a vulture."

Clearly, many people would suggest I get off my soapbox on entitlements. But I can't do that. I have learned that if we want to solve America's economic problems, we must include entitlement reform. And to bring about reform, we must start by talking about it—despite the eye-glazing effect of the unimaginable dollar amounts and the arcane rules and procedures through which Washington distributes these hundreds of billions to millions of citizens each year.

My involvement with the entitlements issue began when I helped to found the Bipartisan Budget Appeal. The five former secretaries of the Treasury and I were all concerned about the explosion in federal spending, but I wanted to truly understand why it was happening. Thus began an arduous journey through the little-understood realm of entitlement programs, especially those doled out without regard to financial need. These entitlements—"non-means-tested," in budgetary parlance—make up the vast majority of our benefit spending. Some of my early conclusions were presented in 1982 in an article for *The New York Times Magazine,* which the editors called "No More Free Lunch for the Middle Class." I argued then that "unless we . . . launch a counter-revolution against middle-class and upper-class entitlements, budget control and economic recovery will continue to elude us." Furthermore, I warned that "we are setting the stage for a very ugly generational conflict."

With runaway federal spending, as with so many other matters, we always seem to be looking for scapegoats. The favored scapegoat of the left, I noted, was the wasteful Pentagon. There was a kernel of truth in this view. Clearly, the generals should not be left alone in the candy store to spend at will. Military spending should reflect a bottom-up assessment of genuine security threats. That was true when the Cold War was still on, and is certainly still true now. Yet the numbers themselves told me that, even if we uinlaterally disarmed, we were never going to find enough defense cuts to solve our long-term budget problem and finance large increases in productive investment.

The favored scapegoat of the right was the "welfare cheater." I explained to readers that *if* we could cut *all* of the programs for the poor by 25 percent, it would save only 3 percent of the budget. We would run out of "unworthy" poor people long before we balanced it.

THE ENEMY IS: US

The scapegoats, popular as they may have been, were, of course, not the real problem. The real enemy, as Pogo put it, is us: the great American middle-class majority, whose non-means-tested entitlement subsidies far outweigh the benefits we direct at the poor.

During a dinner at what one could safely call the "liberal" Hamptons salon of my friend Jason Epstein, senior editor of Random House and a founder of the generally "progressive" *New York Review of Books,* I found myself participating in a dialogue of the deaf with some of Jason's guests. People were repeating one garbled myth after another about entitlements, particularly that Social Security was a "sacred contract," an "insurance" program that simply repaid "needy" beneficiaries "their" money. As I have said, I have always thought of myself as a moderate Republican, a conservative on fiscal matters, but a liberal on social issues. That night, I felt as if I were coming across to these sincere and otherwise sophisticated people as some kind of Neanderthal by attacking the very notion of welfare for the well-off (and most certainly for people like myself), and this despite the fact that my program of reform suggested *supplementing* benefits to the poor.

Jason suggested I write a series for *The New York Review of Books* on Social Security and Medicare. This was one of those counterintuitive ideas—me, a Republican, writing for that bastion of "liberal" thinking. But as I thought about it, if not there, where, and if not then, when? Bob Silvers, a gifted editor, was enthusiastic and most generous in the space he provided—enough for a long, two-part series that offered both a diagnosis of the problem and a program of reform.

The response was extraordinarily heated. When the series appeared late in 1982, Bob Silvers reported such an avalanche of protests that a liberal magazine had given so much space to a Republican "reactionary" that he felt something far beyond the usual follow-up via "letters to the editor" was required. What caused that unprecedented response? Was it simply that I was so misguided? Was it that a Republican businessman had trespassed into one of the most sacred territories of liberal policy wonks—the Social Security system? Or did the visceral tone of the protests suggest that I had not merely crossed policy swords, but committed a form of blasphemy?

In any event, Bob had an extraordinary idea. Why not devote an entire issue of *The New York Review of Books* to the responses? And so it happened in 1983. The issue was entitled "The Great Debate: Peter G. Peterson Replies to Critics."

Since one of my critics had questioned the "pessimism" of my analysis when I pointed out how our overall Social Security system—sooner or later—was headed for bankruptcy, I asked A. Haeworth Robertson, a former chief actuary of the Social Security Administration, to review my numbers. He thought I had tended to *understate* the magnitude of the problem.

But beyond the debate about the facts, what sticks most in my mind is a line of argument made by an especially well regarded critic, economist Alicia H. Munnell. She wrote that programs for the poor tend to be poor programs. To avoid this problem, Social Security should be explicitly designed to ensure that *everyone*, including the well-off, is "entitled."

I responded as follows:

> This is stunning. Benefits to the elderly poor are, as they should be, sacrosanct. But Munnell wants to protect them by bribing the elderly well-off to get on the political bandwagon. Thus the rich must continue

to receive at least the present value of their past contributions in order that the poor receive somewhat more. But if everyone gets on the bandwagon, who will be left to pull it? If everyone receives, who will be left to pay?

This kind of Ponzi scheme is almost certain to self-destruct. If, as I wrote, "everyone makes payments to someone else, not everyone can win the jackpot—unless there is an impossible acceleration in growth of the number or wealth of new players." Back when Samuelson wrote about Social Security in the 1960s, it may have seemed that we could count on that kind of acceleration. Since the early 1970s, we've known for a certainty that we can't. But the country has yet to learn the difficult lesson that our retirement programs can safely grow over the long term only if the economy is growing as rapidly as the retired population.

After these salvoes were exchanged, something else happened that was also unprecedented in my career of writing about public policy. Five columnists covering the entire political spectrum—left, center, and right—saw fit to devote major space to the debate in *The New York Review*. Anthony Lewis of *The New York Times,* Tom Braden of *The Washington Post,* Morton Kondracke of *The New Republic,* George Will of *The Washington Post,* and William F. Buckley, Jr., of the *New York Daily News.* They were strange bedfellows indeed. Apparently, an approach that challenged the conventional wisdom on entitlements—what some have called the third rail of American politics—touched many sets of nerves.

Thinking over my *New York Review of Books* article and the debate it triggered, I concluded that universal entitlement programs like Social Security had become political sacred cows not because of a humane concern for the poor but because of a political reluctance to impose fiscal restraint on middle- and upper-income voters. I further realized that none of the issues surrounding entitlements can be constructively resolved unless the fog that conceals how the Social Security system works, whom it benefits, and how it will fare over the next decades is dispelled. With real education, I believe we could evolve timely, gradual, humane, and durable entitlement reform. Without it, I would say timely reform and prevention of an inevitable crisis are impossible goals.

ENTITLEMENTS: YESTERDAY AND TODAY

Let's define some key terms and look at some key facts about entitlements. *Entitlements* are any public-sector payments, received by a person or household, that do not represent contractual compensation for goods or services. This definition obviously excludes large portions of the federal budget, from defense procurement to interest on the national debt to purchases designed for America's collective benefit (such as highway construction). But it *includes nearly everything else*— most notably, such dominating fixtures of the American political landscape as Social Security, Medicare, Medicaid, food stamps, federal pensions, unemployment compensation, veterans' benefits, and farm aid.

The most striking single fact about entitlements is their vast cost. Over the course of fiscal year 1993, the U.S. Treasury will mail out benefit checks (directly to individuals or to state agencies and insurance companies that administer benefits) totaling some $800 billion, or about one-eighth of our nation's Gross Domestic Product. That amounts to over half (53.5 percent) of the entire federal budget—or about $6 million every minute of every working day flowing to at least one member of every other American household. These figures, moreover, include only *direct outlays* from the federal budget. They would be even larger if we included tax expenditures—the benefitlike loopholes in our tax code. As we've seen, these indirect subsidies include such items as the home mortgage deduction and the tax exclusion for employer-paid health care. If we count tax expenditures and add the cost of administering entitlement programs—as many economists argue we should to get the full picture—federal entitlements now amount to over *$1 trillion annually* and flow to well over *three-quarters* of all U.S. households.

How and when did entitlements ever get to be so costly?

A very modest, selective version of entitlements began as far back as colonial days when land was routinely granted to veterans of expeditions against the French. In 1818 the U.S. government established the custom of awarding cash stipends to veterans. The first went to the aging ex-soldiers of the Revolution. Federal pensions for career employees began around the same time, but were informal and haphazard until the establishment of the first Military Retirement System in 1861 and the Civil Service Retirement System in 1920. Throughout these years, the number of beneficiaries remained small. The benefits themselves were generally limited to lump-sum payments. They were never indexed to inflation. And they were changeable by Congress at any time. Accordingly, the total cost of entitlements remained minimal: never more than 1 percent of GDP.

Only with the economic collapse of the 1930s did the federal government, under the leadership of President Franklin Delano Roosevelt, initiate a fundamental expansion of entitlements to provide a broader social safety net. First came social insurance (Railroad Retirement, Unemployment Compensation, and Social Security) that promised vast numbers of private-sector workers payroll-tax-funded "insurance" against job loss. Then came the forerunners of today's Aid to Families with Dependent Children and Supplemental Security Income, programs that helped states cope with poverty—a function previously relegated largely to local government or philanthropy. Yet even with all this innovation, low benefit levels still kept the total cost of entitlements quite modest—never more than about 2 percent of GDP—through the end of World War II. When their cost did suddenly spike in the late 1940s, it was for the most traditional of reasons: a new surge in veterans' benefits.

Then the Big Bang hit. Between 1951 and 1976, the federal entitlements bill grew eighteenfold, from $10 billion to $180 billion. Relative to the size of our economy, it tripled, from 3.2 to 10.8 percent of GDP.

Nor, in all the years that followed, has our economy shown any sign of "outgrowing" the cost of entitlements, as many partisans of Reaganomics, along with many liberals, have hoped. Though its relative cost typically rises and falls with the business cycle, our entitlements bill always manages to be higher at the end of each new recession than it was the time before. In fiscal year 1993 direct federal benefit outlays alone will exceed 13 percent of GDP, the highest level ever. Including tax expenditures, the total cost of federal entitlements now amounts to roughly 16 percent of GDP. All official projections, moreover, show that the bill will climb steadily throughout the 1990s.

What makes these projections especially ominous is that they indicate persistent growth in entitlement costs despite three major—though strictly temporary—demographic phenomena that should now be working to push costs down. The first is the huge recent growth in the number of working spouses. The second is the entry of the relatively large Baby Boom generation (born from the mid-1940s to mid-1960s) into its prime earning years. The third is the retirement of my relatively small "Silent" generation (born from the mid-1920s to early 1940s). The first two trends are still enlarging the tax base; the third is beginning to slow *temporarily* the growth in the number of beneficiaries.

THE DEMOGRAPHICS AHEAD

But the favorable age dynamics of what has been called "America's Demographic Indian Summer" will eventually be thrown into reverse. Beginning around the year 2010 when the Boomers start to retire, this large generation will change from taxpayers to beneficiaries. Thereafter, entitlement spending will accelerate into outer space as a rapidly aging population interacts with ballooning health-care costs.

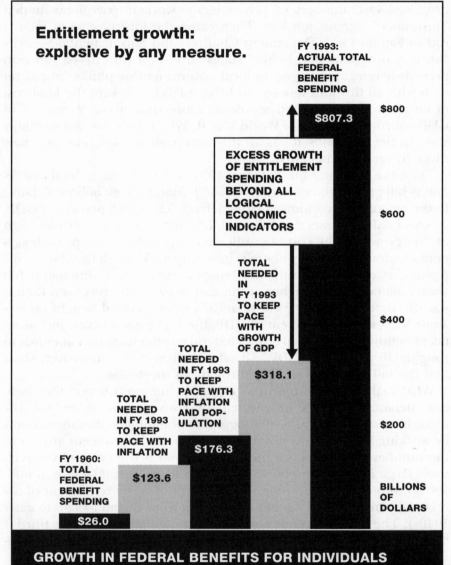

Entitlement growth: explosive by any measure.

FY 1993: ACTUAL TOTAL FEDERAL BENEFIT SPENDING

$807.3

EXCESS GROWTH OF ENTITLEMENT SPENDING BEYOND ALL LOGICAL ECONOMIC INDICATORS

TOTAL NEEDED IN FY 1993 TO KEEP PACE WITH GROWTH OF GDP

TOTAL NEEDED IN FY 1993 TO KEEP PACE WITH INFLATION AND POP-ULATION

$318.1

TOTAL NEEDED IN FY 1993 TO KEEP PACE WITH INFLATION

$176.3

FY 1960: TOTAL FEDERAL BENEFIT SPENDING

$123.6

$26.0

$800

$600

$400

$200

BILLIONS OF DOLLARS

GROWTH IN FEDERAL BENEFITS FOR INDIVIDUALS
FROM FY 1960 TO FY 1993, COMPARED TO
CHANGES IN PRICES, POPULATION, AND GDP
SOURCE: OMB (1993); CBO (1993); BEA (1993); CENSUS (1992)

How rapidly is America "graying"? Between 1946 and 1964, the famed and huge Baby Boom generation was born—76 million strong. Today, there are about 32 million Americans who are sixty-five and over. But by 2020, this number will zoom past 50 million. America will then look like a nation of Floridas. What is more, there will be an unprecedented number of people who are octogenarians and older—a group whose per capita health-care costs are at least twice as high as those of the "young" elderly. In fact, by 2040 there may be nearly as many Americans aged eighty and over as there now are aged sixty-five and over! Alas, the number of workers who will be expected to pay for the benefits of these Baby Boomers turned Senior Boomers will be growing at only a fraction of the pace of the elderly population. If our productivity continues to stagnate, the unimaginable increases in payroll taxes necessary to pay for the coming Senior Boom will be mathematically, let alone politically, unsustainable.

A BENEFITS BONANZA

Another central fact about entitlements is their generosity, indeed largess. Take our federal civil service and military retirement systems, the most generous pension plans in the nation. They cover about 5 million federal employees and soldiers—only about 5 percent of the number of all private-sector workers—yet the benefits they pay out are equal to about half of all payments from all private pension plans. For their enormous cost (over $60 billion in 1993), we can thank a combination of early retirement ages, lavish benefit formulas, and 100-percent-of-CPI COLAs that are virtually unheard of in the private sector. The average retirement age is now about fifty-eight for civil servants, compared with sixty-three for private-sector employees. The average age of retirement in the military is forty-six for officers and forty-two for enlisted men. On average, military retirees now receive monthly benefit checks that are 2.1 times larger than those of private pensioners; civil service retirees receive checks 2.6 times larger. As of 1985, it was estimated that 325,000 of these "royal retirees" were receiving pensions larger than their salaries the year they quit working; 100,000 were receiving pensions larger than the *current* salaries of their *former* jobs! Needless to say, this too is unheard of in the private sector.

All of this might be okay if civil service and military retirees paid for their own benefits. But they don't. Under the Civil Service Retirement System, the "contributions" of participants and their employers cover just a fraction of costs; soldiers contribute nothing toward their pensions. Like Social Security FICA taxes, moreover, any pension "contributions" paid by federal agencies to the U.S. Treasury get spent on general federal outlays as soon as they are received. There are only "paper" trust funds. If the federal government were required to fund its pension plans with real money the way it requires private employers to do under ERISA laws, it would, according to one calculation, have to set aside about $145 billion a year (to pay for newly earned benefits plus a thirty-year amortization of prior-year unfunded liabilities). But no matter. It's more convenient to pretend the bills don't exist—then pass them on to our kids. It's called pay-as-you-go. They pay. We go.

TEN MYTHS ABOUT ENTITLEMENTS

Myths about entitlements are everywhere. They are used—and abused—in the political dialogue in ways that seem to make reasoned debate and reasonable reforms impossible. Let's look at ten of the most common myths.

Myth one: Most federal social spending goes to the poor.

It is important to remember what entitlements have done to reduce poverty. Prior to the New Deal, millions of Americans had no means of support in the event of unemployment, disability, unexpected retirement, or the death of a parent or spouse. At great cost to society and the economy, millions of workers could fall into unsupported poverty and never recover. Vast numbers of children grew up in destitute homes. In 1937, FDR could say, "I see one-third of a nation ill-housed, ill-clad, ill-nourished." Today, entitlements prevent some 20 million Americans (half of them elderly) from falling into poverty.

This is clearly to the good. However, keeping people out of poverty is *not* the cause to which most entitlement spending is directed. In reality, *only about one out of eight federal dollars of social spending serves to lift poor families above the poverty line.* (Even including state and local spending, the figure is just one out of six.) Only about *one of every four federal benefit dollars even flows through programs that use financial need as a criterion for eligibility.* Counting both direct benefits and the value of entitlements conveyed through the tax code, the aggregate amounts received by people above the national median income are simply staggering.* In 1991, about half of all federal entitlements went to households with incomes over $30,000. One-quarter went to households with incomes over $50,000.

---

* Throughout this chapter, calculations of direct entitlements by household income are based on major federal benefit programs for which outlays could be allocated by the income of recipients. These constitute roughly 80 percent of the total.

Looking back over the random, mindless history of upward benefit expansion over FDR's original vision of a benefit floor, a true safety net for the poor, I am reminded not of a safety net but of a well-padded hammock for the rest of us.

Myth two: Entitlement spending helps to equalize incomes by giving more to the poor than to the rich.

Few axioms of American political life find such uncritical acceptance as the belief that social welfare programs effect a dramatic redistribution of wealth in favor of low-income households. It apparently makes little difference that most experts, liberal and conservative alike, have never subscribed to this belief, and that recent data repudiate it altogether.

Back in the sixties, the Nobel Laureate economist Milton Friedman used to shock audiences by asserting that Social Security was actually a regressive program—since the program's mildly progressive benefit formula conpensated neither for its regressive payroll tax nor for the fact that the poor pay taxes over more years (since they tend to start work at a younger age) and receive benefits over fewer years (since they also tend to die at a younger age). Most economists found Friedman's analysis at least plausible; no one has yet disproved it. More recently, the celebrated political scientist Mancur Olson, author of *The Rise and Decline of Nations*, looked over the panoply of American entitlement programs and concluded:

> Most of the redistribution of government is *not* from upper-income and middle-income people to low-income people. Most of the redistribution of income in fact is from middle-income people to other middle-income people, or from the whole of society to particular groups of rich people, or from one group to another where the groups are distinguished not by one being poor and the other being rich, but only by the fact that some groups are organized and some are not.

Income data from the Congressional Budget Office tend to bear out Olson's critique. Total federal benefits to the affluent are at least as substantial as those to the needy. Among Social Security beneficiaries, for instance, households with incomes of $100,000 or more receive, on average, checks that are twice as large as those of households with incomes of less than $10,000. Even when we add in the cash and in-kind benefits disbursed by all of the other federal sources for which we have income data—including "means-tested" welfare and food stamps—we find that households in the top bracket ($100,000 and up) received an average of about $5,700 in 1991, slightly more than the average of $5,600 received by households in the bottom bracket (under $10,000).

But direct federal payments are not the only way in which the federal government distributes benefits. We also have to take into account so-called tax expenditures. These deliberate loopholes in the tax code, designed to favor certain households and bearing no relationship to ability to pay, are the fiscal and economic equivalent of a government check. Most tax expenditures are unquestionably regressive: Many poor households cannot qualify for them—and even when they do, what they receive is smaller, relative to their income, than what goes to the affluent. This year, for example, the Joint Committee on Taxation estimates that the average value of the home mortgage interest deduction for taxpayers with incomes over $100,000 is $3,453. In contrast, the same deduction is worth an average of only $478 for taxpayers in the $20,000 to $30,000 bracket. And even these figures include only those who qualified for the benefit. They exclude many low-income families, including renters and those who opted for the standard deduction, who do not qualify.

When we add together all the direct-benefit outlays and all the tax expenditures, an unambiguous picture emerges. On average, a household with an income under $10,000 collected roughly $5,700 in 1991. On average, a household with an income over $100,000 collected $9,300. This distribution of benefits by income became more—not less —skewed during the 1980s. Clearly, it has nothing to do with economic equality. Let's phrase the issue a bit more bluntly. If the federal government's purpose was to straighten out the national income distribution, it could do a better job by dispensing with all the programmatic rules. Instead, it could simply take all the money and scatter it by airplane over every population center, to be gathered at random by passersby.

Myth three: Social Security and Medicare are an earned right: Beneficiaries are only getting back what they paid in.

Here, the case is open and shut. Most currently retired Americans receive Social Security benefits that are *two to five times greater* than the actuarial value of prior contributions, by both employer and employee. The payback for the Medicare Hospital Insurance program is *five to twenty times greater*. A typical middle-income couple who retired in 1981 has already received back, with interest, not only the total value of their previous Social Security and Medicare taxes, but *also the total value of their lifetime federal income taxes*.

And these actuarial calculations are conservative. They assume that employer contributions "belong" to the beneficiary and that the public must guarantee a "market" interest rate on all contributions, no matter what the condition of the economy or the wages of those who are taxed to make good on this claim. In fact, the Social Security Administration keeps no direct record of how much each person contributes. It just keeps records of each person's wage history, to which a politically determined formula is applied when that person retires.

The politically potent and disingenuous language adopted by the Social Security Administration has contributed to the earned-right myth. The system is described as an "insurance" program, although it is nothing of the sort. References are made to contributors' "accounts," when no such accounts exist.

My father, helped along by years of such misleading nomenclature, went to his grave thinking he was simply getting back "his" money, by which he meant what he had put into "his" account over the years. Since by this logic the benefits *belonged* to him, any proposal to take any of them away was both unjust and immoral. In truth, it was as though the government had a moral obligation to provide a windfall forever. He could only wonder why his otherwise well-educated son thought differently. I could never persuade him. It would have depressed him to find out there was, in fact, no George Peterson Social Security savings account in Washington.

Nor would I have wanted to depress him further with other unpleasant facts about entitlements. My father, as an embodiment of the endowment ethic, was immensely supportive of my wife's work on behalf of poor children at the Children's Television Workshop. He would have been distressed to learn that, in 1986, the last year of his life, America could not afford to fund fully the much-admired Head Start program. Yet merely the *increase* in Social Security's COLAs enacted the previous year would have fully funded Head Start. Had he known the facts, I'm sure he would have been happy to give up his COLA sliver of the huge entitlement pie for such a worthy cause.

Myth four: The elderly, as a group, are poorer than younger Americans.

In reality, the 1990 official poverty rate among the over-sixty-five population was 12 percent, compared with 21 percent among children. When we include the value of all noncash benefits as income, the poverty rate for the elderly is 6 percent, versus 15 percent for children. On this latter basis, poor children outnumber poor elderly in America by five to one. In no other major industrial nation is the poverty rate for children (using identical definitions) anywhere near what it is in the United States.

In view of the myriad problems of young families and children today, it is imperative that we focus much more of our public resources on *investing* in them. They are the truly needy in our society, but they certainly don't get most of the money. In 1990, 63 percent of all direct federal benefits went to the 13 percent of all Americans over age sixty-five, versus 9 percent of benefits going to the 26 percent of all Americans under age eighteen. On a per-capita basis—including all federal outlays that might be called "child benefits," from education to immunization—the ratio of average benefits received was eleven to one: $13,890 to each elderly person versus $1,271 to each child. Even adding in everything spent by state and local governments (for instance, on schools), this ratio still favors the elderly by at least three to one.

It is sometimes argued that entitlements for the elderly merely substitute for transfers of wealth that the young would otherwise make to their parents. That might be true if these programs weren't so lavish. Before Social Security and Medicare, young families did sacrifice for older parents—if and when mom and pop were in need. Yet because today's retirees are, as a whole, so much wealthier than the young, adults aged 25 to 34 now report receiving from their parents twenty times more financial support than they give to them; even for adults aged 35 to 44, the ratio is five to one. Social Security and Medicare, far from replicating traditional family values, have turned them on their head.

Myth five: Social Security is building up a huge surplus that will be available to pay for benefits promised to Baby Boomers.

It is true that Social Security receipts from payroll withholding taxes currently paid into the retirement part of the Social Security system (not the health-care or Medicare part) are higher than Social Security expenditures, and will probably remain so until the Baby Boomers start retiring in large numbers. But this surplus is temporary. What is more, the funds are not being saved or invested. Instead, they are being used to help offset each year's overall federal budget deficit. Thus, these surpluses are transformed into debts held by the Social Security trust funds. Future taxpayers will become liable for the principal and interest.

Let's peer into the future to see what the *real* financial status of our old-age benefit programs is. Recall our earlier discussion of unfunded liabilities, the amounts (in this year's discounted dollars) by which future benefits promised to today's adults exceed all of their future payroll taxes plus the assets currently held in all the governments' relevant "trust funds." The federal government's unfunded liabilities for just four programs—Social Security, Medicare, and civil service and military retirement—come to about $14 trillion. That's a sum several times larger than our official national debt, and one equivalent to roughly $140,000 for every household. That is a system in "surplus"?

I cannot resist railing about the moral issue in all this massive obfuscation and limited disclosure to our children and grandchildren. Are we to accept the morality of the German philosopher who told us "It is the duty of the old to lie to the young"? The morality of slipping this huge hidden check to our own kids for our free lunch? I can imagine few ethical principles more important than honesty and fairness to our children.

As a symbolic gesture, I intend to contribute Social Security's largess toward me—as well as any royalties from this book—to The Concord Coalition's effort to give Americans the straight facts.

Myth six: Today's younger Americans will eventually receive the same health and pension benefits they are providing today's retirees.

Recently, the Senate Finance Committee held a hearing on likely paybacks to various generations. No expert disagreed on the trend (a fact that in itself is unusual): The earliest beneficiaries got by far the best deal, and the deal has been getting worse for each successive generation. By some calculations, some upper-income single males retiring this year may get less out of Social Security than they and their employees put in, plus interest.

Moreover, financing even the reduced returns that are promised to tomorrow's retirees is unlikely to be economically or politically sustainable as America ages. The Social Security Administration projects that, depending on demographic and economic trends, the cost of Social Security and Medicare will by 2040 rise to between 38 and 53 percent of payroll—unless we cut benefits. We can make modest, fairshare sacrifices now. Or we can make wrenching changes later. I believe the only real question is when, not whether, benefit cuts will come.

Myth seven: Retirement benefits are an "inviolable contract" between the generations.

No, Virginia, there is no "sacred contract," at least not according to the U.S. Supreme Court, which has repeatedly ruled that no covered worker retains any rights, contractual or otherwise, over taxes paid into the Social Security system. Perhaps I could be permitted a layman's less lofty legal opinion. As I recall (from a college course in commercial law), one fundamental requirement of a valid contract is a "meeting of the minds" of the parties to that contract: between those who pay and those who receive. But no such meeting of the minds exists. I'm not aware that anyone has consulted my grandson, Peter Cary, now aged

three, about the staggering tax rates that honoring our current entitlement "contracts" will require him to pay when he enters the workforce.

Simply repeating some disingenuous mantra—"inviolable contract," "mandatory," "nondiscretionary," "uncontrollable" payments
—does not change certain truths. What Congress mindlessly giveth can
be taken away. A fundamental reality is that the current system is not
sustainable. If Social Security (or Medicare) is a contract, it is an
unenforceable one.

*Myth eight: Tax breaks for health insurance primarily benefit people who
otherwise could not afford proper health care.*

Maybe this one isn't really a myth, but the regressivity of our subsidies
to privately paid health care is too shocking not to mention. In fiscal
year 1994, exempting employer-paid health insurance from taxes will
cost the U.S. Treasury about $75 billion. Needless to say, of the 35
million or so Americans without health insurance who receive zero
benefits from this huge tax break, most are poor or low-income citizens. Among households that do have insurance, those with the highest incomes and the most generous insurance plans receive several
times as much from this federal tax subsidy as those with low incomes
in a cost-conscious HMO.

*Myth nine: The federal government's major housing entitlement, the home
mortgage interest deduction, promotes homeownership and stimulates the
economy.*

In fiscal year 1994, the cost of the home mortgage deduction to the
U.S. Treasury in lost revenues will be $46 billion, 80 percent of which
will go directly to households with incomes over $50,000. The main
economic effect of the home mortgage deduction is to inflate the price
(and size) of homes, while diverting investment away from more productive sectors of the economy.

Our global competitors, who hear us publicly rail about our
investment-starved economy and our productivity stagnation, politely
ask what conceivable connection this tax subsidy for the relatively well
off has to do with enhancing productivity. Officials in Canada regularly
chide me about the fact that Canada has the same rate of homeownership as the United States without the benefit of this tax subsidy.

Why then do we have it? The answer, of course, does not lie in any
real economic imperative. The subsidy exists because we all think we
deserve it. What's more, it props up one of our most powerful special
interests: the real-estate lobby.

Myth ten: The only reason that Ronald Reagan could not keep his promise to shrink the size of government was the huge rise in defense spending.

Judging by the cheers of his supporters and the jeers of his critics, we might suppose that President Reagan cut deeply into spending on everything but the Pentagon. And judging from the similar partisan bickering over the policies of his successor, President George Bush, we might suppose "the welfare state" remained the victim of further slashing and hacking for another four years after Reagan stepped down.

But the reality is very different: The cost of all direct federal benefits today ($807 billion in fiscal year 1993) is considerably greater than the *entire federal budget* when Reagan first took office ($696 billion in fiscal year 1981). In fact, adjusted for inflation, federal benefits soared by 54 percent from 1981 to 1993—versus zero real growth for all other domestic spending and 15 percent real growth for defense, the one area where everyone supposed the Reagan and Bush administrations had gone hog-wild.

Contrary to popular impression, the advent of the Reagan-Bush era did not signal a decisive shift in entitlement policy. With the exception of the 1983 Social Security amendments (designed by a bipartisan commission), both presidents largely left non-means-tested outlays and middle-class tax expenditures—that is, most entitlements—on autopilot.

Thus, the Reagan-Bush years only reaffirmed that these vast middle- and upper-class entitlements were politically "uncontrollable"—a weasel word behind which Congress and the president can hide their unwillingness to act, since together they can "control" any spending they want.

PROGRAMS WITHOUT A PUBLIC PURPOSE

Perhaps the most depressing fact about entitlements is that, despite their heavy and growing cost, they do such a poor job of accomplishing the public purposes we associate with them. We like to think that entitlements serve mainly to assist households in financial need. So why do about half of all entitlements go to households with incomes above the national median? We like to think that entitlements are a form of social investment—a way in which we all contribute to bettering our common future. So why does the federal budget spend, on average, eleven benefit dollars on each American over age sixty-five (whose life is mostly in the past tense) for every one dollar on each American under age eighteen (whose life is mostly in the future tense)?

But this does not exhaust the questions we should ask, or the ways in which our entitlement programs fail to allocate benefits according to some commonsense criterion of our public interest. Why does our single largest housing entitlement (the home mortgage interest deduction) give 80 percent of its benefits to households with incomes over $50,000—and give nothing to households that cannot afford a home? Why do we pay for the health care of retired tycoons (everything from CAT scans and pacemakers to chiropractic and orthopedic recliners) just because they have reached age sixty-five—while we do nothing for some 20 million lower-income Americans under age sixty-five who lack any health insurance at all? Why do we dole out special benefits to half a million successful peanut growers, dairy farmers, wheat growers, and honey producers—but leave over 3 million children to grow up in households reporting annual cash incomes of less than $5,000? No one argues that Social Security benefits do not prevent millions of households from falling into poverty. But why don't we take just *one-fifth* of all *unearned* Social Security benefits going to households with above-median incomes and bring elderly poverty down to zero? In 1991, households with over $100,000 in income received $30 billion in direct benefit outlays from our major federal entitlement programs and another $19 billion in tax expenditure benefits. Why does it make sense to turn the federal budget into a revolving door— with all the disincentives involved in taxing and benefiting the same affluent households—rather than to give fewer benefits to such households in the first place?

Another issue worth considering is how public benefits change our social and economic behavior in ways that both undermine the benefits' original intentions and increase the benefits' indirect costs. "Moral hazard" is a term traditionally used in the insurance industry to describe policies that tend to encourage the behavior being insured against. For example, collision insurance can encourage careless driving; fire insurance, arson. In recent years, the same term has been transplanted to the public sector, where policy experts have found many examples of the same phenomenon. A classic study of federal flood insurance found that each time the government raised the insured-value ceiling, people would build new houses closer to the Mississippi—leading to more structural damage and higher costs to taxpayers each time it flooded. Something similar was at work in the recent S&L debacle: Because depositors were insured, they sought the highest interest rate, without regard to a bank's creditworthiness.

The moral hazard critique of entitlements maintains that the benefits make people *less responsible*—if not immediately, then after the passage of years—with serious repercussions for both our society and our economy.

Since the late 1970s, this argument has been pressed with special fervor against means-tested benefits. AFDC and food stamps, claim many experts, tend to encourage the very social pathologies (jobless-ness, teen pregnancy, family breakup) they are designed to alleviate. As proof, they cite data indicating that long-term "welfare depen-dency" has been increasing, despite the availability of training and employment opportunities. Although other experts counter that the benefits themselves are not to blame, many state legislators are taking the critique to heart and are introducing behavior-based reforms (such as "workfare," "wedfare," and "learnfare").

It is remarkable that the same critical energy has not been leveled at the moral hazard associated with many *non*-means-tested programs—which, of course, are much greater in size. The effects have been just as amply documented. Social Security benefits persuade people to retire earlier. Farm aid leads to unproductive cultivation. "Cost-plus" Medicare reimbursement invites hospitals and doctors to overtest, over-prescribe, and overbill. Our federal tax code encourages people to take out larger mortgages and to accept more expensive health insur-ance policies from their employers. In each case, the concept of moral hazard reminds us that we have to balance how benefits help with how benefits can hurt. We shouldn't mind the occasional malingerer in a program that insures against total disability. But what about policies that bribe us into spending more on housing or health care—espe-cially when we know Americans are already such profligate consumers of these items? They certainly cost us far more (in direct fiscal and economic terms) than dead-end welfare dependency. Since social in-surance programs make promises to pay future income, and since most of these promises are not "funded," perhaps the most serious moral-hazard charge is that entitlements discourage household savings. After all, no one who anticipates a windfall saves as much—especially if the windfall is big.

It is symptomatic of our entitlement addiction that we can clearly appreciate the negative consequences only when they seem remote from most of us. Who can forget Ronald Reagan's anecdote about the cost of providing food stamps to mink-wearing welfare mothers who use them to buy vodka? Yet it is also symptomatic that we flinch from any reminder closer to home. Who can recall any politician complain-ing about the incomparably larger cost of subsidizing home-equity loans to rising young stockbrokers, of granting free medical care, PX cards, and half-pay for life to ex-colonels at age forty-two, of passing out farm aid to affluent agribusiness owners, or of writing checks to globe-trotting senior citizens that are forwarded to Bermuda? During the 1980s, accordingly, it was easier to crack down on those who might actually deserve some public assistance than it was to re-examine the claims of those who don't really need it. The assumption that free lunches corrupt only the underclass has become yet another crutch for our politics of denial.

Entitlements cost a lot today and threaten to cost much more to-morrow. They favor the rich over the poor, the old over the young, and consumption over savings. They dump random windfalls on many who don't need them and pass over others who do. Even while growing every year, they fail to carry out our heartfelt convictions about giving a fair measure of personal security and social justice to every American. For any number of reasons, federal entitlements have become a central manifestation of our inability to make meaningful choices. Is it any wonder they belong at the very top of the nation's policy agenda?

We must go beyond the objective of merely controlling the growth in the dollar cost of federal benefits. We have to rethink the underlying social and economic relationship between these benefits and our behavior, attitudes, and expectations. *We must invent a new entitlement system that will not just pay us affordable benefits when we need them, but will also encourage us to save more for the future, care more for our own children and parents, and take more responsibility for our own health.*

As America itself grows old, perhaps the most vital changes in our entitlement system will be those that encourage a positive new vision of aging. Entitlements for the elderly must promote an active, economically self-sufficient lifestyle for elders who are able. We will no longer be able to afford a system that equates the last third or more of one's adult life with a publicly subsidized vacation.

The worst aspect of our entitlement addiction is how it subtly fixes our attention on how much we are going to get now—and how it obscures any thought of what we have received from others and what we intend to pass on in our turn. *It is time for America to begin unlearning its entitlement ethic and begin relearning its endowment ethic.* At some point, we must decide how much we are willing to give up today in order to save for and invest in a tomorrow of rising living standards for ourselves and, of course, our children. Entitlements are as the very core of this ultimate tradeoff.

4

Health Care: Where the Buck Never Stops

In recent years, poll after poll revealed that Americans were fed up with gridlock in Congress and wanted to throw all the rascals out. But most felt the congressman in their own district was doing a good job. Something rather similar is true in health care. Ask Americans whether they are happy with the care that they personally receive from their doctors and the vast majority answer "yes." Ask them whether they are pleased with how our health system works and three-quarters say it needs to be fundamentally changed or even scrapped or rebuilt. Just one-quarter say it works "pretty well." Schizophrenia?

Not really. Public opinion about health care in America is a minefield of contradictions—and for good reason. We have the best medical technologies in the world—and use them far more often than other countries. From fetal surgery and gene therapy to ultrasound and microwave scalpels, the list of recently or soon to be realized medical miracles makes anyone like me who grew up in the world of country doctors reel from future shock. Most of us also enjoy a freedom in choosing where we get care that is the envy of foreigners. Well-to-do Americans don't hop the border to get the very best that modern medicine can offer in Toronto. Canadians—and Germans and Japanese—come here.

But Americans are outraged at our system's extravagant costs. For years, these had been invisible to most people. Medical bills were paid for on a largely first-dollar basis by employers and government. But now the costs are beginning to show up in household budgets. As they do, polls indicate that Americans think they are paying too much and are worried about getting too little. What most Americans don't realize—but must—is that what they see today is still just pennies on the dollar.

Indeed, runaway medical costs threaten our entire economy. In 1993 the bills for the lavish style of medicine we practice soared over $900 billion. *That's about $3,400 per capita—more than three and one-half times as much in real dollars as we paid twenty-five years ago.* America devotes well over double the share of its economy to health care now than back in the mid-1960s and spends well over half again as much as other major industrial countries spend on average as a share of *their* economies. With U.S. automakers ponying up an estimated cost of $500 more per car in health insurance premiums than their Japanese counterparts, businessmen like former Chrysler chairman Lee Iacocca tell us that our health-care profligacy is crippling our international competitiveness. Governors like Thomas Kean of New Jersey have called health care the "Pac-Man" of their state budgets because it devours scarce resources and robs other pressing priorities. Runaway medical costs are also the single most important reason that federal spending and federal deficits have now become "uncontrollable." Unless we cap medical costs, President Clinton warns us, America faces economic disaster in its future.

Then there are the tragic feast-or-famine ironies that no other medically advanced nation tolerates. The elderly Pete Petersons of America are entitled to receive limitless "free" medical care at public expense after reaching the magic age of sixty-five. That is a right. Yet we allow one million young women to come to term each year in the United States without benefiting from even a single prenatal visit. Despite the hundreds of billions of tax dollars we throw at doctors and hospitals, some 35 million mostly working Americans and their children do not have even minimum insurance against catastrophic illness. Just a short stay in the hospital could bankrupt them. Millions more worry about losing coverage if they change their jobs.

Yet perhaps most disturbing is the nagging sense we aren't getting our money's worth. Health statistics tend to confirm this suspicion. Although the per-capita cost of health care in other major industrial countries is only about half of that in the United States, most of our allies and competitors enjoy a life expectancy that is as high or higher than our own.

All of this reminds me of the famous airline television commercial: "We must be doing something right." In the case of health care, I would have to reverse that: "We must be doing something wrong."

But what? I've been accused of many things in my life. Excessive humility is not one of them. Yet I confess I've found writing about health care daunting. In other areas of our public and private lives where we need to change course, there are—or so it seems to me—rather clear answers to our problems. We can means-test the cash entitlement windfalls we now dish out to middle- and upper-income Americans. We can curb our outsized appetite for energy by taxing it. I can even think of relatively straightforward reforms that will limit the litigiousness that is hobbling our economy and shattering our sense of community. But once you start talking about what we really need to do in health care you run smack into issues no one even wants to talk about. The right to live and the right to die. Playing God.

Part fiscal, part economic, part political, part psychological, part ethical, and part cultural, our health-care crisis, in my view, confronts us with the most complex choices America has faced in my memory. How we handle this crisis will shape our future as a nation. We should congratulate Bill Clinton for having had the courage to tackle issues that President Bush simply prayed would go away. They deserve all the attention and talent that Hillary Rodham Clinton and her Task Force on National Health Care Reform have brought to them. Our new President's goals are certainly the right ones. We must, as he says, tame our health-care cost spiral if we are to stand a real chance of balancing the budget or renewing the rise in U.S. living standards. And we must extend health insurance to those who now lack it and can't afford it. As Henry Aaron of the Brookings Institution put it, universal access is simply "a standard perquisite of citizenship in modern developed nations."

But, alas, there is one final difficulty. Polls reveal that most Americans believe "waste, fraud, and abuse" or "greedy" doctors, hospitals, and drug companies are entirely responsible for runaway medical costs. It's them, not us, is our attitude. There *is* lots of waste in our health system. Medical professionals *do* "profiteer"—if what that means is that they can often charge higher prices than they could command if subject to the normal discipline of the marketplace. Yet all the experts know that there is a deeper problem. The underlying causes of our cost spiral are ever-more-sophisticated and expensive technologies, the rapid aging of our population, and heavily subsidized benefit and insurance systems that exempt Americans with a ticket to play the game—and that is most of us—from making almost any tradeoff between health care and other priorities.

As I sat down to write this chapter in the spring of 1993, it was already becoming clear that we weren't ready to face up to the tough choices. The full details of the President's health-care plan had yet to be unveiled, much less debated by Congress. But mostly it seemed to be about expensive new public and private benefits: "Cadillac" health coverage for the uninsured and (perhaps) a long-term care entitlement for the elderly. According to working papers of the President's own Task Force quoted in *The New York Times,* the annual costs of these new benefits could total as much as $100 billion to $150 billion! As for cost containment, we kept hearing about magic bullets (slashing administrative costs was the favorite) that will supposedly allow us to have it all while still saving money. The President appeared to be raising false expectations about what real health-care reform will entail. This seemed to me to be a recipe for disaster.

What *does* real reform mean? It means that we must deny some potentially beneficial care to many people under some circumstances. Costs of genuinely useful technologies are increasing so rapidly that we won't come close to offsetting them even if we get rid of all the waste and redundancy. We can let government do the denying. Or we can let the market do it. But in the end, there will be no way around the "R" word—rationing. As much as we like to think that health care is somehow different, here, just as in every other area of our lives, tradeoffs are inevitable. Some of these tradeoffs will involve forgoing things most of us can agree are purely discretionary. But others will mean making painful judgments about costs and benefits at the margins of life and death. That's the painful prescription. Until we're ready to give something up, we'll never find a solution to our health-care crisis.

UTTERLY UNSUSTAINABLE PROJECTIONS

Since this book is about investing in our future and, above all, the tough choices we must make to find the savings to fund those investments, it will be no surprise that I want to focus the reader's attention on the medical cost spiral devouring America's public budgets, private payrolls, and overall economy.

Let's begin with the federal budget. The short course is as follows. Since 1965—the year we founded Medicare—the cost of federal health benefits has soared from $1.8 billion to about $250 billion, or from an almost invisible 1.4 percent to 16.5 percent of the budget. If we leave current policies on autopilot, the CBO tells us, a decade from now they will be consuming 28 percent of federal outlays. Between 1993 and 2003, the *growth* in Medicare and Medicaid alone is scheduled to add about $450 billion to *annual* federal expenditures. Even without new public spending commitments—and the reforms that the President and Congress are debating are certain to bring these—total federal health-care outlays will jump by 3.4 percent of GDP over that same time span. Along the way, the cost of our federal health-benefit programs will rapidly overtake, then shoot past the cost of Social Security, that great-granddaddy of all our entitlements.

These ballooning federal health-care costs are a nightmare for us deficit hawks. Even if we miraculously balanced the budget next year and kept every other program from growing at all, runaway medical bills alone would just about put us back where we started by the end of the decade. In a word, if we allow business as usual to continue in health care, even the most earnest efforts to eliminate the deficit or launch "imperative" new investment agendas will be doomed to failure.

But the potential of medical costs to rob our future is not limited to their impact on the federal budget. From Oregon to Florida, state governments are scrambling to find ways to pay for their share of a Medicaid program that now consumes about 15 percent of their budgets, and whose costs are rising at an annual clip of 20 percent.

And what about the private sector? During the 1980s, hikes in employer health-plan premiums ate up most of the already meager increases in real per-worker compensation in the United States. That was money that could have been pocketed as higher wages—what most Americans think about when they talk of rising living standards. What's more, with these costs showing up in all the goods and services we produce, they also threaten our competitiveness. To get an idea of the sums involved, consider that in the mid-1980s Chrysler Corporation began paying more to Blue Cross and Blue Shield of Michigan than to any other single supplier—including any steel manufacturer.

And what about the direct costs to American families? Despite what people often think, our third-party public and private financing systems shield most of us from paying all but a small fraction of our medical bills out of pocket. In 1992, less than 5 percent of all hospital bills and less than 20 percent of all doctor bills were paid for that way—and that includes what the totally uninsured paid. But it is also true that the growth in health-care spending has been so rapid that the *dollar* amounts people must pay directly to doctors and hospitals have gone up sharply even though the *share* of medical bills they finance out of pocket has not. As costs have shot up, firms that once offered first-dollar coverage are also beginning to ask employees to pay higher copayments and deductibles—and even contribute to their insurance premiums. Along with middle-class fears about losing insurance coverage, that's one reason for the political momentum now driving the calls for health-care reform.

All told the United States devoted an estimated 14.4 percent of its GDP to health care in 1993—a number that in dollars approaches the size of Great Britain's entire economy. Compared with what we spent back in 1965, that's an extra 8.5 percentage points of our economy. That *increase* alone is more than everything we spend today on net domestic investment and civilian R&D combined. Compared with the per-capita average for other industrial countries, the *extra* dollars that we spend would be enough to *double* our net fixed business investment, *double* our total corporate spending on R&D, *double* our total net additions to public infrastructure, *double* our total federal and state cash benefits for the poor, and *double* our total federal aid to child nutrition and education. Not just double each of those things. Double *all* of them.

If the present doesn't scare you, the future surely will. By the end of the decade, health-care costs are projected to rise to $1.7 trillion, over 18 percent of GDP. By then, America's health-care industry will be several times larger than defense, and bigger than farming, energy, utilities, transportation, and construction combined. Further out, the estimates become still more appalling. For the first time last year, the Health Care Financing Administration published official cost projections beyond the year 2000. The number crunchers concluded that if the current interaction of high-technology treatments and cost-plus financing continues into the future as it has over the last few decades, U.S. health-care spending will climb to 22 percent of GDP by 2010, when the oldest Baby Boomers start retiring, and will shoot past 32 percent by 2030, when the youngest turn sixty-five.

Use any word you wish. These projections are unthinkable, unsustainable, impossible. Because the American middle class feels so hardpressed, it is seductive to think that somehow someone else can pick up this tab. But any economist will tell you that we all must pay for it— through forgone cash compensation, higher taxes, reductions in our discretionary incomes, lost jobs, reduced conpetitiveness, and slower increases in our living standards.

We must ask ourselves what will be left of the American Dream if we set aside thirty-two cents out of every dollar we earn to pay doctor bills. There is simply no way we will be able to maintain even today's living standards, let alone invest in the kind of future we want to give our children, while siphoning off anywhere near that share of our income to satisfy our gluttony for health-care consumption.

WHY AMERICANS SPEND SO MUCH

One of my earliest childhood Nebraska memories is of good old Dr. Edwards carrying a black bag filled with all the tools of his trade. If he couldn't help us with his stethoscope or hypodermic needle, we made a rare visit to a community hospital, which may have boasted an X-ray machine. There wasn't much that medicine could do, and most of that wasn't very expensive. As recently as the 1940s, most Americans still died at home, not hooked up to tubes. Back then, I seem to recall, there was still something called "natural death." Each of us spent just $100 annually on health care, about one-thirty-fourth of what each of us spends, on average, today.

It was against this backdrop that a newly affluent postwar society decided to shield most Americans from the costs of much of their own health care. First came company-sponsored Blue Cross and Blue Shield plans with few copayments or deductibles,* then a Medicare program for the nation's then mostly not well-off and not-too-numerous elderly that paid for generous coverage out of a seemingly bottomless reservoir of tax dollars. At the time, we thought insuring against ill health was much like insuring against fire or theft. It would only happen so often, and there was only so much damage to pay for when it did. What no one anticipated was the way that perverse economic incentives embedded in these new benefit systems would themselves *induce* demand for health care, or the way that a combination of unimaginable new technologies and a gathering age wave would further fuel that hot-house-induced demand to create today's medical leviathan.

A Cornucopia of Medical Miracles

In today's world of high-tech medicine, my recollection of Dr. Edwards with his black bag seems quaint. With medicine's advances largely underwritten by the very system of cost-plus subsidies we created back when health care was cheap, doctors today possess an ever-growing arsenal of costly tools and treatments—from organ transplants for diseased hearts, lungs, and kidneys at several hundred thousand dollars a pop to space-age imaging devices like CAT scanners and MRIs that cost a thousand dollars just to turn on.

Most experts tell us that our extensive and excessive use of this cornucopia of technological miracles is the single most important reason America spends so much relative to other countries. While I am a relentless reader of health-care-reform reports, this is something I've also had a chance to confirm firsthand through visits to hospitals in the United States, Canada, Europe, and Japan. Even to my layman's eye, the differences the experts point to were strikingly obvious.

Here are a few of the numbers they cite. In Europe, intensive-care units or ICUs—with all their expensive high-tech equipment—account for just 1 percent to 5 percent of hospital beds. In the United States, they account for 15 percent to 20 percent. On a per-capita basis, the

---

* It's worth noting how two historical "accidents" helped to accelerate the spread of generous company-paid health plans. One was the exemption of fringe benefits from wage and price controls during World War II—a circumstance that meant employers could reward workers by giving them health insurance even if they couldn't pay them more cash. Another was an IRS ruling that exempted most fringes from taxation. Neither decision generated much debate at a time when fringe benefits made up just a tiny fraction of worker compensation. The latter in particular, however, has had enormous unintended consequences in fueling our subsequent spending spiral.

United States has more than seven times as many radiation therapy units and eight times as many MRI units as Canada. We have four and a half times as many open-heart surgery units and three times as many lithotripsy units as Germany. Tally up the bill for our extravagant use of technologies like these and you've gone a long way toward explaining why health-care costs are leapfrogging ahead of inflation. According to some estimates, after adjusting medical expenditures to take into account rises in the general price level, technology explains over *half* of the excess yearly growth in U.S. health-care costs.

When I was at Bell and Howell, we used to assume as a matter of course that new technologies would both reduce costs and improve the quality of whatever it was we were producing. After all, that was often the whole point of developing them. We also assumed that once new, more productive technologies were in place, older ones were headed for the scrap heap. It thus initially struck me (and may strike many readers) as odd that new medical technologies usually appear to *add* to costs—and that old ones, outdoing even old soldiers, rarely even fade away. Part of the explanation is that incentives in our medical marketplace don't reward efficiency, they reward providers who bill the most. And any hospital administrator knows that the way to generate the biggest bills is to buy *expensive* new technologies like MRIs and CAT scanners, then write off the cost by getting lots of patients to use them. Medical professionals are perhaps unique in their ability to do this, since in almost no other industry are the buyer and the seller of a service in effect the same person. (It's also worth noting that expensive new technologies give hospitals the prestige that attracts the best doctors. As one pundit put it, "Hospitals don't have patients; doctors have patients and hospitals have doctors.") And the dinosaur technologies? Why not use them too? Unlike normal markets, the market for medical services isn't overflowing with cost-conscious consumers focused on overall value and ready to discipline providers. Besides, say the practitioners, we'd better not leave any stone unturned since we have to defend ourselves against possible malpractice suits.

But even in a disciplined marketplace, many advances in medical technology would be inherently costly. One reason is that they constantly add to the number and subtlety of conditions we can treat at all. What's more, even when they reduce the per-patient cost of treating a particular condition (which is rarely) they often add to total health-care spending anyway. Consider the case of lithotripsy. By using ultrasound to break up kidney stones, it did away with the need for surgery in many cases. We did save costs on a *per-patient* basis. But since surgery was no longer necessary, these savings were soon overwhelmed by the large numbers of *new* patients with relatively minor conditions who decided to opt for medical intervention instead of trying to pass kidney stones on their own.

With dozens of new technologies like this in the pipeline, health care is rapidly becoming a continuous, lifelong process of diagnostics, monitoring, and fine tuning. Far from saving us money, medical advances are bringing us to the point where there is no extra dollar we can spend that might not confer *some* benefit. Indeed, we ain't seen nothing yet. This is how William Schwartz, one of America's top experts on medical technology, put it: "Everything that's happened up until now in medicine is a prelude. What's really ahead is stunning: a total change in the ways we think about disease. . . . it's going to be very expensive."

Another reason that technology hasn't saved us money has to do with a mystifying-sounding development called the "epidemiological transition." What this means is that thanks to medicine's conquest of most epidemic infectious disease earlier in the century, costly chronic conditions that typically strike later in life have become our major killers and cripplers. Heart disease, strokes, and cancer are not like cholera or polio. They're not really single ailments, but convenient tags doctors give to bundles of related conditions, each of which has complex, multiple causes. We don't know how to cure them yet. We just know how to treat them with sophisticated "halfway technologies." And these usually cost a bundle.

An Aging Society

Which brings us to a second root cause of our cost explosion: the aging of society. You don't have to be getting older, as I am, to know that nearly every measure of illness, disability, and health-care use rises with age. Not just more doctor visits and hospital stays, but more pharmaceuticals and wheelchairs. On average, the number crunchers tell us, each older American consumes over four times as much in medical services as a younger adult and eight times as much as a child. Although seniors now compose just 13 percent of our population, they already account for 37 percent of U.S. medical bills.

If those numbers don't strike you as eye-openers, just listen to what's in store. As we saw in Chapter 3, the aging of the Baby Boom generation will cause the size of our elderly population to soar. By 2040, the share of Americans who are aged sixty-five and over will be at least 20 percent and may hit 25 percent. We will also have to cope with a phenomenon that demographers call the "aging of the aged." While the number of Americans aged sixty-five to seventy-four will grow by 80 to 85 percent, the number of Americans aged eighty-five and over will grow by between 270 and 375 percent. What's so ominous about these projections is that rates of health-care use rise very rapidly even among ascending elderly age brackets. For hospital care, the ratio of per-capita medical spending by the "old old" relative to the young old is about two to one. For nursing homes, the ratio is a mind-boggling twenty to one!

Some imbalance between what we spend on the health care of the old and what we spend on that of the young is of course inevitable. But here too there is a profound difference between America and other countries. To a degree unprecedented abroad, we have tilted our public subsidies in precisely that direction in which medicine's technological revolution makes their impact on costs most explosive: toward the far end of life. Although the elderly are only one-eighth of our population, they receive about three-quarters of all federal health benefits. According to the International Monetary Fund, the U.S. public sector spends nearly eight times as much per capita on health care for the elderly as it does for all people under age sixty-five (and fifteen times as much as for children), while in no other major industrial country is the ratio more than about four to one. And that estimate was made back in 1980. Today the discrepancy is surely even more lopsided.

What do these numbers mean in more concrete terms? Take dialysis on demand. Here the fastest-growing age group among dialysis patients is the seventy-five and over set. It's paid for by Medicare, no questions asked, and no matter what the odds of long-term survival. Abroad, dialysis at that age is practically unheard of. Or consider the totally incapacitated octogenarian stroke victim who suffers a bout of pneumonia. Here he is rushed to the hospital and attended by an army of specialists; in other countries, he is most likely to die at home looked in on by a GP. That's why there's another striking fact about U.S. intensive-care units compared with those abroad. Not only do they account for a far larger share of our hospital beds, but as one observer of the international medical scene put it: "The common patient in an ICU in a major U.S. hospital is an 85-year-old whose heart is failing, whose lungs are failing, who is in need of artificial respiration. The patients [abroad] were different. They were healthier and they were younger." Why do other countries so often limit heroic intervention on behalf of the very old? The reason, of course, is that the demand by the very old for expensive medical treatment is theoretically limitless, and their odds of long-term recovery, almost by definition, are lowest of any age group.

Medicare records tell us that nearly one-third of all hospital spending by older Americans occurs in their last year of life—with much of that incurred in the last month. As recently as 1949, half of all people who died in New York City died at home in bed. By 1989, that number had fallen to just 16 percent. Long before our Senior Boom arrives in full force around 2010, Americans must ask, and answer, searching questions about whether the kinds of efforts we now make to stave off the inevitable are affordable. The issue is so important—not just for budgetary reasons, but for what it says about the kind of society we are—that I will return to it later in this chapter. But first we need to look a bit more closely at how our health system works—or rather, how it doesn't.

A Market Gone Haywire

Other countries face the same potentially explosive technological and demographic cost pressures that we do, but have made tough choices to limit what they spend. It is a myth that national health systems abroad are simply more efficient, don't waste money on paperwork, and keep a lid on doctors' fees, and thus can *both* contain costs and guarantee everyone unlimited access to the very best that medicine can devise. To contain costs, they ensure that not all people always get what they desire. In other words, they ration. In Great Britain, the public health system doesn't pay for kidney dialysis if you're over age fifty-five. To get an arthritic hip replaced, you have to spend years on a waiting list. There are no laws requiring rationing. It's just that the resources government devotes to health care are budgeted, forcing doctors to practice a kind of medical triage to live within those predetermined limits. In Canada the joke is that you had better not get sick in November or December. Your doctor is likely to have earned his maximum allowable fee for the year—and gone on vacation to Florida.

We don't need to have government make all the tradeoffs for us. I believe there are ways to make them more efficiently by using market forces. But in the end we cannot avoid the *types* of tradeoffs other countries are making. Through one mechanism or another, we will have to deny some high-cost, low-benefit care to many people. The problem today is that we have neither government control over health budgets nor a medical marketplace that forces people to think twice about what they spend. We're just not making choices.

To get an idea of how totally haywire our medical marketplace is, take a glance around at how health care is practiced in the United States today and note all the insane variations. Rates for major surgery among U.S. cities: tonsillectomy by age fifteen, 7 percent to 70 percent; hysterectomy for a woman by age fifty-five, 40 percent to 60 percent; prostrate operation for a man by age eighty, 7 percent to 40 percent. Variations in the prices of medical procedures are just as striking. Back in the early 1980s, one study found that hospital charges for treatment of angina in Essex County, New Jersey, varied between $1,800 and $3,650, and the physician charge for a normal birth in Los Angeles varied between $500 and $1,150. Little has changed since then—except, of course, that the prices have gone up. Then consider the results of another study, done for the Chrysler Corporation by a team of physician experts. Among the eight Detroit-area hospitals with the most admissions for lower-back pain, two-thirds of those admissions were judged "inappropriate," as were 85 percent of the total hospital days they resulted in. The admissions, it turns out, were largely for bed rest.

All of these circumstances would be inconceivable if U.S. medical care were subject to the normal discipline of the marketplace—or just to the criterion of common sense. Think about what would happen if a Chevrolet dealer in Essex County, New Jersey, was pricing cars twice as high as his competitors. He'd be out of business overnight. The last time I was in Maine, I didn't notice any difference between the men in Bangor and those in Portland. Yet the latter apparently "need" nearly four times as many prostate operations by age eighty-five! Forgive me if I insist on bringing a businessman's perspective to this. But if we had a functioning market, there would be few variations like the ones I noted above. Costs would also be lower. But ever since we made our fateful decision to set up a system in which most people are personally shielded from bearing the cost of their care—and indeed, in which everyone has a right to whatever technology is available—assessing tradeoffs between costs and benefits has been the last thing on doctors' or patients' minds.

First, look at the incentives that patients face. As recently as 1965, over half of U.S. health-care spending was paid for out of pocket by patients; today that share has plummeted to just over one-fifth. What's more, of what remains much comes from uninsured households or goes for nursing homes, dental care, and pharmaceuticals. That, incidentally, is why drug companies are taking so much heat right now. Pharmaceuticals (even including over-the-counter drugs) account for less than a dime out of our health-care dollar and haven't risen as much in price as most other medical services. But we still pay for them the old-fashioned way—nearly three-quarters out of pocket. As prices keep shooting up, doctors, to be sure, are also beginning to take a bit of heat from outraged patients. We pay for nearly one-fifth of their bills out of pocket. But for hospitals, where most of the expensive technology is and the biggest slice of our medical dollar goes, that share is down to less than 5 percent. The rest of the bill is picked up by "someone else"—namely employers, insurance companies, and government.

The result? We have little incentive to question the value of the care we receive—and what incentive we do have drops toward zero once we've exceeded the annual stop-loss amount in our insurance plan. The decisions we make about treatment ultimately drive the cost of our insurance premiums and taxes up and the share of our compensation we receive as cash take-home pay down. But when we are at the doctor's office or the hospital, those outcomes are not apparent to us.

Then look at the incentives that medical professionals face. We generally pay them on an open-ended, fee-for-service, after-the-fact basis—meaning that they simply tally up the prices of whatever tests and treatments they have ordered, then put the bill in the mail. Needless to say, this is unheard of in almost every other industry. In effect, doctors and hospitals tell us what we owe after we've already agreed to pay it. This kind of reimbursement is the single most important reason we have a cost-plus health system—with the larger the cost, the larger the plus. Doctors and hospitals earn more by doing more and charging more, not by practicing medicine more efficiently. When we learned about this kind of cost-plus billing at the Pentagon—$800 wrenches and gold-plated toilet seats—it caused national outrage. In health care, we hardly seem to give it a second thought.

Recent trends in what the media never tire of calling our "increasingly competitive health-care marketplace" should not deceive us. Only about 15 percent of Americans are now enrolled in HMOs—prepaid plans that make more by being more efficient. Most of today's so-called managed care—with its alphabet soup of IPAs and PPOs—amounts to little more than bargain hunting by large payers. Its cost-containment tools—volume discounts and utilization review—don't do much to change the underlying cost-plus incentives providers face. What's more, much of what those payers who can play this game do save simply gets shifted as higher costs to other payers with less market clout—in other words, to small businesses and to individuals.

An Open Spigot of Entitlement Dollars

How did we get a health system that's like a car with a jammed accelerator and no brakes? An important part of the explanation lies in the massive public subsidies we direct at it. First and foremost, there is the open spigot of direct entitlement dollars. All told, public budgets now pay nearly 45 percent of U.S. medical bills. No matter whether they're poor or rich, beneficiaries in Medicare's Hospital Insurance (HI) program receive five- to twentyfold paybacks on their and their employers' lifetime payroll taxes plus interest. Under Medicare's Supplementary Medical Insurance (SMI) program, general revenues finance about three-quarters of all outlays. And what about Medicaid, our means-tested benefit program for the poor? First-dollar coverage without even a token deductible to discourage the casual use of medical services (something like calling an ambulance to get an aspirin). In a recent exchange of ideas with Dr. Fred Plum, chief of neurology at New York Hospital and an enormously thoughtful observer of our health-care system, he indicated that even a fifty-cent cost-sharing requirement could deflect many unnecessary cases from our emergency rooms.

In looking for a way to sum up our cost-plus public approach to health care, I can't help recalling a remark that Social Security commissioner Bob Ball made back in 1965. At the time, the government was trying to gain the support of doctors who were opposed to the new Medicare program on the grounds that it might open the door to "socialized" medicine—in other words, that it might *curtail* the incomes they could earn in our "free enterprise" system. Its "main principle," he explained, is that "costs will differ . . . from place to place, and we will reimburse whatever it turns out to be." We are still paying for what has sometimes been called a great "bribe." Since health benefits are simply the sum of what each of us—with the advice of his or her physician—decides to purchase in a market for ever-more-sophisticated and expensive forms of medical treatment, they have become uncontrollable in an even more fundamental sense than cash benefits. As I have mentioned elsewhere, when LBJ signed the Medicare act, he said the extra $500 million in spending would present "no problem." Today Medicare costs three hundred times that original estimate!

But direct federal benefits are not our only health-care entitlement. Government also tells us to indulge our appetite for health care by exempting employer-paid insurance from taxation. An indirect subsidy that will cost the U.S. Treasury about $75 billion in 1994, this huge tax loophole helps explain why, despite the obvious interest of employers and insurers in squeezing inefficiencies out of our health system, cost-plus fee-for-service pricing remains the norm in the private sector.

My own experience at The Blackstone Group is a case in point. At the beginning, we offered a health plan that cost our employees virtually nothing out of pocket. We had the full menu of services—psychiatric, dental, eyeglass prescriptions—all with de-minimis cost sharing. In hindsight, we should not have been surprised that our employees feasted on this free lunch. But I must say, when we looked at the size of the bill, we were shocked. Over just five years, the per-employee premiums we were being asked to pay shot up by nearly 250 percent.

What was the excuse for our imprudence? Here's the logic. Our industry pays large cash incomes. A relatively high proportion of our employees are in the top tax brackets. Health-care benefits are tax-deductible to our firm and tax-free to our employees—thereby making the federal government a major partner in our imprudence. Why not pay our employees relatively more of their compensation as health-care benefits, relatively less as cash wages? Since many who work at our firm must pay total marginal income tax rates of 40 percent, we could buy $1.40 worth of health care for every dollar of cash wages we paid them.

All of our employees, fat-cat bankers included, dined on this rich cuisine. But even a profitable Wall Street investment bank has its limits. Faced with astronomical hikes in our health-care bills, in 1993 we cut some benefits (eyeglasses are history), significantly raised both per-doctor-visit and annual deductibles, and asked employees to pay directly for a share of their premiums.

Unfortunately, not everyone has learned this easy lesson: When we give people a credit card, then don't even ask them to look at the statements, they become irresponsible shoppers. Ironically, President Clinton's new higher marginal tax rates may simply throw more gasoline on the fire by increasing our incentives to spend through our tax loopholes for things like gold-plated health-insurance plans.

In the last two sections, I've been talking about why our medical marketplace lacks what economists call a "budget constraint." Without a doubt, that's the main reason it doesn't work right. But it's by no means the only one.

It's Up to the Doctor

When I was chairman of Lehman Brothers, I remember walking down the hall one day. The next thing I knew I woke up in an ambulance, then found myself in a hospital bed. As a workaholic overachiever, I assumed the symptoms were my body's way of telling me to slow down. The initial diagnosis, to say the least, was shocking. I listened as a doctor explained the odds were 90 percent plus I had a malignant brain tumor and perhaps "sixty good days left." Naturally, my attitude was the costs be damned: Find me the best neurologist there is. (I got him: Dr. Fred Plum.) In the end, the tumor turned out to be benign— and since the surgery (over fifteen years ago now) I have suffered no symptoms (though some of my critics may deny that). Still, I'll never forget the unaccustomed sense of helplessness I felt.

That's a feeling almost anyone who's been seriously ill has experienced. Since medicine requires specialized expertise, we make doctors our proxies in judging today's bewildering array of high-tech treatments. Such delegation of authority is of course characteristic of all relationships between laymen and professionals. People entrust large sums of money to my firm, presumably because they believe we can make more money for them. But we are questioned all the time about nearly everything: investment sectors chosen, prices paid, and most certainly, fees charged. Most patients (and not just fat cats like me) have little reason to care about how much they spend, and hence little reason to question their physician's decisions. The result, almost every expert who has looked at this issue concludes, is that medical professionals enjoy great latitude in generating whatever volume of services they must to target the incomes they think they deserve.

There is hardly a physician in the country who will admit that this is so—and those who act this way are probably not even aware that they are doing it. Doctors, after all, are their patients' advocates, and their overriding ethical imperative is to do whatever is in our best interests, regardless of cost. But what economists call physician-induced demand is real, and we, as patients, shielded from costs and eager to have our doctors do whatever is feasible, are coconspirators.

If we need proof, all we have to do is look at the bizarre inversion of the usual laws of supply and demand in our medical marketplace. Since the mid-1960s, the number of physicians in America has doubled, far outpacing the growth in our population. (That, by the way, is another of LBJ's legacies. In view of shortages in rural areas, he thought we needed a lot more doctors, and directed vast public subsidies to medical schools. As it turns out, few of the new doctors ever took a trip to the country). Ordinarily, we would expect a greater supply to lower prices. Have the relative incomes of doctors fallen? No. Doctors were more than able to maintain their income expectations by increasing their service volume—as in "see me next week" instead of "see me in six months."

That patients and doctors don't enjoy equal access to information is hardly surprising. What seems truly astonishing to me is that the scientific basis of much of today's clinical practice is so imperfect that physicians themselves often have no real idea of the medical effectiveness—much less the relative costs and benefits—of different treatment options. According to Paul Ellwood, the head of a well-known health-policy think tank, perhaps "half of what the medical profession does is of unverified effectiveness." Economic self-interest and medical culture—with its imperative to diagnose, then try to cure, whatever the costs or odds of success—already predispose doctors to do more rather than less. The lack of data about what really works and what doesn't is yet one more reason why most do more.

Our system of tort law further reinforces the cost-blind incentives in our health system itself. Since I return to this topic in Chapter 6, I'll save some of my ammo. Here let me just note that malpractice premiums themselves are bad enough. They just drove my wife's gynecologist into early retirement. But these are only the tip of a cost iceberg. By putting physicians at risk of expensive and capricious suits, we force them to practice "defensive medicine"—in other words, to protect their backsides. According to some estimates, totally unnecessary tests and treatments that doctors perform to leave a "paper trail" for trial lawyers now account for one-fifth of all physician expenditures. But that isn't all. Our malpractice system also discourages almost any form of cost-saving innovation. New tools, tests, treatments, and procedures can always be added to standard clinical practice. But old ones are rarely eliminated lest that be construed as defective medicine by the courts.

To sum up, the theory behind much of what doctors do today seems to go something like this: It might help. It probably can't hurt. Besides, it protects my backside. What's more (okay, I'll be honest), I get paid more, and by the way, so does the hospital.

Heedless of costs, we have also acquiesced in allowing doctors to cement their control of markets by regulating the terms of their own competition. The result: a maze of protective regulation on a par with the medieval guild system. It encourages overspecialization and ensures that medical procedures are usually performed by the most expensive practitioners in the most expensive settings. For example, one study found that pediatric nurses have the skills to treat 95 percent of first-time infant visits. But the cost-plus regulation that governs our health system rules this kind of efficient substitution out of bounds.

With all of these incentives pushing medical costs in the same upward direction it should not surprise us that they have become a cancer consuming our economic future. Nor should it really astound us that once costs spun out of control, all of our attempts to rein them in have failed. It was our purpose all along to shield people from making tradeoffs. We have never seriously expected doctors or patients to give anything up, so we have always allowed the cost-containment game to be rigged so that we could avoid changing our choiceless behavior.

Here's just one example of how that works. During the early 1980s, the government switched Medicare's HI program from after-the-fact, fee-for-service billing to a case-based prospective payment system in which reimbursement was set in advance according to a patient's "diagnostic related group" or DRG. As was intended, the rise in HI costs slowed. But meanwhile, costs in Medicare's SMI program—as well as in employer-paid health plans—soared. What happened was this. Physicians shifted procedures—and costs—to Medicare outpatient settings, where business as usual could continue, or recouped their "losses" by increasing billing to private payers. A "freeze" was then declared on SMI prices. But since there was no limit on their allowed *volume* of billing, doctors could just order new services or creatively "unbundle" old ones. In the end, everybody (except, presumably, the taxpayer) got what they wanted.

Our insistence on having everything in health care is one more manifestation of our underlying entitlement ethos. Seduced by modern medicine's technological capabilities, we have become persuaded that health itself—perhaps the thing we value most—is something we can always purchase on demand at a doctor's office or hospital. Not surprisingly, we ended up not only with an extravagantly expensive health system, but one that embodies all the skewed priorities of our entitlements system as a whole. It favors consumption over investment, puts the needs of the old before those of the young, and writes blank checks to those most able to pay while often passing over the truly needy.

OUR ENTITLEMENT ETHOS AT WORK

Nineteen ninety-three was the year of the policy wonk—and nowhere was this more evident than in our health-care debate. From "medical IRAs" to "managed competition," reform schemes that no one but a handful of health economists had ever heard of suddenly became the talk of the day—in op-eds, on Capitol Hill, and, or at least so it seemed, at breakfast tables across America.

But policy-wonk fixes are just part of the answer to our crisis. Ultimately, the solutions must also rest on changes in our cultural values and expectations.

In the years since my Nebraska childhood, Americans have developed almost infinite expectations of medicine's ability to deliver "care" or "cure." Unlike other countries, which budget spending on doctors and hospitals, we have yet to arrive at any consensus on how to value health relative to other goals. The reason we have a cost-blind health system is that we have demanded one that shields us from the necessity of making painful tradeoffs. I'm convinced that until there's a sea change in our underlying values and expectations, it won't matter much what reforms we adopt. We'll come no closer to a solution.

My ideas along these lines have been profoundly shaped by discussions I've had with my old friend Dan Yankelovich, that dean of U.S. pollsters. Among all the insightful things he's told me, one in particular leaps to my mind. According to Dan, the vast majority of Americans view health care as what he calls a "maximum right." We all think that we deserve the best that money can buy regardless of our own personal means. The reason this is so striking is that we view almost everything else as a "minimum right." Take food, for example. We can all agree that in an affluent nation like ours it's unconscionable to let people starve on the streets. But when we think about feeding hungry people, we don't have in mind taking them to lunch at Four Seasons. The same goes for education. Not every person, simply because he or she is an American, deserves a subsidized education at Yale. A good state university will do just fine. As we confront flattening real incomes, high debt, and an uncertain job outlook, most Americans are becoming more value-conscious than they were during the spendthrift 1980s. But this attitude applies to buying clothes at the Gap instead of Bloomingdales. It rarely occurs to us to extend it to our doctor's waiting room.

A kind of corollary to this "maximum right" attitude is the notion that "someone else" should always pay. One August night in 1989, Americans who tuned in the evening news got a close look at this mentality in its purest and most politically potent form. The scene: a mob of enraged Silver Eagle oldsters besieging House Ways and Means Committee Dan Rostenkowski's car, then pelting it with rotten tomatoes. The incident was but the most newsworthy in a wave of protests that saw mostly well-off seniors inundate the congressional post office and swamp Capitol Hill phone lines with threats of political reprisal. Its upshot was the hasty and embarrassed repeal of Medicare's Catastrophic Coverage Act just a year after it had been signed into law amid self-congratulatory handshakes, both Congress and the White House convinced they had a sure-fire winner in a benefit package that filled in Medicare's remaining gaps.

What backfired? Strapped for funds, lawmakers had designed the new program to be self-financed by its beneficiaries—with well-to-do seniors paying the costs of their less affluent peers—rather than by another payroll tax hike on working-age families. "Catastrophic" was indeed a catastrophe, and the act itself may well have deserved repeal. It provided expensive new public wrap-around coverage that the great majority of seniors did not need: They had private Medigap insurance. But the storm of protest that "Catastrophic's" financing provisions triggered perfectly captures our "someone else" should always pay attitude. If the benefit had been payroll-tax-financed (that is, "free"), there isn't a Washington observer who believes for a moment that there would have been even a peep of protest.

HEIRS OF PONCE DE LEON

But the "Catastrophic" story is instructive for still another reason. It gets right to the heart of the future-denying bias underlying so much of what we do in health care. There are some 35 million working-age Americans and their children today without *any* health-insurance coverage. But when Congress decided to think up a new benefit program, did it turn to them first? No. Its first thought was to give still more to those who already had the most generous entitlements.

America is the only society in the world to sanction a collective solicitude for the health of the old that is vastly greater than that for the health of its young. Thanks to Medicare, virtually all Americans over age sixty-five are insured at least once for the lion's share of their medical expenses. (Fully 80 percent also have a private Medigap policy or a *second* public health-care entitlement.) Less than 1 percent of the uninsured are elderly; 40 percent are under age twenty-five! Another result of the generational imbalance in our public policy is that America's overall mediocre showing in health status actually masks widely divergent outcomes at different ages. With the highest infant mortality rate of all major industrial countries, America is the least healthy place to be very young. But with the greatest life expectancy at age eighty-five, it is the best place to grow very old.

Quixotic heirs of Ponce de León in search of the fountain of youth? Perhaps that's too harsh. But the United States, alone among western nations, refuses to put any limits on what we spend for the hopelessly ill.

It's not just the elderly, of course. There's life-support for brain-dead auto-crash victims. There are second liver transplants for alcoholics. And the list goes on and on. Sometimes the bills are paid with tax money. Sometimes private insurance picks them up. Whether the decisions are about life and death or just about quality of life, our attitude always seems to be "spare no cost." As a British doctor put it, Americans never say there is "no surgery that would help, no drug that is advantageous, and no further investigation that is required. There seems to be an irresistible urge to *do something*." An American internist interviewing European physicians reports a similar astonishment at our style of medicine. Doctors over there would often say: "I studied in the U.S. Your teaching hospitals are excellent, your technology is superb, but you don't know when to stop."

But how, most Americans will ask, can we possibly put a value on a human life? The answer is that we do it every day. We just don't like to think about it that way. Some people buy off-road vehicles that flip over—others buy Volvos. Whenever we put up a stop sign instead of a traffic light, whenever we decide that it is worth the cost of making cars with bumpers that will absorb the impact of collisions at fifteen miles per hour but not at forty, whenever we decide to pay for one policeman on the beat instead of two, we are implicitly placing a value on the lives that may be lost.

Along with Dan Yankelovich, Dr. Fred Plum has played a key role in helping me crystallize my thoughts about our health-care crisis. He is universally regarded as one of the nation's premier neurologists, and I found in him not just a brilliant doctor, but a good personal friend and a health-policy mentor. I think the reader will benefit from hearing what he has to say as much as I have, so I've included a letter here that he wrote me in response to my relentless inquiries.

June 6, 1993

Dear Pete:

You and I have been talking about America's fiscal crisis for more than a decade and, in particular, America's health-care cost crisis. You asked me to summarize my views on our health-care crisis with a diagnosis of the problem and some prescriptions for possible solutions.

These may seem to be drastic steps, and they undoubtedly will be unpopular inasmuch as each one will draw strong criticism from many sources. Nevertheless, if one wishes to exercise true leadership in furthering the improvements in both our economic future and our medical care that the American people seem to wish, I see no alternative to facing up to these very tough kinds of choices.

1. *Current intensive care practices are excessively expensive.* They are pursued in perhaps 50 percent or more of cases for many days after patient outcomes become hopeless. Furthermore, in the United States highly expensive critical-intensive-care units devote a large proportion of their resources to aged victims of disabling illnesses with hopeless prognoses. By contrast, other industrialized countries limit admissions to such units to predominantly younger persons suffering from diseases or injuries with good prognoses. Excessive use of critical-care units for hopeless or terminal cases has contributed hugely to current American expenses for terminal care. Perhaps 25 percent of all medical health costs are incurred during the last three months of life. Prognosis figures are available to physicians on a disease-by-disease basis, but few doctors pay attention to them, much less advise families early on about highly probable outcomes and the futility of further effort.

We must strengthen the concept of "futility," that is, the uselessness of heroically treating illnesses in which death is inevitable within a matter of days or a very few painful weeks. Only a few states have statutes that enable physicians (with family consent) to suspend treatments having no medical benefit. Most states, including New York, limit the futility application to patients who are predicted to die within forty-eight hours. Given present resuscitation equipment, it is almost impossible to predict death with such accuracy unless one withdraws life-supporting machines. Many patients spend pain-racked or machine-supported days of suffering or semiconsciousness before merciful death finally stops the clock and the cost explosion. To achieve the goal of limiting futile care, doctors must be allowed greater discretion in considering further medical care as having no benefit in restoring personality or significantly extending life. I believe the sensible solution would be to extend the futility time span to two weeks, at a minimum.

2. *Excess surgery remains a common problem, especially in certain geographical areas.* Reports by the Rand Corporation and others on a disorder-by-disorder basis indicate that as many as 50 percent of certain high-cost surgical procedures may be unnecessary. In my own field this applies particularly to carotid artery and coronary bypass surgery. Falling within the same category is a great excess in the use of tests carried out nowadays by specialists in particular areas. Gastroenterologists do

far more high-cost endoscopy studies than conditions warrant. I would estimate the excess as high as 75 percent. Similarly, cardiologists often use redundant tests that inflate their costs by three to four times the amount required to diagnose and treat patients with routine cardiac problems. Other doctors, including neurologists, may own expensive imaging equipment, which they apply excessively to their self-referred patients.

3. *Neonatal rescue is an important but excessively overapplied specialty.* Neonatologists vie with one another to win the prize for rescuing the smallest newborn fetus. This often requires several weeks and even months of highly expensive, intensive hospital care plus a substantial risk of permanent neurological damage and total social dependency in the future.

4. *To reduce costs effectively and humanely, attention must be given to the multi-billion-dollar problem of permanent care of the hopelessly, mindlessly demented.* This group includes many patients overwhelmingly traumatized by head injuries produced by traffic accidents or other trauma. Even larger, however, is the number of "old-olds"—a group that is growing rapidly compared to the rest of society. All told, close to 2 million persons are now institutionalized because they have lost the fundamental capacities of even caring for themselves. Many of these invalids can recognize neither themselves nor their families. Attention to the problem will require enormous efforts in dealing with ethics, developing societal explanations, and working out practicalities. At the very least, one could begin immediately to refuse reimbursement for acute medical treatment of the totally, permanently incapacitated when they develop what used to be called "the old man's friend"—intercurrent infections, heart attacks, and similar complications.

5. *Consideration should be given to establishing national, inexpensive health-screening programs addressed at health augmentation and illness detection (the "regular check-up").* It is widely recognized that in the absence of dangerous symptoms, an annual review of the history, a blood pressure determination, a test of ocular pressure, mammogram, Pap test, and screening blood analysis can be done by a trained nurse practitioner with a practical accuracy and effectiveness equal to that of physicians. The same person can provide counseling on preventive health measures such as diet, exercise, and alcohol intake. Expensive medical care should be reserved for the sick.

6. *Based on means tests, all persons, irrespective of socioeconomic status, should be responsible for at least a small payment toward their medical care.* At present, our emergency room often is filled with indigents on Medicaid who have trivial complaints but nowhere to go and nothing to do. Even a 50-cent minimum would deflect many of these nonmedical demands from our costly health system. At the other extreme, millionaires over age sixty-five expect full, time-consuming,

luxury medical treatment but expect Medicare to carry the full expense, which it never does. Among this wealthy group, means testing should require that, except for truly catastrophic illnesses, all would have to be self-insured or pay costs directly rather than be granted a free entitlement.

In sum, the more that medicine offers, the more the people demand. Meanwhile, all levels of the society believe more or less strongly that someone other than the consumer must pay. And they tend to blame evil forces rather than our own excessive social demands. Until these primary medical excesses are curbed, costs will rise no matter what kind of system one develops. With "full medical care" applied to everyone, the deficit five years from now will go up and not down. Only rationing, or a similar cap on health-delivery costs, is going to work. Limitations must necessarily be placed by age, by disease, and by thoughtful adjudication.

Sincerely,

Fred Plum, M.D.

As you can see, Fred is at least as skeptical as I am about the ability of policy-wonk fixes alone to solve our problems. One of the points he insists on is that Americans must first develop a sense of the "futility" of briefly extending the terminal stage of acute, fatal diseases in which the end is inevitable within a matter of a few painful days or weeks—or of constantly yanking back from the brink of death frail, disoriented people who suffer from severe dementia. In half the cases or more, Fred says, current intensive-care practices are pursued well beyond the point where the outcomes have become hopeless. He also mentions what used to be called "the old man's friend"—the heart attack or bout of pneumonia that once mercifully ended lives bereft of meaning.

In Japan, I'm told, doctors often practice a graceful art of selective disclosure by encouraging terminally ill people to believe they'll recover, then sending them home to die with dignity. Here too we disclose the truth selectively—but with a difference. We try to make our pretense come true by hooking terminally ill people up to tubes in what can only be described as a prolongation of death. Many tens of thousands of Americans die that way each year, without dignity, able to recognize neither "themselves nor their families," as Fred puts it—and all, of course, at vast expense. Even when doctors, at the urging of loved ones, want to do the right thing, fear of legal sanctions all too often prevents them. This preoccupation with postponing death seems to me to be the quintessential expression of Americans' no-limits mentality. We can't even accept the ultimate limit—death.

HEALTH ON DEMAND

Another striking hallmark of Americans' approach to health care is our emphasis on after-the-fact intervention, which, to say the least, is not the most cost effective way to deal with a host of medical cases and conditions that now burden our health system. I'm told that the well-known health economist Victor Fuchs began a recent lecture at Stanford University by writing the following equation on the blackboard: "Health equals medical care." He then quickly erased it. His point, of course, is that prevention and a few simple lifestyle choices can have a potentially greater positive effect on our health than almost anything high-tech medicine can do for us. We ruin our lives, then ask doctors to fix them.

From alcohol and drug abusers to gunshot victims and crack babies, many of the tragic cases that end up in our hospital wards represent the human fallout of poverty, broken families, and a fraying social fabric. Until we address these underlying problems directly, our health-care system can do nothing but supply expensive Band-Aids.

But our "medicalization" of social problems is by no means just an issue of the poor and disadvantaged. The great American middle class has far more control over the risks incurred in daily life, yet often fails to take even minimal personal responsibility. Medical experts tell us that among the most crucial determinants of health are the delayed benefits of individual lifestyle choices about things like diet, smoking, alcohol and drug use, exercise, and seatbelt use. Indeed, the U.S. Public Health Service estimates that alterable lifestyle factors account for some 54 percent of all deaths from heart disease, 34 percent of all deaths from cancer, and 50 percent of all deaths from strokes. Experts also stress the vast benefits of modest investments in preventive care. Hypertension screening and treatment programs, for instance, cost as little as $2,000 per life-year saved. Dealing with the eventual complications of hypertension through organ transplants and dialysis, on the other hand, costs between $50,000 and $150,000 per life-year saved. Yet our pervasive consumption bias has persuaded us to throw money at the latter type of approach while leaving the former starved for funding. In fact, what we spend publicly on prevention only amounts to about one penny out of every dollar in federal health-care outlays.

As a recent report by former Surgeon General C. Everett Koop's new institute points out, "One of the best ways to cut health-care costs is to avoid using the health-care system." The report goes on to stress that there is something fundamentally wrong with our priorities when government and private health insurance companies willingly "cough up $150,000 for an operation to remove a cancerous lung, but refuse to provide $60 for a smoking cessation class that could have made the lung operation unnecessary." Perhaps the most egregious instance of our neglect of prevention, however, is in the area of prenatal care. The C. Everett Koop Institute explains that "a critical part of preventive health care is prenatal care. It costs only $900 to provide basic prenatal care. That's only a fraction of what we now spend on premature and low-birthweight babies." Perfectly aware of where our cost crisis is leading us, the Koop Institute philosophically observes that "The day may come when you cannot afford a quadruple bypass, but you can always afford prevention."

None of this is to say, of course, that the hundreds of billions of dollars we spend on health care have bought us nothing. American octogenarians, as we have seen, are the longest-lived in the world. Or consider the flip side to our deplorable infant mortality rate. Part (though by no means all) of the reason it is so high is that American hospitals classify extremely premature infants as live births. Neonatologists then vie with one another for the prize for rescuing the smallest baby. When they die, as they often do, they show up in our infant mortality statistics. Doctors abroad more often save the costs of this heroic intervention by classifying these births as miscarriages. It's also important to remember that much of what we pay doctors and hospitals for has as much to do with the "quality" of our lives as with cure. Hip-replacement operations for arthritis sufferers—often rationed as elective surgery abroad—are just one example. They give many older Americans a new opportunity to lead active lives. Yet the benefits *fail* to show up in our aggregate health statistics.

Still, it is true that a few collective investments in preventive and public health (chiefly vaccination and sanitation), plus a few breakthroughs against major killing diseases (chiefly the discovery of antibiotics), deserve most of the credit for the improvement in health we have experienced this century. Along with personal lifestyle choices, it is this low-tech health care, the cost of which is quite modest, that largely determines the health of nations.

FACING THE PAINFUL TRADEOFFS

Somewhere in the laws of economics it is written that infinite expectations must inevitably be constrained by finite resources. Since we cannot pay for everything, it is imperative that we begin to ask searching questions about our legitimate public interest in subsidizing health care. What types of health care truly represent investments in our collective future, and hence are inarguably deserving of public subsidy? What types of health care represent pure consumption? And when it is a question of pure consumption, what—if any—level do we deem it in our public interest to guarantee?

It is far from clear how we will choose to deal with the inevitable
tradeoffs. But the nature of those tradeoffs *is* crystal clear. Often they
will involve decisions about how much to pay to avert very low risks. Placing every patient in intensive care even after routine surgery (at a cost
of several thousand dollars per day) would undoubtedly save a few lives,
since frequent blood tests, electronic monitoring, and round-the-clock
personal surveillance would occasionally detect emergencies no physician could have foretold. But such a practice would add billions of dollars yearly to hospital outlays. Or consider the issue of when to use
expensive tests, such as biopsies or CAT scans. Often we test thousands
of patients at a cost of millions of dollars for each serious condition that
we detect. In such cases, how are we to decide precisely where "conservative" treatment ends and "wasteful" treatment begins?

Then there is the different set of tradeoffs surrounding low-
probability cures. Sometimes we confront them when dealing with the
very young. The cost of keeping alive a three-months-premature infant
(who has a poor chance of survival) can easily run over $20,000 per
week. Most often such low-probability-of-cure tradeoffs surface with the
very old.

As we grapple with these tradeoffs, we must learn to think of them
in concrete terms. A dollar spent on one priority is a dollar that cannot
be spent on another. Should a state government spend $100,000 on
heroic intervention for an elderly Medicaid beneficiary in her last year
of life? Or should that same money be allocated to pay for prenatal
care for as many as one hundred low-income women? Should the
money spent on futile efforts to preserve the life of a crack baby with
AIDS instead be devoted to paying for modest home care for a couple
of dozen elderly widows? What value, in short, do we place on quality
of life for the many versus life (prolonging death, really) for the few?

We also need to consider carefully how we define insurable health
care itself. Should it include everything that makes us feel better?
(Cosmetic surgery for a socialite? Knee arthroscopy for a serious jog-
ger? Psychiatric sessions for a demoted employee?) Which of America's many social pathologies are really amenable to medical solutions?
Finally, and most fatefully in terms of costs, where should personal and
familial responsibility end and public responsibility begin in providing
long-term care for the frail elderly?

Changing our thinking will be difficult. A society that spends so
profligately on our type of health care is a society fixated on the
present at the expense of the future. Which brings us to the biggest
health-care tradeoff of all: How much do we feel comfortable spending
on health care for ourselves, and how much do we instead want to
devote to investments in our collective future, such as productivity-
enhancing R&D or a better education for our kids? It's as much a
choice of problems as solutions.

At issue are not only political choices about where we can save money, but cultural choices about what share of the American Dream should be bequeathed to those who live beyond us.

THE SEARCH FOR MAGIC BULLETS

In a recent article in *Fortune*, Dan Yankelovich described the stages through which public opinion on complex and potentially divisive national issues typically passes. In the early stages, there is a growing awareness that a serious problem exists, the development of a sense of urgency about addressing it, and a tentative exploration of policy options. At a certain point, however, denial, a search for scapegoats, and wishful thinking about painless solutions usually set in. Only after the magic bullets have proved illusory do we finally come to grips with the real issues and choices. In health care, Dan says, we have yet to move beyond denial and wishful thinking. Unfortunately, I believe that he is right, and that a cloud of unreality still fogs today's health policy debate.

Can we bring health-care costs under control without real sacrifices? Many who should know better find the political appeal of magic bullets irresistible and insist that we can. Get rid of the "pure waste" in our system, some tell us, and we can have much cheaper care with no restrictions at all on the best available technology. Others put their faith in greater administrative efficiency. As evidence of the cost-saving potential, they point to the huge savings in "paperwork" we could supposedly realize if we had a single-payer health system like Canada's. In a replay of failed 1980s budget-cutting logic, some even suggest that getting tough on fraud and abuse is the answer to all our problems.

The problem with these fixes is not that they're necessarily bad ideas. It isn't even that some of them might not save large amounts of money. It's that they're not magic bullets. None of them changes the underlying cost-plus economic incentives shaping patient and provider behavior in our health system, or alters the ways in which new technologies and new expectations interact to constantly fuel our spending spiral. It is this equation that explains why real per-capita health-care costs are *growing*. Unless reforms change this equation, even if the savings they yield are large, those savings will soon be overwhelmed by new cost growth.

Take the most popular of today's magic bullets: getting rid of excess paperwork. Here we've found the perfect villain. It's not us. It's totally impersonal. It's hard to say whether patients or doctors hate it more. The GAO estimates that in 1991 we could have saved about $70 billion if paperwork had consumed no larger a share of America's medical dollar than it does of Canada's. It sounds as if there's a painless solution to our health-care crisis here if we just cut administrative costs. Some are so convinced this is true that they cite it as a compelling reason to switch to a national health system in the United States. Unfortunately, advocates of this fix neglect to tell us a few things.

The first is that most of the mountain of paperwork in the U.S. health system is designed to *control* costs. True, these cost-monitoring forms filed in triplicate waste vast amounts of time and (yes) cost a lot of money, but without them a doctor would hear few complaints about charging a thousand dollars for a checkup. For the most part, our "excessive" paperwork costs are directly attributable to keeping track of copayments and deductibles and to reviewing doctor and hospital bills. If we eliminated this paperwork without changing the underlying incentives in our system, we would see a *redoubled* spiral in costs due to still greater induced demand. (Even the GAO admits this is a likely outcome.) And the paperwork that isn't designed to control costs? Much of it is designed to protect providers from malpractice suits.

But let's assume that we really could have slashed $70 billion in administrative costs in 1991 without unleashing *new* cost pressures. We'd still have all the *old* cost pressures. Indeed, in terms of total spending we'd be back where we started in about twelve months! The problem is that the underlying equation of new technologies, new expectations, and cost-plus incentives is now causing U.S. health-care spending to grow by about $70 billion a year.

What can we realistically expect in terms of administrative savings? According to the Committee for a Responsible Federal Budget, the widespread adoption of consumer "smart cards" and uniform electronic billing and claims-processing systems could save us a couple of billion a year. Maybe other kinds of administrative streamlining could save us a good deal more. Outside of the Beltway, a couple of billion is still a lot of money. This is saving we could desperately use for new high-priority public and private investments. We should certainly implement such reforms. Tomorrow. But we must also understand that they won't bring us much closer to a long-term solution to our cost crisis or let us off the hook when it comes to painful tradeoffs.

The same is true of getting rid of wasteful and redundant medical procedures. I'm not saying that *that* couldn't save enormous sums of money. It could. But here too there's a problem. How exactly do we know "pure waste" when we see it? If one expert's idea of it is usually another physician's (or patient's) idea of "necessary care"—and it is—who gets to make the final judgment? Unless we change incentives so that patients and providers care more about how much they spend, pure waste will be no easier to squeeze out of our health system than it is to locate as a federal budget line item. What's more, even if we can all agree on what pure waste is and then manage to identify and eliminate all of it, the introduction of new medical services that aren't "wasteful" (in the sense that they have at least *some* benefit) will continue to drive our spending spiral. As big a problem as pure waste is, it's not our biggest problem. The biggest problem is that we refuse to put in place any mechanisms that compel us to weigh the costs and benefits of medical care that is both expensive and *marginally useful.*

Consider our previous experience with "painless" solutions to our health-care cost spiral. Back in the 1970s, it was widely thought that we could realize huge and permanent cost savings by eliminating excess hospitalization. Since then, America has managed to achieve the shortest hospital stays in the western world. That's why Medicare beneficiaries complain about being released "quicker and sicker." For a few years in the 1980s, the drop in hospitalization did suppress the growth in our national health-care spending. But that was all. Afterward, the underlying equation of technology, expectations, and incentives kicked in, causing total costs to climb as far as or faster than before.

Then there's a different kind of magic bullet. We don't really have a cost problem at all, many claim. We have a profits problem. If only overpaid doctors, mercenary hospitals, and profiteering drug companies would behave, everything would be fine, thank you. Medical professionals in America do exercise monopoly pricing power. That's one reason U.S. doctors earn 5.4 times the average wage in our economy, compared with 4.3 times the average in Germany and 3.3 times the average in France. That's also one reason that, on average, U.S. surgeons today charge about eight times as much to remove an appendix, gall bladder, or uterus as their counterparts in Europe and five times as much as their counterparts in Japan. But we must also bear in mind that physicians' net income accounts for under one-fifth of U.S. health-care spending. Other countries have strict medical wage and price controls and *still* must ration to control costs. Unless we change the incentives providers have to spend money on *our* behalf, ratcheting down their incomes a notch or two won't bring us much closer to a solution either.

Why have I gone on about fixes that *won't* do the job? There's a good reason. The real challenges in U.S. health-care reform are cultural and political. Much of the American public believes there are magic bullets that will allow us to have everything and save money too. We have to understand that our search for magic bullets is really just another way of making excuses—of avoiding the need to choose. It's a manifestation of how we focus on the self and on the present, not on the community at large, or our children, or the future. Other cultures understand the difference and make the tough choices. We have to relearn that habit.

TEN GUIDING PRINCIPLES FOR REFORM

In health care, as in every other dimension of our lives, the surest cure for our politics of denial is honest talk. I for one am convinced that if the American public is educated about the real nature of the choices that confront us, they will be far better prepared to make farsighted sacrifices on behalf of the future. If I didn't believe that, I wouldn't have written this book.

Our political leaders, however, appear to lack that faith. As the President's Task Force on National Health Care Reform went about its work in 1993, there was, to be sure, a process that passed for consensus building. But that was mostly about touching bases with every conceivable special interest among the American people that hoped to gain something from new federal spending—veterans, the elderly, the disabled, and so on down the long and varied list. There were lots of moving (and true) stories about people unable to afford even basic medical care. But when it came to the matter of who will have to give something up, there was hardly a hint of the painful tradeoffs ahead. There was no direct talk of how those who are able will simply have to pay for *more* of their own care. There was certainly no mention of the "R" word—rationing. The administration simply pointed to a health system bloated by profiteering, waste, and inefficiency and promised, in effect, to squeeze it.

Waste there is in plenty. But to cap our medical spending spiral we must also develop mechanisms for restricting access to *useful* care whose costs are not justified by the benefits. The reason is that rapid cost increases due to new technologies with some benefit will continue. But opportunities to offset those costs by squeezing waste and redundancy out of our health system will eventually be exhausted. Here let me once again remind the reader of just how grave our situation is. An enormous (and impossible-to-achieve) $70 billion in overnight administrative savings would now buy us only one year's respite from new cost growth—and just as with any cancer, it's the *growth* we must stop if we are to find a cure.

What we must ask ourselves is this. When the time comes for the administration and Congress to call for sacrifice, will they have the mandate? Unless the President first articulates a clear vision of what real health-care reform will mean, I don't believe they will. And that should set off alarm bells. As we've seen, some experts think that the *new* benefit expansions the Clinton administration is considering could cost as much as $100 billion to $150 billion a year in extra public and private spending. Unless we're prepared to make sacrifices we're unlikely to get compensating cost containment. More likely, we will get still faster cost growth as a result of still more induced consumer demand. Needless to say, new spending commitments of this magnitude could make the funding of other "imperative" new investment agendas impossible.

I certainly don't profess to have all of the answers. What I do have are some clear ideas about the right and the wrong directions we can take in health-care reform. Along the way, I think the following principles should guide us.

1. Go Slow and Allow Room for Experimentation

Let me start with a word of caution to the President. *Go slow and allow ample room for experimentation.* We actually know far less than we like to think about the cost-saving effects of alternative approaches to reform. Our medical marketplace is enormously complex and, with new technologies sprouting up almost daily, is getting more complex all the time. What's more, unlike the market for PCs or VCRs, the market for medical services is one in which people react subjectively and emotionally. When it comes to health care, we'll never get people to behave quite like the classic *homo economicus.* Health economists, to be sure, can crank out numbers that purport to tell us how people will respond to different changes in incentives—but to say that these elasticity estimates are more than guesstimates is, to indulge in a pun, "stretching it."

What we can be reasonably certain of are two things. If history is any guide, we will greatly overestimate the savings of whatever reforms we enact. After we introduced DRGs in the early 1980s, health-policy wonks will recall, HHS secretary Margaret Heckler could claim with a straight face that we had finally "broken the back of the health-care inflation monster." But of course we hadn't. We also know that there is an iron law of fringe benefit programs: It is far, far easier to add to than to subtract from benefit programs once they are in effect. All of this tells us that experimentation is crucial. To my mind, it also suggests *we should be cautious about large new benefit expansions until savings are in place.*

The states provide a natural laboratory for health-care reform—and, what's more, they are already a jump ahead of Washington. While the federal government dithered during the Bush administration, state governments took the lead on this mother of all domestic policy issues. The headline-grabber, of course, was Oregon, which developed a controversial plan to cut Medicaid costs by refusing to pay for certain high-cost, low-probability-of-cure treatments. The idea was to use the savings to extend basic health-care benefits to the state's totally uninsured. (Originally denied its needed federal waiver by the last administration on the grounds that it violated the Americans with Disabilities Act, the plan had to be watered down to gain approval by this administration.)

But Oregon has not been alone. Maryland is experimenting with statewide fee schedules for hospitals and doctors. In an entirely different approach to cost control, Florida is about to implement a reform plan that leverages the market clout of health-care buyers by pooling employers, government, and individuals into Community Health Purchasing Alliances. A score of other states have enacted or will soon enact less ambitious reforms that change the way the market for small-group insurance works. Their purpose is to make basic health coverage more affordable for individuals and small businesses who now find it prohibitively costly. *It would be a mistake for the federal government to squelch these state initiatives with a one-size-fits-all reform plan.* "My worst nightmare," as Florida governor Lawton Chiles phrased it, "is that Washington will tell us what to do."

Health care, then, is a case where the approaches taken by different states add to our knowledge and understanding of how best to deal with our national problem. In searching for the best way to treat an aggressive cancer in individuals, doctors try different approaches: chemotherapy, radiation, surgery, even a change in diet. It makes sense to apply the same logic to treating the health-care cost explosion consuming our economy. Only through experimentation will policymakers learn what works best. Above and beyond what it teaches the experts about the nuts and bolts of cost control, experimentation will have another benefit. It will afford the *American people* some needed catch-up time to learn, adjust, and rethink priorities as we move beyond denial and magic bullets and begin to come to terms with the real choices before us.

It's not that we have no idea at all how costs might be controlled. Other countries budget spending on health care. They then enforce those limits through government regulation. In practice, this means wage and price controls as well as rules about what kinds of technologies will be funded and which providers can use them. There is no denying that command and control regulation of this sort has helped other nations hold the line on health-care spending. What we know much less about is how to control costs in ways that don't do undue violence to American cultural and political instincts and institutions.

2. Preserve What's Good in Today's Health System

Which brings me to another key point. As we get serious about health-care reform, *we must be careful to preserve as much as possible of what's good in our current system.* It's easy to say let's do a Canada or let's do a Germany—as if we could import the technical cost-containment apparatus these countries use without importing the cultural attitudes and political institutions that underpin it. More than any other, America is a nation shaped by free-market traditions and distrust of government bureaucracy. Presidential campaigns have been launched and won on platforms whose substantive message sometimes amounted to little more than "Let's get Washington out of our hair." I don't think Americans will ever become comfortable with systematic government micromanagement of our health system.

And here let me add another word of caution to an administration that has reportedly considered imposing medical price controls as a kind of shock therapy for our health system. As someone who had the unhappy experience of implementing government price controls during the Nixon administration, take it from me: In an economy as vast, diversified, and complex as our own, their unintended effects will be legion—as will the ingenious ways that providers invent to evade them. Command and control regulation inevitably becomes a nightmare of inefficiencies: shortages, waiting lists, and squandered and misallocated resources. Short-term price controls also tend to become permanent, locking in these inefficiencies. Many countries in Europe are now recognizing that this is the price they have paid for cost control and are seeking to introduce efficiency-promoting competition into their national health systems. It would indeed be odd if America turned its back on the market just as other countries are beginning to court it.

I guess it won't come as a surprise that I believe *market forces will have to play a central role in shaping any new U.S. health system that is at the same time affordable and acceptable to most Americans.* How can we introduce market discipline into today's cost-plus system? The answer, of course, is that we must change its incentives so that patients or providers— preferably both—are confronted with the tradeoffs they will always avoid as long as cost-free options remain open to them.

3. Give Individuals Incentives to Be Cost-Conscious

One way to change our cost-plus behavior is to require that we as patients directly pay for a larger share of our medical bills with our own checkbooks. I'm not talking about the brutal all-out-of-pocket gambit now faced by the totally uninsured. What I have in mind are significantly higher copayments and deductibles. People hate these. But major studies by prestigious think tanks such as the Rand Corporation have confirmed what is just common sense: Cost sharing makes a real difference in how we spend money on health care. It does so for two reasons. On the one hand, it makes each of us weigh the value of a second thousand-dollar test against less costly alternatives. On the other hand, it helps to keep us at home when our ailments are trivial (a common cold, for instance), or, indeed, when we're not suffering from any medical condition at all. Fred Plum tells me what many people seek from their physicians is little more than TLC. Some have nowhere else to go and nothing else to do—and a visit to the doctor may lighten their wallet less than a movie.

When it comes to our public benefit programs, Congress can simply legislate higher cost-sharing requirements. Naturally, the scope for higher copayments and deductibles is greatest in a non-means-tested program like Medicare. But Congress should consider some cost sharing for all—even for participants in Medicaid. (I've already mentioned the 50 cents cost-sharing requirement Fred Plum suggested; according to a recent CED proposal, three dollars for an office visit and one dollar for a prescription would be appropriate.) The objective, of course, is not to get poor people to pay for their own health care, but to discourage the casual use of medical services. As for private insurance, Congress can effectively mandate higher copayments and deductibles by limiting the amount of our tax exemption for employer-paid health care to lower-priced insurance plans that feature them. Today, the sky's the limit. The cost of any plan is fully deductible, even if it's gold-plated and complete with first-dollar coverage.

But cost sharing has its limits. If consumers are spending their own money, they will think twice about a follow-up doctor's visit when they've had the flu, a sinus infection, or a sprained ankle. Heart attack victims are less likely to question the value of a hospital stay—or their physician's decision to operate. The same goes for people with brain tumors. Then there is another matter to consider. Although two-thirds of U.S. medical bills are for "little" or "mid-ticket" tests and procedures totaling less than $5,000—and hence, one might suppose, could be subject to the discipline of cost sharing—it is also true that in any given year one-fifth of Americans account for four-fifths of all health-care spending. Just 4 percent account for half of the total. Some of us just get much sicker than others. The purpose of greater cost sharing is to cause us to weigh our spending decisions more carefully than when we have first-dollar insurance coverage, not to undo the protection that insurance affords against catastrophic medical costs.

The same logic, incidentally, explains why *we will also have to restrict the current underwriting practices that allow health insurers to "segment" their markets.* Because some of us get sicker than others, risk pooling on a community-wide basis is essential. The young must help pay for the old and the healthy for the ill. If we allow insurers to "cherry pick," many of us who are sick—or who are deemed likely to *get* sick—will end up in separate plans. Needless to say, the costs of these plans will soar. In the insurance industry, that's called a "death spiral." Others of us, as is now the case, won't be able to find coverage in any plan at any price. From the standpoint of young and healthy individuals, and of insurance companies trying to make a profit, cherry-picking good health

risks and shunning those who are sick or likely to get sick may make
sense. But from the standpoint of society, it's a practice we can't allow.

How, to return to my previous point, can we get around the limits
inherent in cost sharing? One way is to *create incentives that also ensure
that consumers will be cost-conscious purchasers of health insurance when
they're still well, not just of medical services when they're already at the doctor's
office or hospital.* Patients may not be well prepared to scrutinize the
costs and benefits of alternative high-tech treatments while being
prepped for surgery. However, consumers *are* able to weigh the costs
and benefits of different levels of insurance coverage when budgeting
their household expenses before the fact. To turn consumers into
cost-conscious health-insurance shoppers, we would need to give them
a stake in the money they save by opting for lower-priced plans—
something they rarely have today. One promising idea is to replace our
current tax exemption for employer-paid health benefits with a system
of individual tax credits. Such a change would make it crystal clear to
people that they're spending their own money, not their employer's.
What's more, any savings people realized by choosing a lower-priced
plan would go directly to them. As for public benefit programs, we
could restructure them as voucher systems. Participants would be given
fungible "shopping cards," then be refunded any difference between
their voucher's value and the price of any lower-priced plan they decided to purchase.

Another strategy is to require that all insurance (whether bought
directly by individuals or by employers or government acting on our
behalf) be purchased through statewide or regional health-care coop-
eratives. These would negotiate premiums (and standards) with insurers and providers, then offer us a menu of competing (and qualifying)
plans. That's the core idea behind the "managed competition" model
we've heard so much about recently. It's not a bad one. But unless it's
coupled with caps on our open-ended health-care subsidies and other
tough measures, it is not going to contain medical cost inflation after
the initial "bargained" reductions in insurance premiums.

4. Make Providers Accountable for How They Spend Our Money

However we decide to discipline the demand side of our medical
marketplace, we must not forget that it is providers who must often act
as our proxies in making spending decisions—and who also get our
money. Physicians' net income may account for under one-fifth of all
U.S. health-care spending, but doctors' decisions about testing, hospitalization, medication, and other aspects of our care determine over
three-quarters. In a real sense, our lavish direct and indirect public
health-care subsidies are not entitlements for patients at all. They are

entitlements for doctors and hospitals. *Providers must be made account-able for how they spend our money. The best way to do this is to pay them a fixed amount in advance to deliver care to a population of patients—and then make them live within their budgets.*

In practical terms, *shifting our health system toward prospective payment will mean encouraging or requiring more people to join HMOs.* In such ar-rangements, doctors and hospitals make more by doing less, not by racking up bills for as many expensive tests and treatments as possible, then passing them on to third-party payers. But because HMOs have to compete with each other—and hence must please patients—they also face incentives to deliver care more efficiently, not just to cut costs. As a result, some experts believe, a health system dominated by compet-ing HMOs would not only send the right signals to doctors and hos-pitals, it would also send the right signals to technology markets by shifting demand toward innovations that deliver the most health for the dollar and away from those that add the next increment of "qual-ity," costs be damned.

Many Americans object to HMOs on the grounds that they limit our choices and encourage providers to restrict our access to high-cost care. And indeed, if they didn't have to compete head-on with heavily subsidized fee-for-service plans in today's cost-plus legal and regulatory environment, that is precisely what they would do. That's the point. We must have some mechanism that compels us to weigh tradeoffs in health care. The choice is what kind. The overall "budget constraint" created by HMOs is preferable to the main alternative: government micromanagement of the price and available quantity of each discrete service in our medical marketplace. In HMOs, hands-on decisions about how to allocate scarce resources would by and large be left to medical professionals—where they belong. Although doctors fear that HMOs will limit their professional autonomy, they might actually mean less interference in clinical practice than is the case with today's sys-tems of retrospective utilization review. All of us should think hard about who we want making life-and-death decisions. Our physicians? Or public and private bureaucrats?

Although I come to the idea reluctantly, I'm convinced that if we are to be successful at cost containment, *another key element in our overall strategy must be a global federal health-benefits budget with annual spending targets.* The trick will be to impose that budget in ways that are as consistent as possible with market competition. Once again, I believe the best solutions will be those that avoid regulatory micromanage-ment. Congress, for instance, could set capitated budgets (so much for each beneficiary) for its funding of state Medicaid programs. How individual states implemented their programs would then be their own business. Today state governments expend a lot of imagination trying to win more Medicaid matching funds from Washington. It's called "leveraging" their Medicaid dollar. With prospective federal budgeting, the incentive would shift entirely to using resources efficiently. To contain costs, many states might require that beneficiaries join HMOs or other types of managed-care arrangements. (Arizona has already done this with some success.) The result would be a lockstep series of capitated budgets from the federal level on down.

And what about Medicare? It could, as I've already suggested, be switched to a voucher system. Beneficiaries would be given capitated vouchers whose prospectively determined value would constitute the extent of the federal government's spending commitment. With or without vouchers, Congress could also mandate that beneficiaries join a basic benefits insurance plan or an HMO. It could then set an upper *ceiling* on what it would pay for a beneficiary's premium, thus capping total costs.

Some indict prospective budgeting because it encourages constant political wrangling among different interests—the Gray Lobby, the Veterans Lobby, AIDS advocates, spokespeople for the disabled, and so on—and someone inevitably loses out. But that is just one more reason we should have a global benefits budget for federally funded health-care programs. It will get the interests out in the open and force us to decide what share of our tax dollars we wish to devote to health care for whom, and how much we want to allocate to other goals. As a wit once quipped, "Europeans do not see how a budget can be anything but prospective."

In advocating global federal budgeting, what I'm insisting on, of course, is that we use public resources prudently. People who are able to spend more on their own than what we subsidize publicly would still be able to. With our maximum-right notions about health care, many Americans will find this hard to accept. But that is the way setting limits works in every other country—and that is the way it will have to work here.

5. Extend Basic Health Insurance to Those Who Cannot Afford It

Much concern in today's health-care debate is focused on extending insurance coverage to the 35 million mostly working Americans (and their children) who now lack it. A fair number of these Americans do not really need public help—or at least not much. About two-fifths of the uninsured have incomes of more than twice the poverty level; more than one-fifth have incomes of at least three times the poverty level. Even modest insurance market reforms that restrict price discrimination against individual and small-group buyers would make affordable insurance accessible to many of these citizens.

But I couldn't agree more with the President that *ensuring those Americans who cannot afford it access to our health system must be a primary goal of any reform package Congress passes.* In principle, I don't have anything against any of the major possible approaches to tackling this problem: a purely government program, a mandate that private employers offer coverage in conjunction with an expansion of Medicaid for the nonworking poor, or so-called play-or-pay schemes. This last option, which the Clinton administration seems to favor, requires that employers offer private coverage or pony up a payroll tax to fund a new public program.

Where I differ is in my insistence that we must not saddle either taxpayers or employers with another hugely expensive Medicare-type program. We must remember that iron law of fringe benefits—and the political arithmetic of public entitlements: It's far easier to add to than subtract from benefit programs once they are in effect. If we're richer in the future, we can always decide to add more. In the meanwhile, let's start by giving the uninsured what they need most. Not free dental care, or psychiatric care, or prescription drugs, or cosmetic surgery. But protection against catastrophic medical costs. And of absolutely crucial importance, let's also be sure that we achieve savings elsewhere so that we can fund such a program without further bloating the outsized shares of public budgets and private payrolls that already go to health care.

As for the other main benefit expansion now being debated—a new long-term-care program for the frail elderly and the disabled—I'm much more skeptical that we need it. Medicaid already offers means-tested long-term-care coverage with generous eligibility requirements. For those of us who are able, saving for and providing long-term custodial care should be a matter of individual and family responsibility. The last thing in the world we need is a new middle-class entitlement.

6. Rethink the Rationale of Our Existing Health-Care Entitlements

As we look for the most cost-effective ways to extend coverage to the uninsured, *we must also re-examine the rationale behind our existing health-care entitlements.* Our medical cost crisis is so serious and our need to find new funds for public and private investments is so great that we simply cannot permit continued welfare for the well-off in the federal budget.

The most important change we can make is to adjust Medicare benefits according to financial need. One way to do this is to tax their insurance value. (Since our tax code is progressive, benefit taxation constitutes a kind of implicit means test.) Another is to use a sliding-scale "affluence test" to withhold benefits from upper-income retirees on a steeply progressive basis. It is unconscionable that the average U.S. working family earning just $30,000 must pay ever-increasing payroll taxes to finance huge Medicare windfalls for golf-playing retirees living on several times as much. An aging America cannot keep subsidizing the health-care consumption of millions of affluent seniors we encourage to pretend have earned that right.

While on the subject of the largess we lavish on the well-to-do old, it's important to make a related point. In budgeting public entitlement outlays, it's crucial to think in terms of the *total* resources—health and nonhealth—we direct at particular age groups. A. Haeworth Robertson, a former chief actuary of Social Security and long-time advocate of entitlements reform, once summed it up this way: Insisting that the Social Security retirement system is in fine shape while ignoring Medicare is like a doctor telling a patient that his heart is okay but forgetting to mention he's dying of emphysema. As far as working-age Americans are concerned, both Social Security and Medicare are part of the same payroll-financed benefit system. All the money goes to the same people. It makes no sense to insist that Social Security is off limits while letting Medicare spin out of control. Back in 1982 when Social Security was running a deficit and Medicare was in "surplus," we kept hearing from defenders of the entitlements status quo that the two programs were indeed part of the same system—and that we should "borrow" from Medicare. Well, they still are! If health care for the elderly is such a high priority that we must spend more on it, why not cut the subsidies that seniors receive as cash retirement income?

But old people aren't the only ones getting a free lunch. For the life of me, I can't see any reason well-off veterans should receive "free" care for non-service-related medical conditions simply because they have done their duty as citizens by serving their country.

Then we come to our poverty policy in reverse: the tax exemption for employer-paid health insurance. This wasteful and regressive subsidy is worth most to Americans like me in upper-income brackets. Those working for minimum wages without any health insurance receive nothing from it at all. We should cap this exemption. One sensible way to do so is to peg the value of the subsidy to the lowest-priced option among a menu of competing health plans. Another is to peg it to the average cost of an insurance policy. In either case, to qualify for the subsidy at all, health plans, as I've already said, should also be required to feature significant copayments and deductibles.

7. Ensure That Saving Is Real Saving, Not Cost Shifting

Another challenge we face will be finding ways to *ensure that the public health-care costs we save are not simply shifted to the private sector.* When doctors and hospitals respond to government's attempts to clamp down on health-benefit spending by increasing their billing to private payers—as they've repeatedly done in the past—we might save money publicly. But total national health-care spending—and the overall burden on our economy—remains largely unchanged. In the future, we must try to minimize cost shifting. One way to tackle this tough problem is to require by law that each provider charge all his customers the same rates. This is just another way of saying that we should forbid price discrimination, something that in most other industries is considered a violation of antitrust law. However, such an "all-payers" system need not—and, indeed, should not—*fix* the rates that providers charge.

8. Make It Safe for Doctors to Do the Right Thing

Along with the kinds of changes in economic incentives I outlined above, there are other types of fundamental changes we will have to accept as well. Perhaps most important, *we will need to make it safe for doctors to do the right thing by doing less for us. One essential step will be the reform of our malpractice system.* The benefit: We relieve the upward pressure of defensive medicine on health-care spending. The tradeoff: We restrict our traditional liberty to sue before a jury of our peers.

Another step will be institutionalizing new attitudes toward death and dying. All Americans should be encouraged to sign living will agreements—something my wife, Joan Ganz Cooney, and I have done. Although the vast majority of Americans (89 percent) say they themselves would want to have a living will, only a tiny fraction (9 percent) have made such advance directives. Following through is an act of social responsibility, in that it saves precious resources. But my wife and I also thought about it as a way of escaping a grotesque, undignified, and ultimately inhuman death and, above all, as an act of personal responsibility in excusing our children from making agonizing decisions on our behalf. We have talked to them often enough to know that they, like many others, have little problem with the abstract principle of limiting care, but they would find it hard to act on that principle with loved ones.

9. Invest in Developing Better Knowledge About Costs and Benefits

Our chance of success at cost containment will also be greatly increased if we *make a concerted effort to develop much better knowledge about the relative costs and benefits of different medical treatments.* Much "outcomes research" is already under way. But most studies are simply aimed at determining the "medical effectiveness" of particular treatments—in other words, at finding out whether they indeed help or perhaps even harm patients. Systematic attempts to rank alternative medical procedures in terms of their relative costs and benefits (gains in "Quality-Adjusted Life Years"—or QUALYs—for instance) are hardly off the ground. Research along these lines is one of those genuine investments on which we should not hesitate to spend more public money.

Indeed, health-outcomes data are crucial if we are to leverage a wide range of cost-containment strategies. With much better—and widely disseminated—knowledge about what works and what doesn't, and at what cost, it will be easier to empower consumers as cost-conscious health-care purchasers. With scientifically based practice guidelines in place, utilization review by third-party payers would become a much more effective tool. Medical malpractice reform would be easier to implement. Reform of our costly system of guild regulation could also go faster and further. If practice guidelines allowed the routinization of even a core component of medical services, doctors could delegate countless tasks to "physician extenders," or encourage more self-care. As Dr. Plum put it in his letter, "Expensive medical care should be reserved for the sick."

10. Recognize That Medicine Is Not the Answer to All Our Health Problems

Finally, *we must recognize that throwing more dollars at most types of medical care not only jeopardizes America's economic future, but it may not even be the best solution to many of our health problems.* I'm thinking, of course, of the incalculable benefits of greater attention to prevention and healthy lifestyles. As far as a solution to our *cost* crisis is concerned, the experts, it's true, caution us not to look for a magic bullet in this direction. Smoking-related illnesses, for instance, now add many tens of billions of dollars to America's annual health bill. But if everyone quit smoking, we might not realize all the long-term savings that many anticipate. The reason? Some people would be spared a quick and relatively inexpensive heart attack at age fifty-five, but then put at risk of a costly and protracted nursing-home stay at eighty-five. Still, as I said earlier, all the experts do agree that *a few simple habits over which we have personal control have a greater influence on our health than anything doctors can do.*

Americans today are of course already paying much greater attention to healthy lifestyles than just a decade or two ago. Consider one statistic: Since 1965, the share of the adult population that smokes has plummeted from well over 40 percent to under 30 percent. Yet in some areas of our lives, our behavior has actually changed less than we might think. Despite the proliferation of spas and fitness centers, only one out of ten Americans reports engaging in vigorous exercise three or more times each week; the percentage of overweight eager eaters in our population has remained unchanged over the past thirty years. Moreover, the overall declines in self-destructive behavior like smoking and alcohol and drug abuse that we've registered in recent years actually mask divergent trends among different income groups. The shift toward healthier lifestyles has had much less impact among lower-income than middle- and upper-income Americans—and has barely touched the underclass. If we are to make across-the-board progress, a concerted public education campaign will have to be a big part of the solution. Thankfully, we have some excellent models to look to in the efforts of both private-sector groups like the Partnership for a Drug-Free America and public-sector campaigns like the "Healthy People" program launched by former Surgeon General C. Everett Koop.

The Partnership for a Drug-Free America, for example, reports declines in overall illicit drug use of as much as 50 percent since the mid-1980s. A major factor in this turnaround has undoubtedly been better education and awareness among young people about the devastating effects of substance abuse. The Partnership's own $1.5 billion pro bono advertising campaign has been a powerful catalyst in this heartening change. This highly effective television advertising campaign reached an estimated nine out of ten American homes with a daily anti-drug message in recent years. If we consider the relationship between substance abuse and health-care costs (according to most counts, a person with an alcohol or drug problem uses the health-care delivery system several times more frequently than a person without such problems), the potential "bang" for the educational "buck" becomes clear.

STARTING DOWN THE WRONG ROAD TO HEALTH-CARE REFORM

Norman Ornstein of the American Enterprise Institute crisply summarizes the dilemma of health reform: "The public defines health reform as *more services for less money,* while every other plan, from left to right, defines health reform as *fewer services for more money.*" The American people are not yet prepared to face the real choices that lie ahead in health care. Even many months into the national debate triggered by the Clinton administration's reform efforts, we remain a nation full of ignorance, myths, and denial about both the real problem and the real solutions.

Thus, it should be no surprise that the President's headlong and headstrong rush into a "comprehensive solution" is contributing to a renewal of the old gridlocked politics in Washington. Achieving true comprehensive health-care reform will be the "mother of all political battles," but we have been ill prepared for the fight.

I believe a preferable course would have been for the President to begin by laying out the parameters of the problem and educating the American people about the possible solutions. A national debate could then have taken place with more of the right kind of public input than has been the case with Hillary Rodham Clinton's Task Force. The advantages and disadvantages of various solutions could then also have been presented as part of the search for the right answers, not an attempt by an administration already seen as disconnecting from the public to force a costly and preconceived plan down the country's throat. More experimentation with a wide range of solutions would have been invaluable in divining the correct answers to a problem where even the top experts disagree so fundamentally about solutions. As part of this process, the President might also have considered issuing annual White House reports setting cost-containment goals and summarizing the results of federal, state, and private initiatives. These would have helped promote the kind of dialogue we need while focusing the public's attention on the real issues before us.

This educational, incremental, experimental process, using the immense power of the presidential bully pulpit, might have taken several years or more to complete. But it would have been time very well spent. As I have tried to make clear in this chapter, our health-care crisis is simply another piece of more than a quarter century of a you-can-have-it-all-without-paying-for-it hubris. Beyond hubris, trying to solve a problem this long in the making at a single stroke is but another symptom of our "short-termitus."

The Clinton plan is thus in danger of becoming a premature and false start down the road to health-care reform. Although the Clinton White House deserves praise for breaking with the politics of neglect that characterized the past, it has not yet shown it can provide the leadership necessary to educate Americans about the real problems we face, then weld a national consensus around real solutions.

Finding our way back to the right road again requires us to first understand and then face up squarely to the real choices before us. And making real choices in turn requires acceptance of some tough new realities. Consumers will find that they don't always have their accustomed freedom of choice. Physicians, too, will wake up to the fact that they can no longer do business as usual. As Pulitzer-prize-winner Paul Starr summed it up, "A variety of forces—political, economic, and cultural—are converging to limit . . . the autonomy the [medical] profession has enjoyed from the discipline of the market and the state."

Most unsettling of all, we will discover that "rationing" of one sort or another is inevitable. We may choose to make it explicit along the lines of the Oregon plan. Alcoholics get first liver transplants paid for at public expense, but not second ones, and so on down the list. Some say that such legalistic guidelines may be the only thing that satisfies many Americans' traditional sense of the importance of clear rules of the game. But no other country rations health care in quite that way. And small wonder. What politician would want to be associated with such a list? (Here it is worth noting that Oregon's tentative step toward rationing is limited to the poor—and the most vulnerable of the poor at that: welfare mothers and their children. *Elderly* Medicaid beneficiaries do not come under the new rules.) More likely, rationing in America, just as is the case abroad, will take place on an implicit ad hoc basis within the constraints of limited public and private resources. But whatever the exact route we choose, and whatever the precise roles we assign to government and the market in making decisions, we can be sure of one thing. We will not be able to afford everything that medicine's advances will make possible.

Most Americans are horrified at the very mention of rationing. But to say that we will have to ration health care is just another way of saying that we will have to set limits. And to say we will have to set limits is itself another way of saying that we will have to make choices if we are to build the kind of America we are trying to build and be the kind of Americans we want to be.

Building that America will require deep changes in our attitudes and expectations. It will mean a new way of thinking about what constitutes consumption in health care and what constitutes investment. It will mean a new acceptance of the ultimate limit—death. Can we make all of these changes without doing undue violence to American cultural and political instincts and institutions? I think so—if we have a positive vision of what change will mean. We need our leaders to give us that vision. If ever there was one, now there's a truly presidential task.

5

Cheap Gas and Apple Pie

Like most Americans, I have vivid memories of the events triggered by Saddam Hussein's invasion of Kuwait on August 1, 1990. As oil prices doubled, helping to tumble a faltering U.S. economy into recession, the White House forged an international coalition that mounted the most ambitious international military campaign since the Korean War. On January 17, 1991, we all tuned in the evening news to watch Baghdad light up like the proverbial Christmas tree. Just eleven hundred hours later—hours in which families anxiously awaited news of the half a million young Americans whose lives were on the line—Operation Desert Storm ended amid unforgettable scenes of triumph and destruction: the burned-out hulks of four thousand Iraqi tanks strewn across the desert; the pall from six hundred oil-well fires blackening Kuwait's skies; an oil slick sixty miles long and twenty miles wide oozing down the Persian Gulf to the Indian Ocean.

America, of course, had many motives for going to war with a ruthless dictator who was bent on empire building and about to acquire nuclear capabilities. Yet whatever else was at stake, as we watched the smart bombs and Tomahawk cruise missiles explode over Baghdad, Americans knew that a bottom-line cause of the war was oil—or, to be more precise, the threat that an oil cutoff posed to our economy. As then Secretary of State James Baker put it in an all-too-candid remark, the three biggest reasons the United States rushed into the Gulf crisis were "jobs, jobs, jobs."

GLUTTONS FOR ENERGY

The Gulf crisis served as the starkest kind of reminder not just of the dangers of America's dependence on foreign oil but, more generally,

of the costs of feeding our outsized appetite for energy—the root cause
of this dependence. Other industrial countries also must rely, to a
greater or lesser extent, on imported oil, and hence had much at stake
in the Gulf War. But America is the world's greatest energy glutton.
That gluttony is evident everywhere—by land, sea, and air.

- *America uses energy far less efficiently than most other countries do.* In fact,
  total per-capita energy consumption in the United States is 1.5 times
  the average for other major industrial countries. Japan's economy
  is able to obtain about 2.5 times as much physical output per barrel
  of oil as we do. If we're looking for reasons that U.S. business finds
  it tough to compete today, that's one. Our comparatively less efficient use of energy is a drag on our overall economic growth, can
  help feed inflation, and, of course, hurts our competitiveness.

- *America's energy profligacy also makes us the world's greatest CO_2 polluter.*
  All told, the U.S. economy now generates about 5.8 tons of carbon
  emissions per capita each year, compared with an average for other
  major industrial countries of about 2.8 tons.

- *America consumes far more oil than any other country—and is particularly
  profligate in its consumption of gasoline.* In fact, though we have less
  than 5 percent of the world's population, one-tenth of all the
  world's oil output gets pumped at our gas stations alone! On average, Americans consume about 2.6 times more gasoline per capita in their automobiles than people in other major industrial
  nations—making us far and away the world's leading gas guzzlers.

- *America's dependence on imported oil is growing rapidly—even as other
  countries are trying to cut back on the habit.* America's net oil imports
  in 1992 averaged about 6.9 million barrels a day—or 40.5 percent
  of our total oil consumption. That is a higher percentage than in
  1973, when the first Arab oil embargo warned us we should change
  course. Despite the recent experiences of Desert Storm, there is no
  sign that there will be a turnaround anytime soon. The U.S. Department of Energy projects that by the year 2000, net oil imports
  will hit between 9.1 and 13.5 million barrels a day—or 49 to 65
  percent of our total consumption. The bill? Between $70 billion
  and $95 billion. By 2010, official estimates of our import depen-
  dency rise to levels as high as 17 million barrels per day—or 72
  percent.

As a business globe-trotter, I often find myself at gas stations in
Tokyo, Paris, Milan, London, Hamburg, and elsewhere. Wherever I

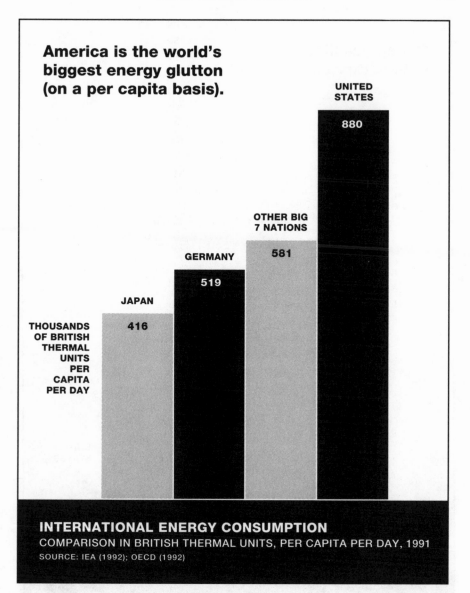

America is the world's biggest energy glutton (on a per capita basis).

UNITED STATES

880

OTHER BIG 7 NATIONS

581

GERMANY

519

JAPAN

416

THOUSANDS OF BRITISH THERMAL UNITS PER CAPITA PER DAY

INTERNATIONAL ENERGY CONSUMPTION
COMPARISON IN BRITISH THERMAL UNITS, PER CAPITA PER DAY, 1991
SOURCE: IEA (1992); OECD (1992)

look, I find fresh evidence of the degree to which America is different from other countries in our insistence that limitless consumption of cheap energy is a birthright—almost on a par with eating apple pie.

Almost everywhere in the world, gasoline is taxed heavily to encourage conservation, reduce pollution, and—not so incidentally—fund government budgets. My curiosity about how foreign countries handle their energy policies led me to compile the data in the chart on the next page. It depicts the latest gasoline taxes and prices in major

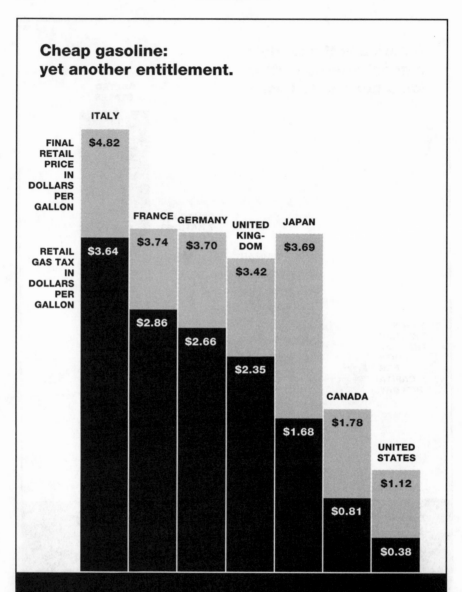

Cheap gasoline:
yet another entitlement.

INTERNATIONAL RETAIL GASOLINE TAXES
COMPARISON IN DOLLARS PER GALLON
NOTE: BASED ON 1991–1992 AVERAGES. "LEADED PREMIUM" DATA USED FOR
EUROPEAN COUNTRIES; "UNLEADED REGULAR" DATA USED FOR U.S.,
CANADA, AND JAPAN. SOURCE: INTERNATIONAL ENERGY AGENCY, OECD;
INTERNATIONAL FINANCIAL STATISTICS, IMF

industrial countries and strikingly illustrates just how anomalous America's belief in "cheap gas" really is.

Since the oil shocks of the 1970s, many other developed countries have made great strides in using energy more efficiently and in reducing their oil dependency. For Americans, living in a country of relative oil plenty (the United States, we sometimes forget, is one of the world's biggest oil producers), it is instructive to examine the performance of Japan, a country with virtually no oil of its own. As recently as 1980, Japanese oil imports weighed in at about 5.5 percent of GNP and oil accounted for over 40 percent of its total import bill. By the end of the 1980s, oil imports had fallen to only about 1 percent of GNP and made up less than 15 percent of its import bill. What happened to explain the dramatic change? Japan knew it had to reduce its tremendous reliance on foreign oil or remain indefinitely vulnerable to cutoffs in supply. Perhaps no statistic better captures the benefits of Japan's decision to face up and seek real solutions than this one: *In 1990, just a decade and a half after the beginning of the sustained industrial restructuring that followed the first OPEC oil embargo, Japan was producing 2.4 times the real output with the same energy input that it had been able to manage back in 1974.*

What a contrast to our own response to oil dependency! When OPEC played its hand again in 1979 and sharply raised prices, triggering the second great oil shock, the United States temporarily decreased its oil consumption and increased domestic oil production. But the decrease in consumption was over by 1983 and has since reversed direction. The good news about energy production was over by 1985. While governments in other countries made conservation a top priority—and stuck to it—we Americans changed our ways only until the immediate crisis subsided. It reminds me of my own diet history. All my life I've been an eager eater, and for much of my earlier life I was on one short-lived and failed diet after another.

The Gulf War once again got our attention. Yet as soon as the parades were over it was back to business as usual. There was, to be sure, much empty talk about the need to increase our energy efficiency and wean ourselves from our addiction to foreign oil. The Bush administration trotted out a new "National Energy Strategy." Congressional hoppers suddenly overflowed with energy bills. But a couple of years had to pass before, amid breast-beating and cries of "draconian sacrifice," we steeled ourselves to enact a few timid measures. After blasting Paul Tsongas for proposing a new gasoline tax, President Clinton did an about-face and included a broad-based energy (or BTU) tax in his first budget proposal. But with an impact on gasoline of just 7.5 cents per gallon at the pump, most economists agree it was far too small to make much difference in curbing our energy appetite. At 4.3

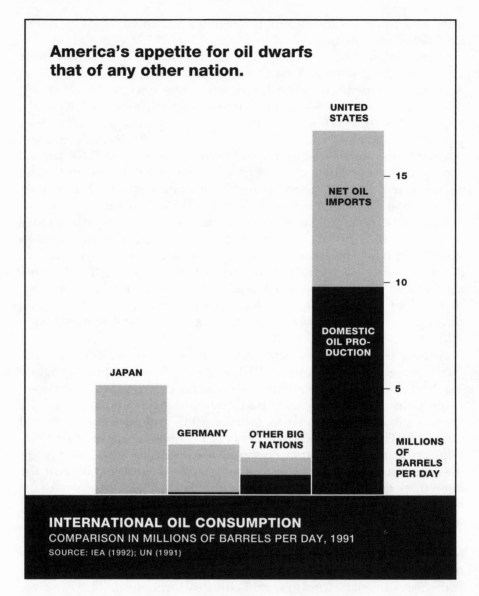

**America's appetite for oil dwarfs
that of any other nation.**

UNITED
STATES

NET OIL
IMPORTS

— 15

— 10

DOMESTIC
OIL PRO-
DUCTION

JAPAN

— 5

GERMANY   OTHER BIG
7 NATIONS

MILLIONS
OF
BARRELS
PER DAY

INTERNATIONAL OIL CONSUMPTION
COMPARISON IN MILLIONS OF BARRELS PER DAY, 1991
SOURCE: IEA (1992); UN (1991)

cents per gallon, the gasoline tax that Congress ultimately passed is
smaller still. Compare all that to the recent German imposition of an
additional fifty-cents-a-gallon gasoline tax to rebuild the former East
Germany—a tax presumably enacted under the quaint notion that a
country should pay for what it deems to be in its best national interest.

Apparently Americans still prefer to view cheap gasoline as yet another entitlement (over the past dozen years, the real price of gasoline
in the United States has actually declined by more than 40 percent

from its 1981 peak!)—no matter what the costs to our economy, our national security, our environment, or our children.

ANOTHER UNFUNDED ENTITLEMENT

Like me, my readers doubtless know someone who consumes quantities of a particular product that far exceed what they themselves can imagine needing or wanting. Perhaps it's CDs, soap operas, or fashionable clothes. But we're not in the habit of calling them "gluttons." And we certainly wouldn't suggest that we target them with special taxes aimed at curbing their "excessive" consumption.

Why do other countries view energy differently from CDs or Calvin Klein jeans? And why is it imperative that in the United States we begin to do the same?

The answer is that some activities we engage in privately impose public or "social costs" on the rest of us that aren't included in the prices of the goods and services we buy, but that must be paid for in some fashion. To the extent that individuals or businesses don't pay for those indirect costs, the rest of us are subsidizing them. However, by taxing those activities that impose indirect costs on our economy and society—what economists call "externalities"—we can both reduce those costs (more taxes mean less consumption) and more equitably distribute them. Take the case of highway tolls. We may gripe about them, but we can all understand their rationale. They help to pay for repairing crumbling roads and sagging bridges. Anybody who drives a car contributes to the wear and tear on our highways. It only makes sense that motorists contribute at least something more to their upkeep than people who take a plane or a train.

Yet when it comes to the environmental, economic, and national security costs of our profligate consumption of oil, we don't seem to get the connection, perhaps because they are less direct than a pothole. That they are less jolting does not mean they are small. They are huge. By not paying for them in the price of oil and gasoline we buy, we have in effect created yet another unfunded entitlement.

We don't think of cheap gasoline as a subsidy to consumers. But almost all economists agree that it *is* one, and a particularly inefficient and perverse one at that. Some of the subsidy's costs are paid for directly by the public treasury—in the Pentagon's budget, for instance. Some show up as lost productivity when we sit idling in traffic jams. Others come out of our pockets when oil-shock-triggered recessions leave all of us poorer. Still others, such as the damage we do to our environment, are passed on to future generations. According to one partial estimate of these "externality" costs that excludes defense outlays, the social costs of driving that motorists themselves don't defray through gas taxes or highway tolls come to as much as $300 billion a year.

Let's first look at the environmental costs of our energy gluttony. Experts may differ on the precise extent of the damage caused by everything from auto emissions to coal-driven acid rain, but when we take into account the quality of the air we breathe, our poisoned rivers and lakes, and the threat to forests and wildlife, not to mention the possibly catastrophic impact of global warming in the next century, all agree that the costs are vast. Ever since the environmental movement of the 1970s, Americans in principle take for granted that private industry should curb and help pay for the costs of its pollution. With this in mind, we have passed regulations that require businesses to bear the costs of controlling a host of noxious industrial emissions. But when it comes to the millions of cars that clog our roads, spewing out thousands of tons of hydrocarbons and volatile organic compounds each day, we don't seem to recognize that we are *all* collectively paying for the costs we individually impose on others. The press routinely lambastes the tobacco lobby for protecting an industry whose products add an estimated $50 billion to today's annual health-care bill. As a matter of public policy, most Americans agree that 100 percent excise taxes on cigarettes are justified. Yet few extend the same logic to America's massive "car drivers lobby"—or demand that drivers be held accountable for the damage they cause.

What are we to say to our children about our insatiable appetite for energy? Clearly, we will be unable to tell them it was good for the air they breathe or the climate in which they live. Americans are good, to be sure, at lamenting the effects of headline-grabbing environmental catastrophes like those unleashed by Saddam Hussein's "ecological terrorism" or the wreck of the *Exxon Valdez*. We must learn to devote as much imagination and energy to mitigating the gradual and insidious long-term impact of air pollution, acid rain, and global warming.

Then consider the more immediate economic costs that our energy gluttony imposes when we suffer an unanticipated oil cutoff. Sudden spikes in oil prices can cause recessions because they not only increase the cost of filling up at the gas station and heating our homes, they make the goods produced by every industry that uses petroleum in its manufacturing process more expensive. Faced with higher prices, consumers make fewer purchases; getting fewer orders, businesses lay off workers. The potential economic losses can be enormous. During each of the oil shocks of the 1970s, total world GNP dipped about 6 percent below where it otherwise would have been. Other industrial democracies recognize and try to mitigate this cost through taxes and other policies that discourage excessive reliance on oil. We prefer to ignore it until it stares us in the face.

An additional economic cost of our oil dependency is that it will make it harder for the United States to close its trading deficit in goods and services—something we will almost certainly have to accomplish in the late 1990s if we are to wean ourselves from our dangerous and costly reliance on foreign capital. America's overall deficit in goods and services (that is, the shortfall between everything that we sell to foreign consumers and everything that we buy from foreign producers) weighed in at $41 billion in 1992. If our oil deficit, which has already climbed back to $45 billion from its low of $31 billion in 1986, worsens by $25 to $50 billion between now and the year 2000 (as official government projections say it will), the only way we can eliminate our overall deficit in goods and services will be to improve our trading balances apart from oil by some $65 to $90 billion. Excluding U.S. farm products and raw materials—which, over the long term, stubbornly resist contributing to a major or sustained improvement of our trading balance—this would mean a 14 to 19 percent real increase in our exports of other goods and services, *without any increase in our nonoil imports.*

Rather than allowing an unchecked rise in net oil imports to put obstacles in the way of closing our overall trading deficit, we need to put energy policies in place that will moderate our appetite for oil and help improve our net export position. The alternative to closing our trading deficit—accumulating still more debt to foreigners—is not an option that America, already the world's largest debtor nation, should willingly contemplate.

But as Desert Storm reminded us, there are other costs to our energy gluttony as well. With the politically volatile Persian Gulf countries now producing one-fourth of the world's oil and sitting atop two-thirds of the world's known reserves, concern about the security of our energy supplies continues to hold our foreign policy hostage. First of all, there is the year-to-year expense of maintaining military preparedness for an adequate response to a new crisis—and this at a time when Americans desperately need to invest more resources in solving pressing domestic problems. Let's recall that, even after Iraq's crushing defeat, its actions have forced us to deploy and redeploy our air and naval forces. Even while we're at peace, the security costs of our oil habit are thus playing a crucial role in the evaporation of our much-vaunted peace dividend. Then, of course, there is the ultimate cost of going to war—measured not just in material but in lives.

I have asked my foreign policy mentors what could spark a new crisis in the Middle East. Almost anything, the answer comes back: the Arab-Israeli impasse, the festering wounds of previous wars, especially that between Iran and Iraq, Islamic fundamentalism run amok, or our own concern about nuclear proliferation, to name a few prime candidates. Desert Storm certainly did not eliminate the historical causes of instability in the Middle East. Paradoxically, the end of the Cold War may also have made the situation more volatile by removing a potential safety catch. Neither the former Soviet Union nor the United States now has the same compelling reasons for using its muscle to prevent a blowup.

To those who believe that the United States can simply relaunch Desert Storm at the next sign of Middle Eastern trouble, it is worth considering the unusually favorable circumstances that aided our cause during the Gulf crisis. One reason the Bush administration was willing to intervene so decisively was that it knew any resulting shortfall in oil supplies to the United States could be made up by Saudi Arabia and other friendly sources, such as Mexico. The availability of substitute supplies was also why oil prices stabilized so rapidly, and goes a long way toward explaining our political will in maintaining the Iraqi embargo. What's more, Desert Storm cost few American lives, and much of its $50 billion price tag was ultimately picked up by our allies, including, once again, Saudi Arabia. It would be foolhardy to assume that the price of future interventions will be so small.

Finally, we come to the most intangible cost of our energy gluttony: a tarnished world image that saps our influence in global affairs. This cost shows up most obviously in our foreign policy. To paraphrase a former French foreign minister's quip, it's hard to take seriously a nation that could ease one of its biggest national security problems with a substantial gasoline tax. A United States that cannot control the twitches of its own appetite for oil at home is also a nation that is finding it increasingly difficult to be disinterested in its dealings abroad. From the Wilsonian crusade to make the world safe for democracy to the Marshall Plan and beyond, America's foreign policy has been molded by ideals and goals that transcended our narrow self-interest. Today the rest of the world is beginning to see a different America.

When Saddam Hussein invaded Kuwait, we played every diplomatic card at our disposal to muster international support, then wielded massive military force. No amount of talk about restoring the "sovereignty" of the Kuwaiti people could disguise what was really at stake: protecting our oil lifeline. Now, as what was once Yugoslavia sinks into fratricidal chaos, we have dithered—unwilling to get "bogged down" and openly citing as a rationale for inaction that we have no vital strategic interest there. With the Cold War over, such ambiguities promise to leave our credibility as leader of the free world in tatters.

And what about our international image as a polluter? With America's vast wealth, natural resources, and technological know-how, we should be leading the civilized world into the next century by forging economic policies that make protecting and improving the environ-

ment a top priority. But other industrial democracies are instead leading the way while we, the laggards, indulge in a profligate consumption
that the rest of the developed world is ready to give up. From the
empty rhetoric offered by U.S. representatives at the UN's "earth summit" in Rio de Janeiro in 1992, we already know how poorly justified
our energy habits appear. Once again, our influence in global affairs
suffers.

Wherever we look, whether to our economy, our national security,
or our environment, the signs all point to the same familiar bottom
line—the need to make tough, strategic choices.

ENERGY CHOICES

Other industrial democracies have made real choices in energy policy—all of them difficult, none of them politically costless. It's time
that we faced up and followed suit.

I believe the place to begin is with a hike in the federal excise tax on
gasoline of fifty cents a gallon that would be phased in between 1995
and the year 2000. As politically problematic as the measure might
seem, it is the simplest and most equitable way to help defray the vast
social costs of America's unfunded gas entitlement. It will also have
fewer adverse effects on our competitiveness than a broader-based
energy tax that would raise the costs of our manufactured products—
something that's crucial to avoid at a time when we must reduce our
overall trade deficit.

One good reason for a substantial gasoline tax, of course, is that it
would help reduce the federal deficit. But such a tax would also lower
the volume of our trade deficit in oil by restraining total U.S. oil
consumption, and indirectly it would also help to lower our dollar
trade deficit by moderating growth in world oil prices. This last effect
is important. While fearing OPEC's power to push up prices, Americans have seldom understood that we, as the world's largest oil consumers, possess sufficient buying power to pull down prices, if only we
would use it. With a substantial gasoline tax, we could at least try to do
just that—playing the traditional OPEC game in reverse.

A gasoline tax of fifty cents a gallon would raise about $50 billion
yearly in new federal revenues. It would also cut our oil-import deficit
while still leaving us with far lower gasoline prices than almost any
major western nation. Even with a new U.S. gasoline tax of fifty cents
a gallon, people in the other leading industrialized countries, where
the average gasoline tax is over two dollars, would still be paying two
and one-half times more tax than Americans would.

But we also need to go much further in encouraging more efficient use of oil and the development of alternative clean energy sources. Here we must consider not only the risks of dependence on oil imports and the dangers of a swollen foreign debt, but also the growing national consensus that fossil fuels pose serious environmental hazards.

Yet on this front too, the United States has been lethargic in devising ways to reduce its oil gluttony. Consider just two foreign examples. By switching to alternative fuels, Japan since 1973 has decreased oil's share in its total energy consumption from 77 percent to 58 percent. It has also, as we have seen, boosted the total economic output it obtains per barrel of oil to a level 2.5 times higher than what we get—a stupendous accomplishment, because it not only saves resources directly, but lessens the impact of oil-price shocks on economic growth and inflation.

France is also facing up to its energy challenges. The French understood that doing nothing—that is, relying too heavily on oil and in particular on imported oil—involved costs and risks that were intolerable. So France decided to focus on developing its nuclear power program—certainly not a riskless proposition. But in the French view, nuclear power put their economy and national well-being at less long-term risk than too heavy reliance on Middle Eastern oil producers. At last count, France gets over 70 percent of its electrical power from nuclear energy, and it has set a goal of getting 100 percent by mid-decade. Its nuclear power industry has had no major safety problems so far and has even enabled the French to reduce some of the worst effects of burning fossil fuels for power generation, including damage to the health of their coal miners.

Meanwhile, in the United States, there was just more of the usual national somnolence. Liking every kind of alternative energy except the ones that are available, we have witnessed an endless tug-of-war between industry special interests, taxpayer lobbies, and environmentalist groups that leaves our energy policy gridlocked. In a replay of what happened with VCRs—American companies developed the technology and Japanese companies then profitably produced the machines—other industrial countries (such as France) have invested heavily in the development of new and safer nuclear power technologies whose principles were first worked out in the United States. Yet we cannot even decide where to dispose of the waste from our own limited (and now antiquated) nuclear power industry. No new nuclear power plant has been ordered in the United States since 1974, and as license renewals for those constructed in the 1950s and 1960s come up for review, all indications are they will be denied.

I'm not arguing that we should rely on nuclear power over other sources of energy. I'm simply saying that we can't afford to spurn all alternatives to oil as we do now. Squabbles about how acid-rain-control legislation should affect the future use of emerging clean-coal technologies have stymied their development. Despite progress in the 1980s, a maze of regulation continues to create artificial shortages of natural gas, another abundant domestic energy source that is cleaner than petroleum. As a result, U.S. utilities are turning back to oil to provide generating capacity. This of course will simply add to pressures on oil prices and our import bill, not to mention the bad effects on the environment. The point is that we need to make a choice and a commitment to finding real, workable alternatives—whether cleaner fossil fuels or entirely different sources of energy. Concern about the economy and the environment are not so mutually contradictory as is often claimed.

Finally, in view of the potential for new crises in the Middle East, I am forced to conclude that we must pay more attention to the security of our energy supplies. But there are more ways to enhance security than by keeping our military on red alert. We should reach agreement with the other industrial countries to coordinate policies for dealing with energy emergencies within the International Energy Agency, which was set up in response to the oil crisis of 1974 and has since been largely neglected. We should also enlarge our Strategic Petroleum Reserve—which now gives only about three months' protection against an oil cutoff—and should further consider a new, long-term arrangement for low-cost "leasing" of oil for this reserve from selected OPEC sources, under which we would, in effect, rent the oil we store.

At the same time, we should seek to build more *genuine economic interdependence* with the moderate Gulf states (as well as with other low-cost oil producers, such as Mexico and Kazakhstan). This is not only in our interest, it is also in theirs—and the Gulf states know it. I am repeatedly told by the Middle East scholars at the Council on Foreign Relations that countries like Saudi Arabia and Kuwait wish to build ties of true "interdependence" with the United States and, within that framework, are willing to pursue moderate policies on the production and pricing of oil.

If we foolishly turn away from them, there could be trouble ahead, but trouble of a subtle sort that we may at first find hard to recognize. One lesson the Gulf states have learned over the past decade is that very sharp increases in prices unleash market forces that both limit demand and encourage the production of competing supplies—and both of these developments work against their own long-term interests. Equally important, they may have observed that while Americans often act decisively in the face of an obvious crisis, they appear likely to tolerate trends, such as chronic trade or budget deficits, that are insidious and gradual. An astute OPEC strategy would be to let both production and prices rise steadily in the years ahead—feeding our addiction, not triggering a violent withdrawal. On our current trajectory, then, the alternative to a "sudden cutoff" might be a "slow bleed."

How can we build economic interdependence? In recent years, European Community members have exported four times as much in goods and services to the Gulf states as we have. They have also encouraged joint investment projects with some of the OPEC countries and just before Desert Storm had opened negotiations on a free-trade pact with the Gulf Cooperation Council. Americans may be surprised, as was I on a trip to the Gulf in 1990, to learn that British employees in Saudi Arabia outnumbered Americans by 40 percent. As recently as ten years ago, there were about eighty thousand Americans in Saudi Arabia; by 1990 the number had shrunk to about twenty-five thousand. Increasingly in the years before Iraq's attack on Kuwait, the United States paid little attention to improving its relations with OPEC members in general or with the moderate Gulf states in particular.

The most obvious way to forge closer links with the Gulf states—and at the same time reduce our trade deficit with them—is to do as the European Community countries do and export more to them. Until the United States gave up a huge arms contract for Saudi Arabia to Britain in 1985–86, we still behaved as though we were aware of the value of closer economic relationships, including two-way investment. America, of course, has more potential influence over emerging policies in the Gulf states than Britain, since it can link economic cooperation with defense assistance to any friendly state, especially Saudi Arabia, that has a plausible need for it. We should use that influence more consistently. In February 1990, well before the Gulf War, Saudi and Kuwaiti leaders were privately expressing to me their rising concern about a potentially aggressive Iraq—clearly with good reason.

"But, Pete," say my economist friends, "how can you preach energy security through increasing our *interdependence* with the moderate Gulf states and, at the same time, preach energy security through *independence* by stressing emergency oil storage?" They wonder whether the United States "can have it both ways."

I think we need a national policy that walks on both tracks. On the one hand, great nations like ours should not put their destinies into the hands of others, particularly militaristic, violent, radical states subject to outbreaks of Islamic fundamentalism. We must lessen our oil dependence in all the ways we can—above all by being more efficient users of energy.

But at the same time, we are most unlikely to ever be able to do without oil entirely, and as oil economists at the Institute for International Economics remind me, the world's low-cost suppliers of oil will continue to be in the Arabian Peninsula—or in places like Kazakhstan. Economic theory and experience, in turn, show that nations should pursue those activities in which they have the greatest comparative advantage. We cannot and should not try to produce all of our own oil. And we certainly should not put the U.S. government in the industrial policy business by having it subsidize and prop up high-cost domestic producers. Such efforts would be just as quixotic as President Carter's Project Independence, and would be just as doomed to failure. In short, we will continue to need foreign oil for the foreseeable future, and that makes the case for interdependence compelling.

It also underscores the most fundamental energy-policy lesson of all that we have yet to learn. Even when Americans agree that we need to reduce our dependence on oil—in particular foreign oil—they typically think in terms of energy autarky and high-cost energy alternatives. But we must also strive to reduce our energy bill by reducing our overall consumption of energy. Our gluttony is at the heart of the problem.

The stakes are great. America's energy gluttony is not just another short-term concern that, like the S&L debacle, will one day go away. It is part of a much deeper problem: our national tendency to indulge in excessive consumption at the expense of our future. My friend and colleague in the Nixon White House, Herb Stein, once wryly observed: "If something is unsustainable, it tends to stop." With cheap gas no less than with other entitlements, the real question is not whether we will decide to change course, but when—and after how much more harm to ourselves and our children.

Americans face a choice. We can begin to work out policies that increase our productive use of energy, improve the environment, avert the risk of crisis posed by our dependence on foreign oil producers (whether through a "sudden cutoff" or a "slow bleed"), and at the same time help to erase our trade and budgetary deficits.

Or we can do nothing. And when our children ask why we didn't act, we can tell them: "Despite the fact that in 1993 our national appetite for energy was far out of proportion to our population or our productivity, we deemed any reduction on your behalf to be too great a sacrifice." Better yet, we can say: "We left the outcome up to the free choice of the American consumer and, too bad, you lost." Clearly we will be unable to tell them that our energy and oil gluttony was good for the air they will breathe, for the climate in which they will live, for their influence in global affairs, or, indeed, for their economy.

6

One Nation—with Lawsuits and Settlements for All

A man injured trying to board a city bus in the middle of the street wins a $619,000 award from a Washington, D.C., jury—though he was admittedly so drunk at the time of the accident that he could not recall what happened. A woman, claiming that a CAT scan robbed her of her psychic powers, receives a million dollars from a Philadelphia jury. With the meter still running, U.S. manufacturers have already shelled out about $9 billion for asbestos litigation. The plaintiffs? Often not even their customers or employees, but men who worked in naval shipyards during World War II when the health hazards of asbestos were little understood and when some of the companies now paying damages had yet to be founded.

Enter Pete Peterson, a "candidate" for a New York jury, along with about fifteen others. The case: a woman who had slipped on a wet sidewalk at Kennedy Airport and allegedly suffered an "injury," minor at best. The city—in other words, all of us jury candidates—was being sued. The questioning dragged on interminably. Finally, my moment arrived. The plaintiff's lawyer asked if there was any reason that I did not feel "qualified." As my children would say, I lost it. Assuming that he was a contingency lawyer, I told him I was a relentless observer of America's productivity decline. It seemed to me we were here witnessing one contributing factor to that decline—perhaps two dozen people consuming untold hours of otherwise productive time on an obviously trivial issue, something our international competitors would at best find indulgent. I was quickly dismissed from further consideration.

Welcome to the front lines of America's litigation crisis: an explosion of lawsuits that clogs our courts, hobbles our economy, and fragments our sense of community.

Americans have become far and away the most litigious people in history. With 5 percent of the world's population, we have 70 percent of its lawyers. Japan has just 11 attorneys for every 100,000 inhabitants, England 82, and Germany 111. We have 281. In the District of Columbia, one out of every ten working people you meet on the street (and every other member of Congress) is an attorney. From child custody and sex discrimination to product liability and medical malpractice, Americans now file about 18 million suits each year—one for every ten adults. And this number is growing by leaps and bounds. In federal courts, filings have nearly doubled since 1970 and tripled since 1960. By some estimates, about 90 percent of all civil lawsuits in the entire world are filed in the United States.

The vagaries of our litigation system make the stuff of newspaper headlines—"junk-science" testimony; juries that hand out multi-million-dollar awards for "pain and suffering" and punitive damages like so much cash in a lottery; lawyers who tirelessly search for novel pretexts to sue and "deep-pockets" defendants to pay, then bank a lion's share of whatever their clients collect in court as contingency fees.

But the vast costs that litigation imposes on our economy and society at large are the real reason to worry. One conservative estimate puts direct spending on lawsuits and liability insurance at $80 billion a year. And this is just the ante. Threatened with bankruptcy by mostly groundless lawsuits, whole U.S. industries, such as small aircraft, have simply thrown in the towel and gone out of business. Because of liability fears, safe and useful products that promise to improve our welfare—from new generations of contraceptives to better child restraint seats—have never been developed or marketed. To avoid frivolous malpractice claims, doctors practice "defensive medicine," adding billions of dollars of unnecessary care to our national health-care bills. With insurance either unaffordable or unavailable, vital services from town dumps to day-care centers have closed their doors.

And what have we bought in return? Feast-or-famine justice. Once an individual right is formally discovered and defined, once infringements of that right are publicized by interest groups and measured or at least quantified, and once a deep-pockets defendant can be found to pay the damages, then and there the wheels of our litigation system begin to spin. But if not? Well, you had better fend for yourself. This same pattern of feast or famine, moreover, shows up in the systems of health, safety, and environmental regulation we have put in place to protect our rights. On the one hand, we measure trace amounts of environmental toxins in parts per billion. On the other, the best that we can do about cigarettes is—without success—to forbid their sale to children.

Such outcomes leave all of us poorer. They also point to the fundamental problem behind America's litigation crisis: a mentality that pays exclusive attention to discovering and protecting individual rights while forgetting the interests of the wider community. Even as lawyers and regulators worry about small risks to our individual welfare, we stand by helplessly as crime and a host of other pathologies fray our social fabric. We can watch workers labor to remove asbestos from the basements of schools—though most experts agree leaving it in place would often actually be safer—while just outside the legal system can do little to prevent kids from being shot dead in broad daylight.

America may be the only country in the world to pay so much attention to the rights of individuals while ignoring those of the community. It wasn't always so.

AMERICA'S RIGHTS REVOLUTION

The original purpose of our legal institutions was settling differences between people in ways that promoted the long-term good of the community. They performed quite satisfactorily throughout our history until well into the postwar era. But then we shifted our focus. We took these same institutions and, without changing their names, used them to further a different agenda. We set out to discover, define, and enforce a much vaster range of personal rights for their own sake, without any thought for whether this change of direction would work to the public good, or what it would cost the economy.

To the right of injured parties to receive compensation for such economic damages as property losses and doctor bills, we added the right to collect awards for such intangible damages as pain and suffering and mental anguish. (In a late-breaking development on this front, Pfizer, the manufacturer of the Shiley heart valve, is now being sued on the grounds that the mere use of its product can cause *fear* of possible injury. Apparently pain and suffering now need not even be *associated* with a real harm.) On top of our traditional rights not to be assaulted or libeled, we piled hundreds of new rights under such rubrics as age, sex, and job discrimination. Government agencies began to measure trace amounts of toxins in parts per billion and issue tens of thousands of pages of command and control regulation setting safety standards for everything from stepladders to water fountains.

At the same time, courts suddenly turned long-standing legal doctrines on their head to make it easier for plaintiffs to collect damages. Until the mid-1960s, firms could only be held liable for harm caused by their products if they had failed to conform to a "reasonable standard of care" in their design and manufacture—in other words, if they had been negligent. Under our new doctrine of strict liability, the defective condition of a product is in and of itself sufficient to establish guilt. We also abandoned the rule of contributory negligence—which held that a plaintiff who was himself partly responsible for a mishap could not sue for damages—and expanded the doctrine of "joint and several liability"—which holds that a defendant partly responsible for a mishap can be required to pay the entire bill. The goal? To open up the bank accounts of deep-pockets defendants.

The point is not that many of these developments did not further worthy social goals. Certainly protecting the rights of disadvantaged Americans should be a major concern of U.S. law and regulation. Great victories have been won in assuring the rights of many groups previously victimized by systematic discrimination. The problem, however, is that we often pursued our new rights agenda in ways that failed to add up the costs and consequences for society at large.

Why did the demands of the wider community seem to matter so little? One explanation lies in America's affluence at the time our rights revolution first took off in the 1960s. With our GNP headed for the stars, the costs of doing a better job of protecting individual rights hardly seemed to be an issue. After all, we could afford to send a man to the moon, fight a war in Asia, and launch the Great Society—all at the same time. Another explanation lies in the cultural climate of the times. The consciousness revolution then sweeping America celebrated differences and grievances between individuals and groups and tended to view institutions geared toward promoting the common good as benighted, even pathological. If the community was doing so well, and if individual rights were everywhere being denied, it seemed only fair that more and more risks should be borne not by people themselves, but by government, corporations, and other large impersonal institutions.

So in the end, Americans came to believe that almost every conceivable harm to an individual has legal redress—and that there is always someone to pay the bill. Victimization had become more than a defining link in our society; it had become Big Business. But, of course, no one has legal redress for an economy that is now grinding to a halt and a society that threatens to fly apart at the seams. Adam Smith talked about the "invisible hand" that operates in the marketplace to ensure that the free play of individual economic self-interest ends up making all of us richer. One pundit recently described our litigation system as an "invisible foot."

A SYSTEM OUT OF CONTROL

Take a walk through the minefield into which litigation has turned our society, and almost anything can set off an explosion. Maybe you've decided to mow your lawn. Your mower could kick up a rock that hits someone in the head. Or if you leave it lying around, a neighbor's child might play with it and lose a toe. Either of these mishaps could mean a costly injury suit—including, say, a million dollars for pain and suffering. Are you liable? Maybe yes and maybe no. Can the lawnmower's manufacturer be sued? You bet. If he took every precaution to ensure that the machine was as safe as state-of-the-art knowledge allowed, will that limit his liability? No way. Can he at least estimate the financial risks he is exposed to? Of course not. He might win a half-dozen suits hands down—then be hit with a several-hundred-thousand-dollar verdict because an obese man had a heart attack while straining to start his mower, as actually happened to one manufacturer in the mid-1980s.

It is the capriciousness of our litigation system that is perhaps its most visible failing. Even when a case is weak, a sympathetic victim, an underemployed lawyer, and a deep-pockets or well-insured defendant to sue can be a recipe for a multi-million-dollar windfall—with the precise figure more or less picked out of a hat. Take payouts in malpractice suits. Among those plaintiffs who receive compensation, a mere 2 percent account for two-thirds of the dollar value of all awards—a lopsided distribution that cannot possibly reflect the actual merits of the cases involved.

Exacerbating this capriciousness is what one observer has called "junk science." We have already met the soothsayer whom a Philadelphia jury awarded a million dollars for being put out of business by a CAT scan. "Expert" witnesses have persuaded other juries that trace amounts of environmental toxins cause "chemically induced" AIDS, that obstetricians are frequently to blame for cerebral palsy, and that nonexistent design flaws cause Audi 5000s to accelerate at random and crash, or Cessna and Piper planes to fall mysteriously from the sky. As Donald Elliot, former general counsel of the Environmental Protection Agency, summed it up, the law today "extends equal dignity to the opinions of charlatans and Nobel Prize winners, with only a lay jury to distinguish between the two."

But above and beyond mere capriciousness is a more fundamental problem: a pervasive uncertainty in both law and regulation about what our individual rights and mutual obligations really are. This uncertainty makes it impossible for anyone to know in advance when they're about to step on a hidden landmine. And it invites constant lawsuits to test and define what we're entitled to.

We can all agree, for instance, that the elimination of sex discrimination, an avowed goal of federal legislation, would be a good thing. But what exactly is "sex discrimination"? Does stamping it out mean that single-sex schools must be abolished? Or that athletic departments must offer boys' field hockey teams? Then take the Occupational Safety and Health Administration, whose mandate is to order firms to do whatever is "reasonably necessary for safe or healthful employment." But what does "reasonably" mean? Or again, consider the 1990 Americans with Disabilities Act. It calls for the removal of all barriers to the disabled in public places and businesses where that "removal is readily achievable" and the expense not "unduly burdensome." Litigants are already flocking to court to explore the limits of this new law.

Which brings us back to the driving force behind America's litigation explosion: our discovery of whole new categories of rights to protect. A novelty just a few decades ago, age and sex discrimination suits have become prominent fixtures of our legal landscape. Now it is the rights of the disabled and alternative families that are at the cutting edge of legal controversy. As the tide of litigation continues to rise, old areas of law are also expanded to include new concerns. Employers face suits for drug testing, wrongful dismissal, and wrongful failure to promote. Doctors face suits for wrongful birth. Product liability lawyers continue to find new perils in toasters and toys. Palimony plaintiffs get equal billing with spouses in divorce court.

Often these new rights directly conflict with each other, creating still more confusion—and litigation. One example involves a recent spate of cases in which workers were fired for sexual harassment. Sexual discrimination laws often require employers to take prompt action in such cases—yet such action can run directly afoul of other laws that forbid employers from firing workers without due process. Many of these workers are suing their employers for "wrongful dismissal"— and winning.

But it is not just that the number of rights we seek to protect has multiplied. The costs of infringing them has also soared. Between the early 1960s and early 1980s—the most recent period for which comprehensive statistics are available—the average judgment in U.S. tort cases rose more than fivefold in real dollars, from $50,000 to over $250,000. Juries now deliver over four hundred million-dollar-plus verdicts a year, up from under twenty in the mid-1970s. Then there are the skyrocketing bills for liability insurance. Among doctors, who are hit especially hard, neurosurgeons can pay as much as $200,000 a year.

One reason for this cost growth is the proliferation of awards for pain and suffering and mental anguish—themselves involving new types of rights. A plaintiff's doctor bills and lost income while laid up in a hospital can be fixed with some accuracy. But the dollar value of these subjective damages is highly arbitrary—so it is easy for juries to hand out awards in multi-million-dollar dollops. Punitive damages are another reason for our litigation cost spiral. Once reserved for cases involving wanton or malicious conduct, punitive-damages verdicts are now routinely fired off by juries. According to one study, the real average value of punitive damages in trials in Cook County, Illinois, rose from $43,000 in the mid-1960s to $729,000 in the early 1980s.

These huge pots of money create yet another problem by tempting lawyers to game the system for their own gain. Most of us understood why Bart Giamatti had to send Pete Rose packing for betting on baseball: moral hazard. If athletes were allowed to gamble on the sports they play, they might throw games. We would all also reject out of hand any suggestion that doctors be permitted to bet on their patients' recovery by billing only those who get well. Sick people certain to recover would be overcharged, well people might be told they were sick, and difficult cases would be shunned.

Yet we allow lawyers to take clients on a contingency-fee basis—a practice unknown in virtually every other industrial democracy. The result? A scramble to find "victims" with rights to vindicate and a torrent of frivolous suits in which the weakest claims get pursued as long as they involve big bucks. The search for victims has recently been made easier by our decision to lift traditional bans on legal advertising, an about-face that has in effect legalized ambulance chasing, something lawyers once went to jail for. Today's ambulance chasers of course insist that contingency fees are essential to guarantee a day in court for those of us who could not otherwise afford it. Other countries get around this problem by having the losers in legal battles pay the winners' costs—the so-called English rule, but really, as one wit has put it, the "everywhere-but-America rule."

In their pursuit of contingency-fee windfalls, American lawyers are aided by legal doctrines that enable them to raid the coffers of deep-pockets defendants on the slenderest of pretexts. The most important is the joint and several liability rule, which provides for the apportionment of blame among different defendants, then allows the whole settlement to be collected from any of the guilty parties, even if he is judged to have had a token 1 percent share in responsibility for a mishap. When a Los Angeles man high on drugs ran a stop sign—to cite a headline-grabbing case—it was the city that had to cough up almost all of the $2 million that was awarded the victim of the accident he caused. The reason? It had failed to trim roadside shrubbery that may have blocked the driver's view around the corner unless he first bothered to stop, then look.

More frequently, this rule has been used to allow lawyers to make end-runs around social institutions that we originally put in place to avoid costly litigation. An employee unhappy with what he gets from workers' compensation (a no-fault benefit system under which he cannot ordinarily sue his boss) can still collect big bucks from the manufacturer of the forklift—or scaffolding or conveyer belt—whose use (or misuse) caused his injury. In fact, the majority of large product liability payouts are now for workplace injuries. But what if blame cannot be attributed with any certainty—not even a token 1 percent share? Courts came up with the so-called Sindel rule, the ultimate twist on joint and several liability. It enables the consumers of generic products—whose manufacturer often cannot be identified—to sue all manufacturers of that product, with liability set according to each firm's market share. Although some means of redress in such cases is needed, once again the result has been to make it easier for lawyers to raid the coffers of deep-pockets defendants.

Finally, we come to the crowning indictment of a litigation system gone haywire. Even when the right people get compensated, as a mechanism for getting money to those who have been injured the system is incredibly inefficient. One study concluded that 30 percent to 40 percent of awards and settlements in the United States end up in the bank accounts of law firms, with another 20 percent to 30 percent chewed up as administrative costs of the court system. That leaves about a third for claimants. Other studies have calculated that when everything is added up, lawyers' take in our litigation lottery is still higher.

No other country has a litigation system remotely similar to our own. It is both enormously expensive and shockingly inefficient. It capriciously bankrupts or enriches those who come into contact with it. And it imposes vast costs on our economy and society at large.

COSTS AND CONSEQUENCES

On August 13, 1991, Dan Quayle entered the lion's den of the American Bar Association to outline the Bush administration's new "Agenda for Civil Justice Reform." During his keynote speech at the association's annual convention, he questioned if America "really needs 70 percent of the world's lawyers"—a bit of lawyer bashing that provoked a widely reported row with ABA president John J. Curtin, Jr. What was most noteworthy about Quayle's address, however, was not the fireworks it set off, but its characterization of our litigation crisis as a serious economic problem—as a "self-inflicted competitive disadvantage." Why would a tort reform proposal have originated in the President's Council on Competitiveness that Quayle headed up? The reasons are not hard to find.

By all accounts, Americans take each other to court more often and spend far more money and time doing it than any people on earth. According to one study, compared with Great Britain, a country with similar common-law heritage, the overall cost of tort claims in the United States totals ten times more per capita, the cost of malpractice claims thirty to forty times more, and the cost of product liability claims a hundred times more. At as much as 2.6 percent of GDP, according to another study, the total cost of America's tort system weighs in at about five times the average for other major industrial countries. That *difference,* by the way, is roughly equal to our total investment in commercial R&D. In other words, if our tort system's cost were reduced to the level in other industrial countries, the released resources would be sufficient to double what we spend in this crucial investment area.

Who bears these costs? All of us do—not just those of us who are unlucky enough to be dragged into court. U.S. businesses, as Vice-President Quayle noted, can suffer in competition with foreign firms whose liability insurance premiums are typically just 5 percent of our own. The result? Lost jobs, a bigger trade deficit, and more dependence on foreign capital. American consumers must also cover the costs in the purchases they make at the sporting goods store or the drugstore, and in the prices of thousands of other goods and services bought and sold throughout our economy. Liability now accounts for 5 percent of the cost of an automobile, one-quarter of the cost of a tour bus ride, more than half the cost of a football helmet, and 95 percent of the cost of a flu vaccine.

Product liability is the area of tort law that poses the greatest potential threat to America's competitiveness and overall economic prosperity. It is also among the fastest-growing types of U.S. litigation, with the number of new suits in recent years shooting up ten times faster than the number of other types of tort cases that come before federal courts. The problem is not just that the total costs of product liability are vast. If we had tried systematically to litigate—or regulate—risk out of every corner of American life, businesses could perhaps have learned to adapt efficiently. But we haven't. Instead, we let the burden of litigation fall haphazardly, generating outcomes that can be as perverse as they are costly.

In industries that have come under the heaviest fire, more often than not the result has been to deprive us of safe and useful products, not improve our welfare. Consider one instance from pharmaceuticals, an industry that could provide us with countless other examples. Forced to pay a flood of astronomical product liability judgments against vaccines that at most posed dangers to a handful of individuals, drug companies started abandoning that business. As a result, many vaccines, including the one for polio, that have saved thousands—even millions—of lives are now made only by a single manufacturer. The upshot? Skyrocketing costs, declining rates of vaccination, and a grow-ing danger of shortages.

The demise of America's small aircraft industry furnishes another casebook study in unintended outcomes. Until recently, the United States led the world in small airplane sales. But then came a spate of mostly groundless liability suits. With the cost of legal defense averag-ing several hundred thousand dollars a case and with total damage claims exceeding the net worth of Cessna, Piper, and Beech combined, all three U.S. manufacturers decided to stop making small airplanes. Meanwhile, as fewer new models were introduced and as our general aviation fleet aged, what had actually been a safety success story came to an end. After dropping steadily for decades, crash and fatality rates suddenly leveled off.

Still more important have been the chilling effects of capricious liability verdicts on innovation, which is so crucial to competitiveness and rising living standards. By threatening to neutralize expected prof-its, the mere risk of suits against new products can discourage research, development, and investment. Even more perversely, the introduction of improved products can suddenly leave old ones vulnerable to suit. After all, courts may interpret improved products as evidence that the old products were defective—something that automobile manu-facturers have learned to their regret. The potential effects of these disincentives are enormous. In the early 1970s, thirteen U.S. pharma-ceutical companies were engaged in developing new contraceptives and fertility drugs. Today there is just one. This outcome is by no means unique. The risk factor has been cited as a "go slow" incentive by top managers in many industries. According to the Conference Board, 25 percent of firms have discontinued some forms of research and development because of liability concerns.

But the harm that litigiousness does to America's economy is by no means limited to product liability. Medical malpractice is another fast-growing area of tort law that has generated huge and entirely unin-tended costs.

As we saw in Chapter 4, the inflationary impact of physicians' insur-ance premiums on the total cost of medical care is just the tip of a cost iceberg. In some specialties, the majority of physicians have been taken to court. For instance, 70 percent to 80 percent of obstetricians have been sued at least once; 20 percent have been sued three or more times. No wonder that doctors practice "defensive medicine," recom-mending tests, performing surgery, calling in consultants, prescribing drugs, and ordering hospitalization even when they know these steps are really unnecessary. In one survey, 41 percent of doctors reported prescribing extra tests because of concern about lawsuits; 27 percent said they provided additional treatments.

No one disputes that malpractice suits have exposed occasional quacks and compensated many deserving plaintiffs who failed to receive competent medical care. Product liability awards have also penalized irresponsible manufacturers and provided redress for individuals who have suffered real harm. Society must have some mechanism for achieving these goals.

But in these areas, and in fact throughout our legal and regulatory systems, we must ask ourselves whether the results of our haphazard attempts to protect individual rights are justifying the huge costs and whether we are actually devoting resources to solving the problems that pose the gravest threats to our welfare. I'm confident we'll agree that at times—as in racial discrimination and other civil rights cases where broader issues of social justice are at stake—the costs do justify the results. But often we'll find that the economic burden of litigation and regulation is unmatched by any commensurate payback.

FEAST-OR-FAMINE JUSTICE

Everywhere we look, we can find the same pattern: We hit small problems with a sledgehammer, while doing nothing to address much larger ones. The FDA won't let a new drug on the market that hasn't been tested for ten years and will yank off the shelves a tried-and-true one that benefits millions at the slightest hint it might pose health risks to one in ten thousand users. But because the FDA has no jurisdiction over agricultural products, aflatoxin, a common peanut mold and one of the most carcinogenic substances known to man, is entirely unregulated. At great cost, we measure and seek to eliminate minute trace amounts of such environmental toxins as PCBs. Although asbestos ranks close to 100 on the EPA's "Priority List of Hazardous Substances," it is the leading cause of health and safety litigation. Why? Because asbestos manufacturers have—or at least had—deep pockets.

Americans now live in a society with the highest rates of violent crime and the largest prison population in the developed world. Dysfunctional families, illiterate high school graduates, epidemics of drugs and teenage pregnancy, crumbling inner cities, and a debilitating syndrome of multigenerational poverty all create huge social costs that we are passing on to future generations. Accused criminals get their day in court—and rightly so. Yet when we are deprived of a public good whose value is incalculable (when, for example, we cannot go out at night without fearing for our lives), we seem to have little redress. These outcomes betray the lie behind our pretense: that by selectively protecting individual rights we are making this country a better place to live in.

What concrete steps can we take to correct the worst failings of our litigation lottery? Here are a number of possible steps.

- *Place a ceiling on huge and arbitrary awards for pain and suffering.* Although it may not be possible, or even sensible, to revert to traditional American legal doctrines by eliminating awards for pain and suffering, we certainly can stop the headlong rush toward unlimited damages. It is possible to devise more objective standards for awards for pain and suffering and mental anguish as well as to set more realistic absolute limits on compensation.

- *Limit punitive damages.* Justice does not require that we put into the hands of sympathetic juries the virtually untrammeled power to award any amount of punitive damages they see fit. Limits on awards could be imposed that would still achieve the desired deterrent effect without placing an impossible burden on our nation's economic resources. And whatever the cap, punitive damages should be limited to situations involving a degree of criminal negligence or shocking disregard of a duty to others.

- *Modify the doctrine of joint and several liability.* We need to strike a balance between protecting the rights of injured parties to receive damages, on the one hand, and limiting the degree of financial responsibility of defendants only marginally responsible for injuries, on the other. One sensible way to do this is to modify our current doctrine of joint and several liability by reintroducing a fault standard into product liability cases. A standard of comparative fault, for instance, might be applied in cases involving many defendants.

- *Restrict use of contingency fees.* Circumstances in which contingency fee arrangements are permitted should be curtailed. It is not necessary to allow the widespread use of such fees in order to ensure access of worthy litigants to the legal system. In many areas, such as bankruptcy and proceedings in surrogates' courts, legal fees are now subject to court approval. This system could be expanded, with the proviso that courts might award "bonuses" over standard rates for exceptional efforts and results. Such incentives would preserve much of what is best in our current contingency fee system without creating the "blank check" fee incentive that now exists.

- *Consider the English rule of court costs.* In many types of cases, it may be desirable to adopt a system like the English rule. Losers would pay the winners' legal expenses. Such a change, most experts agree, would have a restraining effect on frivolous lawsuits.

· *Encourage alternatives to formal litigation.* Recent advances in alternative dispute resolution should be encouraged and in many cases made mandatory. The advantages of certainty and quick resolution will be attractive to litigants apart from the benefit to society as a whole. But the benefits to society will be large indeed.

What all of these steps have in common is that they demand society face a choice: Someone must give up some kind of right if the community as a whole is to regain some rights of its own. To make this choice, we must develop a new mentality. In a crucial respect, our attitude toward litigation reflects the same cultural bias that underlies our entitlement ethos. Americans find it difficult to admit that doing something positive for an individual can have negative consequences for the community. Yet in our litigiousness, just as in our addiction to entitlements, private gain has often come at the expense of the public good.

We have made the United States a dangerous place to do business or—as many a doctor who has stopped at the scene of a traffic accident can attest—to be a Good Samaritan. And in our zeal to protect individual rights, we have allowed a massive infringement of other individual rights. Once again, Americans face a choice.

7

After the Cold War: Our Real National Security Interests*

For much of the postwar era, Americans thought of national security in military terms and as a matter of foreign policy. In my own life outside the business world, I have for several years served as chairman of two organizations—the Council on Foreign Relations and the Institute of International Economics—whose memberships, missions, and agendas in the past were often treated as mutually exclusive. Yet economic and foreign policy now substantially overlap. Our real security as a nation requires hard choices involving concerns we are used to treating as separate: military and nonmilitary, domestic and foreign.

This recent evolution brings us back full circle to a broader conception of U.S. national security that prevailed briefly after World War II. When our National Security Council was created in 1947, its mandate was to serve as a forum for integrating "domestic, foreign, and military policies relating to the national security." The NSC's early working definition of our national security is as appropriate now as then: "*to preserve the United States as a free nation with our fundamental institutions*

---

* This chapter is a much-expanded and revised version of a formal paper presented to a symposium of the American Assembly in May 1992, and later published as "The Primacy of the Domestic Agenda," by Peter G. Peterson and James K. Sebenius, in *Rethinking America's Security* (New York, 1992).

and values intact." This goal implied a combination of military, political, and economic objectives. Back in those days, such issues as America's role in rebuilding the shattered economies of Europe and Japan were routinely discussed at the NSC as priorities on a par with the creation of NATO, the U.S.-Japan security agreement, and other Cold War military matters. Additionally and significantly, our concept of national security at the time encompassed not just foreign military and economic considerations, but domestic threats and interests as well.

"HIGH POLITICS" AND "LOW POLITICS"

By the mid-1960s, however, national security policy meant *foreign* policy in general and *military* policy in particular. Rarely, if ever, were domestic economic challenges seriously considered part of our national security agenda. When I joined the government in the early 1970s, "high politics," to Henry Kissinger and its other masters, meant the metaphysics of MIRVs and other such seductive issues of managing the superpower balance of terror. By contrast, my responsibilities as the President's assistant for international economic affairs focused on trade, productivity, and the dollar—matters consigned to the realm of "low politics." I recall how Kissinger once chided me about being preoccupied with "minor commercial affairs." I retorted with surprise that he was being uncharacteristically redundant. In his world view, were there any *other* sorts of commercial affairs?

Throughout those years, whenever "economics" clashed directly with military "security policy," the United States gave precedence to the latter. Not so for other less affluent countries, whose military costs we often paid. They rarely subordinated economic to military concerns and delighted in being able to single-mindedly focus on building competitive economies.

In 1971, fresh from my private-sector experience in the intensely competitive camera and photography business, it seemed obvious to me that the ability of American companies to compete in world markets would be under increasing pressure. It seemed equally obvious that continued declines in our competitiveness would ultimately affect vital national interests, including "national security." It did not then seem too much of an intuitive leap to argue for a comprehensive, global, early-warning system to monitor our competitiveness. This kind of early-warning system, however, could simply never be put in place unless our most senior national security officials, including those at the economic intelligence unit of the C.I.A., were active participants. Nor could it happen if key government departments—Labor, Commerce, Treasury, the Federal Reserve—were unwilling to share their precious separate allotments of information turf. But my proposal was deemed a MEGO—a Nixon administration acronym for "my eyes glaze over."

The Japanese government was clearly orchestrating an industrial policy aimed at maximum penetration of U.S. markets. The French government was involved in commercial espionage directed against U.S. companies. Yet neither the White House, nor the State Department, nor the Pentagon was about to allow such concerns to interfere with the "overriding" importance of maintaining Japanese and European cohesion against the perceived threat from the Soviet Union.

Today, two decades later, it is even more obvious how *our own* economic concerns and constraints are beginning to influence, if not dictate, America's relations with others. For some time it has been clear that U.S. national security interests must include the development of policies that will increase our economic strength and domestic stability. Economics has been at the heart of the U.S.-Japan relationship in highly visible ways for more than a decade, but now it is also at the heart of the U.S.-Russia relationship, the U.S.-China relationship, and the U.S.-EC relationship.

A new definition of national security is now needed that recalls the vision of 1947 but augments it with more forceful economic and domestic policy components. I doubt that any foreign challenge of the 1990s will affect America's security as much as what we do—or fail to do—about pressing economic and social issues at home. We should not forget Eisenhower's admonition—exceptional in its time and place—not to "undermine from within that which we are seeking to protect from without."

With the Cold War over, our failure to have made progress on our pressing domestic agendas now threatens America's long-term national security more than external military threats. While the world remains a dangerous place requiring us to maintain military strength, our failure to invest in productive capacity, R&D, infrastructure, American education, our beleaguered underclass, and other domestic problems will have a greater *direct* impact on "the United States as a free nation with our fundamental institutions and values intact" than threats from abroad, whether ever more remote, such as the possibility of Russian nuclear attack, or quite real, such as the possibility of another Persian Gulf War. Moreover, continued failure to address and advance these domestic priorities will entail a progressive loss both of political will and of economic capacity to take actions abroad that are vital for our national security.

We have traveled far enough down this wrong road. In the future, the domestic and economic components of national security must be accorded the same level of importance as military issues and foreign policy concerns. To its credit, the Clinton administration has made an important move in this direction through the creation of the National Economic Council (NEC).

Let's reflect a bit. During the Bush administration, whenever there was an international crisis, most Americans, no matter what their political stripe, felt comforted by the President's expertise and the time he spent on foreign affairs. We were also encouraged by the level of competence brought to bear. Seeing Jim Baker, Dick Cheney, Larry Eagleburger, Colin Powell, Brent Scowcroft, and the President "working the issue" gave one a sense of confidence that the situation was in good hands. With respect to domestic affairs, it was just the opposite. Who has any idea who had responsibility for our imploding inner cities, our failures in education, or the dramatic rise in racial violence in recent years—let alone the economy? Wouldn't it have been nice, I often thought, to see the President come into the Oval Office in the morning and say, "I don't want to see my national security advisor. I want my domestic policy team in here to give me a briefing on the state of affairs at home." But that was wishful thinking. Foreign policy was still seen as "high politics"—and more receptive to presidential intervention and accomplishment.

To separate "foreign" from "domestic" policies is less and less possible. As we more effectively integrate these policies into a more coherent view of national security, the primacy of the domestic agenda in our national security will become evident. This broadened and more integrated national security agenda can no longer be treated as incidental to our "real" national security policy. It must now play a central role. Equally crucial is sustained presidential leadership to persuade the American people that the end of the Cold War has not exonerated us from the need to make tough and effective national security choices. If anything, that need is even more pressing today.

A NEW GENERATION OF THREATS

No one can dispute that the postwar world has been a dangerous one for the United States. With Soviet nuclear weapons and military adventurism, North Korean and Chinese aggression, assorted menacing regional conflicts, an expanding nuclear club, and the increasing threat of terrorism, "eternal vigilance" has been a necessity. Our experience with Iraq's malevolence and military capacities, still fresh in the public mind, sounds a current warning against complacency or neo-isolationism.

Yet the world is changing. With the breakup of the Soviet Union and the startling disintegration of its military establishment, any threat of a massive conventional attack on Europe has ended. Former defense secretary Harold Brown has said that we would have about five years of political warning of a new military buildup in the service of renewed Russian expansionism. Clearly, some of the old threats have diminished.

Beyond the now-defunct Warsaw Pact, consider China as a specific example of a receding threat. Quaint as it may sound today, much of our Asian defense policy was formulated with a keen remembrance of "hordes of Chinese" pouring across the Yalu River during the Korean War. I vividly remember, as a private citizen member of the President's Arms Control Advisory Board, hearing presentations by the Joint Chiefs of Staff even in the late 1960s about the threat of a Chinese nuclear first strike against us. China was an unambiguous and dangerous enemy. Today, however, American companies are rushing to trade with and invest in China. Without minimizing the political risks in China's future, or the implications of its expanding military powers, or its destabilizing sales of advanced missiles to countries like Iran, or its sponsorship of Pakistani nuclear ambitions, it is safe to say that America's ability to compete with Japan for Chinese markets is now a far more worrisome issue to America than the possibility of a Chinese nuclear first strike.

It is not that there are no developments abroad today that concern us militarily. Here, for example, is Defense Secretary Les Aspin's thoughtful assessment of the major current foreign threats to our security:

- Regional aggressors like Saddam Hussein in the Middle East, Southwest Asia, North Korea, and elsewhere
- Contagious conflict arising from ethnic or religious problems
- Nuclear proliferation and the spread of weapons of mass terror and destruction in Third World countries
- Conventional and high-tech terrorism
- Drug trafficking

But we must also be concerned with an emerging security threat of a different character: the self-inflicted *economic* weakness that now indirectly undermines our national security.

ECONOMIC WEAKNESS AS A NATIONAL SECURITY THREAT

Despite America's decisive action and seemingly effortless success in the war with Iraq, the 1990s will be a decade of new and increasing tension for the United States between international needs and domestic economic constraints. These constraints are caused by budget def-

icits, balance of payments deficits, growing foreign debt and debt
service costs, paltry levels of investment, anemic productivity growth, a
loss of technological leadership in cutting-edge industries, and a general decline in our global competitiveness. The awkward but enduring
fact is that, taken together, the claims of our various national interests
and global obligations will far outrun our available resources to sustain
or defend them. As the full implications of being the world's largest
debtor dawn on us *and* on the rest of the world, the gap between our
interests and our capacities will become larger, more obvious, and more
painful. As Eisenhower sought to teach us, military and economic security over time depend on each other; countries that lose control of
their economic destinies also lose control over their foreign policies.

New Resource Constraints and Threats

In the Gulf War, we saw the embarrassing anomaly of Uncle Sam
brandishing a saber in one hand while rattling a tin cup with the other.
It is hard to stand tall, as it were, on the bended knee of a financial
supplicant. One wag has noted that the new art of "collective leadership" involved America both leading *and* collecting. But perhaps that
is too kind; to many, it must have seemed like begging.

Over the last decade, we have already seen the effects of chronic
budget stringency on foreign policy interests: State Department allo-
cations (even to maintain embassies and consulates abroad) dropping
and under further siege, administration proposals for massive cuts in
foreign aid (except to Egypt and Israel), our virtual inability to offer
meaningful financial support to a newly democratic but fragile Philip-
pine government (a meager $50 million at a time Corazon Aquino
appeared before a joint session of Congress), and our financial paralysis in the face of enormous Eastern European changes (for example,
President Bush's embarrassing offer of $25 million at the time of his
visit to Hungary).

Just as cutting back on infrastructure maintenance during its 1970s
fiscal crisis ended up costing New York City vastly greater sums to later
repair the damage, the costs to the United States of its increasing
inability to respond constructively to changing opportunities and
threats abroad will grow still larger over time. America today faces
constraints on its policies that are very serious for a great power. These
constraints are spreading slowly, like a silent, progressive disease, and
the long-term effects are both cumulative and debilitating.

If we want to look at the kind of security threats that might confront
us over the next generation, we will have to open our minds to a range
of scenarios that have not been covered by Pentagon plans.

Mexico, for instance, presents a caldron of potential threats that
could easily become immense national security problems for the

United States—if Mexico's impressive recent progress should falter or if the North America Free Trade Agreement (NAFTA) should prove a stillborn or hopelessly compromised initiative. Political, social, demographic, economic, and financial trends combine to make an "explosion" south of our border much more likely than a nuclear war. If Mexico fails to grow economically in step with its population, which just passed 90 million on its way to a projected 130 million in the year 2010, Mexico's problems will become *our* problems. Needless to say, some 40 million *more* Mexicans, many unemployed and just across our effectively open border, could greatly accelerate illegal immigration. Just imagine the humanitarian and policy disaster if conditions in Mexico were to become as hopeless as those in Haiti!

Such outcomes might easily place Mexico—as well as certain other Latin American and Caribbean countries—among the external sucurity challenges that we face. Beyond the valuable, though partial, step of the North American Free Trade Agreement (and the Caribbean Basin Initiative), we would have to think about more comprehensive policies that include further debt restructuring or relief, immigration reform, investment flows, economic development programs, and a major, coordinated attack on drug problems.

In the future, the United States will face a bewildering array of new threats to its national security. Yet we have not come to grips with the nature of the post–Cold War era. While none of the new generation of threats are of the magnitude represented by the former Soviet Union's nuclear potential, many not only pose real concerns, but they may also prove especially difficult to defuse since they cannot be addressed by conventional foreign policy and military means. Such is obviously the case with the potentially destabilizing effects of explosive population growth in many Third World areas. I've already mentioned Mexico, but we also need to pay more attention to Algeria, Egypt, and the Sub-Saharan states of Africa. Refugee movements also present a major challenge that will be extremely difficult to handle.

Though I believe that most observers sense the importance of creative new initiatives in these areas, there seems to be a conspiracy of silence. Even at the cost of ignoring emerging threats to our national security, most avoid speaking out since doing something requires answering an awkward question: *Where will the money come from?*

Before the decade of the 1990s is out, I predict a further surge of domestic budgetary pressures leading to loud calls to bring home U.S. troops from Europe, Korea, and far-flung bases and ships. Ideally, this fiscal necessity should present major opportunities for enhanced security at lower cost. But on our current course the likely outcome will not be so desirable: We may have to take these steps as a result of fiscal crisis and in an atmosphere of severe trade tension.

Pressures to cut our military commitments will likely intensify just as the United States is striving to increase its share of world exports and to further reduce its current account deficit. Undoubtedly, the Japanese and Europeans—who, especially after the Gulf War, will increasingly be seen by resentful Americans as the affluent beneficiaries of long-time military free rides—will also be struggling to *retain* their trade positions as their economies emerge from their current recession. The chilly press conference following President Clinton's first blunt meeting with Japanese prime minister Miyazawa—what the Nixon administration would have euphemistically referred to as a "frank and constructive exchange"—underlined this festering and divisive trade tension. Moreover, as GATT's continuing deadlock warns us anew, competitive attempts to win global market share could give way to an antagonistic mercantilism. These economic conflicts will put serious strains on the cohesiveness of our military and political alliances. Acrimonious debates over allied military burden sharing that turn into fundamental questioning of collective purposes threaten the foreign policy landscape. It will be very difficult to keep trade wars limited to trade issues alone.

If we move to get our own budgetary house in order and attempt to further increase our exports, we will need to exert strenuous diplomatic efforts to induce other countries to adopt complementary economic policies to expand world trade. (The alternative of deep global recession or depression might also "solve" our trade and current account problems: We had a trade *surplus* nearly every year during the 1930s.) But such coordination will be very difficult to sustain in an atmosphere strained by either foreign policy disagreements or a slowly growing world economy.

New Vulnerabilities

There also are other risks inherent in running huge deficits and relying on foreign investors to fund them. Though it is unlikely to occur in a brazen form, a decision by foreign investors or central bankers to sell their large holdings of dollar-denominated securities or to cease buying additional ones—for economic *or* political reasons—would put us in deep trouble. We have generally played down such a possibility, often pointing to our potential leverage over Japan, a generally unflagging purchaser and holder of dollars. After all, roughly one-third of Japanese exports have come to our markets in recent years. Yet if we took serious protectionist measures aimed at the Japanese, they could threaten powerful retaliation by ceasing to fund all or a major part of our deficits. This could cause a dollar plunge, an interest rate surge, and a deep recession along with a host of other unpleasant consequences. While we have successfully navigated the late 1980s, when this scenario came closest to occurring, the underlying conditions that could trigger it are still present (and could once again be exacerbated as world economic recovery leads to rising U.S. and global capital demands).

Such action by the Japanese or others could parallel a dramatic 1956 foreign policy incident. Shortly before the U.S. elections that year, the British surprised the United States by orchestrating an invasion of Egypt in tandem with the French and the Israelis. Opposing this "risky, imperialistic" gambit, which was a response to the nationalization of the Suez Canal by Nasser, the United States forced the invading armies to withdraw by threatening to dump the pound sterling and cut off British access to international credit—measures that could have caused a steep devaluation of the pound, not to mention necessitated such highly unpopular policies as gasoline rationing. In our current position as the world's largest debtor nation, it is sobering to recall that America took these actions despite the fact that we were alliance partners and "special *friends*" of the British.

Commenting on the huge run-up in foreign debt that so hamstrung British foreign policy, historian Susan Strange observes that in effect Britain eventually became "the ward of the other developed countries of the non-Communist world. They constituted a creditors' club exercising the same watchful concern over the British economy that the Aid Consortia exercised over those of India, Indonesia, or Turkey." British financial observer Michael Stewart adds, "Given the stream of postwar balance of payments crises to which Britain has been subjected, I am amazed at the insouciance with which the United States has quietly amassed such an astronomical foreign debt." Yet Stewart should not be so amazed. The painful lessons of great debtorhood were hard for the British to perceive. As Susan Strange sums it up:

> . . . at a time when the British had amassed by far the largest government foreign debt per head of population of any country in the world . . . Most Britons . . . did not seem too sensitive to the "crushing burden"—either on their pockets or on their consciences. Their regret seemed a trifle perfunctory, their concern superficial, and their appreciation of the scale and urgency with which the creditors required repayment very vague indeed.

Economic reality in Britain, however, soon translated into harsh wage freezes and incomes policies as well as unpleasant constraints on public expenditures—just as has been the case in more recent years with many developing countries trying to work their way out from under staggering debt loads.

Of course, the United States is not postwar Great Britain. Among many differences, our debts are mainly in our own currency. Charles de Gaulle used to lament the "extravagant privilege" accorded the United States by our reserve currency status—our ability to repay foreign borrowing in our own currency. It was this special position that in part allowed us to avoid steep tax hikes in paying for the Vietnam War and that permitted our recent defense buildup, entitlement increases, and tax cuts to occur without still higher interest rates.

Further, should the Japanese (or other major buyers or holders of dollars or dollar-denominated assets) seek to exert direct foreign policy leverage on the United States today as a result of their newfound creditor position, they would simultaneously inflict grave costs on *themselves* from the resulting dollar plunge, huge foreign exchange losses, the likelihood that their exports would be sharply curtailed, the risk of global recession, and worse. But nowhere is it written that countries, in emotional political spasms, will not act in ways that prove counterproductive. And though governments and central banks tend toward relatively measured action, the herd mentality and psychological panics may sweep the private investing community, adding to underlying volatility and danger. (History has plenty of examples of speculative booms and busts, including the South Sea Bubble and "tulipmania.")

In sum, worldwide economic risks are increased by the domestic economic predicament in which we now find ourselves. Ironically, with the possibilities of lethal economic and financial action, reaction, and counterreaction, we now face the possibility of an economic version of MAD, or *M*utually *A*ssured *D*estruction, with which we uneasily lived in the military security realm throughout the Cold War.

Less dramatic than our "debt mountain," but more troubling in some ways, is the gradual decline in America's technological leadership. Indeed, even many of our most impressive new feats of military technology, from "smart bomb" targeting to new materials used in military aircraft, now rely quite heavily on engineering breakthroughs and component-sourcing in Japan. As we saw in Chapter 5, our increasing dependence on foreign sources of oil also has consequences in both the economic and national security realms.

All of these developments raise a still broader concern. Above and beyond the threat of a creditor strike or vulnerability to oil exporters or dependence on foreign sources for key components in military technologies, U.S. economic weakness will cause a subtle but very real worldwide shift in *political perception* of America. It is perhaps ironic, but in a world that is increasingly multipolar and complex the need for collective action still puts a great premium on the capacity of the United States to exercise leadership. As the Gulf War coalition showed, the United States is the only candidate for such a role. Yet as our finances become "leaner" and our domestic economic problems mount, we risk becoming both more reluctant and "meaner" in the exercise of our world leadership.

Today, many Americans are deeply troubled by our inaction in the face of the tragedy in Bosnia. Our Secretary of Defense has said that regional, ethnic, and religious conflicts are likely to be among the most dominant features of the "new world order" landscape—and that we must be prepared to meet the threats they pose. Yet, face-to-face with just such a crisis, we find ourselves setting the awful moral example of doing nothing. What signals does our inaction in Bosnia send to the rest of the world about our potential for continued moral and foreign policy leadership? How likely is it that our inaction will encourage the proliferation of other regional, ethnic, and religious conflicts around the globe? Finally, to what extent has our stance—or rather nonstance—on Bosnia been dictated by a perception at the White House that "it *really* is the economy, stupid." With so many pressing economic concerns on our domestic agenda, his advisors must have reminded President Clinton that he could not risk squandering his political capital on such a controversial foreign policy "diversion." If the U.S. economy were in better shape—and if our fiscal house were in order—it's difficult to believe we would not be taking a stronger stance.

Our capacity to exert leadership will surely be undermined to the extent that increasing domestic and economic failures cause us to be taken less seriously abroad. An extreme but instructive analogy, of course, is the effect of domestic failure in the former Soviet Union on the reality and perception of its global influence. Since perception can govern action, I believe that we will see our "friends" take more independent stances and our enemies act with less restraint, and generally, will see our presence, stature, and security diminished—unless we get our economic act together.

This is certainly not a time for America to stop leading; no one else will take our place. It is a time for a different and difficult kind of leadership. It is a time when we must lead by rallying a sometimes indifferent and often passive world. It is a time when we must supply the will, if not the wallet.

DIRECT DOMESTIC THREATS TO NATIONAL SECURITY

As I assess the changing character of external threats, I am struck by the emergence of powerful domestic trends that also threaten our security. Economic weakness and relative decline may *indirectly* constrain essential action abroad and increase our vulnerability. Yet other

domestic trends, if unchecked, may progressively and *directly* threaten
the basic character of our society's institutions and values.

Without dreams of a better life for our children, what kind of society
will we become? Can a stable center hold in the face of widening and
divisive income gaps between the rich and the poor, the old and the
young? Will citizens at the bottom exercise their civic and political
responsibilities when their basic economic security is threatened? Can
our freedoms and our fundamental values and institutions—that is to
say, our national security—remain intact?

We all remember what happened in Los Angeles in April 1992. The
days of rioting there that followed the acquittal of the police officers
accused of beating Rodney King were like a national televised warning
about the true dimensions of our insecurity in an increasingly polarized and divided society. Meanwhile, in New York, where I live, the
collective anxiety over a possibly devastating repeat of the World Trade
Center bombing is barely below the surface for many people. As I and
millions of other New Yorkers daily ascend into our multistory office
towers, we cannot help wondering about our safety. How do the conditions that give rise to these realities of daily life in America today
square with our forefathers' goals of providing for domestic tranquil-
ity, let alone national security?

My friend Dan Yankelovich, a most insightful pollster, wrote the
following words—before the Los Angeles riots—that bear repeating:

> [Our] situation is a formula for social and political instability. The
> history of this century shows that there is no more potent negative po-
> litical force than downward mobility. If the American Dream becomes a
> mockery for tens of millions of vigorous young Americans who, it should
> be remembered, represent mainstream American youth, not just inner
> city minorities, the nation can expect rising levels of violence, crime,
> drug addiction, rioting, sabotage, and social instability. The surge of
> racial tension between young whites and blacks is already an expression
> of it. We will be lucky if this is the worst of it.

REDEFINING THE TRADITIONAL NATIONAL SECURITY AGENDA

Members of the foreign policy establishment must look afresh at sub-
jects that have traditionally been outside their purview and study the
links to national security of intensely domestic and "political" topics.
Even reforms to grubby and unfamiliar particulars of our national
political life can matter a great deal to the attainment of our emerging
national security agenda. We may conclude, for example, that major
campaign-financing reform to limit the explosive growth of special

interest PACs is essential. These PACs direct vast resources to programs and purposes that often have little to do with our true national security priorities—while what ought to be our most pressing concerns, because they lack the same special-interest representation, often go starved for funding. Or we may decide that it is crucial to make adequate free television time available to political candidates. We have the most expensive campaign system in the world. In 1988, the typical candidate for the U.S. Senate raised and spent $3.7 million in the election bid. Since much of this money is raised from special interests, cutting "their" programs to fund investments in the general interest becomes particularly difficult.

Wherever we come down on these specifics, however, the general point is clear: National security demands a focus that looks well beyond traditional foreign policy and military issues. A strong foreign policy requires a strong economy; a strong economy depends on farsighted domestic policies. Thus, the interests that are most important on our domestic front should find their way onto the agendas of "foreign policy types." But by the same token, those who have up to now focused exclusively on issues that are overtly domestic and economic must broaden their angle of view to include traditional national security concerns.

I might add that there is no hard-wired barrier to taking a broader view of security concerns—even among the highest priests of traditional strategic thinking, such as Henry Kissinger. I well recall an incident in the summer of 1972 when I was in charge of the U.S.-Soviet Commercial Commission that was responsible for trade, most-favored-nation discussions, investment to develop Soviet energy and timber resources, Export-Import Bank credits, Lend-Lease repayment, and so forth. In the Nixon administration, we had *implicitly* linked all these issues to progress on foreign policy concerns (such as arms control and a Vietnam settlement). By then, it had become clear that economic issues were rapidly growing in importance to the Soviet Union and that they needed us in this area far more than we needed them.

Kissinger was to meet with Brezhnev and needed to understand the specifics of my mission. I sent him a dense, forty-page memo on all these economic and commercial issues and flew out forty-eight hours later to San Clemente (the Western White House) to meet with Nixon (but mostly with Kissinger). In that intervening period, he had boned up on the issues in the memo and, without prompting, went through them one at a time. I was immensely impressed at how Kissinger had woven them into what before might have been a pure foreign policy focus. Today, a far wider range of economic factors must be incorporated into national security policy.

AN INTEGRATED NATIONAL SECURITY BUDGET

Herb Stein, whom I've long admired from our days together in the White House, once wrote the following: "America is a very rich country. We are not rich enough to do everything, but we are rich enough to do everything that is important."

So I think the starting point is to ask ourselves: What is really important? This requires a much stricter definition of our national interest and security than in previous times. National interest must be defined, not in the context of what we would like to do, or have been doing, but in the context of what we must do. We must start with *zero-based* definitions, put both domestic and foreign threats down together, and select those programs that we find truly necessary. In short, we must make choices.

We have to consider threats to our national security on an *integrated* basis—domestic and foreign. In a rational world, what we should do, it seems to me, is list a series of possible threats and analyze each in terms of several criteria: How likely is the threat to materialize? What would be the negative effects if it does? What would be the cost of doing something about it? What would be our likely success if we decide to do something about it? And what happens if we do nothing?—a question usually not asked and rarely answered.

One of the pitfalls in developing such an integrated look at threats and opportunities is that foreign policy professionals are rather like medical professionals: They like to practice their specialty. They think of tradeoffs within "their field." Questions are typically posed in terms of stealth bombers versus less expensive aircraft or sea-based missiles versus land-based ones—never as a new generation of aircraft versus a new underclass program in Los Angeles.

Now we must find informed and humane generalists—as well as create a decision-making structure—that can traverse these diverse fields and determine real priorities. Which is more crucial, the Committee for Economic Development's $11 billion program to give underclass children a basic start in life or, at equivalent cost, maintaining some 65,000 troops in Europe? Or, since we now spend only about $100 billion annually on civilian-sector R&D—arguably a key to post–Cold War economic security—have we considered the security cost of a 10 percent reduction in defense compared to the 25 percent increase in civilian R&D that reallocating those funds might represent?

One thing we urgently require is a new comprehensive national security guidance document. Despite a number of attempts at delineating a "national security strategy" (the White House publishes one annually), these forays have generally produced little more than a compendium of interests, threats, and responses representing everyone's hobbyhorse and subjected to precious little incisive analysis or prioritization.

The nation has not produced a truly comprehensive guidance document since 1950 when the famous NSC-68 was drafted and published. Appropriate for the emerging bipolar superpower confrontation, NSC-68 laid out a coherent response to the major threat then facing the United States. And NSC-68, in essence the document spelling out the doctrine of "containment" of communism, served us well in guiding our national security policy for several decades. Today, with the collapse of the USSR, the disintegration of the "international communist movement," the reunification of Germany, and the rising importance of economic and domestic concerns, isn't it time the White House took the lead and drafted a new coherent and comprehensive strategy document addressing our *real* national security challenges?

Whenever the Pentagon has enumerated and analyzed national security threats in recent years, the implication seemed to be that these threats could all materialize, and that some of them could materialize simultaneously, necessitating the use of ground forces in several theaters at once. I very much doubt that that's the way such a multiple contingency would arise or be handled. The "two-and-a-half-wars" scenario of the last few decades is one the Pentagon has taken literally, preparing to field huge military forces in several parts of the world simultaneously. Given the changed nature of the world and our pinched purse, letting such a broad-gauge approach drive our defense spending would represent a choiceless relic of our past habits of making decisions. (As this book is going to print, Secretary of Defense Les Aspin was announcing the outlines of a new strategy to fight and win *two* regional wars simultaneously.)

There are many experts who certainly know much more than I do about the anatomy of our defense budget. However, I have read many recent studies of the subject, including Defense Secretary Aspin's interesting papers. I have also paid special attention to fellow Council on Foreign Relations directors Harold Brown and Admiral William Crowe, the former head of the Joint Chiefs of Staff. I came away from these discussions and analyses with the strong impression that we can meet our legitimate and very important external security needs with a defense budget substantially smaller than the one we have now. What we need, obviously, is to engage in a budgeting process that starts from a zero basis and builds up from the bottom only according to actual needs and the most pressing and realistic threats.

Once we have gone through this exercise, we should implement our new policies by way of *multiyear* rather than purely annual budgets. Moreover, along with an integrated national security budget should come serious consideration of the institutional changes needed to formulate and execute it. President Clinton's National Economic Council is a useful step in this direction. Yet we need to go further, asking what changes may be needed in the structure and operation of the associated congressional committees and in other areas to achieve what we must: a comprehensive, integrated strategy that combines our foreign and domestic interests *and* compels us to make tradeoffs.

RECONFIGURING THE MILITARY

Clearly, we need a different military structure in a post–Cold War world, but we ought not to simply engage in a top-down, across-the-board shrinkage of the military establishment that would leave us with the equivalent of the force we fielded during the Cold War, only one-quarter to one-third smaller. Drawing heavily on the views of thoughtful and experienced military experts such as Harold Brown, it strikes me that some of the right questions to ask about reconfiguring America's military are:

- *How do we achieve the proper balance between our active forces and reserve forces?* Congress and the administration want to place much more emphasis on reserve forces because they are supposedly less expensive than active forces. But these savings may be a false economy. For example, the Pentagon states that while these forces are cheaper, it takes an inordinate amount of time to bring reserve *combat* forces up to par. Indeed, according to testimony from the Army Chief of Staff, it takes nearly a year's training and preparation. Clearly, this kind of lead time will create serious problems in an overall national security strategy that must rely on rapid response to emerging global contingencies. In any bottom-up assessment of our security needs, we will find that we need both active and reserve forces. The question, then, is one of striking the optimal balance.

- *What is the proper tradeoff between sea-based and land-based air power?* Or to put the question another way, do we still need twelve expensive aircraft carriers and attendant surface fleets or can we make do with less? Operation Desert Storm reinforced the lessons learned in other wars: that land-based air power can generate more combat sorties, carry far heavier payloads over much longer distances, and do it far cheaper than carrier-based air power—if land bases are available. The Navy's large sea-based air force may have been important during the Cold War, but it appears likely that land-based air power, particularly long-range bombers such as the B-1 and B-2, can indeed make up for a reduction in expensive carrier battle groups. Many experts believe there is no rational case for maintaining a force of twelve carriers other than to show the flag and maintain a forward presence. Such concerns are not inconsequential, but we can surely address them with fewer carriers.

- *What kind of land forces do we need and what is the proper balance between the Army and Marines in this area?* Last summer, Senator Sam Nunn raised the issue of whether the Army and Marines should field duplicate expeditionary forces. This is a terribly important question since the strategy of the United States is now focused on responding to regional wars. For the last half century, the Army's main role was defending Europe from Soviet attack. But since that mission has been rendered moot by the end of the Cold War, it now is touting its ability to rapidly move Army forces to global hot spots. This sounds remarkably like the traditional mission of the Marine Corps, which has grown so large that it is now one-fourth the size of the entire U.S. Army. Perhaps it is time to decide whether the country needs two land armies often competing for the same mission.

- *Do the Marines need their own independent fixed-wing air force, or can the Navy and Air Force provide that support?* The Marine Corps maintains a fixed-wing tactical air force based on the maxim that the Marine air-ground team is so unique that only the Corps can provide the high-quality, close-air support needed by the Marine ground elements. This reasoning may have been acceptable in the past, but needs serious study in this era of tight defense dollars. If it turns out that the Navy is capable of providing air support to the Marine ground elements ashore, we may conclude that the Marines do not need their own independent fixed-wing air force and that we could save billions by using Navy fighter aircraft to do the job.

- *How can we better coordinate and eliminate overlap among our three independent tactical air forces?* In the event of war, there is always a difficult argument about whether there should be a unified air commander. There usually is, but he is less efficient than he could be, since this eventuality is not planned and coordinated. One approach would be to let the Air Force see to our long-range interdiction mission, even with tactical air, and then force it to trade off between long-range bombers (that fly from the United

States to anywhere in the world) and forward-deployed, land-based systems. The Navy might then handle a degree of battlefield support with the Air Force providing some close air support—with both understanding from the outset that they would be subject to the Army commander. Further, they might be assigned in the same way that the Marine division air wing now works, with command directly given to the ground forces.

- *How many expensive new aircraft development programs can we afford?* In a study by the Congressional Research Service (CRS) last year, analysts stated that the cost of tactical aviation programs alone could amount to $350 to $400 billion over the next two decades. Senator Sam Nunn, chairman of the Senate Armed Services Committee, recently told Defense Secretary Les Aspin that the United States simply cannot afford full funding for the tactical aircraft programs the administration is proposing in its fiscal year 1994 defense budget.

- *What kind of air defense of U.S. territory do we need and what kind of missile defense program should we fund?* Sadly, current law provides little guidance. For example, the law governing roles and missions for the Pentagon does not even mention ballistic missile defense. As a result, all services have extremely vague responsibilities for the air defense of the United States itself. This confusion in turn has allowed the services to build redundant forces and capabilities. The Air Force and Army maintain completely separate high-altitude air defense capabilities and command structures. In addition, the new Ballistic Missile Defense Office is now developing a Theater High Altitude Air Defense (THAAD) for the Army that further blurs the line between what are called "point and area defense systems," and which will undoubtedly intensify jurisdictional disputes between the Air Force and Army. A further example involves air defense carried out by the Air Force with interceptor aircraft and by the Army with surface-to-air missiles and antiaircraft weapons. This split makes operational control and coordination more difficult. Without advocating who should get the mission in any particular case, it is clear that such issues of duplication and coordination need re-examination.

In July 1992 Senator Nunn delivered an important speech aimed at the Pentagon and calling for a fundamental *reform* of roles and missions, not merely another tepid endorsement of the status quo. The chairman of the Joint Chiefs, General Colin Powell, publicly released the Pentagon's long-awaited report on roles and missions the following February. It contained many recommendations for improving training and support responsibilities and some important suggestions regarding the command and control of combat forces. But those essentially cosmetic matters aside, it left the core of the services' functions—and the consequent duplications and redundancies—intact. Very little in the report focused on consolidating duplicate—and sometimes triplicate—service responsibilities. Not surprisingly, Senator Nunn and the new chairman of the House Armed Services Committee, Representative Ron Dellums, have expressed their disappointment over Powell's report. This debate is extremely important for the country because it raises questions that have not been seriously addressed since the 1948 Key West Agreement. Powell's report was a useful first step, but this review process needs to go much further.

Above and beyond the kinds of changes I've already discussed, we must develop a more effective institutional response to the reality that we will often have to work with multinational forces (as in the Persian Gulf War). If UN sanction will be needed for intervention in regional conflicts, we should think through how best to rationalize the command, role, and mission implications of such forces. This will be particularly true to the extent that countries begin to earmark force units in advance for use in UN-sponsored or -sanctioned multilateral peacekeeping efforts.

I am not saying that all of the potentially ambiguous and conflicting roles and missions of the armed forces necessarily require change, but that they need a thorough re-evaluation and assessment in order for the overtly military component of our security to be efficiently provided. Rationalizing these roles and missions will inevitably involve hard choices. Defense Secretary Les Aspin has thought carefully about such issues and has proposed an initial military budget that moves toward reform—though he had to retreat on certain key provisions, since even liberals and longtime military critics such as California congressman Ron Dellums balk when facilities in *their* districts are candidates for cutting. This kind of politics threatens to leave us mired in our usual choiceless state of affairs.

Let me now shift gears and add an absolutely crucial caveat. Even given the decline of traditional external military threats to our security and the rise of internal, economic, and social threats, we certainly cannot allow ourselves to become so preoccupied with domestic threats that we *ignore* the continuing need for adequate military resources. Indeed, there can be no greater or more important role for government than ensuring that the nation is safe from external attack and that its vital interests abroad are protected. We must avoid the kind of wholesale disarmament on which we embarked after both world wars as well as after Vietnam when we ended up with a "hollow force"—tanks that didn't run, planes that didn't fly, ships that didn't sail. All of this then had to be reversed on a crash basis at vast cost.

We must have the right forces for this post–Cold War era, *ready* to fight despite the downsizing in personnel and budgets. The Clinton administration has proposed a very taut defense budget over the next five years. By 1998 defense outlays are expected to account for only about 3.2 percent of GDP—a smaller share of our economy than at any time since Pearl Harbor. That will mean that the defense budget will have declined in real terms by about two-fifths from its late-1980s peak, with our overall military force structure reduced by at least one-quarter and key areas like weapons "modernization" hit much harder.

Significant cuts in defense spending are certainly warranted given today's global environment. Such reductions do demand, however, that we drastically revamp how we conduct our defense management, especially with respect to acquisition and defense industrial policies. Now more than ever waste and inefficiency will threaten our ability to equip our forces with state-of-the-art armaments.

We must therefore think hard about the specific steps we need to take to ensure that we do not wind up again with a "hollow force." Our military is staffed by top-flight talent equipped with outstanding instruments of war. That could quickly erode unless we take a more businesslike approach to defense management. In this vein, I have learned much from discussions with the senior staff of Business Executives for National Security (BENS),* an organization representing over 1,500 business leaders across the country. They advocate a reform agenda in part built around the following initiatives:

1. *Reducing Overhead and Infrastructure.* Always resistant to change, our stateside military base infrastructure, even after the June 1993 announcements of base closings, is being reduced only 15 percent while personnel levels are being cut by as much as a third and "modernization" budgets by 50 percent from their late 1980s peaks. The most difficult challenge is to close unneeded military bases and facilities in the face of tremendous congressional pressure to keep installations open in members' districts. BENS played an important role in promoting the creation of the Base Closure and Realignment Commission and has actively supported its efforts to shut down unneeded facilities.

2. *Wholesale Reform of Acquisition Practices.* Deputy Secretary of Defense

---

* I am particularly grateful to Tyrus Cobb, President, and Bob Gaskin, Vice President for Policy and Programs.

Bill Perry estimates that as much as 40 percent of our acquisition costs are attributable to management overhead (versus 10 percent to 15 percent in commercial enterprises). Overhead costs must be reduced. In addition, continuation of procurement programs based on service-defined requirements is unacceptable today; instead, increased centralization of acquisition activities is needed. Layers of oversight bureaucracies must be eliminated, complex military specifications reduced, and armies of supervisors abolished. As a rule, the Pentagon should "buy commercial" unless unique military needs dictate otherwise.

3. *Integrate Our Defense and Commercial Technology Industrial Base.* More reliance on dual-use facilities is necessary. Maintenance of costly plants to produce military equipment alone should be avoided except in certain cases where alternative producers are not likely to emerge (e.g., submarine construction). The Pentagon urgently needs to undertake the analysis necessary to determine what sort of "defense industrial base" is really required.

4. *Insist on Real Alliance Burden Sharing.* Simply put, our allies need to contribute a lot more in the way of international burden sharing. Unilateralism in dealing with global crises should be avoided in favor of multilateral cooperation in money and personnel. While there will continue to be no substitute for American leadership, allies such as Japan and Germany must take much more responsibility. We must also rely increasingly on international institutions. Above all, this means the United Nations, whose peacekeeping and peacemaking capabilities we must help build.

In this new world order, burden sharing must also include newly affluent allies such as South Korea, Taiwan, Singapore, and Hong Kong. These countries are in many ways more worried about the present world situation than they were in the U.S.–Soviet Cold War era. China with its rapidly expanding military clout is their next-door neighbor. These smaller countries ask themselves: If China continues to build its military might (or if there is radioactive political fallout from North Korea's efforts to develop nuclear capabilities), can Japan be far behind? Clearly, this region needs new security alliance arrangements.* The United States is still seen as the only major military power that can provide the indispensable elements of *reassurance* and *balance*. We must remain the ultimate guarantor of regional stability. But why should these smaller but affluent countries not share more in the burden? As coincidental as

---

*Such arrangements would most certainly have to include Japan, and, over the long run, could also include China and Russia.

this may seem, I had the opportunity to discuss this very notion with Lee Kuan Yew, Senior Minister of Singapore, in the summer of 1993. I was pleasantly surprised to find that this farsighted statesman has already been espousing a doctrine of expanded military burden sharing in money or in kind—and with concrete results. Singapore, for example, is now providing logistical support for our aircraft and ships that were previously maintained in the Philippines.

5. *Toward a Congressional Build-down.* If the armed forces are undergoing as much as a one-third reduction in personnel why should the mammoth system of congressional oversight not be subjected to a similar build-down? As it is now, the Pentagon is "guided" by 100-odd committees and subcommittees exercising "oversight" responsibility. The number of committees must be reduced, staffs trimmed substantially, and intervention—such as the insistence on annual budget reviews—pared back.

Beyond the sheer waste entailed in this kind of "feast-or-famine" approach to military planning, we should remember the effect on morale. Many very talented people have joined the armed forces in recent years on the implicit understanding that they would have military careers. We risk severely damaging their eagerness, enthusiasm, and commitment when we contemplate reducing the size of the military at a rate far in excess of normal attrition but leave so many bureaucrats with their jobs intact.

If we rebuild the military budget from the ground up to meet today's and tomorrow's threats, not yesterday's, we can obtain a military capability that is at once less costly than today's force structure *and* more suited to the challenges we are most likely to face. We could achieve this double blessing if we (1) shift emphasis from today's focus on forces designed to fight the former Soviet Union to the less costly needs of regional and mobile deployment, and (2) enhance and institutionalize the system of financial burden sharing with our allies and, in particular, Japan.

A NEW GLOBAL BARGAIN WITH JAPAN: BEYOND OUR BILATERAL TRADE PROBLEM

Beyond the reconfiguration of our own military forces in a broader national security context, we need to devise creative schemes of burden sharing with our allies in order to achieve a more secure world at lower cost to our budget. In such a new global bargain, while there would be special roles for Germany and the European Community, there is a very strong need for a new type of U.S.–Japan partnership.

Whereas peacekeeping was once primarily a military issue, today's world requires us to think increasingly of "economic peacekeeping." Today's annual investment by Japan in the two types of global security—economic aid and military defense—constitutes about 1.5 percent of its GDP. This compares with about 5 percent in the United States (even after our recent defense cuts) and 3 to 5 percent in most European countries. In the new partnership I envision, Japan should raise its commitment to global security to at least 3 percent of its GDP. Most of this increase in security spending should flow not into Japan's defense budget, but toward enhancing global *economic* security.

In this new U.S.–Japan partnership, our two countries would be equal partners, but with a division of labor corresponding to the comparative advantage of each. Japan would be a senior partner on economic issues; the United States would be a senior partner on political and military ones. But that division of labor, straightforward as it appears, cannot be black and white. The United States cannot be absolved of economic responsibilities to the world order, nor can Japan ignore political and military security issues. Although Japan has in fact recently begun to assume some greater responsibility in military matters, it still needs as full and vigorous a debate about the direction of its foreign policy as America does about its domestic economic agenda.

I am certainly not proposing that Japan remilitarize. Memories of Japan's role in World War II continue to haunt its East Asian neighbors, who strongly oppose a militarily resurgent Japan. Some of Japan's domestic politics and attitudes also sound powerful notes of caution about such a course of action today. Moreover, for Japan to choose a military role comparable to that of the United States would amount to economic folly. Given today's extraordinary global needs for investment capital, especially by countries like the emerging market economies of Eastern Europe, whose very survival remains an open question, it would be foolishly redundant for Japan to invest in a massive military arsenal, and by doing so, perhaps stimulate its worried neighbors to do the same.

For the world's largest debtor nation to protect the world's largest creditor nation is not exactly the natural pattern of things in history. At the moment, such phrases as "new world order" and "new collective security arrangements" sound like empty clichés. But I believe that is only because insufficient intellectual and political groundwork has been done to begin to flesh out and implement those ideas. Both Japan and the United States must make a firm commitment to actualizing a common vision of the new world order.

A key starting point in putting meat on the bones of our new part-

nership should be a new emphasis on the long-term cooperative aspects of the U.S.-Japan security agreement that looks beyond our
shared concerns about the former Soviet Union (and whether it might
remilitarize). Both countries should spell out their long-term security
commitments anew, and these should be endorsed by the U.S. Congress as well as the Japanese Diet.

Japan should also consider whether it wishes to play a greater
burden-sharing role in defending the security of the Asia-Pacific region. While not expanding the geographical scope of its self-defense
efforts, Japan may want to look at issues such as expanding the minimal role its Diet has so far approved for participation in UN-backed
peacekeeping operations or other multilateral security efforts, including regional efforts in both security and economic development.

Perhaps Japan can't and shouldn't send regular troops to conflicts
such as the war in the Persian Gulf. But it can be the *lead investor* in
many multilateral projects of the industrial countries that are just as
vital to world security. I am thinking especially of potential Japanese
leadership in developing alternative clean energy sources on a global
scale. Given the capital shortage in this country, and the billions we're
expending on defending the Middle Eastern oil fields, it is now very
difficult for the United States to take the lead in the massive research
and investment projects that are required to develop alternative energy sources, or to tap the world's remote fossil fuel sources outside the
Middle East, such as those in the former Soviet Union and China. I
recognize that there might be some complications in pursuing this
agenda—including Japan's dispute with Russia over the Kurile Islands
north of Japan. Even so, I believe it is politically feasible for Japan to
play a lead role in funding and even coordinating this badly needed
global energy effort.

Can Japan play a similar leadership role in dealing with the crisis in
global environmental security, and in developing ways to respond to
global warming? Can Japanese companies invest in greenhouse-
friendly energy projects—such as natural gas development in China
and the former Soviet Union? Finally, can Japan also take the lead in
developing solutions to other common problems on the world's
agenda in areas as wide-ranging as earthquake technology and medical
research?

Japan has now emerged as a leader in official development assistance. However, this is only compared to the generally low levels among
other large industrial nations. The question I am posing is: Can Japan
really transfer major resources, including technology and management
expertise, to the countries emerging from communism, so that the
precious momentum toward freedom, democracy, and market economies we have witnessed in the last few years is sustained? Democracy, as

we are seeing in the former Soviet Union, has a hard time flourishing in the midst of economic chaos. With two-thirds of the world in poverty, transferring major resources to the Third World to prevent a further global polarization of haves and have-nots is also urgent. On both of these fronts, Japan has a unique role to play.

I am not proposing a grand version of checkbook diplomacy. Japan should not be seen as some sort of automatic teller machine one goes to every time there is a world problem that requires cash. Such a role would be demeaning for both Japan and America and would ultimately breed mutual resentment. Certainly, the United States, a country founded on the principle of "no taxation without representation," can appreciate that if Japan is to play a leading role in solving world problems, it must have a real seat at the table of global decision making. The United States, as well as the world's other major powers, must make room for Japan to participate fully in that process and exercise its leadership effectively. A partnership in which we try to divide responsibilities, but not power and decision making, is obviously doomed.

Some useful symbolic ways to aid this process would be to create a permanent membership on the UN Security Council for Japan (perhaps this could be done without opening the Pandora's box of charter revision), to have a leading Japanese financial figure as head of the World Bank or the IMF, and to bring Japan in at least as an observer to a redefined NATO. Commensurate with these roles, the world would expect Japan to be a leader in the GATT process, especially through the example of its own market liberalization. We already have a small but encouraging sample of how Japan can respond when it shares in the power and glory of new responsibilities. Since Madame Sadako Ogata became the UN High Commissioner for Refugees, Japan has materially enlarged its contribution to refugee efforts.

As Japan grows out of its former role of "followership," the question becomes not its competence to lead, but rather the content of its leadership. What is Japan's vision? What does Japan stand for or really care about? What is its global ethic? Japan, it would seem, has much the same problem that President Bush admitted to: great difficulty in articulating "the vision thing." When a nation fails to communicate its values, ideals, and goals, the rest of the world understandably sees calculation and self-interest as the sum total of its behavior.

There is indeed a widespread perception that Japan is a free-rider, a taker and not a giver, always begrudging in its contributions to causes that transcend its narrow short-term self-interest. Yet the global challenges we need Japan to take the lead in meeting in the 1990s are enormous: environmental cleanup, clean energy R&D, and foreign aid, to name some of the most pressing. If Japan is to assume the new role in world affairs I have been outlining, it will have to overcome this "imbalance" or "leadership gap," as it has sometimes been called.

With Japan as elsewhere, the United States must of course continue its *own* leadership role. Our role is exceptional: If not us, who? But in terms of fiscal contributions from the United States to tomorrow's global agenda, our constraints at home are obvious. This circumstance could be a great opportunity for Japan *if*—and it's a huge IF—it chooses to embrace its new and fuller role in world affairs. Just as the post–World War II era in many ways represented the finest hour for the United States, given our leadership role in the United Nations, the World Bank and IMF, and the Marshall Plan, so might Japan's finest hour result from its seizing the opportunities now before it.

Japan's reluctance to be proactive sometimes leads people to react to real generosity on Japan's part with skepticism and to focus more on the difficult haggling process it took to get to that generosity. This was clearly the case with public reaction to Japan's ultimate $13 billion contribution to the Gulf War. Many Americans thought Japan did all too little, even though Japan finally did make a major contribution. In other words, Japan's gradual and incremental actions often appear to be grudging. That is something only Japan can change.

I was brought up in a farm town in Nebraska where we murdered the English language. We used to talk about "ambiv-ay-lence" out there. There's a lot of ambiv-ay-lence in Japan and in the United States about ourselves and each other. On the one hand, the Japanese complain endlessly about *gaiatsu* (foreign pressure). And yet many Japanese leaders will privately say that without the foreign pressure, Japan wouldn't have been likely to make any hard decisions to help others.

An experience of my own has probably also influenced my judgment. When I was in the Nixon administration I regularly received delegations of chief executives from top Japanese companies. They would always start by telling me about this "humble little Japanese steel company," this "small island nation," or this "weak resourceless country," as against that huge superpower, the United States—but I knew better. I had been CEO of Bell and Howell, an American company that had already been hammered by Japanese competition in cameras.

The exchange rate for the yen was then 360 to the dollar, as it had been since 1949. I had done many studies for the President showing him the trends in productivity and labor costs in America and Japan over the last ten to fifteen years. Clearly, given Japan's immense progress, an exchange rate set in 1949 was no longer appropriate in 1971. Yet when we raised the issue of the yen being revalued, given these profoundly different circumstances, the reaction we typically got at every level of the Japanese government was a great reluctance to do anything, and an endless rehash of Japan's "humble" status.

Confronted with the fact that the yen was obviously greatly overvalued, having tried every avenue we could to get a revaluation of the yen vis-à-vis the dollar, and facing huge foreign liability claims at a time when we were effectively on the gold standard, I finally came to support, along with others, closing the gold window and imposing an import surcharge. I regarded that surcharge not as part of a protectionist strategy, but rather as a negotiating lever for achieving a more flexible monetary system and a more open trading system. When President Nixon announced this on August 15, 1971, it was presented as a step linked to new monetary negotiations and new GATT trade talks.

But then, as now, we were ambivalent in this country. My own ambivalence about the right amount of *toughness* to use was heightened when I heard our then Treasury secretary, John Connally, speak. Connally seemed to symbolize America's western cowboy roots and our instincts toward unilateralism. He suggested to the President and several of us in the Oval Office that the import surcharge was playing so well in America that we should keep it on for another year, which would conveniently take us through the next election. I won't fully report on the heated discussion that followed, but it showed that these "tough" negotiating agendas are intricate mechanisms that can play into the powerful unilateralist tendencies of a country like ours.

The ambivalence continues in the present. Ask people in the Clinton administration if they want and expect Japan to play a greater leadership role—sharing the environmental burdens, the clean energy burdens, the foreign aid burdens, and so on—and they will say yes, of course, Japan should share much more of the responsibility for global leadership than it has thus far. But if you ask the next question, whether we are prepared to share the glory and yield the power and the prestige—whether we would be pleased to see a Japanese president of the World Bank or IMF, you'll often get silence. The realities, however, dictate that we begin to understand that burden sharing, power sharing, and glory sharing all go hand in hand. America's taste for populist unilateralism must give way to consensus-building and bilateral decision making. This notion of shared leadership is not our thing. Indeed, it is almost "un-American" in some quarters. We are used to being *the* leader. However, we can't sustain new-world-order rhetoric with an old-world-order mentality.

Although I have focused here on the Japanese side of the equation, Japanese leadership initiatives are not, of course, the only ones we need—and cannot exist in a vacuum. Germany, the world's other leading creditor nation, must also take an increasing share in responsibility for economic peacekeeping, as it has already begun to do with its substantial financial aid to the former Soviet Union. The European Community, a key new institution of the multipolar world, will also have a large role to play.

*   *   *

In short, we need to reconceptualize "national security" more broadly
in the terms of the mandate that the National Security Council had in
the late 1940s: "*to preserve the United States as a free nation with our
fundamental institutions and values intact.*" Our national security is no
longer most usefully thought of mainly in military and foreign terms;
it has important economic and domestic components as well. Changing threats, both internal and external, must be soberly evaluated,
keeping in mind that economic weakness at home can sap our political
will and financial capacity to pursue our security interests abroad.

To address these challenges, I have urged four broad steps: expanding our national security agenda to include sometimes unfamiliar domestic priorities that nonetheless bear on our real security, developing
a zero-based "integrated national security budget" in which foreign
and domestic priorities and threats are assessed together, rethinking
the configuration of the military in such a context, and negotiating a
new global bargain that sensibly shares the burdens of economic and
military peacekeeping with our allies, especially Japan. Taken together,
these steps would greatly enhance our security. They are the *real*
choices we must make in an area where we have often behaved as if our
resources were infinite and choices were unnecessary.

PART II

The Choices We Must Make

8

Saving Our Future

The American Dream embodies many different ideas and ideals. Open frontiers. Religious freedom. The melting pot. Equality of opportunity. But a constant of this Dream has always been faith in a future of rising living standards—the expectation that we will do better if we work hard and that the next generation will do better than we did. That was my father's American Dream. It remains the dream of many fathers and mothers today. I'm sure it's a big part of yours.

Today the American Dream is darkening. Living standards have hardly budged in two decades, and for young families with children, they have plunged off a cliff. Middle-class Americans find themselves adopting a siege mentality as aspirations evaporate for a better home or a good college education for their children. When young people today are asked if they ever expect to do as well as mom and dad, most say no. A growing underclass languishes in the basement of our economy. Everywhere we look, we see the need for new investments in our future—to make illiterate school kids literate, to train unskilled workers for our new information-age economy, to develop cutting-edge technologies, to rebuild our crumbling highways and bridges. But we seem to have lost the will to make farsighted choices on behalf of tomorrow. Instead we hunker down and try as best we can to protect what's ours. That's what exploded expectations do to a society.

Imagine for a moment what America might be like if we had never faltered back in the early 1970s—if our economy had remained just as productive and if our living standards had continued to grow at their earlier pace. Measured in today's dollars, the typical full-time American worker in 1973 produced $39,200 in Gross Domestic Product.

(Not all of that, of course, ended up in his or her paycheck; business kept some in profits and dividends.) If our economy had continued to do as well as it did during the American High (1947–73), that same worker would have produced $59,000 in GDP by 1991—an increase of $19,800, or 51 percent! Even if U.S. productivity had just kept up with its long-term (1870–1973) historical average, that worker would have produced $56,000 by 1991—an increase of 43 percent. In reality, the average U.S. worker in 1991 produced only $42,400—an increase of $3,200, or a mere 8 percent.

Such differences are the stuff that dreams are made of. The incomes of American families would have shot up along with per-worker GDP—making everything from housing and health care to college educations and exotic vacations more affordable. It's difficult to believe we would witness the same divergence in fortunes between old and young, rich and poor that the past two decades of stagnant living standards brought. In a rapidly growing economy, a rising tide would indeed have lifted all boats.

And what about the public resources available to carry out collective missions? What about everything from helping disadvantaged kids get a fair start in life to defending democracy to exploring space to protecting the environment? If America's post-1973 economy had kept growing at its long-term historical pace, annual federal revenues in 1991 (at present-day tax rates) would have been about $370 billion higher than they were. We would not have a budget deficit. We would have a large surplus with which to pursue many social goals we now cannot afford.

FAST FORWARD TO 2015

Now run America's history on fast forward. Travel with me into the future, to the year 2015. It sounds like a date in which we might set a science fiction story, but it's not so remote. It's about the time toddlers like my grandson Peter Cary will graduate from college. If the dismal trends of the past two decades persist, per-worker GDP in 2015 will have grown by only $4,300 above 1991's level. Once again, America's living standards will hardly have budged over a span of about two decades.

But let's suppose we could raise the growth rate in output per U.S. worker by just one percentage point per year. That would put it at 1.4 percent annually, up from 0.4 percent since 1973. A modest-sounding goal? Perhaps. Our average in the century before we faltered was 2 percent; from 1947 to 1973 it was 2.3 percent. Our goal would boost us back just *half the way* to what we once achieved. The positive consequences for our future, however, would be profound. With a one percentage point boost, per-worker GDP will have grown by $16,800 in 2015—nearly four times as much as in a status quo future.

If we continue on our current trajectory, our time on history's stage will be remembered with bitterness as the period when America squandered its legacy of positive endowments, and became a second-rate economy and a second-rate world power. But if we take the steps necessary to make the remainder of the 1990s the "Decade of Investment," the turn of the century will become an era of renewed prosperity and influence for America—an era of rising incomes, a more competitive economy, better education, more secure jobs, and the ability to "stand tall" in the world again without borrowing on bended knee. It would signify a fuller and more satisfying future for all generations to follow—a renewal of the American Dream. Posterity would look back and thank us for the sacrifices *we* made.

In talking about why people make sacrifices on behalf of the future, Abraham Lincoln once made this observation:

> Few can be induced to labor exclusively for posterity, and none will do it enthusiastically. Posterity has done nothing for us; and, theorize on it as we may, practically we shall do very little for it unless we are made to think we are, at the same time, doing something for ourselves.

Lincoln's point is that few of us act out of pure altruism and few out of pure self-interest. Most people, most of the time, act out of some mixture of the two. Fortunately, these two motives often overlap. If they didn't, the only workable society would be a community of saints or a community in which everyone must be bribed or punished to behave. The one you'll never find; the other you'd never want to join.

So why should we care about the future? The first answer is: It's the right thing to do. It's right for us as parents to want a better life for our children. It's right for us as citizens to want a better life for those who come after us. But the second answer just as clearly is: By caring about the future we also stand to benefit our future selves. The great majority of us now alive will still be here in 2015! If you're twenty-five your odds are about 95 out of 100. If you're forty your odds are about 90 out of a hundred. Even if you're sixty, the odds are about even you'll see the brave new world. Is there any doubt what kind of future we should strive to make? If we are hard-pressed and hopeless today, how much more so will we be after two more decades of stagnant living standards and shattered dreams?

Later in this chapter, I'll explain exactly how we can attain that future we all desire by engineering a massive shift from consumption to investment. When we examine the numbers, we'll find that in look-

ing for the savings we need to invest in our future, all roads lead to a
familiar place: the federal budget. Our deficits, after all, are just negative public savings. By soaking up our already shallow pool of private
savings, deficits crowd productive investments out of private capital
markets. Indeed, since 1980 financing the federal deficit has been
canceling out between half and two-thirds of all private thrift in the
United States. As far as the benefits to our economy are concerned, it's
as if we had never saved those dollars. At the same time, deficits crowd
future-oriented spending out of the federal budget itself and make it
much harder for us to find the resources to fund collective investments
that we don't leave to private capital markets. When it comes to boosting our own and our children's living standards, balancing the budget
is the surest and the fastest way to get the savings we need. If we are to
realize a positive vision of America's future, we'll have to put our fiscal
house in order. It's an economic imperative.

But there is another compelling reason to balance the budget: equity between generations. It's to this that I want to turn first. The
choices we are making publicly—or rather, the choices we are failing
to make—are not just undercutting our own and our children's future
living standards. The massive debts we are passing on will indenture
our posterity. Thomas Jefferson once said, "The principle of spending
money to be paid by posterity . . . is but swindling futurity on a large
scale."

I'd even go a step further. Our deficits are a kind of fiscal child
abuse. We need to balance the budget not just to help the future but
to stop doing it massive harm—harm that will make a future of merely
stagnant living standards appealing by comparison. Call that a *moral
imperative.*

AN AMERICAN NIGHTMARE

There is, it's true, a handful of economists who say that deficits don't
matter. Some of them point to the fact that other industrial countries
have been known to run budget deficits that (measured as a share of
their economies) are as large as ours, yet have enjoyed rapid living
standard growth. Even Japan ran deficits for a time during the early
1980s. (From the mid-1980s until Japan's recent recession, it's worth
noting, Japan's central government *added* to the country's pool of
private savings by running large budget *surpluses.*) But what these economists neglect to tell us is that these other industrial countries save two
or three times as much as we do privately! They can afford to run large
deficits because their net national savings—the savings left over for
private investment after the negative savings of deficits is subtracted—is
more than enough to meet their investment needs. We can't.

Other deficit defenders claim that there's no reason to worry because American families will somehow automatically compensate for our negative public savings by increasing what they decide to save on their own. I have to admit that's an ingenious, if perverse, justification for our collective profligacy. The problem is, there isn't a shred of evidence to support it. Indeed, as federal deficits have ballooned over the past dozen years, household saving has done just the opposite of soar. It has plummeted to its lowest level in our postwar history.

The vast majority of economists do of course believe that deficits matter. Even some of them, however, occasionally question why deficit hawks like me insist on balancing the budget. You keep talking about "the deficit" as though it's one number, they say. Surely you know it's more complicated than that. We've got on- and off-budget deficits. We've got different deficits in different federal trust funds. We've got deficits adjusted for inflation, adjusted for investment, and adjusted for "full employment." Once you look at the whole range of possible deficit numbers, how can you be sure the real number isn't actually a fairly low one? Why do you view the goal of a balanced budget like some kind of Holy Grail?

In answering these queries, I sometimes feel like paraphrasing Samuel Johnson: Obfuscation is the last refuge of a scoundrel. Yes, it's true that there are many alternative ways of calculating the federal deficit. But it's also true, though little noted, that the most sophisticated of these alternatives points to a deficit that is considerably greater than the official number. Take our "official" federal deficit in fiscal year 1992: $290 billion. It's a pure cash-in, cash-out number. As any good accountant will tell you, we will learn more about the health of our federal balance sheet if we instead look at the deficit on an accrual basis that takes into account changes in government assets and liabilities. Let's first take the big downward adjustments that might be allowed for net federal investment, net federal lending, and the amount by which inflation lowers the "real" value of the national debt. These might slice $100 billion off our official deficit. But then take the big upward adjustments: treasury borrowing of our retirement trust fund "surpluses," the accumulation of unfunded liabilities for future benefit payments, estimated insurance payouts, and estimated loan defaults. These push the deficit back up by at least $200 billion. So what should we be looking at? An official "cash-flow" deficit of about $300 billion? Or an "accrual" deficit of at least $400 billion?

Either way, the cumulative economic harm that deficits of anywhere near these magnitudes promise to inflict on tomorrow's workers and taxpayers can only be described as appalling. A decade from now, the net interest on our official national debt alone is scheduled to shoot past $475 billion a year, up from $200 billion in 1992. By then, the bills for consumption that we've already enjoyed will account for nearly one-fifth of all federal outlays and preempt nearly half of all federal income tax receipts. But with the GAO now projecting that deficits will continue to soar to 21 percent of GNP by the year 2020 (compared with deficits in the range of 3 to 6 percent since 1985), that, of course, is just a prelude to what lies ahead. Or consider the staggering future costs of our Social Security and Medicare entitlements. To pay these, official forecasts now reveal, workers in the next century will eventually face a tax bill equal to between 38 and 53 percent of payroll.

Is there a way that we can total the costs of our buck passing, then compare the burden that different generations of Americans will be called on to shoulder? Until quite recently, none existed. But a couple of years ago, economist Larry Kotlikoff of Boston University pioneered just such a method. He calls it "generational accounting," and the results are now published by the U.S. Office of Management and Budget.

In tallying up his generational accounts, Kotlikoff assumes that all Americans born before 1992 get all the benefits they are scheduled to receive under current law, but pay no more than the taxes they are already scheduled to pay. In exempting all but today's infants from any future tax hikes (or benefit cuts), we thus let the full costs of our buck passing fall on Americans as yet unborn and unnamed.

The findings? To support today's workforce in its retirement with today's benefits, keep up with interest on the national debt, and finance all the other obligations of government, Americans born in 1992 and the years to come would have to pay 71 percent of their employment income in *net* taxes! ("Net" here means total taxes paid in *excess* of total benefits received.) Compare that with what Americans born from 1900 through 1991 would have to pay through the course of their lifetimes: from 22 to 34 percent of their employment income in net taxes to all levels of government, with the youngest paying the most and the oldest the least.

A German philosopher once said, "It is the duty of the old to lie to the young." But numbers like these will in the end leave us no room to dissemble. There are two ways that you can look at them. On the one hand, you can say that our current system of intergenerational transfers is based on an injustice so vast that Thomas Jefferson would be left gasping in his efforts to describe it. What could we possibly call a future in which we asked workers to pay nearly three-quarters of their lifetime income in net taxes and all they received in return were today's status quo and declining levels of functionality in our social systems? I'd call it an American Nightmare. On the other hand, you can say that such a system is economically and politically unsustainable and must inevitably be reformed before to-day's infants reach the prime of their working lives. The second interpretation is just as correct as the first. We will not be able to hold ourselves harmless from future benefit cuts or tax hikes. We will not be able to push off all our bills onto our children and our children's children. We *will* change course. We can do so now, prudently and hopefully, or we can do so later—amid wrenching economic crisis and generational strife. The real question is not whether reform will come. It is how many more years of damage to our future and of insult to our conscience we will suffer before we act.

A FORGOTTEN MORAL LEGACY

Most of us like to think that we have at least a passing acquaintance with the social ideals of America's founding statesmen. Yet rarely do we recall how much their devotion to liberty, democracy, and material progress was tied to stern principles of honest and prudent public accounting. Nearly all of them associated balanced budgets with principled leadership, a virtuous citizenry, and a prospering economy. Chronic deficits spelled corrupt leadership, political decadence, and economic ruin.

George Washington may have disagreed with Alexander Hamilton about certain issues, but he never doubted the advice of his first Secretary of the Treasury when it came to the federal debt. Hamilton insisted "there ought to be a perpetual, anxious, and unceasing effort to reduce that which at any time exists." Washington's successor, John Adams, similarly warned in his inaugural address that "the consequences arising from a continual accumulation of public debts in other countries ought to admonish us to be careful to prevent their growth in our own."

As for our third president, Thomas Jefferson, *there* was a zealous and lifelong enemy of deficit spending in any form. "The public debt is the greatest of dangers to be feared by a republican government," he wrote on one occasion. "To preserve our independence, we must not let our rulers load us with perpetual debt. We must make our election between economy and liberty, or profusion and servitude," he wrote on another. To Jefferson, a generation that incurred a public debt without paying it off was actually in violation of "natural law" (that unwritten but universal law that many philosophers have believed tells us what is just and what isn't), for this raised "the question whether one generation of men has a right to bind another." In the letter to James Madison that I quoted in the Introduction, he summed it up this way:

> . . . the earth belongs to each [new generation] during its course, fully, and in its own right. The second generation receives it clear of the debts and incumbrances of the first, the third of the second, and so on. For if the first could charge it with a debt, then the earth would belong to the dead and not to the living generation.

The very birth of our nation, in short, was attended by leaders whose opposition to chronic deficits was both deep and principled. And this opposition did not end with the Founding Fathers. About the time of Jefferson's death in 1826, a new generation of "Jacksonian" Democrats took up the antideficit banner. For Andrew Jackson, the national debt was "a national curse." It would let no American rest easy until it was entirely paid off. As far as all of Jackson's immediate successors in office were concerned, the United States (as James Polk once declared) "owes to mankind the permanent example of a nation free from the blighting influence of public debt."

During the Civil War, the Union had no choice but to borrow vast sums from the public. But after the fighting stopped, "paying off the debt" became a popular slogan throughout a three-decade tenure of war-veteran presidents—all the way from Ulysses S. Grant to William McKinley. In an 1869 article called the "National Debt," the secretary to the British legation in the United States noted that "the majority of Americans would appear disposed to endure any amount of sacrifice rather than bequeath a portion of their debt to future generations." Later, the "Progressives" of Teddy Roosevelt's era took pride in new rational accounting methods that helped keep outlays in line with revenues. Still later, the "Normalcy" Republicans of the 1920s made balanced budgets a bedrock principle of their economic policymaking.

It's often assumed among Americans younger than I am (in other words, among those who lack even a child's memory of the early 1930s) that FDR and the Great Depression brought a sudden end to our traditional animus against deficit spending. But the truth is that from Black Thursday through D-Day, the American public endured deficit spending only for reasons of dire necessity. They hated every minute of it. In fact, Franklin Roosevelt first gained the White House in 1932 by castigating President Hoover for his profligate borrowing. Throughout the rest of the decade, FDR was forever defensive about the deficits his administration incurred. ("I have said fifty times that the budget will be balanced for the fiscal year 1938. If you want me to say it again, I will say it either once or fifty times more. That is my intention.") In 1939, an opinion survey confirmed that the majority of Americans—even majorities of the poor and unemployed—preferred spending cuts to more borrowing. As soon as World War II was over and the era of national emergency past, most Americans rejoiced that the country would no longer have to borrow against its future. As recently as the mid-1960s, opposition to deficit spending was still so strong among a vanishing breed of older Americans that when Barry Goldwater promised to cut Social Security, it helped him win the elderly vote.

Was all this just a legacy of talk? Not at all. It was a legacy of living principles—really, informed habits—that shaped our public behavior year to year, decade to decade. If you look back at the federal budget from George Washington through Dwight Eisenhower, and exclude only years of declared war or catastrophic depression, the record is remarkable: 106 years of budget surpluses and thirty years of budget deficits. Even these deficits, on average, did not exceed 0.5 percent of the size of our economy. Since 1960, however, the record has undergone a radical shift: just one year of budget surplus and thirty-three years of budget deficits. What's more, as a share of our economy our modern budget deficits now routinely run in the 3 to 6 percent range.

What could account for such a startling sea change? The answer, I believe, is part of the story of America's fall from grace into choice-lessness that I traced earlier in the book. As a have-it-all hubris and an I-deserve-mine rights revolution came to shape our current entitlement mentality over the past few decades, we forgot a principle that earlier generations of Americans took for granted: The opportunity of those who come after us to start their own lives unencumbered by the cost of "our rights" is itself a right of a higher order. We should by all means debate what we're entitled to. We should by all means argue over which of our own rights are real and which are imaginary, which of our own rights are deserving of public subsidy and which are not. But wherever the chips fall, let's once again agree on a simple ground rule: The right of our children and their children to a fresh start in life must be a right that supersedes any entitlement we may claim for ourselves.

Without exception, all earlier generations of Americans engaged in furious battles over those two great questions of political life: Who benefits? Who pays? Farmers battled it out with bankers, southerners with northerners, proslavers with free-soilers, westerners with easterners. Unions squared off against corporations, small businesses against trusts, Populists against gold bugs, New Dealers against Liberty Leaguers. Yet throughout those debates, no one ever questioned that the issue would eventually have to be settled, one way or the other, among the living. No one ever stood up and said: "Wait a minute. I'll tell you what. Why don't we *both* just take what it is we want and stick our kids with the bill?" Surely the temptation must often have been there. Just imagine the devastation left behind by the Civil War, or the widespread desperation in the wake of the Great Depression. But most Americans just said no. They would not be party to any choice that would nullify their collective aspirations as a society and a nation.

Today we often hear talk about a "sacred generational contract"—
the contract that supposedly guarantees those of us who are now older
a right to publicly subsidized retirement and health-care benefits and
obligates our kids to pay whatever the bills turn out to be. Within the
limits of what we can afford as a society, it is reasonable and equitable
that we collectively cushion individuals against many of the vicissitudes
of life, including a poverty-stricken old age. But as we saw in Chapter
3, such a public decision does not create an inviolable legal contract,
much less a "sacred generational contract." Despite all the rhetoric
about "earned insurance," Social Security is, at bottom, a tax and
benefit program. What Congress giveth, it can also take away.

The real sacred generational contract that ought to govern the relations of the old and the young in our society, or in any society that
plans to prosper and be long for this world, is the one that promises to
hold the future harmless, not ourselves. What a long road we have
traveled since the days of our Founding Fathers!

So important was this original understanding of generational equity
to what our country is about that from our earliest days as a nation
Americans have from time to time considered incorporating it explicitly within our Constitution. Thomas Jefferson himself leaned in this
direction. Less than a decade after the Constitution was ratified, he
wrote to a friend: "I wish it were possible to obtain a single amendment
to our constitution . . . an additional article, taking from the federal
government the power of borrowing." Later, Jefferson modified his
proposal, suggesting instead that all public debts be entirely paid off
within a term of nineteen years—a period that he figured was the
duration of a single generation's tenure in power. Jefferson's ideas had
some real influence at the state level. In the wake of a financial crisis
in the 1840s and 1850s that caused many states to default on their
credit, "balanced budget amendments" were added to most state con-
stitutions. But such was our national aversion to debts and deficits that
a similar measure was deemed unnecessary at the federal level—at
least until recently.

Today, of course, Jefferson's proposal for a federal balanced budget
amendment is back on the table—and for obvious reasons. When we
can no longer agree tacitly to uphold basic moral principles, it's only
natural that concerned citizens should think about writing explicit
rules that aim to compel us to be responsible into law.

A BALANCED BUDGET AMENDMENT?

At the risk of startling some readers, let me say that I have mixed
feelings about the wisdom of a balanced budget amendment. Its great

virtue would be its symbolism. It would announce that our *intent* is to do the right thing for the future. But we must be aware that in that very symbolism there is also a danger. It might persuade us to think we have solved our problem and thus divert our attention from the real business at hand: making choices.

At its best, a balanced budget amendment will be no panacea. It will not tell us *which* choices to make. We will still have to relearn the habit of weighing tradeoffs ourselves, or accept automatic, across-the-board spending cuts that make no distinction between those public outlays that are worthy and those that aren't. At its worst, it could simply be evaded, while allowing us and our leaders to claim that we're being virtuous even as we defer the tough choices. For a balanced budget amendment to avoid this trap, it must feature ironclad safeguards that preclude accounting gimmicks. Here we're talking about everything from moving programs off-budget to using overoptimistic spending and revenue forecasts, then saying "oops." It would also have to require that whatever spending cuts and tax hikes are needed to eliminate the deficit be enacted at once—not, for instance, after the next election—even if their implementation is phased in.

Another difficulty of a constitutional balanced budget amendment is its reliance on the Supreme Court for enforcement. The Court is the least knowledgeable of the three branches of government when it comes to the federal budget. Yet enforcing budget balance would require it to settle the thorniest of budget questions. Who pays for deficit increases arising from a weaker-than-projected economy? Who pays if a tax increase raises less revenue than expected? The Court would soon find itself assuming the powers of the purse, which the Constitution expressly reserved for the people's elected representatives.

I'll leave it to sincere advocates of a balanced budget amendment like Senator Paul Simon of Illinois to figure out whether a realistic and enforceable balanced budget amendment for the federal government can be devised and implemented. Certainly I wish them success. Likewise, I'll leave it to legal scholars to explore whether other constitutional means of redress can be employed on behalf of future generations.

One interesting option is to deem our children and grandchildren to be a "protected" group under the due-process rubric of the Fourteenth Amendment. Where else does the Supreme Court allow us to impose trillions of dollars in taxes on a group that has no vote—not even a voice—in our political system? If I remember my grade school civics correctly, that's called taxation without representation. A couple of years ago, one such class-action suit on behalf of future generations was filed in our federal courts—and lost on the grounds that tomorrow's taxpayers do not enjoy "legal standing" and that we must rely on paternalism (that is, our natural concern for posterity) to protect their interests. Perhaps other suits will be filed and won. But whatever the outcome, there's a lesson in that initial ruling.

No law or rule or budget process will work until most Americans retrieve some measure of the unwritten principle that our children and their children have the right to inherit an economy unencumbered by our own debts. That is the same moral imperative that tells us not to leave behind polluted rivers or nuclear waste or depleted groundwater, and that is embodied in what in today's environmentalist movement is called the principle of "sustainable growth." It is the natural law that tells us, in Jefferson's words, that the earth is merely "in usufruct to the living." What that archaic-sounding phrase means is that we ourselves can fully enjoy the benefits of being Americans today but must leave our country in good shape for the next tenants. What we are talking about, in a word, is the ethic of stewardship.

The ideal of generational stewardship has a close cousin in another ideal I've discussed in this book: endowment. If the ethic of stewardship tells us not to squander our patrimony and mortgage our future, the endowment ethic tells us that we should strive to do something extra as well. We should leave behind *more* than we were bequeathed. And that of course brings us back to where we started: the need to save for and invest in a renewed American Dream of rising living standards.

GETTING HOLD OF A POSITIVE VISION

A number of years ago I made a visit to a successful physician, Dr. Herbert Spiegel, who specializes in weight control. He explained why eager eaters like myself often will not stay on a diet. Most people cannot sustain any regimen based solely on a negative vision, that is, the notion of self-denial, unless their very lives are at stake, and even then they must have a positive goal: life itself. The doctor then asked a few questions: What did I want to weigh? How important was it to me? Why was it important to me? If for reasons of health, precisely what was the "better health" that I wanted to enjoy? If for reasons of appearance, did I have a positive vision of what I wanted to look like?

After some thought, I set a goal of 175 pounds—a seemingly impossible target given my then-current weight of 215 pounds! Dr. Spiegel then had me stand in front of an ingenious mirror that changes the visual proportions of the body without the grotesque distortions typical of amusement-park mirrors. He dialed in 175 pounds. There I stood, a much leaner and, if I do say so, more physically appealing Pete Peterson. He told me to study this positive vision, try to lock it in my mind, and retrieve it often as a concrete image of my ultimate goal. In the following months, I lost thirty pounds.

Are there similar tangible payoffs we can focus on as a nation? Consider just one. Economists tell us that the real net rate of return to much of our stock of business plant and equipment runs at roughly 8 percent a year. What this means is that if America were to forgo consuming and instead invest a single dollar of income each year, by the tenth year we would generate, in each future year, an extra dollar of national income (to consume or keep saving as we choose); by the fifteenth year, we would be generating two extra dollars; by the eighteenth year, we would be generating three extra dollars!

Saving for the future is hard work. It takes patience. It means going without immediate gratification for the sake of incremental rewards that take time to add up to anything substantial. Although moral principles point the way, human nature requires that when we undertake such work and exercise such patience we do so for something more than thou-shalt or thou-shalt-not imperatives. We must feel that we are moving toward something tangible we desire—like that long-term one- or two- or three-dollar boost to our future consumption. We must be confident that if we make sacrifices they will enhance our own lives— maybe directly, perhaps just indirectly by making us happier parents or prouder citizens. What we need is the wisdom of the diet expert, Dr. Spiegel, who teaches his patients to reconnect the act of self-denial with a higher sense of our own future well-being and self-worth. What we need, to borrow again from Abraham Lincoln, is a concrete sense of how, by benefiting posterity, we are also benefiting ourselves. Americans, in short, must once again get hold of a positive vision of their own and their nation's future. To paraphrase the famous line from *South Pacific*, if we don't have a dream, how are we ever going to make a dream come true?

The "vision thing" is not just important for the success of presidential administrations, as George Bush learned too late. Nations with positive visions of their future tend to prosper. Those without them falter and decline. The differences may not be apparent year to year. History can move like a glacier. But it nonetheless moves decisively. Consider the following tale of two countries.

Back in 1870, Great Britain was widely known as "the workshop of the world." It enjoyed the highest standard of living of all nations on earth. Its plant and equipment were the most advanced, its workers the most literate, its engineers the best trained, its scientists the most renowned. On every continent, the British sterling set the standard for sound currency; on every sea, the British Royal Navy set the standard for great powers. The United States at that time, though a dynamic and promising republic, was clearly not in the same league. Its average

wage level lagged at least 10 percent behind that of Great Britain. Its
labor force was relatively unschooled and toiled mainly in agriculture.
Few of its scientists had an international reputation. The U.S. "greenback" was considered a frontier currency; the Union Army had its
hands full fighting Indians on the (still empty) Great Plains.

Yet there was another difference between these two countries. Sometime around 1870, Great Britain began to lose a positive vision of its
future. It first began to take its position of world leadership and its
rising living standards for granted, then to doubt they were worth
making sacrifices to maintain. In the last decades of the nineteenth
century and the early decades of the twentieth, Great Britain's savings
and investment rates began to falter and fall behind those of its competitors. The education of its workforce, the dynamism of its scientific
research, and the scale of its commercial infrastructure gradually
seemed less impressive by comparison. Squabbles over how to divide a
slowly growing economic pie soon led to debilitating class strife. As
everyone hunkered down and tried to protect what was theirs, the
widespread attitude became "I'm all right, Jack. You take care of yourself."

Meanwhile, America's faith in a future of open frontiers, boundless
opportunities for individual advancement, and ever-rising living standards grew stronger. In the decades following the Civil War, U.S. rates
of savings and investment climbed to unprecedented heights. Quality
education became universal at older and older ages—not just in gram-
mar school and the "Three Rs," but also in high school. Billions in
public and private dollars poured into railroads, bridges, harbors, electrical grids, industrial R&D, assembly lines, urban sanitation, and rural
reclamation. America gradually became famous for its world-class universities and cutting-edge scientific research, for its well-educated workforce and brilliant inventors.

Year by year, these differences in direction were subtle. Until the
end of the nineteenth century, they seemed insignificant compared to
the colossal gap in ostentatious wealth and global reputation that continued to separate the two countries. Year by year, the differences in
concrete economic results were also subtle. For the hundred years that
followed 1870, output per worker in the United States grew only 0.6
percent per year faster than output per worker in Great Britain. Yet
over that century, these differences led to vast consequences indeed.
By the 1950s, Great Britain had become just another industrial nation
of declining economic importance. The United States had become the
world's foremost economic giant. By 1970, output per worker and
average wages in the United States towered over those in Great Britain
by some 75 percent. The U.S. greenback set the standard for all currencies. America's armed forces set the standard for great powers.

The typical historian will doubtless point out that this tale of two countries is more complicated than I make it seem. America and Great Britain did not enjoy the same natural resources. There were differences in class structure. There were differences in political culture. And there were vast differences in the toll exacted by this century's two world wars. All of these contributed to America's dynamic rise and to Great Britain's decline. That's true. As for the typical economist, he might observe that this story is no more than an object lesson in the power of compound growth rates. Six-tenths of one percent compounds into an impressive 85 percent over a hundred years. Indeed it does.

But the rest of us might glimpse a bigger moral. Those societies that work patiently for the betterment of their future flourish. Those that lose their positive vision falter.

Since the early 1970s, as we have seen, the United States has been experiencing the bleak side of this equation. Recall the productivity growth gap that once separated Great Britain and the United States: 0.6 percent per year. Now consider the gap that has separated Japan and America over the past two decades: about 2.5 percent per year. That means we've been falling behind our foremost competitor at four times the speed at which Britain once fell behind us. Japan, of course, has its own special problems—including a weak and uncertain political leadership, too much regulation in its economy, an uncompetitive service sector, too little mobility in its workforce, and a massive senior boom that's already in the present tense, not on the next century's horizon. Its current recession has also stalled its productivity boom. But that's what recessions do. The kinds of comparisons in productivity I'm making here are long-term averages that take into account both booms and busts in the business cycle. To be sure, Japan has its own "facing up" to long-term problems to do. But I believe that Japan's economy will be growing again soon. Given Japanese investment patterns, I expect it will grow faster than ours.

There are, of course, a couple of different ways that economies can grow. There may be lots of new entry-level workers (a Baby Boom). It's also possible for a larger share of the population to work (more women in the labor force). But in the end, sustaining a rising living standard comes down to increasing productivity. The astute MIT economist Paul Krugman once summed it up this way: "Productivity isn't everything, but in the long run it is almost everything. A country's ability to improve its standard of living over time depends almost entirely on its ability to raise its output per worker." If Krugman is right—and he certainly is—Americans have good reason for concern.

But now return again with me to that future of rising living standards I sketched at the start of this chapter. Let's focus for a moment on that prosperous 2015 we can have if we raise the growth rate in U.S. output per worker by one percentage point per year above its recent trend— just half the way back to what we once achieved. If we manage it, the time required for American living standards to double will shrink from centuries to just decades. By 2015, we'll be well on our way toward doubling them within the lifetimes of our children. If we manage it, our industries will remain internationally competitive. If we manage it, America, together with its democratic ideals, will surely remain a dominant influence in global affairs. Both personally as individuals and parents and publicly as citizens, we will have done better for ourselves and feel better about ourselves. We will have averted national decline and restored the American Dream.

KARL MARX MEETS ADAM SMITH

How can America trigger and sustain a new productivity boom? The answer, quite simply, is through a renewed emphasis on savings and investment (and, in particular, investing smartly)—the things that made our productivity zoom upward in earlier eras.

Nearly every economic thinker who has reflected on the matter, from Adam Smith to Karl Marx and John Maynard Keynes, agrees that "capital formation" is the key to productivity growth and rising living standards. Capital formation is a term that economists use to refer to both savings and investment. It encompasses not just warehouses and smokestacks, but (at least in theory) any resource that we dedicate to the task of enriching our future. Spending on public infrastructure, research and development, and education can all classify as capital formation. Looked at another way, capital formation is the aggregate measure of everything that society, either privately or publicly, refrains from consuming today in order to realize a higher payoff tomorrow. According to some economists, a country's rate of capital formation, counting human as well as physical capital, may account for as much as two-thirds of its rate of growth in real output per worker.

To be sure, nothing in life is as simple as it sounds. Sometimes productivity surges forward (the transistor is invented) or backward (oil prices jump) for reasons that have little direct connection to capital formation in prior years. Sometimes societies think they're engaging in productive capital formation, but they're not. The Soviet Union spent prodigious sums of money on dams and steel mills that raised the percentage of their GDP that was measured as investment—but that hurt their living standards because the resources were not efficiently allocated. They invested dumb, not smart. And sometimes, even when we engage in genuine capital formation, we still have no reliable way of calculating its benefit. Few would deny that raising honest and drug-free kids constitutes a genuine economic benefit to our national future. But few economists would ever dare quantify that benefit.

Even if we allow for these caveats—and even if we just look at physical investments, because we can't measure human capital accurately—history has repeatedly borne out what economic theory suggests: There is a strong link between capital formation and productivity. Since the early 1950s, the productivity growth rate in each of the major industrial market economies has been very closely correlated with its rate of investment. Situated at the extreme high end of the investment "input" and productivity and earnings "output" distribution, of course, is Japan. At the extreme low end—you guessed it—is the United States. Starting in the early 1970s, moreover, the dramatic slowdown in America's productivity and living standard growth has closely tracked our declining rates of net savings and net domestic investment.

If we could accurately measure and consistently compare rates of *total* capital formation in different countries, most economists believe, the link between investment and productivity would appear still stronger. Recall that along with the plunge in America's rate of investment in physical capital, our investment record in human and intellectual capital has flagged as well. To cite just a few examples that underscore how far we are falling behind our competitors, one recent study concluded that the average Japanese high school graduate is more proficient in reading, mathematics, and science than our average four-year college graduate. With a population just half the size of our own, Japanese colleges now confer 10,000 more engineering degrees than we do. In a historical first, Japanese industry in 1990 outspent U.S. industry on R&D—not just as a share of GDP, but in dollars!

Differences such as these have played a key role in our productivity slowdown over the past two decades and will become even more crucial determinants of U.S. living-standard growth in the next century's emerging information-age economy. We must at all costs invest in more and better tools for tomorrow's workers. But we will also have to improve the skills of our workforce itself, while increasing the share of our resources that we devote to the scientific and industrial research that spurs productivity-enhancing innovations in the first place.

How much extra capital formation does it take to generate a given improvement in productivity? So central is this question that I've asked it of practically everyone I know who might shed some light on it—economists, business executives, policy experts, and historians. The prudent rule of thumb, I've learned, is that to get an extra one-quarter percentage point in productivity growth ordinarily requires somewhere between 1.5 and 2 percent of GDP in extra savings and investment. Like most rules, this one comes with a couple of basic assumptions. It assumes that we're not looking for results tomorrow, but over the long term (at least a decade). It presupposes that most of the new investments we make will be allocated in efficient ways throughout our economy (no Soviet GOSPLAN). And it rules out—or better, averages out—good and bad "surprises" in our future (the discovery of room-temperature fusion or an environmental catastrophe).

Let's do the arithmetic and get to the bottom line. If we want to be reasonably sure of boosting U.S. productivity growth by a full percentage point, we will have to allocate an *extra* 6 to 8 percent of our GDP to capital formation. Since the mid-1980s, U.S. net saving available for new investment has languished between a mere 2 and 4 percent of GDP. To achieve our positive-vision future, we will have to roughly triple what we've been saving, to between 8 and 10 percent of GDP!

In terms of today's GDP, we're talking in aggregate dollars about shifting some $375 billion to $500 billion annually from economy-wide consumption to savings. (This is where the minimum target of $400 billion in new annual investments I talked about in the Introduction comes from.) In more personal terms, we're talking about shifting approximately $3,750 to $5,000 per U.S. household in the same direction. That's how much the average household will temporarily need to give up in consumption. The sacrifices can come in the form of spending cuts and tax hikes that help balance the budget and end our negative public savings, or they can come in the form of more private savings. But one way or the other, that's what they must add up to in order to achieve our goal.

The prospect of undertaking a savings and investment agenda that costs $3,750 to $5,000 per U.S. household may have some of my readers gulping, and it should. But lest I be misunderstood, let me clarify a few points. Averages, of course, are just that: averages. Those who have the most in our society can, and should, be called on to make much larger than average sacrifices. Those who are poor or near-poor need make only small sacrifices or none at all. We should also keep in mind that in moving toward our savings and investment targets there are types of consumption we can cut that few of us think of as our own consumption and that few of us will miss (redundant battleships and redundant CAT scanners, for instance). Still, however we look at $375 billion to $500 billion, the numbers are huge. Consider that (in inflation-adjusted dollars) even the smaller of those two figures eclipses our largest 1980s defense budget by some $20 billion.

Are sacrifices of this magnitude really necessary to get the kinds of productivity and living standard results I'm talking about? An enormous body of economic theory supports my 8 to 10 percent of GDP savings and investment target. But there's also the experience of other countries, as well as our own history. Let's skip the theory, which is pretty tough going, and look at some real-world numbers.

If America succeeded in raising its net savings rate to 10 percent of GDP, that would put us roughly on par with the average for the major European industrial countries over the past twenty years. These countries have their problems and most Americans wouldn't want to live there. But there is no doubt that their higher savings and investment rates have been translated into higher rates of living-standard growth, as American tourists are now learning to their surprise. Indeed, on average over the past two decades, nearly all of these nations have enjoyed growth rates in per-worker GDP that are 0.5 to 1.5 percentage points higher than the U.S. rate. This is about what we would expect given our rule of thumb of an extra one-quarter percentage point in productivity growth for each extra 1.5 to 2 percent of GDP allocated to savings and investment. And what about Japan? Once again, the differences are about what we'd expect. Since the early 1970s, the Japanese have saved an average of 18 percent of GDP and enjoyed a per-worker GDP growth rate that is roughly 2.5 percentage points higher than our own.

Now look at our savings and investment target in terms of America's own historical experience. Ten percent of GDP is just about the average for total U.S. net national savings (including public-sector investment) during our fastest-growth postwar decade, the 1960s. (In making my calculations, I've prudently assumed that a 10 percent net national savings rate won't in the future get us the same incredible return that it did in that earlier period of less global competition. If it does, we will do much better than I project, and we may even close the gap with Japan.) A 10 percent of GDP savings rate, moreover, would still be well under our long-term historical average throughout the half-century preceding the 1930s. Clearly, 10 percent of GDP is at least what America was devoting to savings and investment back when we were doing things right. Clearly, it's the goal we want to attain in the years ahead. To get there, we're going to have to tighten our belts. The money's going to have to come from somewhere. But where?

INTRODUCING THE SAVINGS AND INVESTMENT AGENDA

At first blush, there may appear to be an odd coincidence about the amount of new dollars America would have to save and invest to meet our 8 to 10 percent of GDP capital formation target. Earlier in the chapter, we saw that the *total* liabilities we are shifting to future generations through deficit spending now amount to about $400 billion a year. And what would achieving an 8 to 10 percent rate of capital formation require? Taking between $375 billion and $500 billion away from current consumption and instead allocating it to productive investments that will benefit tomorrow's living standards.

The extra funds we would need to save and invest in order to realize

a positive-vision future for America are thus roughly equivalent to the
debts we would have to stop accumulating to obey Thomas Jefferson's
injunction not to harm the future by pushing public liabilities off onto
our children. This overlap of economic and moral agendas is of course
not really coincidental. The federal deficit is the main cause of our low
rate of capital formation. *Balancing the budget is what we will have to do to
get most of the savings we need.*

Private saving in the United States, it's true, has fallen sharply over
the past couple of decades—from an average of 8.2 percent of GDP in
the 1960s to an average of 5.3 percent since 1985. But our deficits
(negative public savings, really) have ballooned even faster than private saving has dropped. In 1992, our negative public savings drove the
net national savings rate of the United States down to the shocking
level of 0.6 percent of GDP, far and away the lowest in the postwar
period. It's not that individual American families aren't trying to do
anything positive for their own and their children's future. The single
biggest problem is that all older people (collectively) have been consuming more than we can afford as a society by borrowing from all
younger people (collectively). The result? What each parent is struggling to do individually for his or her own children is being undermined by what adults as a whole are conspiring, unwittingly, to do to
everyone's children.

But the way in which our official federal budget deficits now instantly cancel out the lion's share of all U.S. private savings is only part
of the story. Many economists believe that the off-the-books unfunded
benefit liabilities we have been accumulating for future retirement and
health-care consumption are an important reason that private saving
in America has become so scarce to begin with. Why? Because a couple
of generations of Americans have been convinced that government
was doing much of their saving for them in our Social Security and
other public "trust funds" and have therefore cut back on their own.
But as we've seen, there's no money saved in these trust funds. They're
just accounting entries. There's nothing there to fund productive investments today. And there will thus be no returns tomorrow to help
defray the costs of future retirements or the thousand other needs and
dreams that might have been made affordable had real savings been
set aside.

When I stress how absolutely crucial balancing the budget is to our
savings and investment agenda, I'm not saying that making every possible effort to increase private thrift in America isn't also important. I
couldn't agree less with radical free market economists who assume
that individuals and families always make the right decisions in weighing the demands of the future against those of the present—that somehow whatever we end up saving privately is by definition the right

amount. As we've just seen, people can be misinformed about the real amount of saving going on on their behalf. It's also possible for individuals and families—indeed, for an entire society—to forget that making dreams come true means saving for them. Although younger Americans are now catching on to the fact that our system of intergenerational transfers is a Ponzi scheme that's bound to unravel, they've yet to start saving more again on their own. Increasingly, Americans of all ages fear for their future, but, even more, we seem to fear *doing something* about the future. Many of us appear unable to kick the consumption habit and start saving and investing in a better tomorrow. How can public policy help?

The most obvious answer, of course, is that it can stop hurting savings so much. Other industrial countries tilt their tax codes to favor savings. Ours penalizes it by double-taxing dividend income. It also implicitly rewards certain kinds of profligate consumption (gold-plated health plans and luxury housing) with tax breaks. We need to reverse these perverse incentives. At the same time, we should increase the opportunities that individuals and families have to contribute on their own or through their employers to tax-favored retirement plans like IRAs and 401ks—as well as to allow them to use those funds for genuine household investments like education that have nothing to do with retirement.

In recent years, Congress has restricted who can contribute to such savings plans. It has also capped what people can set aside. One reason, of course, is that lawmakers have been searching under every bush for new tax dollars. But this is a shortsighted approach to raising revenues. In effect, we've been cutting back on tax breaks for genuine savings that might fund productive investments in order to allow our unfunded retirement and health-care entitlements to continue growing unchecked.

Actions—to say nothing of tax code changes—doubtless speak louder than words. But sometimes words and ideas help, too. In the early 1960s, the reader may recall, the cadre of New Economists that President Kennedy brought with him to the White House launched a concerted "education" campaign to get rid of America's irrational "Puritan ethic." The notion was that we were a savings-obsessed society and that what our economy really needed was more consumption. The times, I guess, were ripe for that kind of let-it-all-hang-out message, and the New Economists' antisavings crusade got a positive reception from the American people. With so many incentives already telling us to consume (everything from 100 percent deductibility of credit card interest to 100 percent deductibility of home mortgage interest), we ended up convinced that we could spend our way to prosperity.

IT'S TIME FOR A LITTLE MORE PURITAN ETHIC AGAIN

Today we could sure use a bit of that old Puritan ethic back. Just maybe the times are now right for a prosavings crusade. Just maybe the American people are ready to listen to a leader who uses the bully pulpit of the presidency to say, loud and clear, that our very future as a nation now depends on tightening our belts. Such a crusade would require frank talk about where we really stand as a nation and where we're headed if we don't change course. President Clinton has already made a "new beginning" at that. But even more, it would demand equally frank talk about what we will need to give up and what expectations we will have to modify if we are ever to get our future back.

Our leaders need to tell the American people that our current system of intergenerational transfers is unfunded, is unsustainable, and one way or another will ultimately become less generous. They need to send a clear message that genuine savings must henceforth play a greater role in our retirement planning. (How about having the Social Security Administration send out slips telling all Americans what they would need to set aside each year, given prudent assumptions about things like interest rates, in order to enjoy targeted levels of retirement income at different ages? I'm sure there's hardly an American family that wouldn't be shocked to learn how inadequate its current saving really is.)

Beyond this, our leaders need to say that we must, at all costs, forge a new and more positive vision of the role of older people in our society that de-emphasizes leisure and dependency and re-emphasizes productive citizenship—that extends the number of working and saving years while rolling back the number spent in subsidized leisure. They need to tell us that we'll have to begin rethinking "health" more in terms of lifestyle and prevention, less in terms of death-prolonging space-age technologies. Above all, our leaders must explain persuasively that the only way we're going to be able to enjoy more of *all* types of consumption in the future is to save and invest more today—and that to do this, we're going to have to learn to get by with less of certain types of unsustainable consumption. These are all things that Americans, willy-nilly, will eventually learn on their own. But it will be much better for our own future living standards and for the nation our children will inherit if we learn them sooner.

It took America a quarter-century or more to become a low-savings society. Obviously, it is unrealistic to expect that we can relearn our traditional thrift ethic overnight. The kind of savings crusade I am advocating must be a long-term, sustained effort, not a fad like the energy conservation program of the 1970s that faded as soon as fuel prices fell. Although focused leadership from the White House will be essential, it can't just be a presidential effort either. It must be a bi-partisan campaign developed in full cooperation with congressional leaders and private-sector representatives. Finally, it can't be just words. A successful savings crusade will have to be backed up by legislated tax incentives. To have either credibility or a lasting positive impact on our national balance sheet, it would also, needless to say, have to proceed hand in hand with reforms that balance the budget and stop our negative public savings.

As we think about how to launch and follow through on a savings crusade, Japan's experience provides an instructive example, if for no other reason than that it shows us it can be done. Faced with the daunting task of rebuilding their country after World War II, the Japanese set about developing and implementing a national savings campaign. They created new government agencies to coordinate it, including the Central Council for Savings Promotion, the Savings Promotion Department of the Bank of Japan, and the Savings Promotion Center of the Ministry of Finance. These agencies organized savings workshops, offered financial guidance, sponsored children's banks, and appointed private citizens as savings promotion leaders. They also produced magazines, leaflets, posters, advertisements, and even films that promoted the virtues of thrift. (Some Americans might feel uncomfortable with this kind of "propaganda," yet, interestingly, we feel no such compunction when it comes to government brochures or radio and TV ads that constantly remind us of our "earned insurance" entitlements to public benefits like Social Security.)

At the same time, the Japanese ratified the message of this education campaign by writing a set of unambiguous financial incentives into their tax code (no taxes at all on personal savings up to substantial levels and very low tax rates on capital gains, for instance). Although some of its prosavings tax breaks have been scaled back in recent years, Japan's private savings rate still remains extraordinarily high. Once learned, it seems to have become about as difficult for the Japanese to kick their saving habit as it is for us to kick our consumption habit.

What are the real prospects that a country with more than 300 million general purpose credit cards (and a gross dollar credit card volume that since the late 1980s has grown about twice as fast as our economy) will renew its household thrift? I've often said in this book that America is now aging rapidly. More precisely, it's "middle-aging" and will continue to do so until the huge Baby Boom generation passes through its forties and fifties. Personal savings rates ordinarily peak in middle age. Most of the big purchases that starting a family involves are by then already behind us and the need to draw down a part of one's life savings in order to pay for retirement is yet to come. Having delayed, as they have, so many of life's passages, the Baby Boomers have gotten off to a late start as savers. But that's all the more reason they will want to be saving a lot in the years ahead. Some will still face the prospect of sending kids to college at an age when their own parents had already retired to leisure communities. Most are aware that as a generation they'll never enjoy the kinds of Social Security (or home equity) windfalls their elders did. If we give them half a chance, they might just surprise the rest of us and lay to rest that me-generation label they've been carrying around since the 1970s.

But whatever degree of success we ultimately enjoy in increasing private thrift, by itself it won't come close to getting us enough savings to meet our overall capital formation targets—or at least not fast enough to turn things around anywhere near as soon as we should want to. As almost any economist will tell you, the magnitude of household-savings responses to changes in tax incentives is notoriously difficult to predict. No matter how energizing the moral suasion of a savings crusade might be, the voluntary changes households make in their consumption habits will take time to occur. If we're thinking about getting things back on track by the end of the 1990s, I doubt there's a reputable economist alive who believes we can count on anything like 6 to 8 percent of GDP in new private savings. So, once again, we end up right back where we started: with our budget deficit.

THE DANGERS IN BORROWING FROM ABROAD

"Just hang on a minute, Pete Peterson," I can hear some unreformed and unrepentant 1980s supply-sider saying. "There's a third way. Why not borrow the savings we need to invest from abroad?" But the supply-sider would be wrong to suggest this course for at least as many reasons as I have fingers on my hand.

To begin with, borrowing abroad may not even be a *practical* option. Many economists now predict that we are heading toward a "global capital shortage" in the late 1990s in which the ready supply of recycled dollars we enjoyed in the 1980s just won't be there at acceptable interest rates. The last decade's two biggest capital exporters, Germany and Japan, are both turning off the spigot. Faced with reconstructing the former East Germany, Germany has suddenly become a net borrower. During its recent recession, Japan, meanwhile, has been engaging in fiscal stimulus, investing heavily in public works, and shoring up the battered balance sheets of its financial institutions, leaving less "excess" savings for investment abroad. In the longer term, it faces the mounting public costs of a massive senior boom and may never again lend as much abroad (nearly 5 percent of GNP) as during the late

1980s. Post Desert Storm, the Middle East in general (and Kuwait in particular) has obvious new development needs and is unlikely to be the reliable source of capital it was in the past. If we want to do much investing during the rest of the 1990s, we'll just have to grow much more of our own savings.

That's a good thing. Foreign-financed investment is certainly better than none, but massive borrowing like that of the 1980s is an unsustainable proposition—and remember, it is our *long-term* economic predicament we must confront. History shows that over the long run high-investment economies are also high-savings economies. Experiments in investing without saving just don't last very long since they can't outlive the speculative fever of investors at home or the fragile trust of lenders abroad. What's more, the main purpose of economic activity in the United States ought to be to create wealth for our own citizens, not foreigners. When our domestic investments are financed abroad, let's not forget that foreigners get the returns to their capital and that we and our kids must ultimately pay off whatever it is we've borrowed.

Great nations also do not remain great nations by putting their economic destinies into the hands of other countries whose own priorities may change—and in any case are different from theirs. Inevitably, the domestic economic policy of debtor nations comes to be dictated in the halls of foreign parliaments and the boardrooms of foreign central banks. Inevitably, the foreign policy of debtor nations, as we saw in Chapter 7, is also held hostage to the political agendas of creditor nations.

Then there's a final point. Investments with long-term payoffs—and that's what we must encourage—will depend crucially on low long-term interest rates. These rates, in turn, are directly affected by our supply of domestic savings. More domestic savings means lower long-term interest rates, which means more long-term investment. For all of these reasons, it would be folly to count on the savings to fund our investment agenda anywhere but at home.

FROM SAVINGS TO INVESTMENT

And what about that investment agenda? Up to now I've been talking about where our new savings must come from. Do we want to give a lot of detailed thought to exactly where that savings should go? When it comes to the private investments we make—and private-sector investments, as opposed to government-mandated investments, should be far and away the lion's share of all of our new investments—the answer is no. We don't need or want an "industrial policy" that puts government in the business of micromanaging our private sector. If we create the right kind of overall economic climate for investment, private lenders and borrowers will allocate our savings more efficiently than any congressman or bureaucrat can. That, after all, is what markets do.

What's the essential ingredient in the "right" kind of economic climate I'm talking about? The answer, of course, is confidence. Businesses and financial markets must be sure that we're really getting our long-term economic act together if we are to have more long-term investments with large long-term payoffs and less of the feverish speculation and short-termitis we saw so much of during the 1980s. In my capacity as president of The Concord Coalition, I recently asked DRI, that most credentialed of econometric consulting firms, to forecast the impact a credible and enforceable plan for balancing the budget might have on the future of long-term interest rates. The answer surprised even a deficit hawk like me. As I noted in the Introduction, DRI believes long-term interest rates would gradually decline by a whopping 2.5 to 3 percentage points beneath what they are forecast to be in a business-as-usual scenario in which our deficit continues to balloon out of control. Now that could really stimulate an investment boom!

As for public investment, yes, we need more of that too. Private capital markets simply don't exist for some of the highest-return investments we can make as a society—in basic research, in education, in worker retraining, and in the health and skills of underclass kids, to mention a few of the most important. But here, unlike in the private sector, we *do* want to think in detail about how we target our new spending. As I stress in the following chapters, we should be careful to restrict our public investments to those things we know the private sector can't do better. And we must be careful to focus them on the kinds of programs we're confident will pay high returns in the future, even if we can't precisely measure those returns. There's simply no room in America's investment agenda for a new pork barrel.

THE TIME FRAME AND THE BOTTOM LINE

What's a realistic and sensible time frame for reaching our savings and investment targets? For both economic and symbolic reasons, I'm convinced that the year 2000 is what we should be aiming for. Getting there that quickly will take enormous determination from Congress, the President, and the public. It may also mean a number of tough years as we wean ourselves from unsustainable consumption habits. But if the going gets tough, we must keep reminding ourselves of the price of not getting there: *many more* tough years in the future.

Now let's take a look at the bottom line at the end of the 1990s. How exactly will the numbers add up? A balanced budget in the year 2000 will mean an additional 4.5 percent of GDP available for new private investments. If we also devote an extra 1 percent of GDP to new public investments, that gets us to 5.5 percentage points of GDP. That leaves 0.5 to 2.5 percentage points to come in the form of more private thrift if we are to meet our capital formation targets. As we go about reducing our unfunded public benefit liabilities, we may well get more private savings than that—which is just one more reason to attack our budget problem head-on. All roads indeed lead to the federal budget. We know that's broken. And, though we can debate the details—or even some of the broad brush strokes—we've got a pretty good idea how to go about fixing it. As my grandson Peter Cary might say, "Just do it."

THE PETERSON SACRIFICE TEST

How to get that job done is what the rest of this book is about. In the next chapter, I'll lay out a set of general principles that I think should guide us as we go about the business of budget reform. In the final chapter, I'll present a detailed action plan that shows how we can balance the budget in accordance with those principles.

In the broadest sense, what we'll be doing, of course, is shifting much more of our economy's resources from consumption to savings and ultimately to investment. At each step along the way, making that shift will require decisions about *whose* consumption is to be cut. When we talk about rates of savings and investment and productivity and a rising living standard, it can sound very abstract. But there's nothing abstract about it. Saving our future and restoring the American Dream for ourselves and our children tomorrow demand that we give up something today. We will constantly have to ask ourselves that most brute of all questions: Who pays for it? As we're asking it, it will be helpful if we also keep in mind the flip side of the equation: What do we get in return? We will all be more willing to make the sacrifices we need to if we have a tangible vision of the concrete investment rewards we can enjoy.

Let me now flesh out some details of what I have in mind, along the lines of the "Peterson Sacrifice Test" I described in Chapter 1. In the examples below, I start out with a series of possible consumption sacrifices that will get us a fair way toward balancing the budget. For each one, I note the savings we will realize in the year 2000 if we make the sacrifice, then match that savings with investments we could use it to pay for. As we will see, at times the sacrifices are also their own rewards.

Sacrifice 1. Cap our home-mortgage interest deduction at $12,000 for individuals and $20,000 for joint-filing couples. *Rationale:* This lavish tax subsidy encourages scarce savings to flow into residential housing and away from productive business investment. *Reward:* $6 billion— what we would need to pay for a 10 percent permanent tax credit for business research and development. *Objective:* To spur business investment in the development of cutting-edge technologies on which U.S. competitiveness and the improvement of American living standards increasingly depend.

Sacrifice 2. Gradually raise the Social Security retirement age to sixty-eight between 1995 and 2006. *Rationale:* An aging America will need more of its seniors to remain productive contributors to our economy and will not be able to afford to fund limitless end-of-life leisure. *Reward:* $16 billion—more than enough to pay for *both* a 10 percent permanent R&D tax credit *and* a 10 percent worker-training tax credit. *Objective:* To spur business investment in cutting-edge technologies and in the skills of a U.S. workforce that is now ill-prepared to meet global competition in the next century's economy.

Sacrifice 3. Raise federal "sin" taxes on cigarettes to one dollar per pack and on alcoholic beverages to sixteen dollars per "proof gallon." *Rationale:* To reduce the health, social, and economic costs attributable to smoking and alcohol abuse. *Reward:* $22 billion—nearly twice as much as we would need to pay for a comprehensive early childhood development program for all low-income children (prenatal care, immunization, and Head Start–type care) along the lines recently proposed by the Committee for Economic Development. *Objective:* First, to avoid the much larger social, economic, and health costs we will have to pay later if we fail to make modest investments now. Second, to reap the huge social and economic benefits of a better-educated, healthier, and more productive workforce. According to studies cited by the CED, spending on early childhood intervention has enormous demonstrated returns: three to six dollars, for instance, for every dollar invested in preschool education.

Sacrifice 4. Cap our current open-ended tax subsidy for employer-sponsored health care at the average cost of insurance coverage. *Rationale:* This subsidy encourages excess health-care consumption, contributes to our health-care cost explosion, and does nothing to help those who don't have and can't afford insurance. *Reward:* $40 billion—enough to pay for extending medical coverage to lower-income American families that lack it. *Objective:* To help guarantee all Americans access to our health-care system—something Henry Aaron of the Brookings Institution has called "a standard perquisite of citizenship in modern developed nations."

Sacrifice 5. Phase in an increase in the federal gasoline tax of fifty cents per gallon between now and the year 2000. *Rationale:* To encourage energy efficiency, reduce our dangerous dependence on foreign oil, and improve the environment. *Reward:* $47 billion—nearly enough to pay for the R&D tax credit, the worker-training tax credit, and the childhood development program, as well as to fund an expanded Earned Income Tax Credit (EITC) for the working poor and an expanded SSI benefit for the disabled and the elderly poor. *Objective:* To increase the productivity of our physical and human capital and to provide a better floor of income protection.

Sacrifice 6. Implement a steeply progressive "affluence test" or "graduated entitlement benefit reduction" that would, as I propose in Chapter 10, withhold a portion of federal benefits from households with incomes above the U.S. median. *Rationale:* There is no room for welfare for the well-off in the federal budget as long as we are passing on huge unfunded benefit liabilities to our kids. *Reward:* $71 billion—over four-fifths of what we would need to meet my 1 percent of GDP target for new public spending on high-return investments in rebuilding our decaying infrastructure, recapturing our global lead in science and technology, and improving the health, skills, and welfare of our children, our most compelling reason to care about the future.

Sacrifice 7. Make all of the above sacrifices. *Rationale:* Because we have decided the tradeoffs are justified. *Reward:* $202 billion—enough to fund *all* the above-mentioned public investments *and* to increase our rate of net private investment. *Objective:* To reinvest in a future of rising living standards and to restore the American Dream.

When it comes to proclaiming our intention to do the right thing for our future, we all sing in unison. But when it comes time to actually give something up, all we hear is a deafening silence. It's time we faced up.

9

How to Think About Budget Reform

Otto von Bismarck, the German chancellor whose name is virtually synonymous with realpolitik, once said that there are two things people should avoid watching close up: the making of sausages and the making of laws. Based on my own hands-on experience with policymaking during my brief tenure in the Nixon administration, I sometimes suspect that Bismarck intended his quip as an insult to butchers.

No one who's serious about balancing the budget can ever afford to forget just how messy a business lawmaking in our nation's capital really is. There are the open demagoguery and hypocrisy and the secret deals. There are polling results to weigh and media spin to fret about. Then there is the awesome clout of our current consumption lobbies. They're always there in the wings, ready to reward with campaign funds or to punish at the polls. When all the dust has settled after a legislative session, I never wonder why the results are less than perfect. I sometimes find myself asking how they end up having anything to do with our public interest at all.

Obviously, we don't live in a philosopher's kingdom like the one Plato described in his *Republic,* where all the laws are made by perfectly wise men. We live in an open democracy that lurches from one constituency concern to another, and from one election to the next. Our system is noisy, even chaotic. But we wouldn't want it any other way. As Winston Churchill once put it in what has become a modern cliché, "Democracy is the worst form of Government except [for] all those other forms that have been tried from time to time."

Still, there are turning points in history when any political system, and especially a democracy like ours, must rise above the usual "politics of sausage making." At such moments, great national challenges demand that we think more about the general interest and less about special interests, more about pulling together to achieve future goals we all share and less about the rewards each of us stands to win today for himself or herself alone.

As a people, Americans have always been ready to pull together and sacrifice when a hostile power has posed an immediate threat to our national survival. Our failure to save for and invest in our future is ultimately every bit as menacing to what it means to be an American as any foreign army we've ever confronted. Yet, perhaps because our economic malady is long-term and home-grown, we seem unable to muster the sense of urgency and shared conviction needed to act decisively. I am reminded of a telling metaphor in a story I once heard about frogs. If you throw one into a pot of boiling water, it will jump out, scalded but alive. If you instead put it in cold water, then slowly turn up the heat, it will swim around until it's too weak to jump—then get cooked.

If ever there was a time when Americans needed to apply some of our famous can-do spirit at home, it's now. As we approach the next century, nothing is more vital to our survival as the kind of people we want to be than engineering a massive shift from consumption to investment. And nothing is so crucial to realizing that goal as stopping our negative public savings. If we fail to act now, the America our children inherit will be not only one of stagnant living standards at home and diminished stature abroad but a less generous, less compassionate, less liberal society than the one in which we now live. People will simply have far less to spare for any ideal that transcends the business of just getting by in life.

The reforms we will need to balance the budget will test the limits of our political system. Stemming the rising tide of red ink and restoring the American Dream for our children will require patience and long-term planning in a system that stresses immediate results. It will require across-the-board sacrifice in a system fixated on protecting the consumption claims of entitled constituencies. It will require honest dialogue and honest accounting in a system where double-talk and burying the bottom line now pass for statesmanship.

Washington insiders tell me all the time that it can't be done. No administration or Congress, they say, will be able to ask for the needed sacrifice. The "Happy Time" Republicans made a virtue of vice during the 1980s because they didn't have the courage to bring the ominous deficit issue directly to the public. President Clinton ran on a platform of reinvesting in America's future but hasn't been able to offer us a credible plan for balancing the budget because he just can't ask for real sacrifice where he has to—from America's broad middle class. Presumably (or so many political pundits think), Ross Perot would have fared little better had he been elected.

But I simply refuse to believe that doing what's right for our future is politically impossible. With a positive vision of the concrete benefits that reform will bring us, and with the conviction that our sacrifices will really matter, I'm convinced that the American people will find the will. Staying the course certainly won't be easy or painless. But few things really worth doing ever are.

In the next chapter, I'll lay out a step-by-step plan for balancing the budget. But before I invite you to look at the plan's details, it's essential that I explain its overall logic. If any reform effort is to succeed, it will need a lot of things working in its favor—including skilled leadership and a committed public. But perhaps most of all, it's going to require agreement about fundamental principles. Without that, we won't be able to avoid false steps that defeat us at the outset. In short, we need an overall framework for reform that tells us why we're doing what we're doing at each step. I believe we should adopt the following twelve principles. If we do, the specific reforms we enact will be sounder and fairer and will stand a better chance of economic and political success.

1. *Always remember our ultimate purpose: raising U.S. living standards by boosting our rates of savings and investment back to world-class levels.* Although some critics will doubtless misunderstand me, I am not an advocate of sacrifice for sacrifice's sake. I don't insist on balancing the budget because I think the pain will somehow make us better people. I insist on it, as we all should, because it's the fastest and surest way to find the savings we need to invest in that future of rising living standards which we want for ourselves and our children. As we deal with the difficult tradeoffs that balancing the budget will involve, we must keep reminding ourselves that the reason we're giving up something today is so that we can all have more tomorrow.

Let me recap the logic we walked through in the last chapter. If we ever hope to enjoy again the rising-living-standard growth we recall from the 1950s and 1960s, our goal should be to boost the share of GDP we devote to net capital formation to between 8 and 10 percent by the turn of the century. That's up from 2 to 4 percent today. There's hardly an economist alive who'd bet money on our ability to increase what we save privately by anywhere near 6 to 8 percentage points of GDP that quickly. We can get most of the way there by balancing the budget. A balanced budget in the year 2000 will mean that the approximately 4.5 percent of GDP the government now borrows to finance the federal deficit will be available for private investment. If we also devote an additional 1 percent of GDP to future-oriented public spending—something I stress in my budget action plan—that brings us up to 5.5 percentage points of GDP. We would only have to bank on renewed private thrift for between 0.5 and 2.5 percentage points of GDP in extra savings. That's why we must balance the budget. That's why we must go all the way. And that's why we must start soon.

2. *Balance the budget by the end of the 1990s.* America needs as much new savings and investment as possible as early as we can get it. On this count alone, it is crucial that we bring our "official" federal budget deficit down to zero by the end of the 1990s. But there are other good reasons we should insist on this target and time frame.

In the first place, reaching balance in our so-called unified or consolidated federal budget is actually a more modest goal than it might seem. Even if we balance our total federal budget, we would still be using our Social Security "surpluses" to cover current spending. If we really want to save and invest these surpluses to help cover the costs of our future retirements, we would also have to run a large surplus, equal to the Social Security surplus, in our consolidated federal budget!

Then there is the matter of something called public confidence. Half measures simply won't serve to rally most Americans around the cause of shared sacrifice—even if they hadn't already seen enough failed budget-balancing schemes to last several lifetimes. There's nothing inspiring about a promise first to cut the deficit in half, then to let it grow by leaps and bounds again after the next presidential election—as President Clinton's first budget plan does. Without a clear goal and confidence that we can reach it, lasting reform will elude us. When I talked about the need for clear goals at the beginning of the book, I quoted Congressional Budget Office Director Robert Reischauer, who has aptly likened a budget plan without a clear goal of budget balance to an Apollo program whose stated objective was to send a man 239,000 miles somewhere into space and have him return. Our leaders need to promise us the moon itself—then actually deliver it.

But it's not only public confidence we need to be concerned about. There are also the financial markets to consider. During the 1980s we liked to tell ourselves it was never the right moment in the business cycle (or the political election cycle) for cutting the deficit. In the years ahead, the imperative of reducing our debt burden and raising our national savings rate to world-class levels will constantly remind us that it's always the right moment. For the rest of the 1990s, telling the financial markets that they must absorb a higher dose of federal debt will be like telling an exhausted marathoner to run another mile.

Only steady progress toward eliminating the deficit will maintain investor confidence, keep long-term interest rates headed down, and keep our economy growing. Steady progress, of course, does not mean that we should do it all this year or next. If we are to avoid too bumpy a ride as our creeping recovery gathers momentum, we must phase in our reforms gradually. But the greatest danger is not that we will go too far. It is that we won't go far enough. I can imagine few things more damaging to America's economic prospects than the collapse in market confidence a return to "not-nowism" and gridlock will cause.

If we make that progress toward balancing the budget, moreover, it promises to set up a virtuous circle of lower interest rates and higher investment. As any economist will tell you, low long-term interest rates are crucial if we are to stimulate new investment. As any budget watcher knows, low interest rates will at the same time reduce the cost of servicing our national debt, thereby further shrinking our federal budget deficit.

Finally there is perhaps the most compelling reason for acting now. As America's age wave hits in earnest early in the next century, the explosive growth in today's system of retirement and health-care entitlements promises to make our 1990s budget problem look like a picnic. If we leave current policies on autopilot, the number crunchers over at the GAO tell us, we're looking at unthinkable deficits of 21 percent of GNP by the year 2020. If we don't begin to prepare for tomorrow's immense challenges now, the narrow window of opportunity we enjoy in the 1990s will slam shut. When change does come, and it inevitably will, it is likely to be truly wrenching, draconian, and enacted amid economic crisis and intergenerational strife. That is a scenario we must avoid.

3. *Face up to the need for both tax hikes and spending cuts—but get most budget savings from spending cuts.* Let read-my-lips conservatives be forewarned. Any responsible plan for balancing the budget will require raising new revenues above and beyond those President Clinton has already called for. The revenue raisers I've included in my plan are substantial ones. Among other measures, I keep President Clinton's higher marginal tax rates and add a phased-in fifty-cents-per-gallon federal gasoline tax and a 5 percent national retail sales tax. Why do I insist on raising new revenues? Simple pragmatism is one reason: Tax hikes must be part of any reform effort that hopes to forge an effective political coalition. Simple arithmetic is another: We won't be able to cut spending enough to balance the budget without sacrificing programs that should be high national priorities.

But let tax-and-spend liberals take note. During the 1990s, spending cuts will have to get us much of the way toward a balanced budget—

and in the more distant future they must exceed tax hikes by wider and wider margins. Why? I've talked about the main reasons earlier in the book. Much of what the federal government does today is to mail benefit checks to middle- and upper-income households. Excluding interest payments, non-means-tested entitlements alone now account for about 45 percent of all federal spending. It simply makes no sense to turn the budget into a revolving door by continually raising taxes to pay for benefits that go to all of us.

What's more, over the long run it just won't work. Built-in structural increases in entitlement spending—due to the aging of our population, soaring health-care costs, and 100 percent-of-CPI benefit indexing—are now scheduled to add 3 percentage points of GDP to federal outlays over the next ten years. By 2020, even in a relatively favorable demographic and economic scenario based on official Social Security Administration forecasts, our total entitlement bill would hit 19.5 percent of GDP, up from 12.5 percent today. By 2040, our entitlement bill would be closing in on one-quarter of GDP. Just to cover these locked-in increases in entitlement costs—without making any new commitments or fulfilling any new public purposes—we would have to schedule a new Clinton-scale tax increase *twelve* more times over the next half century! There is no way we can do so without ruinous harm to our economy and our kids. Inevitably, we will have to reorder our priorities and learn to *spend less*.

4. *Focus on spending cuts that generate long-term savings.* It is absolutely crucial that we lock in permanent and compounding savings in those areas of the budget that, if left on autopilot, will cause deficits to balloon in the next century. That means entitlements. We should, to be sure, save as much as possible wherever else we can. When it comes to cutting defense, my plan goes as far as President Clinton's does—and that's pretty far. There is also some room left to trim in the small "discretionary" domestic spending corner of the budget. But in the end, nothing we do in these areas—even if we do everything—will begin to add up to a balanced budget.

From phasing in higher Social Security retirement ages to cutting welfare for the well-off to capping our open-ended health-care subsidies, many of the specific reforms in my budget action plan will begin to yield significant savings in the 1990s and then go on to save us much, much more in the next century. Unless a reform plan emphasizes structural entitlement changes like these, the sacrifices we make today will be largely in vain. Even if we manage to balance the budget in the near term (and that's not likely), deficits will explode again in the long term.

5. *Structure reforms to require across-the-board participation in meeting our goal of a balanced budget.* As we think about ways to reorder our priorities

and spend less, it is of paramount importance that we call on all groups of Americans who are able to make a real contribution. Across-the-board participation is fair. It's the only way we will ever get the budget numbers to add up. And it's a political necessity. Building consensus means that no set of programs or special interests can be singled out. It also means that none can be spared. In my plan, seniors get their Social Security and Medicare taxed. But yuppies get their mortgage and health-insurance tax favors cut back. Private-sector retirees face a hike in their eligibility age for Social Security. But civil service and military retirees get a "diet COLA" instead of 100-percent-of-CPI indexing. Farmers get their subsidies trimmed. But everyone from corporate jet owners to pleasure boaters pays higher user fees for government services that are now largely "free."

If one group (the nonpoor elderly) bears a somewhat disproportionate share of the sacrifice in my plan, it's because they now receive a vastly disproportionate share of our public largess. If another group (the poor, no matter what their age) is exempted from any overall material sacrifice under my plan, it's because equity in this case demands no less.

6. *Within the framework of across-the-board participation, ask for sacrifice according to financial means.* Although it is crucial that all of us who are able contribute, we should also structure our overall approach to reform so that the sacrifices Americans are called on to make take into account their financial means. The broad American middle class will have to make real contributions, or balancing the budget will be impossible. But as incomes rise among middle- and upper-income Americans, so too must their contribution. When it comes to new revenues, the truly well-to-do must pay a much fuller and fairer share. As for entitlement benefits, there is no justification for welfare for the well-off.

7. *Reinforce our floor of protection for the poor.* If we are to create the kind of America we are trying to create, budget reform cannot be only about budget balance. It must also be about reinfusing everything we do publicly with a more legitimate public purpose. Nowhere is that lack of purpose more evident today than in our indiscriminate system of entitlements and tax subsidies. They benefit the rich at least as often as the poor, and along the way scatter huge windfalls on everyone in between. In 1990, just $110 billion of the $681 billion in total government benefits (including state and local spending) helped to bring U.S. households out of poverty. But an extra $43 billion in targeted spending would have eliminated poverty in America.

As this is being written, certain senators are proposing "caps" on entitlement spending and COLA reforms. The charge immediately comes back that these measures would savage the "elderly" and the "working poor," creating the absurd impression that all seniors and working Americans are poor! But if we insist on simply defending our entitlements status quo, we will never find the budget savings to reinvest in our future, nor will we ever find the resources to provide more generous public assistance to those who do need and do deserve it: frail elderly and disabled Americans who are poor and unable to work; Americans who are working or who have shown their willingness to work, but who remain in poverty; and, above all, children, regardless of the reason they are poor.

Providing such targeted assistance is a central purpose of my budget plan. For the elderly and the disabled, there is an increase in benefits under our means-tested Supplemental Security Income (or SSI) program. For families juggling jobs and babies to make ends meet on poverty and near-poverty wages, there is an enhanced Earned Income Tax Credit. For underclass kids, I advocate large new public investments in their health and skills. For all Americans anywhere near the poverty level, there will be a guarantee of health insurance coverage. The bottom line? Despite the nearly $500 billion in federal outlays my action plan will be saving a decade from now, poverty in America will decline. The payoff? We must remember that it's not just charity. If we simply leave them to fester, the problems of the disadvantaged in America will increasingly undermine the cohesiveness of our society and the competitiveness of our economy. Here too, much of what we are really doing is investing—in a healthier, safer, more stable, more productive, and more hopeful America.

8. *Change the ways we tax and spend in order to create future-affirming economic incentives.* One crucial step will be to raise as much of our new revenue as possible from taxes that target consumption. By taxing consumption (as opposed to income), we of course create incentives that favor household savings. To a greater or lesser extent, every other major industrial country tilts its tax code in this direction. As we've seen, we do just the opposite by handing out tax breaks for consumption (such as gold-plated health plans and luxury housing) and by double-taxing dividend income. Reversing this bias is one of the many reasons I favor a large federal gasoline tax. (The others are also future-affirming: limiting the economic and security costs of our energy gluttony and improving the quality of the environment.) It is also why (despite its regressivity) I include a national retail sales tax in my budget plan. But this measure, let me stress, is intended to be temporary. What we really need to be thinking about is how to gradually replace today's entire income-based tax system with one based instead on a *progressive* consumption tax.

Whether or not we go the whole nine yards, we will certainly want to
limit the ways our tax code now heavily subsidizes certain types of
profligate consumption. Here I have in mind, above all, our huge tax
favors for health care and owner-occupied housing. Without any compelling public policy rationale, they channel scarce economic resources
away from potentially more productive uses by encouraging people to
spend much more than they otherwise would on space-age medical
technologies and vacation condos in Florida. My action plan sensibly
caps our open-ended tax exemption for employer-paid health insurance and taxes a portion of Medicare benefits. It also limits our mortgage interest deduction for affluent homeowners. In our national
economic accounts, it's true, Beverly Hills mansions are classified as
investments. But they're not economically productive investments that
increase our incomes over time and are no more deserving of limitless
public subsidies than the lavish kind of health care we practice.

As we curtail these consumption-oriented tax breaks, we should
think about using some of the savings to favor instead private economic activities that will benefit us all by accelerating the rise in U.S.
living standards. In my budget plan, I advocate two productivity-
enhancing tax breaks that most economists agree will yield large returns over time: worker-training tax incentives and a permanent R&D
tax credit. As a further measure to favor productive economic activity,
I also provide for the indexation of capital gains (excluding those on
investments in real estate, art, and collectibles).

Along with incentives that favor consumption over investment, there
is another set of biases in our public policies that we should also seek
to reverse: those that encourage dependency instead of productive
contribution to society. Saying we should do more for the poor is not
suggesting that they deserve a free lunch with no questions asked. We
must continue to think about ways of restructuring welfare as "workfare" and "learn fare." And we must do everything possible to ensure
that low-earning Americans with jobs have every incentive to keep
them. That's why I endorse the President's proposed expansion of the
Earned Income Tax Credit as a way of reinforcing our floor of protection for the working poor. It is more than just a form of means-
tested income support: It is also a *work* incentive.

When we talk of unproductive dependency, we almost invariably
think in terms of welfare and our underclass. But that entirely misses
the most important work disincentives of all in our society—those that
encourage most Americans to spend the last third of their adult lives
in subsidized leisure. We need higher retirement ages to help cap
entitlement costs. But changing the ways in which we encourage retirement is not just a matter of saving money directly. It's about persuading more of those elderly who are able to remain active
contributors to our economy. One win-win thing we can do is to get rid

of our onerous Social Security "earnings test" that now penalizes seniors for staying in the workforce by reducing their benefit checks. The cost to the federal budget of paying working seniors full benefits will be modest. The paybacks of sending the right signals to the elderly are incalculable. Aging too must be part of our new positive vision of America's future in the next century. Indeed, it must be at its core.

9. *Spend more on high-return public investments.* Along with changing the ways in which we tax and spend to encourage wealth-producing private economic activities, we should also redirect more of what we spend directly through public budgets to the attainment of future-oriented goals we all share. That, if I'm not mistaken, is what government in democratic republics was once supposed to be all about. Unlike some Republicans I know, I've got nothing against collectively investing in our nation's future. It's essential—and the way we lag behind our competitors on this score already threatens our global competitiveness. Up to this point, I've obviously been singing from the same hymnal as President Clinton. Now let me stress where I seem to differ.

We can never afford to forget that economic resources are scarce and that dollars are fungible. Whatever budget savings we redirect toward new public investments are savings that could be handed back to private capital markets for productive investment there. Too much of the "investment" agenda President Clinton proposed had nothing to do with productivity-enhancing activities that will benefit tomorrow's living standards. It was social pork. We must be sure that all our new public investments are productive. Where we decide to invest more publicly, moreover, it should be only in investments that the private sector is least likely to make—projects that are too huge for single enterprises to undertake, or in which large returns accrue to the public while payoffs for particular businesses are small or risky. We're talking, of course, about such things as basic research and rapid transit—or preschool education and prenatal health care. How can we be sure that what we spend publicly is truly invested in areas where the returns are high? One idea I advocate is to require a "productivity impact statement" for each new public investment program, just as we now require that environmental impact statements precede the groundbreaking for large public and private ventures alike.

10. *Phase in spending cuts and tax hikes gradually.* The changes we'll need to make an economic moonshot are large, and we'll have to begin as soon as possible if we want to get there. But real reform doesn't have to mean wrenching adjustments in either individual incomes or expectations. Indeed, one of the most compelling reasons to begin now is to avoid the necessity of draconian measures later. Grad-

ualism will give people time to plan, to increase their household savings, to delay a new purchase. With only a few exceptions, all of my proposed reforms begin to be implemented in 1995. Many, however, are not fully phased in until the year 2000, some not until the early years of the next century. Compared to conventional wisdom, the time frame may seem radical. But it's not. It's realistic. Take my proposed three-year hike in the Social Security retirement age. It's scheduled to begin in 1995 and proceed by three months a year until it's fully phased in in 2006. Back in 1983, Congress enacted a two-year retirement age hike to be phased in between the years 2000 and 2022. No one needs thirty-nine years to prepare for such a modest change!

11. *Observe the principles of honest accounting, prudent forecasting, and credible enforcement.* There is no room in any responsible budget plan for smoke and mirrors. Not only will gimmicks get us no closer to our goal, they will undermine the most crucial element in any reform effort: public confidence. We've had enough of rosy economic scenarios that never come true. We've had enough of sleight-of-hand changes in the timing of spending and taxing that allow us to squeak in under a budget target one month, then exceed it the next. We've had enough of moving programs off-budget. And we've had enough—I hope my colleague David Stockman will forgive me—of magic asterisks to indicate unspecified spending reductions. To his credit, President Clinton got rid of the rosy scenarios and most of the phony numbers when he drew up his first budget proposal. His plan doesn't get us where we need to go. But we should be thankful for that higher level of honesty.

Above and beyond honest accounting and prudent forecasting, maintaining public confidence will require that any budget plan meet a further test. If the broadly shared sacrifice that our leaders must call on the American people to make is to be forthcoming, there must be faith that the plan we adopt will be fully implemented and will really do the job. No one wants to see his or her taxes raised only to have the money disappear down a black hole. No one wants to have his or her benefits cut only to learn that the budget deficit is once again allowed to balloon out of control.

If the past dozen years provide any lesson, unfortunately it is that there is no *procedural* mechanism we can employ that will compel us to make the right choices if we have not already determined to make them. Deficit targets that leave the details of how we are to meet them unspecified simply don't work. There is always some way to evade or postpone the tough decisions. What we must do is to agree *now* on what sacrifices will be required. We need to spell out in advance *precisely* what spending will be cut and what taxes will be raised. And we need to pass our *entire* reform package all at once, even if the implementation of particular measures in it is to be phased in over future years. *Then* we should put in place the strongest enforcement mechanisms we can devise.

In the end, the best enforcement mechanism of all may be an informed electorate prepared to vote politicans out of office if they fail to demonstrate fiscal responsibility. As our own contribution to public education and political accountability, The Concord Coalition, its Chairmen, President, impressive staff, and collection of Vice-Chairmen, such as Bill Gray (former Chairman of the House Budget Committee), Paul Volker (former Chairman of the Federal Reserve Board), and John White (former issues director of the Perot organization), plan to issue regular "Budget Watch" reports. These reports will set goals, scrutinize budget projections, determine whether spending cuts are real and revenue forecasts are based on prudent assumptions, sort out the pork from true productivity-enhancing investments, assess our progress toward balancing the budget, and rivet attention on the costs of business as usual.

A few years ago at a dinner party, I heard Governor Jerry Brown quip that "there is no constituency for fiscal responsibility." Sadly, he has been all too right. The more advocates for the future the American public hears—and the more groups with overlapping balance-the-budget agendas—the better. We need private watchdog organizations and "budget truth squads" of all types to speak out loud and clear if we are to stand a chance of creating the kind of climate in which real reform can occur—then keep it on track.

An essential part of what needs to happen is that *young people themselves*—the ultimate victims of our choicelessness—must gain a more effective political voice. This is why The Concord Coalition has been happy to encourage the efforts of Lead . . . or Leave, a grass-roots organization of twenty-somethings that last year persuaded ninety congressmen to sign a pledge to either cut the deficit in half in four years or leave office. When members of Lead . . . or Leave recently picketed the AARP, that most powerful bastion of the gray lobby, they were reportedly invited in for milk and cookies. That may not seem like the most auspicious beginning to a dialogue that must ultimately head off an age war in the next century. But big things often have small beginnings. It's indeed heartening to learn that other groups of young people, such as Third Millennium, are now speaking out about deficits and generational equity as well.

12. *Always focus on the ultimate bottom line: our national balance sheet.* As we think about the sacrifices we will need to make, we should keep in mind a final point. There is far too much emphasis today on how particular programs are doing, whether their paper "trust funds" are

running a temporary "surplus," and whether they are thus "paying their way." What really matters is the aggregate impact of all our taxing and spending on America's balance sheet, today and tomorrow, and the net savings left over for our children and our future after all the shell games are played out and all the accounts are summed.

This principle brings us back full circle to where we started: the imperative of raising our rates of national savings and investment to world-class levels. All countries—even the ones that save a lot—consume most of what they produce. It's that thin sliver of national income that isn't consumed which constitutes any country's lifeline to the future. Whether we will choose to widen the sliver of national income we save and invest is the question on which the future of the American Dream depends. Balancing the budget is crucial because it's the only sure way we know of widening that sliver anytime soon. As we go about the task ahead, all programs and all priorities must be on the table.

At times when great national challenges demand that we rise above our usual "politics of sausage making" and bend history to a new course, experience shows that a high-level commission with the right mandate, credentials, and bipartisan membership can sometimes work wonders in ending gridlock. In thinking about how best to proceed at today's juncture, I can't help recalling the key role the Committee on Economic Security played during the mid-1930s in masterminding the New Deal. During their year of deliberations, the high-level federal officials, business leaders, and prestigious academics who made up the committee designed the entire legislative package that became the Social Security Act of 1935, including unemployment insurance, old-age insurance, and the forerunners of today's SSI and AFDC programs. Recently, faced with a smaller but politically no less daunting challenge, we witnessed the success of the Base Closure and Realignment Commission in forging consensus about how best to share the pain of downsizing our military.

Now that Bill Clinton's first and partial deficit-cutting exercise is behind him, I believe the time has come for the President to appoint a high-level commission whose specific mission it would be to hammer out a plan that faces up to both the economic imperative of balancing the budget by the year 2000 and the moral imperative of ending our fiscal child abuse. I sometimes wonder whether the creators of our original New Deal safety net for the poor would even recognize the well-padded hammock for the middle and upper classes that our vast entitlements edifice has become. I'm sure most would agree that today we must forge a new covenant between citizens and government for the sake of the future—a covenant every bit as history-bending as FDR's New Deal. Indeed, we face another rendezvous with destiny.

Properly empowered and operating on a purely bipartisan basis, the kind of national commission I have in mind would, at the least, move us in the direction where the types of essential but politically all-too-toxic reforms I lay out in the next chapter will become possible. For the President, it is a chance to recapture a squandered opportunity and, as President Kennedy, one of his heros, did with the 1960s Apollo program, inspire and rally the nation behind a cause that will make sure this is not the last American Century.

10

The Peterson Budget
Action Plan

The budget plan I now present is an honest effort (at least, it's my honest effort) to balance the federal budget, thereby boosting America's rates of national savings, private capital formation, and living standard improvement. At the same time that it puts our fiscal house in order, it redirects public resources toward worthy public goals, including alleviating poverty, providing health insurance for those who cannot now afford it, and funding high-return investments in infrastructure, human capital, and the development of cutting-edge technologies.

In looking for a name for my plan, I at first hesitated to call it the *"Peterson* Budget Action Plan,'' as I thought that might seem pretentious. But my colleagues persuaded me to go ahead and do it. What they had in mind, I suspect, was that people would then know to blame me and not them. The name issue aside, my plan consists of policy recommendations that begin to go into effect in fiscal year 1995. These recommendations, of course, are not meant to be exhaustive. Nor is this particular mix of reforms the only possible mix that would allow us to balance the budget and remain faithful to the guiding principles I outlined in the last chapter. My budget plan is a demonstration model, not the production model. Its purpose is to show, by broad strokes, how Americans can—if we so choose—reclaim the better future we all desire.

Let me begin with a few highlights.*

- **The Peterson Budget Action Plan will balance the budget by the year 2000.** Under the Congressional Budget Office's business-as-usual baseline projection, the federal budget will be running a deficit of $457 billion in the year 2000 and $742 billion in 2004. If my plan is implemented, the consolidated federal budget by the year 2000 will show a comfortable surplus—about $30 billion—which will gradually rise to nearly $50 billion by 2004. (Given the uncertainties inherent in all projections, plus the especially difficult problem that controlling health-care costs poses, it is only prudent to aim for some surplus.) As a point of comparison, if President Clinton's original budget plan had been enacted the deficit would still have been $295 billion in 2000 and $465 billion in 2004.
- **My budget plan's savings are entirely structural.** There are no phony accounting tricks (like juggling the timing of tax receipts and benefit payments) or one-shot bonanzas (like sales of federal assets). The entire budget saving under my plan comes from durable long-term adjustments in the size and function of national defense, in our personal expectations of future federal benefits, and in our tax structure. Many of the reforms (such as those that adjust our expectations about retirement or slow the growth in health-care costs) will not only lock in permanent budget savings; they will generate savings that continue to rise rapidly in the next century.

Consider, for example, that as America "grays" over the next fifty years, the total number of federal beneficiaries is expected to at least double and the number over age eighty-five is expected to triple or quadruple. Any permanent percentage savings in benefit costs that we achieve will therefore naturally grow substantially over time. The entitlement dollars saved by my plan already come to 1.9 percent of GDP (or about $150 billion a year in today's dollars) by 2004—yet keep growing, to 3.4 percent of GDP (or about $350 billion a year in today's dollars) by 2020 and to 5.3 percent of GDP (or about $700 billion a year in today's dollars) by 2040.† That's what I mean by structural budget savings.

---

* Throughout the rest of this chapter, all years in budget projections refer to federal "fiscal years." All "savings" figures refer to savings relative to the January 1993 Congressional Budget Office (CBO) baseline projection through fiscal year 2004. It is this projection that forecasts what federal outlays and revenues will be in the future if we make no policy changes. All budget functions ("entitlements" and "domestic discretionary," for example) are CBO-defined, and may differ slightly from the OMB-based definitions sometimes used elsewhere in the book.
† All budget numbers for beyond the year 2004 cited in this chapter refer to projections that are based on the official (1993) Social Security Administration demographic and economic scenario through the year 2040.

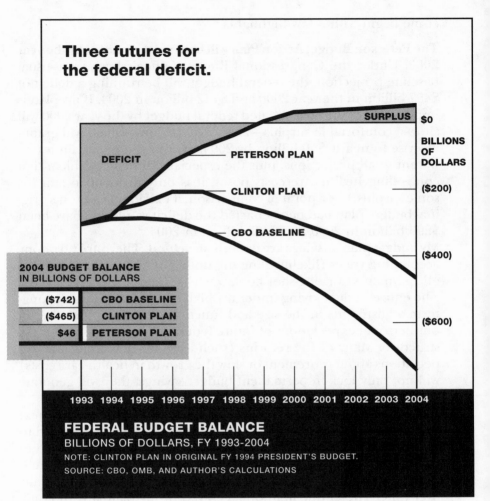

Three futures for the federal deficit.

SURPLUS $0

BILLINGS OF DOLLARS

DEFICIT

PETERSON PLAN

CLINTON PLAN ($200)

CBO BASELINE

($400)

2004 BUDGET BALANCE
IN BILLIONS OF DOLLARS

($742)	CBO BASELINE
($465)	CLINTON PLAN
$46	PETERSON PLAN

($600)

1993 1994 1995 1996 1997 1998 1999 2000 2001 2002 2003 2004

FEDERAL BUDGET BALANCE
BILLIONS OF DOLLARS, FY 1993-2004
NOTE: CLINTON PLAN IN ORIGINAL FY 1994 PRESIDENT'S BUDGET.
SOURCE: CBO, OMB, AND AUTHOR'S CALCULATIONS

· **Even as my plan balances the budget, it will cut the U.S. poverty rate and improve the living standards of America's lowest-income households.** The expansion of Supplemental Security Income in my plan will guarantee access to a poverty-level cash safety net to every American who is over age sixty-two or disabled. The expansion of the Earned Income Tax Credit will guarantee the same to every American parent with two or more children who works full-time for minimum wages. And my expansion of Medicaid will guarantee access to health insurance to all lower-income households with incomes up to twice the poverty line. Some of the proposals in my plan (the national retail sales tax and higher "sin" taxes, for instance) will impose some burden on lower-income households. But on balance, for all poor and near-poor Americans, the total cost of such changes will be exceeded by the new cash and health-care benefits they receive. The principle of fairness to the poor is of the utmost importance to me. I have asked leading experts to calculate the impact that all of the benefit cuts and tax hikes I propose would have on Americans in various income brackets. Using the same computer models Congress does for this purpose, this is what they found: Not only does my plan shelter the poor and near-poor from most sacrifice, but, on average, families with incomes of less than $10,000 would come out ahead of where they are now by a meaningful 26 percent.*

· **From middle-class and affluent Americans, my budget plan asks for sacrifices that rise along with their income.** In hypothesizing about how to balance the budget, most people assume that any plan that gets the job done must inevitably be regressive. But beyond sheltering poor and near-poor households, the size of the sacrifices my plan asks of middle-class and affluent Americans rises steadily as incomes increase. The reason is that many of its reforms have been carefully designed so that they will have little (or, in some cases, no) impact on American families with incomes beneath the national median but will call for sacrifices that are genuinely progressive for those over the median. Included among these are a comprehensive "affluence test" that uses a sliding-scale to withhold the entitlement benefits of above-median households, increases in the taxability of entitlement benefits, caps on our tax subsidies for health care and housing, and higher marginal income tax rates on the top 1 percent of U.S. tax filers.

When it comes to how sacrifice is shared under my plan, I think the following numbers sum it up best. Americans who are not officially in poverty but who have incomes well beneath the national median would make only a small contribution toward deficit reduction. (The 13 percent of Americans who earn $10,000 to $20,000 bear just 1.7 percent of the total sacrifice, for an average sacrifice of about $200 per family). By the time we get to the middle of America's middle class, the contribution is significant. (The 13 percent of Americans who earn $30,000 to $40,000, for instance, would bear 13 percent of the sacrifice, for an average of about $1,800 per family.) At the upper reaches of America's middle class, the contribution would be much larger. (The 5 percent of Americans who earn $100,000 to $200,000 bear 16 percent of the sacrifice, for an average of about $5,600

---

* In budget savings calculations in this chapter, "family" refers to related people living together *or* to an individual living alone or with other unrelated people.

per family.) Once we arrive at the truly affluent, the contribution amounts to a much fuller and fairer share. (The 1 percent of Americans who earn $200,000 and over bear 14 percent of the sacrifice, for an average of about $23,300 per family.)

· **My Budget Action Plan observes the principle of gradualism.** All policy changes that ask for sacrifices from any but the wealthiest 1 or 2 percent of Americans will be phased in gradually over no less than six years and do not become fully operative before 2000. In contrast, policy changes in my plan that ask for sacrifices exclusively from the rich—or that target additional cash benefits to lower-income households—become effective immediately.

· **Spending cuts under my plan will greatly exceed tax hikes.** By 2004, budget savings from cuts in entitlements, defense, discretionary domestic programs, and interest on the national debt will exceed total new revenues by 1.8 to 1. (Although I prefer not to split hairs over what to call a spending cut and what to call a tax hike, I should point out that if we exclude from the tally revenue raised by closing tax loopholes and capping benefitlike tax subsidies, cuts in federal spending exceed revenues from new taxes and higher tax rates by an even more impressive 2.6 to 1.) As time passes, moreover, the accelerating savings in entitlements and interest will tilt the ratio of spending cuts to total new revenues increasingly toward spending. By 2020, that ratio becomes 4.5 to 1; by 2040, 11.5 to 1. The primary long-term impact of enacting my plan would thus be to halt the hemorrhaging of federal spending that is already built into current policy.

· **My budget plan will greatly increase the resources that America dedicates to investment.** The main purpose of balancing the budget, of course, is to stop our negative public savings and thus free up national savings for productivity-enhancing new private business investments. Under my plan—and even discounting the possibility of a rise in private-sector savings rates—U.S. savings available for private domestic investment will climb by 4.7 percent of GDP between 1994 and 2000 and by 4.9 percent of GDP by 2004. But we will also need to make new, productive public investments. By 2000, my plan will boost federally funded spending on such crucial priorities as child education and health, high-tech research and development, and public infrastructure by $85 billion, or by 1 percent of GDP. All told, this will double or triple America's current level of real-dollar public investment in such critical, high-return areas.

· **My plan extends health-insurance coverage to the uninsured.** Another pressing social goal my Budget Action Plan achieves is helping ensure that Americans who can't afford it have access to our health system. Under my plan, expanded Medicaid benefits for lower-income households plus mandated employer coverage will extend health insurance to the vast majority of those who now lack it and to nearly everyone anywhere near the poverty line.

· **My Budget Action Plan will alter economic incentives in ways that boost America's private savings rate and encourage long-term productive investments.** By reducing unfunded public benefit liabilities for future retirement and health-care consumption, my plan is almost certain to result in more private savings. By shifting our tax base from income to consumption, it will also create incentives that favor savings and investment. Moreover, when it comes to the types of investments we make, my plan will tilt the playing field away from residential housing and toward productivity-enhancing investments in business start-ups, plant and equipment, commercial R&D, and worker training.

How are most politicians and lobbyists likely to react to what follows? I am a realist. I am familiar with the shrill charges ("Unthinkable!" "Draconian!") that are so often heard whenever any sacrifice is asked and with the crocodile tears that appear whenever the status quo is challenged. But I am also an optimist. I believe that most Americans understand that our current economic trajectory is both immoral and unsustainable. And I'm convinced that they will be willing to make reasonable adjustments in their habits and expectations if they are certain that it will make a real difference and if they feel that the sacrifices they make are fairly and broadly shared.

And that's the last but most important selling point of my Budget Action Plan. It *will* make a difference. It will get the job done. Barring a major war, a depression, or some other national catastrophe, it will balance the budget and triple our rate of net national savings. It will put our economy back on track toward a positive future.

"THE DEVIL IS IN THE DETAILS"

Let's review the overall budget targets that I set in Chapter 8 in light of the CBO baseline projections through the year 2004—our benchmark forecast that tells us what is likely to happen if we do nothing and just let the entire budget career into the future on autopilot.

First, let's focus on our primary objective: balancing the budget by 2000 and keeping it balanced thereafter. In 1994, the year before my plan goes into effect, the CBO projects a deficit of 4.4 percent of GDP. Our goal calls for budgetary savings of at least that magnitude over the six-year period beginning in 1995. Next, let's recall our secondary objective: boosting federal investment outlays by one full percentage point of GDP. This raises to 5.4 percent of GDP the savings we must find in all noninvestment areas of the budget. Designing reforms that meet these targets would alone be a tough job. But now get ready for another challenge that makes the job even tougher: From 1997 on, the CBO projection shows a "baseline" deficit that deepens as a share of GDP. Even while we change policy, growing entitlement and interest outlays will raise the deficit cost of "doing nothing" at an accelerating pace. By the year 2000, in fact, the baseline budget deficit hits 5.4 percent of GDP. By 2004, it hits 7.4 percent of GDP—or, for those of you who prefer to view it in the clearest, starkest terms, $742 billion.

The bottom line? Our goal must be to save 6.4 percent of GDP in all noninvestment areas of the budget by the year 2000. By the year 2004, we must be saving at least 8.4 percent of GDP relative to baseline. This amounts to savings of $542 billion and $843 billion, respectively. Even allowing for inflation, these are gigantic numbers. Then recall that our strategy must also be consistent with all our reform principles, from fairness to the poor to gradualism. It must also rely on prudent economic assumptions. To get an idea of how important prudent forecasting is if we are not to fall short of our targets, consider this: If real annual GDP growth between 1993 and 1998 were to weigh in one percentage point under what the CBO now projects, it would add $106 billion to our 1998 budget deficit.

It's worth emphasizing that the CBO baseline assumes only lukewarm employment, productivity, and real wage growth over the next ten years. (That's hardly surprising, since it also assumes our deficits will continue to mushroom.) My plan should push us toward a faster growth path—which would itself help raise revenues and shrink the deficit. I have declined, however, to incorporate such "positive feedback" into the economic projections. In the interest of credibility and prudence, my plan is designed to achieve its goals even in the absence of any economic improvement over current expectations for the next decade. If we do better than expected, our budget surpluses might be used to finance more of our unfunded federal retirement trust funds. Or (if the surplus is large enough) we might be able to justify slightly more spending or slightly less taxing. Needless to say, we should waste no time worrying about such choices. They will be easy. This book is about the real and the tough choices that face us today.

Concentrating on projections is challenging but essential. Abstract theories about reform cannot substitute for a hard look at the numbers and a realistic appraisal of the concrete choices required to overcome them. As Ross Perot explained on national television when asked about budget plans: "The devil is in the details."

TWENTY-FOUR PROPOSALS TOWARD A BALANCED BUDGET

My plan takes on the devil on his favorite ground. Its twenty-four proposals are organized around eight major budget categories: one for defense, one for domestic discretionary spending, four for entitlements, and two for general revenues. There is also a ninth category for interest costs. For each proposal, I indicate the year or years during which it will be implemented or phased in. I also indicate the budget savings (less spending, more revenue, or both) or the budget cost in the years 2000 and 2004.* These savings numbers do *not* refer to *cumulative* savings between now and 2000 or 2004. Unlike the politicians who typically cite cumulative savings figures because the numbers are larger and make it seem that they are doing more to cut the deficit, my numbers refer to the *annual* savings this plan will realize in those particular years. Also note that my savings numbers refer only to federal *budget* savings; they do not reflect any savings our private economy may realize if my plan is implemented (slower growth in health-care costs, for instance).

The Defense Budget

Ever since the Cold War began winding down in the late 1980s, there has been widespread agreement that America can enjoy a "peace dividend" by scaling back what it spends on national security. That scaling back, of course, is already well under way. In 1986, defense spending amounted to 6.5 percent of our GDP. Every year since, that share has fallen, and by 1993 it had dropped to 4.8 percent of GDP. When it comes to defense, the real question is not whether to cut but how much further to cut.

Reform 1. Keep cutting defense—prudently and sustainably.

Implementation: 1995 to 1998. Savings in 2000: $53 billion. Savings in 2004: $60 billion.
My budget plan assumes that we can still cut defense substantially. Its recommendations for defense spending track President Clinton's recommendations downward through 1998; thereafter, defense spending rises only fast enough to keep pace with inflation. This means that what

---

* Many of my proposals are interactive, which means that the savings for any one proposal may be affected by other proposals. The savings from taxing Social Security benefits, for instance, will be reduced by raising the Social Security retirement age. In the savings calculations in my plan, each proposal therefore assumes the enactment of all prior proposals. The savings numbers are thus arithmetically additive.

we spend on defense will keep sinking as a share of our economy—to 3.3 percent of GDP by 1997 and to 2.9 percent by 2004. One way that we will be able to continue cutting defense is by eliminating the duplication of services and weapons systems in today's armed forces. Another is requiring Europe, Japan, and others to assume more of the global peacemaking burden. But most important, as I discussed in detail in Chapter 7, we can buy a lot more security for a lot less money if we stop letting yesterday's assumptions drive our long-term spending plans and instead begin to shape our strategies around a realistic, "bottom-up" assessment of the new threats America is likely to face in the future.

I am fully aware that many liberals believe that we can cut defense far more than I (and President Clinton) have proposed. But the truth of the matter is that we will be hard-pressed to meet the targets in this action plan. In the first place, a large share of our recent defense cuts were made possible because we had overstocked equipment and ammunition during the procurement binge of the mid-1980s. Today the era of "painless" cuts is coming to an end. There also comes a point when we have to heed the lessons of history. One of those lessons, unfortunately, is that America's investment in defense seems to follow a wrenching boom-and-bust cycle. We don't want to repeat that cycle once again. We don't want to find ourselves with another "hollow force" awaiting some new danger that suddenly forces us to rebuild in great haste and at great cost.

By 1997, according to both my budget plan and the current administration's proposals, U.S. defense spending will be smaller as a share of our GDP than at any time since Pearl Harbor. By the year 2004, it will have fallen below 3 percent of GDP, well under what several other industrial nations now spend as a share of their economies. Yet to meet the kinds of threats we are likely to face, our armed forces must be highly mobile and capable of rapid response to crises in all corners of the globe. Inevitably, this kind of restructuring will require some major new purchases, especially for improved airlift capabilities. In an era of nuclear proliferation and of rising ethnic and religious factionalism, I don't believe we can safely afford to spend less on defense than what I propose.

Domestic Discretionary Spending

"Discretionary" is the term that Washington budgeteers use to describe federal spending that must be voted on and appropriated each year by Congress, unlike most "entitlements," which would keep right on thriving and growing even if Congress took a permanent vacation. Ironically, the domestic discretionary budget category (with its disposable-sounding name) includes practically all the public spending that matters most to our future—everything from infrastructure, education, and crime control to environmental protection, child health, and worker training. It is also a budget category that has shrunk substantially as a share of our GDP since the 1970s—from 4.7 percent in 1979 to 3.7 percent in 1993. In effect, we have been allowing the explosive growth in our politically "untouchable" entitlements to crowd other domestic spending priorities out of the federal budget.

In view of the host of unmet public investment needs now facing our nation—and considering that in my budget plan I propose we spend an additional percentage point of GDP to meet those needs—it's simply unrealistic to expect to achieve *overall* budgetary savings in domestic discretionary spending. What we can do, however, is spend our money smarter. First, let's cut out whatever deadwood remains in our *current* budget. Second, let's be as sure as we possibly can that the new resources we devote to investment spending are targeted where they will yield the highest social and economic returns.

Reform 2. Trim currently budgeted discretionary domestic programs by 10 percent in real dollars.

Implementation. 1995 to 2000. Savings in 2000: $34 billion. Savings in 2004: $38 billion.

During my decades of experience in the business world, I have rarely encountered an organization—especially a large bureaucracy that has never before experienced major restructuring and downsizing—that cannot sustain a 10 percent budget reduction while maintaining (or maybe even improving) the quality of the services it renders. Applying this rule, my plan requires that the *total* cost of all currently budgeted discretionary programs be at least 10 percent lower in real terms in 2000 than in 1994.

How to cut costs? Not by mindless "across-the-board" whacks, but rather by taking a zero-based budgeting approach and looking for areas where our spending is simply not cost-effective—or serves yesterday's priorities, not today's or tomorrow's. Starting with the federal payroll, let's eliminate jobs at overstaffed agencies, cut back on overly generous vacation, disability, and health benefit perks, and (as President Clinton has already proposed) freeze pay for a full year. Here it's not just an issue of direct budgetary savings. The federal government must be able to point to visible, credible examples of its own belt-tightening if it is to enjoy the moral authority to ask the rest of us to sacrifice. Moving on to marginal spending programs, let's just say no to cheap postage for nonprofit junk mail, loan subsidies to favored businesses, pork-barrel "demo" projects, and scandalous "overhead" pay-

ments to universities. Let's do away with educational "impact aid" to
wealthy school districts, outdated grants to the Tennessee Valley Authority, and giveaway loans to utilities that can borrow from the Rural
Electrification Authority. Let's cut back on hit-or-miss housing assistance and haphazard "community development" funding. Let's overhaul or convert the underused VA hospital system. Just maybe the
supercollider is justifiable "basic" research. But maybe the space station is not. In each case, let's ask: Can we justify borrowing to pay for
this project? Sometimes, just like any household, we're going to have
to say no, not this year; maybe later, when we get our finances in order.

**Reform 3. Dedicate a full additional percent of GDP toward a targeted
agenda of public investment needs.**

*Implementation: 1995 to 2000. Cost in 2000: $85 billion. Cost in 2004: $101
billion.*

One percent of Gross Domestic Product is a huge amount of extra
money—$85 billion in 2000, the first year this proposal is fully phased
in. But before Congress starts licking its lips in the hope that these
funds might replace the "pork" it just lost, a few unbreakable ground
rules need to be announced. First, all of this money must go into R&D
and physical and human capital formation programs with demonstrated high rates of return. To help guarantee this, each proposal for
new spending must be accompanied by a "productivity impact statement." Second, no new money is to be spent on investments for which
a reliable and near-term private-sector market exists. Government can
provide an invaluable service to our economy by funding basic research; it should not be in the business of directly funding and managing commercial development. Finally (and it's worth noting that this
is the common practice in Japan), our investment priorities should be
ranked, *in advance* of their funding, by agencies and expert panels
acting independently from our elected representatives. The highest
priorities will be met first, the lower priorities as funding allows. If our
priorities are ranked in advance as I've described, Congress will be
answerable to the electorate not only for what it does fund, but also for
the worthwhile projects it does not. It will also be possible, if fiscal
stimulus is needed, for Congress to move up new projects according to
rational criteria rather than just dish out pork.

Deciding how exactly we spend this 1 percent of GDP must await the
results of productivity impact statements. But it is not unreasonable to
conjecture that half of this sum could profitably go to infrastructure—
not just "old style" investments in roads, bridges, and airports, but also
"new style" investments in things like high-speed rail and deep-water
ports. Perhaps a quarter might be used to support a massive basic

research and development effort (staffed, where possible, with former defense scientists and engineers) that targets cutting-edge industrial technologies. Much of the final quarter could certainly be used to pay for a comprehensive health, education, and neighborhood care program for all low-income preschool Americans. Our children are our nation's most crucial investment, and studies confirm that dollars properly spent on their welfare generate enormous social and economic benefits over time. One study that particularly impressed me is the Committee for Economic Development report I've already mentioned; in it, a group of CEOs concluded unanimously that an additional $11 billion invested annually in the health, education, and skills of underclass kids would have an excellent competitiveness payoff. Ultimately, of course, our children are the primary reason we are undertaking *any* long-term investments at all.

Entitlements: Across-the-Board Reforms

Anyone who harbors the faintest hope that balancing the budget is possible without fundamental changes in our entitlements system— changes that will require some sacrifice from middle- as well as upper-income Americans—should take a close look at the CBO baseline projection for federal spending. It shows that entitlements and net interest payments are expected to climb by 4.5 percent of GDP between 1994 and 2004 (or by a stunning $580 billion in today's dollars)—while all other federal spending is already expected to decline by 1.6 percent of GDP. Since we can't do anything about interest costs except insofar as we reduce the deficit elsewhere, that leaves entitlements, period.

And entitlements aren't about to slow down on their own—no matter how long we wait. Consider that between 1994 and 2020, entitlement spending is projected to *grow* by 7 percent of GDP. That's $1.2 trillion in inflation-adjusted 1992 dollars—enough to pay for everything we now spend on the Pentagon more than four times over! Between 2020 and 2040, entitlement spending is scheduled to soar by another 4.2 percent of GDP. All told, over the next half century, we're looking at *additional* federal benefit costs that amount to at least one-quarter of every worker's paycheck.

My plan's approach to entitlements reform begins with three general provisions that cut across broad cross-sections of the American public. Two provisions will result in large benefit reductions and budget savings: a comprehensive "affluence test" for wealthier-than-average beneficiaries and an expansion in the taxability of most benefits. Both constitute a direct assault on welfare for middle- and upper-income Americans—a taboo-shattering course that some might shun as "politically impossible," but that others may welcome as a means by which an

economically beleaguered mainstream America can regain a sense of
common purpose and shared citizenship. The third provision—an expanded refundable tax credit to low-income working families—carries
a modest price tag but will help correct a major age and income inequity
that afflicts our current entitlement system. We lavish huge public subsidies on the old and the affluent, but do next to nothing to help full-
time working parents who labor in poverty.

*Reform 4. Establish a comprehensive and highly progressive "affluence
test"—or "graduated entitlement benefit reduction"—for above-median-
income beneficiaries.*

*Implementation: 1995 to 2000. Savings in 2000: $71 billion. Savings in 2004:
$93 billion.* *

Whenever I talk about how balancing the budget will inevitably require deep cuts in our current system of welfare for the well-off, I'm
often met with gasps of incredulity. Myths, and especially myths that are
self-serving, die hard, and many Americans still believe that our huge
and burgeoning middle- and upper-income entitlements establishment
is really a safety net for the poor. But as we've seen throughout this book,
it's simply untrue that most federal benefits go to people in dire financial need. Consider that in 1991 about $75 billion in Social Security and
Medicare benefits alone went to households with annual cash incomes
of over $50,000. Most of these benefits, moreover, are "unearned" by
prior contributions: It's not just a matter of "getting back what you paid
in." Consider also that between 1994 and 2004, 70 percent of the increase in total federal entitlement spending will be in programs whose
benefits are disbursed without regard to financial need.

Question: Is there any *comprehensive* way we can scale back welfare for
the non-needy without hurting the poor and without creating a huge
new bureaucracy to establish "need"? Until recently, satisfactory answers were unavailable. COLA freezes and "diet COLAs," the one
widely discussed way to get large across-the-board entitlement savings,
would certainly trim welfare for the well-off. But there's a problem with

---

* The outlay savings calculated for this affluence test reflect only the 80 percent of
federal benefits for which we have accurate data on beneficiary income by household:
Social Security, Medicare, railroad retirement, unemployment compensation, veterans' pensions, food stamps, all means-tested cash and tax-credit benefits, and all federal pensions. The remaining 20 percent includes farm aid and veterans' health
services, for which the affluence test would be sure to generate extra outlay savings
from upper-income beneficiaries. It also includes Medicaid, for which the affluence
test might require special rules to differentiate the truly needy from well-off recipients
of long-term care who qualify by legal subterfuge ("spending down" by setting up
trust funds and making family gifts). In any case, the numbers calculated here are a
conservative estimate of the potential savings from an across-the-board affluence test.

universal COLA cuts. They can't distinguish between the retired widow with a $10,000 annual income and the retired millionaire whose Social Security benefit is perhaps the same but whose income is a hundred times larger. To get around this problem, I've often advocated applying COLA reductions selectively by (for instance) excluding those beneficiaries whose monthly benefit amounts fall below a minimum threshold or by allowing a refundable tax credit to all lower-income beneficiaries. But even with these safeguards, COLA cuts are at best a partial and imperfect way to trim welfare for the well-off.

And the other alternatives? We might, to be sure, scale back subsidies by rewriting the benefit formulas and eligibility criteria of each and every one of our federal entitlement programs. But that would require amending myriad statutes—a process that would have to snake through dozens of congressional committees, could grind on for years, and would be endangered at every turn by interest group lobbies bent on protecting their benefits and ensuring that their ox is not the only one that ends up gored. There's another problem with this approach as well. People have many different sources of income, and piecemeal changes in the benefit levels of particular entitlement programs would leave us uncertain about how we are affecting the *total* benefits and *total* incomes of families in different income brackets.

A couple of years ago, entitlements experts Neil Howe and Philip Longman developed the idea of a single comprehensive means test for all federal benefit programs. In the past, I had turned to Neil for help in many of my entitlements battles, so when it came to developing the present plan, I didn't hesitate to call him. At my urging he enlisted the aid of Pete Davis, another expert, and together they refined the means-testing proposal. *My biggest concern was that it be carefully designed so that it affect no family with an income below the U.S. median.*

The result is the "affluence test"—or "graduated entitlement benefit reduction"—proposed in this plan. As the centerpiece of an overall entitlements reform agenda, it is, I'm convinced, superior to the other alternatives. It would include all federal benefits, both cash and in-kind—not just Social Security and Medicare, but everything from farm aid to federal pensions. In making benefit reductions, it always takes into account the total current benefits and total current incomes of families. It requires no sacrifice of lower-earning American families but asks for progressive sacrifices from families with incomes above the median. It sidesteps many legislative obstacles to entitlements reform. It leaves no doubt that the sacrifice is across the board, so that all Americans who are able make a fair contribution. Last, but not least, the budget savings it will yield are enormous: a minimum of $93 billion in 2004, a sum that will then soar to about $200 billion a year in 2020 and $470 billion a year in 2040.

How would it work? Although it is a benefit cut, pure and simple, the affluence test would be enforced through the tax code. Each year, all tax filers with family incomes above the U.S. median (which is on track to be about $35,000 by 1995, when the test begins to be phased in) will be required to report their estimated combined federal benefits for the coming year. There would be a worksheet to calculate them and a line on the 1040 income tax form to report them. Based on each family's total income, the Department of Health and Human Services would then "withhold" some fraction of those benefits. Benefit reductions, needless to say, would be adjusted in the event that families faced changed economic circumstances during the year or in subsequent years.

And what about the benefit reduction rates? Under the affluence test, families would lose 7.5 percent of all benefits that cause their income to exceed $35,000, plus an additional 5 percent at the margin for each additional $10,000 in family income.* For most types of benefits, the maximum benefit reduction rate would be 85 percent, applicable to families with incomes of $185,000 or more. (All income brackets would be adjusted upward each year to take inflation into account.) Federal pensions are an exception because, at least in some sense, their terms are based on a real contract between government and its former employees. Taking this fact into account, the maximum benefit withholding rate for these programs would be set at just 25 percent.

The table opposite summarizes what the impact of the affluence test would actually be on American families. A glance at the table is enough to show that the test is indeed steeply progressive. If it doesn't finally silence those who endlessly rail that entitlements reform cannot help but ravage the poor, it should at least give them pause. Nothing at all is taken from families with below-median incomes. For families in the $30,000 to $40,000 income bracket (who are receiving benefits and earning enough to be subject to the test), the sacrifice called for averages just $260 a year. All told, this group faces just a 1 percent reduction in benefits—not much when you consider that COLA hikes and health-care cost inflation will still be pushing up total benefits per family by well over 5 percent each year. Remember too that nearly all of the families receiving substantial total benefits (over $10,000) are *retired*. Most of these retirees have considerable financial and real assets. Three-quarters own their own homes, and of these, two-thirds have entirely paid off their mortgages. Very few have any

* Like my budget plan as a whole, this affluence test is a demonstration model, not the production model. According to The Concord Coalition, we could achieve roughly the same overall savings if we applied the test at $40,000 of income with a 10 percent initial withholding rate, then raised that rate by 10 percent for each additional $10,000 of income.

expenses related to work or to raising or educating children. And, of course, most have their health care paid for through Medicare.

For families with incomes of between $50,000 and $75,000, the required sacrifice rises to an average of $2,310, or 12 percent of that income group's benefits. For families with incomes of over $200,000, that sacrifice averages $15,345, or 72 percent of total benefits. Yet at the same time that it is steeply progressive, the affluence test I propose finds the lion's share of its total budget savings where it has to: among America's great middle class. Families with incomes of $35,000 to $100,000 contribute 62 percent of the budget savings. If we count families with incomes up to $200,000, the "middle class" contributes 88 percent. Although individual middle-class families need not make huge sacrifices, the aggregate saving, because they are so numerous, *is* huge.

The affluence test I propose is more than just one way among many to help balance the budget. It also makes our entire system of intergenerational "transfer" programs more equitable and sustainable. In effect, what we will be doing is relying more on *intra*generational burden *sharing* in funding our retirements and less on *inter*generational burden *shifting*. Under my affluence test, the 15 percent share of each family's benefits that is not subject to withholding will ensure that even today's sixty-five-year-old retired millionaire enjoys a (respectable) 3.5 percent tax-free return on all the Social Security FICA taxes he or she personally "paid into" the system. But there will be no windfalls. The retiree with $100,000 in income would receive an estimated 7 percent return. The retiree with a median income (who of course won't be affected by my test) will continue to get a return of about 12 percent.

Effects of the Affluence Test*
(or Graduated Entitlement Benefit Reduction)
on U.S. Families

Family Income	Average Benefit Reduction per Beneficiary Family	Share of Income Group's Benefits Withheld
$0–30,000	$0	0.0%
$30,000–40,000**	$260	1.1%
$40,000–50,000	$910	5.2%
$50,000–75,000	$2,310	12.4%
$75,000–100,000	$4,520	24.3%
$100,000–200,000	$8,050	40.0%
$200,000 & over	$15,345	71.5%

* Calculations in this table include only Social Security, Medicare, and federal pensions.

** In this bracket, only familes with incomes over $35,000 are subject to the test.

As for the poor retiree with $5,000 in income, he or she will get an estimated 13 percent return on past Social Security contributions (and with my expansion of SSI is likely to do even better in terms of overall retirement income). All of these payback calculations, moreover, refer only to Social Security retirement benefits. They do not reflect the more favorable return that all Americans will continue to receive on their payroll contributions for Medicare.

Since many upper-income Americans subject to my affluence test will no longer be receiving a "market" rate of return on their *total* Social Security FICA contributions (both their own and their employer's), they will be helping to pay for the benefits of retirees who are less well-off. Somebody has to subsidize those retirees: If we all insist on climbing on the bandwagon, who will be left to pull it? We can either ask the affluent among our peers to make the sacrifice or we can ask our kids. To insist on doing the latter is to forget Thomas Jefferson's moral injunction to hold the future harmless.

Reform 5. Expand the taxability of most federal benefits.

Implementation: 1995 to 2000. Savings in 2000: $25 billion. Savings in 2004: $33 billion.

The affluence test I have proposed will trim the entitlements benefits now received by middle-class families with above-median incomes and will cut deeply into welfare for the truly well-to-do. But even when fully phased in, affluence testing would still leave an inequity at the heart of many of our largest entitlement programs. This is the favorable tax treatment accorded most federal benefits, the advantages of which mainly accrue to middle- and upper-income families. I can't think of any justification for asking working families to pay both first-dollar FICA taxes and income taxes, while at the same time handing out largely tax-free retirement and health-care benefits to middle- and upper-income retirees. Neither, apparently, can most foreign governments. Throughout the rest of the industrial world, public benefits are generally just as taxable as any other income.

My plan will put most public benefits on a more even playing field with other forms of taxable income. Today, just 50 percent of Social Security cash benefits are taxable, and then only for families with incomes above certain thresholds. Yet if Social Security were taxed like a private pension plan, it is estimated that most beneficiaries would have to pay taxes on over 90 percent of their benefits. Just as President Clinton originally proposed in his first budget, my Budget Action Plan would tax 85 percent of all Social Security benefits. Although this is still generous treatment, a 15 percent tax exemption (the exemption would be calculated on the basis of benefits before the affluence test is applied) can be justified as a means of guaranteeing even today's wealthiest retirees a minimal tax-free rate of return on their personal FICA contributions. But I go a step further than President Clinton proposed by getting rid of the thresholds that currently shield beneficiary couples with incomes below $32,000 (and single beneficiaries with incomes below $25,000) from bearing the same tax burden as wage earners with identical incomes.*

As for Medicare, which is now entirely tax free, my plan will tax 25 percent of its insurance value (that is, the program's average per-capita cost), net of beneficiary premiums. A 75 percent exemption was chosen in order to make the tax treatment of Medicare roughly equivalent to the new tax treatment of employer-sponsored health insurance I propose below. In addition, my plan will extend blanket taxability to several other smaller entitlement programs—most notably workers' compensation—that until now have remained at least partially tax exempt.

Since these changes would affect only households that make enough money to pay income taxes, they would naturally affect no beneficiaries in the lowest income brackets. As for middle- and upper-income beneficiaries, their income tax burden would simply be brought more into line with what all other Americans in the same income brackets now face. An equitable and progressive income tax system is a "means test" from which no citizen deserves exemption.

Reform 6. Expand income assistance to the working poor.

Implementation: 1995. Cost in 2000: $7 billion. Cost in 2004: $8 billion.

Inexcusably, the historical development of America's patchwork "safety net" of antipoverty programs has missed the working poor. We have long had programs for the elderly, the disabled, and the unemployed. But we've had little for parents who work honestly (often full-time and year-round) but whose earnings do not raise them out of poverty. The one exception is a program called the Earned Income Tax Credit (EITC), which—even after its expansion in 1986 and 1990—leaves many working families below the poverty line. The EITC allows families with at least one child to claim a refundable credit that rises with the amount of income they earn. While most types of welfare penalize employment by canceling benefits when people get a job, the EITC serves as a work incentive. Only after earned income rises over a specified limit does the EITC benefit decline. In 1993, a family with

---

* The measure that Congress actually passed, it turns out, did not even go as far as President Clinton's original proposal. For the new 85-percent-of-benefits tax provision, the income thresholds were *raised* to $44,000 for beneficiary couples and $34,000 for single beneficiaries.

two children that earns between $7,750 and $12,200 is eligible for a maximum EITC benefit of $1,511.

To his credit, President Clinton has proposed again expanding the EITC so that no family of four will have to live in poverty in America, so long as at least one parent has a full-time job that pays minimum wages. In 1995, under the proposal in the President's original budget plan, a family with two children that earns between $8,500 and $11,000 will be eligible for a maximum EITC benefit of $3,460. For the first time, low-income workers without children will also receive an EITC benefit that is designed to offset the regressive FICA taxes they pay on their first $5,000 of wages. My plan adopts the President's proposal for an expanded EITC.

Entitlements: Retirement and Old-Age Provisions

Around the year 2010—when a very large (Baby Boom) generation starts retiring and a relatively small (Baby Bust) generation is in its peak income-earning and tax-paying phase of life—America's long-awaited "age wave" will hit in earnest. Practically every public cost associated with retirement will then start shooting upward, much faster than such costs are rising today. If our economy were saving prodigiously and growing rapidly in expectation of these exploding costs, we might be able to pay them without causing intolerable damage to tomorrow's living standards. But our national savings effort has been weakening rather than strengthening. Americans are saving less privately—in part precisely because so many of us expect that government will provide us with ample benefits during our old age. Meanwhile, our public-sector retirement "trust funds" are being spent to pay for current consumption.

Long before our age wave hits, it will be essential that Americans begin to reverse their attitudes toward retirement. Instead of trying to retire ever earlier with ever less financial preparation, we must develop a more responsible (and possibly more rewarding) ideal: the later retirement, the fuller savings account, the better use of maturity and experience in the workplace. We must raise the age of eligibility for Social Security. Instead of proving themselves to be "model employers" by heaping outsized pensions on their employees, government agencies must demonstrate their civic leadership by trimming back today's public pension windfalls. At the same time, we must get rid of current policies such as the Social Security "earnings test" that deter older Americans from working. We also need to do a much better job of ensuring that older (or disabled) Americans are not allowed to fall into poverty. All of these reforms, and the behavior changes that accompany them, will serve us well in a future of unremitting demographic pressure.

Reform 7. Accelerate the rise in the Social Security retirement age.

Implementation: 1995 to 2006. Savings in 2000: $16 billion. Savings in 2004: $36 billion.

In 1983, the National Commission on Social Security Reform recommended—and Congress enacted—a provision to raise the Social Security full-benefit retirement age from sixty-five to sixty-seven. The legislation stipulates that the rise will go into effect, in stages, between the years 2000 and 2022. This was, to be sure, a step in the right direction. But it was also too small and too slow a step. By 2022, life expectancy at age sixty-five will have risen by about six years over what it was in 1935 when Social Security was founded—and this is a conservative projection. Viewed in that perspective, a two-year hike in the retirement age seems quite modest; for those who are concerned about our "generational contract," it's worth noting that this change would only get us a third of the way back to Social Security's original terms. As for timing, no one needs half a lifetime to plan for such a modest delay in end-of-life leisure. It is wrong to ask today's twenty-year-olds to retire at older ages when today's fifty-year-olds could just as easily do the same.

Accordingly, my plan stipulates that the rise in the Social Security full-benefit retirement age begin in 1995 and that it proceed by three months per year until a new retirement age of sixty-eight is established in the year 2006. Eligibility for "early retirement" will rise in tandem, so that today's "reduced" benefits at age sixty-two will ultimately become available at age sixty-five. This provision will generate long-term and permanent budget savings. It does so directly by reducing Social Security outlays. It also does so indirectly, as later retirement adds to income and payroll tax revenue and reduces Medicare outlays (since Medicare is a secondary payer to employer-paid health plans for employees over age sixty-five).

Reform 8. Trim the benefit package for federal pensioners.

Implementation: 1995 to 2000. Savings in 2000: $4 billion. Savings in 2004: $6 billion.

For decades, federal employee lobbies have been demanding "comparability" between federal and private-sector salaries. Thanks to their efforts, cash compensation, which used to lag behind that in the private sector, is now roughly equivalent for most workers with comparable skills and experience. But, as we have seen, fringe benefits, and pension benefits in particular, is an area where any talk of "comparability" has always been avoided. The reason? These pensions and other fringe benefits are far more generous than even those offered lifetime career employees at Fortune 500 firms. But as any businessman who has ever looked at a payroll will tell you, it's nonsense to talk about whether worker salaries are fair unless you take into account *total compensation*—pensions and other fringes included.

My Budget Action Plan will help remedy this inconsistency by modifying the benefit rules for federal pensions. As we make these changes, we should keep in mind that unlike private pensions, our federal pension systems are unfunded. We won't be taking away money that's already been saved; we will be reducing the unfunded liabilities tomorrow's taxpayers must defray.

First, for all nondisabled retirees under age sixty-two, my plan will cut COLAs to two-thirds of the Consumer Price Index. (These retirees, however, will still receive a one-time "COLA catch-up" at age sixty-two to compensate them for the cumulative loss in their pension benefit's real value.) Second, after age sixty-two, the annual COLA will be limited to the inflation rate minus 1 percent for military retirees and to the inflation rate minus 0.5 percent for civilian retirees. (One reason for this slightly different treatment is that civilian retirees are much less likely than military retirees to be receiving fully indexed Social Security benefits in addition to their pensions; another is that civilian retirees have helped pay for their benefits through payroll deductions, whereas military retirees have not.) Both of these provisions, it is worth noting, will still leave all federal pensioners with far better inflation protection than is available in virtually any private pension system. Third, the base pay used for calculating pension benefits will be changed to the highest four years of salary (rather than the highest three) for the Civil Service Retirement System and to the highest twelve months (rather than the salary at the date of retirement) for the Military Retirement System. Finally, the federal matching contribution rate to the "thrift plan" for new civil service workers will be reduced, above 1 percent of pay, to fifty cents (rather than one dollar) for each dollar that workers contribute. (Like the indexing provisions I've proposed, all of these changes will bring our federal pension systems closer in line with the norm in the private sector.)

As modest as they are, these reforms will undoubtedly trigger a storm of protest from our civil service and military lobbies. But the principles of across-the-board sacrifice and total comparability of compensation demand them. Indeed, the American public is likely to view anything less as unfair. Remember that private-sector retirees will meanwhile be facing both higher Social Security retirement ages and larger benefit reductions under my plan's affluence test.

Reform 9. Expand means-tested cash assistance for the elderly and disabled.

Implementation: 1995. Cost in 2000: $20 billion. Cost in 2004: $24 billion.
Of the enormous stream of entitlement benefits (half a trillion dollars annually) that now go to the elderly—often defended as a "floor

of protection" against destitution—less than one-tenth actually serve to lift elderly households out of poverty. In the midst of all this indiscriminate largess, it is especially scandalous that our one cash benefit program explicitly designed to target the elderly and disabled poor (Supplemental Security Income, or SSI) has never been sufficiently funded to offer most of its participants even a poverty-level benefit. Currently the maximum federal SSI benefit for an individual living alone—$5,064 annually in 1992—is equivalent to only about 75 percent of the poverty level. Even with state supplements and food stamps, nearly all of the five million disabled and elderly Americans receiving SSI remain destitute by any ordinary definition of the word.

My Budget Action Plan will take some of the money saved by trimming benefits to upper-income households and dedicate it to raising the maximum SSI benefit to 100 percent of the poverty level. Today, a nondisabled person must be age sixty-five or over to qualify for benefits. Since we will need to provide better safety-net protection for those who are unable to work as the Social Security retirement age rises, my proposed SSI expansion will reduce that eligibility age to sixty-two. (Very few able seniors would actually quit work in order to collect even this enhanced SSI benefit.) To be sure, this reform will not "eliminate" elderly poverty, since many older Americans will choose to avoid the stigma and the complexity of applying for "unearned" means-tested benefits. It is a sad testament to our entitlement ethos that we no longer attach any stigma to receiving our much larger and mainly unearned flow of *non*-means-tested benefits—whether or not we actually need them.

Reform 10. Eliminate the Social Security "earnings test."

Implementation: 1995. Cost in 2000: $5 billion. Cost in 2004: $4 billion.

Because Social Security was designed during the Great Depression as "insurance" payable only in the event of total retirement, it originally stipulated that no one could collect benefits if he or she received any significant wages from work. Although this strict "earnings test" has since been liberalized, it still includes a rule that reduces Social Security checks by one dollar for every three dollars that beneficiaries aged sixty-five to sixty-nine receive in labor earnings over a relatively low threshold (now set at about $11,000) and by one dollar for every two dollars that beneficiaries aged sixty-two to sixty-four receive over a still lower threshold. If they're not really retired, so the rationale went, the elderly should not be receiving benefits. But this test has become counterproductive in a society that must begin encouraging more Americans in their sixties to remain in (or re-enter) the labor force. However well intentioned, it amounts to a costly, demoralizing, and unnecessary tax on the economic contributions of older people.

My plan will abolish it. Supporters of the earnings test often argue that its repeal would transform an "insurance" program into an "annuity" program. Fine. In the first place, it really doesn't make sense to think of Social Security as an insurance program, since its premiums don't come close to paying for its benefits. In the second place, however we think of it, we're better off with a program that does not offer people an explicit reward for permanently forsaking any form of productive labor. Supporters also argue that its repeal would benefit a disproportionate number of high-income working males who would not have chosen to retire at age sixty-two or sixty-five in any case. But remember: The comprehensive affluence test in my plan will severely limit such windfalls. With that test in place, the only unambiguous winners from repealing the earnings test will be middle-income Americans in their sixties who can't afford to forgo benefits but who also want to stay economically active, whether full- or part-time.

Entitlements: Health-Care Provisions

When he delivered his economic plan in February 1993, President Clinton went out of his way to emphasize that controlling the growth in health-care spending is an essential precondition for any long-term economic recovery. He then paused ("let me repeat that") and said it again. The President has spoken the truth: Health-care costs are growing so fast they won't wait for the next century's senior boom before reaching crisis proportions. We have a crisis today. Official projections indicate that national health-care spending will soar past 18 percent of GDP by the year 2000, up from an already staggering 14 percent in 1993. Within the federal budget, health care will be the dominant driver of entitlements growth throughout the next decade. Between now and 2004, just the constant-dollar *growth* in Medicare and Medicaid will be more than everything we spend (now or then) on national defense.

My Budget Action Plan includes a package of reforms that will save the federal government money, help slow the overall growth in U.S. health-care spending, and at the same time extend health insurance to the vast majority of Americans who now go without. These reforms do not pretend to be the final answer to our health-care crisis. But they are at least a start. A first crucial reform will be to limit our current open-ended tax subsidy for employer-paid health insurance. A second important step will be to tighten up on the fastest-growing component of Medicare: the Supplementary Medical Insurance (or SMI) program that pays for physician services for the elderly and disabled. Ensuring that all Americans have access to our health-care system is a social necessity, and my plan contains provisions that do just this in an economical fashion. But to pay for extended coverage, and to further control both public and national health-care costs, we must undertake additional reforms aimed at altering the cost-blind incentives that govern today's medical marketplace. A final component of my plan thus calls for the passage of a federal health-care cost control act.

Reform 11. Cap the tax exclusion for employer-paid health care.

Implementation: 1995 to 2000. Savings in 2000: $40 billion. Savings in 2004: $56 billion.

It is difficult to imagine a more wasteful and perverse subsidy than our current open-ended tax exclusion for employer-paid health care. This lavish tax favor will directly cost the federal government $75 billion in lost revenues in 1994. It encourages private-sector resources to flow into health-care consumption and away from other priorities (like higher wages or new investments). It gives the same preferential tax treatment to the last dollar spent on health care as to the first, and thus subsidizes not just basic health-care coverage, but gold-plated health-benefit plans. But these don't exhaust the list of its faults. Because our tax code is progressive, this subsidy also gives the biggest tax breaks to those who need them the least (upper-middle- and upper-income Americans) while giving nothing to Americans working for poverty or near-poverty wages without any insurance coverage at all. Put into place in an era when medical care was cheap, our open-ended tax subsidy for employer-paid health care is unaffordable today. We must cap it. Doing so will raise significant new federal revenues. It will also contribute to slowing the overall rate of growth in U.S. medical costs. A cap on today's tax subsidy will mean less induced consumer demand for health-care services. If firms (and ultimately beneficiaries) have to pay with after-tax dollars for that share of the cost of insurance premiums that exceeds a dollar ceiling, this will create a cost wedge that will cause many purchasers to switch to lower-priced, more cost-effective plans. It will also encourage providers and insurers to compete on the basis of price to deliver quality care under that dollar ceiling, putting a further brake on runaway medical costs.

Starting in 1995, my Budget Action Plan will limit our tax exclusion for employer-paid health care to $410 per month for family coverage and to $170 per month for individual coverage. (To create further cost-saving incentives, tax-deductible status will also be limited to plans that feature minimum copayments and deductibles.) These caps are set at about the average cost of insurance coverage. The cost of any employer-paid health insurance that exceeds them will be treated as taxable income to individual households. After 1995, the caps will be indexed to the CPI.

Reform 12. Raise Medicare premiums and coinsurance.

Implementation: 1995 to 2000. Savings in 2000: $28 billion. Savings in 2004: $43 billion.

In the early 1980s, Congress responded to skyrocketing Medicare costs by shifting its Hospital Insurance (or HI) component from a traditional retrospective, fee-for-service billing system to a prospective payment system based on each patient's Diagnostic Related Group (DRG). This measure indeed slowed the rate of growth in HI costs. But at the same time, the costs of Medicare's sister SMI program began to soar. What happened was that providers shifted numerous medical procedures to outpatient settings where cost-plus business as usual could continue. Ever since then, SMI has been the chief driver of total Medicare costs. Reining in its growth is essential if we are to control federal health-benefit costs in the late 1990s and beyond.

My plan tackles our SMI cost problem through three reforms. First, it raises the SMI annual deductible that beneficiaries must pay from $100 to $150 and then indexes it to per capita SMI spending. In the late 1960s, the SMI deductible was equivalent to about 45 percent of average annual per capita SMI costs; today, it weighs in at only about 5 percent of the program's per capita costs. Even a modest $50 annual hike in this cost-sharing requirement will help reintroduce a degree of cost-consciousness among SMI beneficiaries. Second, my plan extends 20 percent SMI copayments to the use of clinical laboratory services and home-health and skilled-nursing facilities, none of which now require copayments. This will standardize all SMI copayments at 20 percent, further reinforcing cost-sharing incentives. Finally, my plan raises the SMI premium so that it covers 30 percent of the program's costs, up from 25 percent today. This is only a small step back toward the 50 percent share of program costs that the SMI premium originally covered and would still leave most seniors benefiting from a huge subsidy from the general taxpayer. But by making the real costs of their medical care even somewhat more visible to them, we would be creating an incentive for the elderly—who are not only America's largest health-care consumers but its most active age bracket of voters—to take a political interest in demanding that Congress get serious about cost control.

Reform 13. Extend health insurance coverage to the uninsured.

Implementation: 1995 to 1997. Cost in 2000: $37 billion. Cost in 2004: $53 billion.

Any morally acceptable and politically viable health-care reform package will have to find some means of extending affordable insurance coverage to most of the approximately 35 million Americans who now lack it. The trick is to do so without breaking the federal budget or imposing crippling new costs on small businesses with low-wage workforces—those that are now least likely to offer (and are usually the least able to afford) insurance coverage. In my plan, I adopt a hybrid approach to extending coverage that combines an employer "mandate" with an expansion of Medicaid. It was first proposed by the Congressional Budget Office in 1991 and is less costly than most of the alternatives now being debated in Washington.

Specifically, my plan will require all businesses with twenty-five or more employees to offer health insurance coverage to their workers. Employers would at a minimum be required to cover 75 percent of the cost of the premiums; workers might be asked to contribute up to 25 percent. Both the exemption of businesses with fewer than twenty-five employees and the provision for premium cost-sharing will mitigate the new burden that small firms will face. So too will the special risk pools that will be established through which businesses with high premium costs can purchase insurance. (Alternatively, a "play or pay" plan could be set up that gives firms a choice between purchasing insurance on their own and paying a payroll tax earmarked for a new government benefit program.) In addition to its employer mandate, my plan will raise the eligibility threshold for Medicaid to 100 percent of the poverty level in every state. It will further allow households with incomes between 100 and 200 percent of the poverty level to "buy in" to Medicaid on a sliding scale. Once fully phased in, these reforms will cover roughly 85 percent of all Americans who are currently uninsured—and nearly everyone anywhere near the poverty line.

Reform 14. Enact a comprehensive federal health-care cost control act.

Implementation: 1995 and beyond. Savings in 2000: $22 billion. Savings in 2004: $82 billion.

Controlling health-care costs is without a doubt one of the toughest domestic policy issues that America has ever faced. I certainly don't profess to have all or even most of the answers. Frankly, I don't think anyone does. Finding the answers will require considerable experimentation. But we must start finding real solutions now. If we don't, runaway medical costs will ultimately bankrupt our national economy—not to mention derail any plan to balance the budget.

As far as federal spending is concerned, my plan therefore calls for setting explicit cost-containment goals as part of a health-care cost control act and insists that we meet them. Since 1980, the average annual growth rate in federal health-care spending has weighed in at a staggering 11 percent. My plan's goal is to ratchet that growth rate down by a modest one-quarter of a percentage point a year each year after 1995. As for private health-care spending, I assume in my projections that the reforms I advocate will cause a drop of one-eighth of a percentage point a year. A decade from now these changes would still leave national health-care spending growing twice as fast as our GDP and more than three times as fast as the CPI. Our ultimate goal must be to slow that growth to no faster than the growth of our economy. Even achieving the more limited early-stage goals I have set, however, won't be easy. In the interests of realism and prudent forecasting, it's wise to assume that meeting them is the best we'll be able to do.

When it comes to health-care cost containment, I am fundamentally and firmly convinced that the best approaches are market-based ones aimed at increasing cost-consciousness among both consumers and providers of medical care. This is why the federal cost-containment strategy in my action plan began with measures aimed at altering the cost-blind incentives that riddle today's medical marketplace. As we have already seen, the cap on the deductibility of employer-sponsored health insurance will produce *direct* federal revenues. And the higher Medicare copayments and deductibles will reduce *direct* government outlays. In the same way, my proposals to withhold a share of Medicare benefits under my affluence test and to tax a portion of its insurance value will have *direct* effects on increasing revenues. Yet over and above these direct savings, I believe that this raft of incentives to greater cost consciousness will have significant *indirect* effects in reducing the demand for health services. They thus promise to produce additional *indirect* savings that help us meet our cost-containment goals.

Along with these changes, there are other important reforms that will help medical markets work more efficiently and relieve upward pressures on costs. Near the top of the list must be malpractice reform. Our current malpractice system forces doctors to practice defensive medicine, thwarts cost-saving innovation, and inflates the costs of customary practice. Another key component in our overall strategy must be a concerted research effort in the area of "health outcomes" aimed at ranking the costs and benefits of alternative medical procedures, then incorporating these criteria into practice guidelines. Most experts agree that the lack of hard facts about what works and what doesn't adds tens of billions of dollars to our annual medical bills. If "productivity impact statements" confirm that outcomes research indeed promises to yield big payoffs in health-care savings—and I confidently predict they will—we could earmark a portion of our new investment budget for this kind of basic R&D. While on the subject of reforms that get to the very heart of our health-care crisis, let me also stress the enormous importance of modest new investments in preventive care and public health, as well as the more widespread use of living wills.

The blunt truth, however, is that we don't know exactly how much money will be saved by changing market incentives, or how quickly. And we simply cannot afford to allow our federal health-care cost explosion to continue unchecked. If we are to balance the budget, boost our rates of savings and investment, and restore the American Dream for our children, we must be as sure as we can that we will meet our cost-containment targets. Reluctantly, therefore, I have been persuaded that for federal spending, America, like other countries, must establish a "global" health-care budget with annual caps. In other words, Congress must determine *in advance* what we can spend on our Medicare and Medicaid programs if we are to meet our targets, then do everything possible to live within those limits. I have reached this conclusion despite knowing how difficult it will be to impose *any* top-down cap of this sort in a society as committed as ours is to freedom of choice. But we must remember that our health-care crisis is a national crisis, and crises require extraordinary measures.

How might a global budget for federal spending be imposed? One way would be to impose wage and price controls in government programs and to enact explicit rules about which medical technologies and procedures government will pay for. But after my firsthand experience with wage and price controls in the early 1970s, I have no doubt that a replay would be a political and administrative nightmare. The better approach, and one that is much more consistent with free markets and with experimentation, is to impose government constraints on the *overall* public resources we devote to health care.

What this would mean is greater reliance at all levels in our health system on what is known as "prospective capitation"—in other words, budgeting so many dollars for each beneficiary in advance. Each state, for instance, would receive its federal Medicaid matching funds in the form of a capitated grant. Because the checks mailed out from Washington would no longer be blank, this would save the federal budget money and create incentives for states to get more serious about cost containment themselves. They should be given wide latitude to experiment with how to live within their budgets. Doubtless, however, many will decide to require all Medicaid beneficiaries to join HMOs or else set up cooperative health insurance purchasing pools. As for Medicare, we might consider experimenting with a voucher system. Each beneficiary would receive a fixed-dollar voucher with which to purchase insurance. If the cost of the insurance purchased turned out to be less than the value of the voucher, beneficiaries could pocket the difference, and would thus have an incentive to be more prudent health-care shoppers. With or without vouchers, Congress might also consider requiring all Medicare beneficiaries to join an HMO or other qualified health plan. It could then cap annual costs by setting a ceiling on what it is willing to pay for each beneficiary's premium. All of this is more than an experiment in how best to contain costs. It is an experiment in which the federal government, states, and providers search out the best ways to strike the optimal social, political, cultural, and fiscal balance between the goals of cost savings and freedom of choice and quality of care.

Let there be no doubt about it. Living within a global budget for federally funded programs will be a new and painful experience. To be specific, beneficiaries are likely to face unaccustomed restrictions on access to high-tech, heroic care. But rationing of one sort or another— whether it takes place according to explicit rules or on an ad hoc basis as doctors and hospitals make difficult decisions to live within their budgets—is inevitable. Business as usual in health care is a thing of the past. What we need to be thinking about is not *whether* we need to set limits, but *how best to set them* in ways that do not do undue violence to our democratic and free market institutions and traditions.

Entitlements: Special Benefits and Subsidies

Up to now I've been talking mostly about the two biggest categories of federal benefits: retirement and health care. As far as spending cuts are concerned, I've largely steered clear of a third category, means-tested benefits, since I don't think it's feasible (or in most cases desirable) to generate significant savings by cutting benefits to the poor. But federal entitlement programs come in all shapes and sizes, and there are a large number of benefits and subsidies that don't fall under any of these three headings. A few items in particular are large enough to merit our special consideration: the home mortgage interest deduction, farm aid, and the myriad miscellaneous subsidies that we pass out to favored regions, businesses, or consumer groups by granting them special services whose costs are mostly underwritten by the general taxpayer.

Reform 15. Limit the home mortgage interest tax deduction.

Implementation: 1995 to 2000. Savings in 2000: $6 billion. Savings in 2004: $10 billion.

Rare is the American businessman who travels abroad (and I speak from experience) who is not at some point struck by the comparative luxury of so many of America's houses—and also by the comparative age of so much of America's industrial plant and equipment. One reason is that no other country grants owner-occupied housing such enormous tax favors—favors that effectively steer scarce U.S. capital away from space-age robotics and commercial R&D and steer it instead toward space-age Jacuzzis. The largest of these tax favors is our home mortgage interest deduction, which in 1994 will deprive the Treasury of $46 billion in revenues. Because it hands out over 80 percent of its tax benefits to households with incomes over $50,000, it not only represents a huge cost to the budget, it is also a miserably ineffective means of helping low-income families purchase homes.

My budget plan calls for capping this deduction at $12,000 for an individual, at $20,000 for a joint-filing couple, and at $10,000 for separately filing couples. Assuming an 8 percent interest rate, this means, for instance, that the only affected couples will be those with total home mortgages of over $250,000—a small and relatively wealthy minority of homeowners. In fact, only 1.4 million (or 5 percent) of all 27 million homeowners who claimed the home mortgage deduction in 1990 had deductions exceeding the limits I propose. Likewise, the share of homes whose prices might be adversely affected by these caps (for the most part, luxury homes and vacation homes) is small. This should minimize any near-term disruptions in real estate markets. But because these caps will not be indexed for inflation, the magnitude of our tax subsidy for owner-occupied housing will be allowed to diminish gradually—and the tax savings to increase gradually but substantially—in a way that allows plenty of time for people and markets to adjust.

Reform 16. Reduce aid to farming.

Implementation: 1995 to 2000. Savings in 2000: $4 billion. Savings in 2004: $5 billion.

Eighty years ago, a third of all adult Americans worked on farms. Most of these farmers lived in poverty, and none received federal aid. Today, less than 2 percent of Americans work on farms, and of these very few live in poverty, and each receives (on average) well over $10,000 in federal money—much of which simply serves to prop up noncompetitive enterprises and inflate consumer prices. Commenting on this trend, the Nobel Prize–winning economist Milton Friedman once observed that the size and political clout of interest groups are often inversely correlated: The smaller the group, the larger the potential benefit for each member, and thus the stronger the motivation to fight to win and keep public subsidies. I would never, of course, suggest that the life of most farmers is easy. What I do insist is that our fiscal crisis demands across-the-board, "we're all in it together" burden sharing, and that farmers too must make a contribution.

My plan focuses on curbing the cost of our federal commodity price-support programs—which offer "deficiency payments" to farmers who produce feed grain—by lowering their grain "target prices" by 3 percent per year for five years. In effect, this provision will lower the federal price floor under most grains by nearly 15 percent. Let me add that these same savings could also be found by targeting other agricultural benefit programs for cuts, including everything from crop insurance to our subsidies to wool and mohair producers and honey bee keepers. (To find the rationale for some of these programs, you have to hunt in the history books: Ensuring adequate supplies of wool and mohair for army uniforms, it turns out, was an obscure national security issue during the Second World War!) The sums of money involved here may be trivial in terms of our overall federal budget. But we can't possibly allow such farm-aid priorities to go unexamined and expect the American people as a whole to make sacrifices willingly.

Reform 17. Increase user fees.

Implementation: various dates. Savings in 2000: $7 billion. Savings in 2004: $8 billion.

Railroads. Maritime shippers. State-chartered banks. Nuclear-power utilities. Hydroelectric consumers in the Pacific Northwest. Hardrock miners in the Great Basin. Water-guzzling farmers in California. Open-range ranchers in the Southwest. Media companies that use the electromagnetic spectrum. Airlines and corporate and private planes flying out of busy airports. Oceangoing pleasure boaters. National park enthusiasts. What two things do all of these groups have in common? First, they are all directly benefiting from a federal service or using a resource owned or managed by the federal government. Second, they are not paying the full cost of it.

This plan will ask these (and other) groups to begin to pay a larger share of what such services cost taxpayers. This provision is really seventeen different legislative initiatives that will require agribusinesses (for instance) to pay a realistic scarcity price for their water, corporate patentees to pay for the cost of processing their applications, and yacht owners to pay for the cost of Coast Guard assistance and rescue. Most Americans, I think, would reject the notion of charging individuals special fees in return for public services that help most people in roughly equal measure. But where the favors are large and the beneficiaries are few, most Americans will agree that some payment is both reasonable and fair.

General Revenues: New Taxes and Higher Tax Rates

Liberals must face up to the obvious: Americans have always reviled taxes to an extent unparalleled in any other industrial country (which is why, as a share of GDP, our taxes are the lowest in the industrial world). Our national bias toward private and community initiative—

and against the politics of "tax and spend"—is part of our culture and part of our social and intellectual heritage. U.S. taxpayers will never willingly bear an uncontrolled tax burden. But conservatives must also face up to the obvious: When responsible reductions in spending cannot alone achieve budget balance, raising more revenues then becomes the responsible course of action. To do otherwise would be to cheat our children and to mortgage our nation's economic future. Ever more public debt is an option that Americans simply should not countenance.

My plan therefore calls for tax increases. On the one hand, it endorses President Clinton's steeper marginal income tax rates on America's highest-income households. On the other hand, it greatly expands the use of consumption taxes, not only to raise revenues but to help tilt the economic incentives facing U.S. households in favor of more savings. I propose three types of consumption taxes: a new federal gasoline tax, higher "sin" taxes, and a national retail sales tax. The first two have the additional benefit of targeting types of personal consumption that carry large costs for society as a whole. The third, the retail sales tax, is intended as a temporary measure. Ultimately, we should replace our current income-based tax system with one based on a progressive consumption tax. To this end, I recommend that a high-level commission be established to study the transitional problems involved in such a shift.

Reform 18. Raise top marginal income tax rates.

Implementation: 1995. Revenues in 2000: $35 billion. Revenues in 2004: $41 billion.

In his first budget, President Clinton proposed raising the top income tax rate (for tax filers with total adjusted gross incomes over about $200,000) from 31 to 36 percent; levying a 10 percent surtax on very high income filers (those over about $300,000); and adjusting upward some "alternative minimum tax" provisions. These changes are an appropriate response to the widening distribution of income that has taken place in America since the 1970s, and my plan endorses them. They are one way to ensure that the most affluent Americans bear their fair and fuller share of the burden of deficit reduction. Moreover, the highly progressive tilt of these changes in marginal income tax rates (they only affect the top 1 percent of all U.S. tax filers) balances the impact of the new consumption taxes included in my plan.

The details of these tax rate changes, however, should be subject to a careful review. Some experts (including former chairman of the Council of Economic Advisers Martin Feldstein) believe that such sharp hikes in marginal rates are self-defeating and cannot possibly yield the revenues the Clinton administration anticipates. Affected households, they argue, will find ways to avoid paying the taxes, whether by shifting more of their incomes into nontaxable forms (like municipal bonds), by working less (no one earning $500,000 a year really needs an extra $50,000), or through tax evasion, pure and simple. Other experts believe that since a sizeable share of those earning over $200,000 a year are actually "subchapter S" organizations, these hikes in marginal rates will hurt small business entrepreneurship, an important source of jobs and economic growth.

I believe that these fears are exaggerated. The tax hikes we are talking about will still leave us with marginal rates much lower than most other industrial countries have, not to mention the rates that America itself had throughout most of the postwar period. If we make substantial progress toward balancing the budget, moreover, we will create a healthy macro climate that will help spur economic growth (including the growth of small businesses) and thus boost tax revenues. Still, the concern that all the tax dollars the Clinton plan anticipates may fail to materialize is not altogether unfounded. If careful study shows that guaranteeing our targeted revenues requires us to combine a slightly lower marginal tax rate with a somewhat lower income threshold (say, $150,000) that asks more households to sacrifice something, we should not hesitate to make such adjustments.

Reform 19. Levy a 5 percent consumption tax.

Implementation: 1995 to 2000. Revenues in 2000: $105 billion. Revenues in 2004: $125 billion.

Every other major industrial country relies more heavily—typically, much more heavily—on consumption taxes than the United States does. Not coincidentally, these other countries have higher rates of private savings than we do. As a step toward making our tax system more prosavings, my plan proposes levying a 5 percent tax on most consumption expenditures. In theory, this tax could take the form of either a value-added tax (VAT) or a retail tax. The advantage of a VAT is that it is imposed on all goods and services at each level of production, ensuring equitable treatment of all producers and—not an unimportant consideration—making tax evasion difficult. The advantage of a retail tax is that it is simpler and less costly to administer. Since our ultimate goal should be to fold whichever of these taxes we adopt into a redesigned tax system based entirely on taxing consumption (as opposed to income), we should save ourselves the cost of building a new bureaucracy until we know exactly what our long-term needs will be.

Consumption taxes are often criticized for being regressive. One way to address this problem is to exempt certain types of basic household expenditures—primarily food, housing, and education—from the tax to ease its impact on lower-income families. The 5 percent national retail sales tax that I propose does precisely this. Once the exemptions are taken into account, lower-income households would typically face just a 2.5 percent tax rate on their total consumption.

But if we want to rely more on consumption taxes, and we should, we're going to have to think about how not just to mitigate their regressivity but to make them truly progressive. The best idea is one advocated, among others, by the Strengthening of America Commission cochaired by Senators Sam Nunn and Pete Domenici: a progressive consumption tax on all consumed income. People would get taxed on what they spend rather than what they earn. Or, to put it another way, they would not get taxed on what they save. (Savings would be an adjustment to total income, and people would subtract it before figuring their tax on their 1040 forms.) Consumption tax rates on lower-income people would be low, since they must consume most of what they earn. Going up the income ladder, tax rates on consumption would rise on a steeply progressive basis, both to encourage savings and to ensure that affluent households pay their fair share of taxes.

Although the basic concept is straightforward, most experts agree that many difficult details would have to be worked out before a progressive consumed-income tax could be implemented. One question is how to define what saving is (and how to keep track of how much of it households and businesses actually do). The easiest solution would be to establish qualified savings accounts similar to IRAs for each taxpayer. Deposits to those accounts would be deductible and withdrawals would be taxable. But a large amount of saving takes place in forms that could not be transferred into such accounts—for example, real estate (including the equity people accumulate in their homes); "consumer durables" (some economists count as savings household investments in goods, like automobiles, that last more than a year); little-traded stocks and bonds in small businesses; and intangible assets, such as trademarks, patents, and marketing rights. Establishing proper definitions of which of these constitute "saving" and which constitute "consumption" under a consumed-income tax system will not be easy. But there are other issues to consider. Should only "new" savings be deductible, or "old" savings as well? Once the rules are established, how will they be enforced? (How, for instance, would the IRS ensure that taxpayers don't borrow off the books or inflate asset values to increase the tax-deductible savings they declare?) Finally, where exactly should tax rates on consumption be set to guarantee that the affluent (who *could* save most of their incomes) indeed pay their fair and fuller share of our tax burden? Yes, there are plenty of knotty conceptual and transitional issues. Nevertheless, in view of the enormous benefits to U.S. savings and investment that a shift to a consumption-based tax system would bring, my plan calls for the President and the Secretary of the Treasury to create a high-level commission to help resolve them.

Reform 20. Raise the federal motor gasoline tax by 50 cents per gallon.

Implementation: 1995 to 2000. Revenues in 2000: $47 billion. Revenues in 2004: $58 billion.

Besides helping to balance the budget, higher energy taxes would encourage conservation, reduce pollution, ease traffic congestion, and curtail our nation's dangerous dependence on oil imports from abroad. All of these are "public goods" that Americans should welcome. For the richest of all countries to be quibbling over a 4.3-cents-per-gallon gasoline tax—what the rest of the industrial world would regard as petty cash—is a measure of our political paralysis. To put the number in perspective, 4.3 cents a gallon works out to an average of $27 per driver per year. It is less than half the difference between the cost of full service and self service at many gas stations. Or, if you prefer an international comparison, it's less than 2 percent of the average gasoline tax consumers in other G-7 countries pay.

The real question is not whether we should bring our tax treatment of energy halfway in line with other industrial countries, but how we should do it. There are some good economic arguments in favor of a low tax rate with a comprehensive tax base—in other words, a value-added or "BTU" tax on all forms of energy along the lines President Clinton originally proposed. But I favor a different approach: a 50-cents-per-gallon increase in the federal excise tax on motor fuels alone that would be phased in between 1995 and 2000.

Why a gasoline tax hike? First, it would concentrate penalties on the consumption of energy on the form (oil) that presents the biggest foreign dependency problem for the United States. Second, it would be the easiest to administer and would not require the creation of a new tax bureaucracy. Finally, it would minimize any increases in production costs for U.S. industries and thus not harm their global market share at a time when we will need to be exporting more. In fact, higher gasoline taxes might actually improve the competitiveness of some U.S. industries. By partly closing the gap between our own low gasoline taxes and the much higher ones imposed by our trading partners, we would be encouraging our auto makers to bring the fuel efficiency of their fleets up to global standards.

There are, of course, possible criticisms of a gasoline tax. One that we have often heard recently is that it would place a disproportionate burden on the trucking industry and on rural and western households. A way to partially offset this burden might be to earmark a portion of new gasoline tax revenues for public investment in surface transportation so that high payers would end up getting some of their taxes back in the form of better roads and safer travel.

But however we address these nitty-gritty burden-sharing issues, we should not lose sight of the bigger picture. Fully phased in, a 50-cents-a-gallon gasoline tax would cost U.S. drivers an average of $320 a year, with a regional variation of just $70 above or below that average (and this assumes no change in behavior or fuel efficiency). It is indeed telling that Americans will be quick to raise a hue and cry over a range of this magnitude in state burdens when no one complains about the far greater variation in federal benefits going to different states: about $1,500 per capita, or more than ten times as much. Apparently, we are all far more sensitive about the distribution of sacrifice than the distribution of largess.

Reform 21. Raise federal "sin" taxes.

Implementation: 1995 to 2000. Revenues in 2000: $22 billion. Revenues in 2004: $25 billion.

Throughout American history, public attitudes toward the use and abuse of alcohol and other drugs have gone through several long-term cycles. Back at the turn of the century, the prevailing attitude was toleration. Beginning around World War I, opinions (and laws) turned harsh, and the per capita consumption of alcohol and most types of drugs plunged. From the late 1950s through the 1970s, toleration came back into fashion. But over the last decade, attitudes have once again been shifting into reverse, and after peaking around 1980, most rates of drug abuse (including tobacco) have been declining. This time, the "new prohibitionism" is being reinforced by a tidal wave of statistics demonstrating the vast social cost attributable to "legal" drug abuse—from the auto accidents, broken families, and liver disease caused by alcoholism to the cancer, heart disease, and birth defects caused by tobacco. A growing grass-roots movement is advocating that this abuse be discouraged.

My plan endorses this shift of opinion. By 2000, it will raise the federal excise tax on cigarettes (currently twenty-four cents per pack) to one dollar and increase the tax on alcoholic beverages to sixteen dollars per proof gallon. (Thereafter, both taxes will be indexed to 1994 prices.) One goal of these changes, of course, is to raise revenues. But by increasing the cost of alcohol and tobacco to the consumer, higher "sin taxes" will also accelerate the decline in their consumption. At the same time, my Budget Action Plan also raises revenues through a different kind of "sin tax," one that asks corporations to burden share along with individuals. Specifically, it further restricts (from 80 to 50 percent) the share of all meal and entertainment expenses allowable as deductions from business earnings. In an era of budget austerity, it is only fair to limit the tax write-off for a "business expense" that in at least some measure really represents personal consumption.

General Revenues: Investment Incentives

Clearly, the principal goal of any budget plan should be eliminating the deficit and raising substantially the rate of U.S. net national savings available for private business investment. Yet another goal is also important: encouraging as much as possible of that enlarged pool of national savings to go to those domestic investment projects with the highest economic rates of return. In part, this second goal—what we might call improving the efficiency of capital allocation—will be furthered by many of the proposals I've already described. By boosting federal outlays for basic research, child skills and health, and infrastructure, we will be funding badly needed investments with long-term payoffs for which no private capital market usually exists. By capping our open-ended subsidies to housing and health care, we will be diverting billions of dollars away from two of the lowest-return areas of investment in our economy. Instead of tilting incentives toward swimming pools in every home and CAT-scanners in every clinic, my plan will channel more savings toward the cutting-edge industrial and service technologies that will enhance long-term productivity growth throughout our economy.

Yet even after these reforms, there will remain critical areas where America lacks sufficient investment because the (after-tax) market return to the private investor does not fully reflect the long-term economic benefit. America, like the rest of the industrial world, is finding that creating new jobs is a lot tougher than it used to be. Many raise questions like these: Have the usual links between GNP growth and job growth been broken? Is the *quality* of available jobs in industrial countries fundamentally changing in a world economy in which capital, technology, know-how, and communication are far more global and mobile than they once were? Is there more of a premium today for *intellectual, innovative human capital*—an ever-stronger demand for highly trained workers who can quickly learn to implement innovations? Is the gap between the demands of new jobs and the skills of new workers growing? Is a different kind of "structural unemployment" part of the modern landscape? My answer to all these questions is yes.

We need to recognize that providing jobs in this kind of new world economy where change is the norm will be a far stickier proposition than it *needs* to be if we lose our lead in cutting-edge technologies and if we fail to rise to the challenge of training tomorrow's mobile work-force. At a modest cost in lost revenue, my plan provides for two tax-code incentives—a permanent tax credit for business research and development and a new worker-training tax credit—that will help direct more business investment where we're sure to have a tremendous need for it in the years ahead. It includes another key tax change that will help our future living standards and competitiveness as well: the indexation of capital gains on productive assets.

Reform 22. Enact a permanent tax credit for business research and development.

Implementation: 1995. Cost in 2000: $6 billion. Cost in 2004: $7 billion.

From the invention of the transistor and the superconductor to the development of genetic cloning and fiber optics, great commercial discoveries have generated benefits for the entire economy that far surpass the profits of the discoverer. Most economists have always known this, and many have long advocated preferential incentives for the sort of research and development likely to lead to "public benefit" discoveries and innovations. In 1981, the federal government first set up such an incentive by legislating a 20 percent tax credit for corporate spending on "incremental research and experimentation." Although a step in the right direction, the effect of this credit has been limited. Because the only eligible R&D is "incremental," firms that don't continually expand their R&D budgets often fail to qualify for it. Because eligible spending includes only basic research, commercial innovation goes unrewarded. (While government should not directly undertake commercial development projects, it should encourage business to do so.) Furthermore, because the credit has never been permanent, corporations haven't been able to count on it when drawing up their long-term strategies. Yet almost by definition, budgeting for research requires long-term planning. Over the last twelve years, the credit has nearly "run out" several times, and in June of 1992 it finally did expire.

My Budget Action Plan will make this tax credit permanent. Moreover, it will expand the eligible spending to include all R&D from the first dollar on—not just basic research and not just incremental expenditures. Experience teaches that continuous product innovation is just as important technologically as laboratory work and that R&D in slowly growing or even contracting industries can be just as fruitful economically as R&D in booming industries. The amount of the credit will be fixed across the board at 10 percent of certifiable R&D spending.

Reform 23. Set up worker-training tax incentives.

Implementation: 1995. Cost in 2000: $7 billion. Cost in 2004: $9 billion.

As President-elect Clinton acknowledged in his preinaugural economic summit, the era of lifetime corporate employment is dead: Today's typical young worker, he announced, should expect to change employers five or six times over his or her lifetime. In many respects, the emerging era of the mobile workforce is a welcome development. Only with workers who can shift quickly and comfortably from declining industries to growing industries can the U.S. economy hope to thrive in the ever-changing global marketplace. Yet workforce flexibility also creates new problems. Even as the importance of portable skills and expertise grows the incentive of each business to train its employees will decline. Why, after all, should a business invest heavily in its employees if most of them may soon leave and take their skills to other jobs? Many policy experts have therefore suggested that government find some means of extending explicit rewards to employers who take the trouble (and incur the cost) of training their workers. Reinforcing this recommendation are alarming international comparisons (showing that America spends only a fraction of what many other countries spend on worker-training programs) and dire forecasts about the mismatch between the skill level of today's young workers and the demands of tomorrow's economy.

My plan responds to this new challenge by legislating a permanent 10 percent tax credit for all employer spending on employee education and training programs. It will also allow individuals to deduct the costs of formal education and training programs that help them qualify for a new job—a measure that will aid not just private-sector workers, but federal employees affected by defense downsizing. To discourage abuse, these tax provisions will have to establish clear and enforceable definitions of "training" and "education." Although this could be a slippery problem, our tax code has succeeded in defining many other types of business costs that at first seemed nebulous (such as "research and development"). In any case, the stakes are too high not to make a concerted effort. Few activities generate such large long-term returns over such a wide cross-section of the economy as investing in "human capital"—particularly in an emerging global economy that is far more competitive, technological, and mobile.

Reform 24. Index capital gains to encourage productive investment.

Implementation: 1995. Cost in 2000: $1 billion. Cost in 2004: $2 billion.

Most economists agree that one of the impediments to savings and investment in the United States is that our tax code fails to distinguish between capital gains that are real and those that are merely the result of inflation. The thresholds of our different income tax brackets, our personal exemptions, and our standard deduction are all indexed to prevent the unintended increases in taxes that inflation would otherwise cause. But there is no similar provision for indexing the prices of assets, a bias that tilts household incentives toward consumption and away from savings and investment. Consider this example of how taxes penalize capital gains. With a 7 percent rate of return, a $1,000 investment would double to $2,000 over ten years. On that capital gain of $1,000, a household in our current 31 percent tax bracket would pay $310 in taxes. If inflation averaged 4 percent over that ten years, half of that $1,000 capital gain would not be real. In effect, the investor would be paying a 62 percent tax on his *real* gain.

My plan corrects this problem by allowing the prices of newly purchased assets to be indexed for inflation. In order to focus incentives on productivity-enhancing investments, this indexation would exclude real estate, art, and collectibles. Another idea would be to limit the provision to capital gains on productive investments held for more than some minimum period. But whatever specific approach we take, the goal should be the same: to eliminate the penalty exacted from investors in productivity-enhancing assets when our tax code makes them pay the price of inflation, and thus to get them to focus on the long term.

Net Interest Payments

Short of defaulting on the national debt, interest payments from the U.S. Treasury to outside creditors are beyond anyone's direct control. When the federal government runs a deficit, taxpayers are legally obligated to pay interest to the creditors who cover the government's shortfall. When such deficits are large and growing, the rapid rise in interest costs can itself be a major force behind bigger deficits, which themselves then generate even bigger interest costs. Without any policy change, the CBO projects, the growth in interest costs alone will be adding $128 billion to our annual federal deficit by the year 2000 and $268 billion by the year 2004. But if we make the right choices, we can turn that vicious cycle into a virtuous one. Smaller deficits will mean a slower-growing national debt, which in turn will mean lower interest costs and thus further reductions in the deficit. By saving in the rest of the budget, in other words, we create extra savings in interest costs.

How big are the extra savings? Let's assume that the Peterson Budget Action Plan I've just described is implemented in its entirety. By the year 2000, the federal budget will be saving about $84 billion annually in interest costs. By the year 2004, it will save $221 billion annually.

These vast numbers underscore the permanent favor we are doing both for ourselves and for our children by eliminating the deficit. They represent the debt service we will never have to pay for another decade of debts we choose not to incur.

Yet these figures, large as they are, almost certainly underestimate the interest savings we will enjoy if we balance the budget. If we achieve budget balance by the year 2000, and thereby triple our rate of net national savings, we can expect real (inflation-adjusted) interest rates to fall beneath the levels we would otherwise see if the deficit kept growing. How much they will fall is a matter of dispute. As I indicated earlier, some economists (including those at DRI, the prestigious econometric consulting firm) would predict a fall of 2.5 to 3 percentage points in long-term rates. We hope so. But in the interest of prudent projections, let's stick to an estimate that would strike most economists as an absolute minimum: a total fall of one full percentage point. In keeping with this estimate, my plan assumes that interest rates will gradually drop beneath the CBO baseline by one-sixth of one percentage point each year from 1995 to 2000. Yet even this modest assumption translates into total interest savings ($132 billion in 2000 and $282 billion in 2004) substantially greater than the no-interest-rate-change numbers I cited above.

WHAT THE PLAN DOES FOR AMERICA'S FUTURE

It's time to add up the numbers and look at the bottom line. Allow me to take care of the arithmetic. For the year 2000, the total budget savings from the reforms I've proposed is $483 billion; for the year 2004, $788 billion. Each of these numbers is larger than the business-as-usual baseline deficits that the CBO currently projects for those years—$457 billion and $742 billion, respectively. Yes, we have balanced the budget.

How did we get the job done? Let's look at a few of the overall numbers for the year 2004. Just $222 billion of our budget savings will come from revenue raisers that are unambiguously new taxes or higher tax rates. A huge $569 billion will come from clear spending reductions. (Of these reductions, most are due to cuts in direct entitlement benefits of $191 billion and to interest savings of $282 billion.) Another $98 billion of our budget savings in 2004 will come from reductions in our benefitlike tax subsidies for things like health care, housing, and retirement. As I pointed out earlier, if we don't count these reductions in tax subsidies as taxes (most economists believe they are really benefit cuts), total spending cuts under my plan will outweigh tax increases by 2.6 to 1. Even if we count savings in these "tax

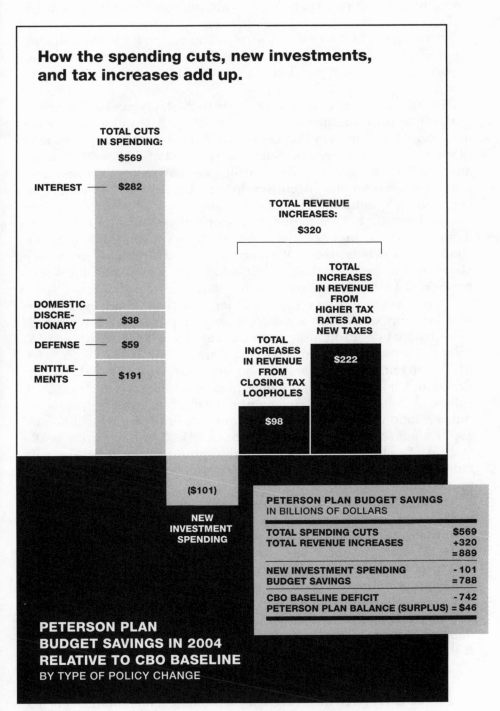

How the spending cuts, new investments, and tax increases add up.

TOTAL CUTS IN SPENDING: $569

INTEREST — $282

TOTAL REVENUE INCREASES: $320

DOMESTIC DISCRE-TIONARY — $38

DEFENSE — $59

ENTITLE-MENTS — $191

TOTAL INCREASES IN REVENUE FROM HIGHER TAX RATES AND NEW TAXES

TOTAL INCREASES IN REVENUE FROM CLOSING TAX LOOPHOLES

$222

$98

($101)

NEW INVESTMENT SPENDING

PETERSON PLAN BUDGET SAVINGS IN 2004 RELATIVE TO CBO BASELINE BY TYPE OF POLICY CHANGE

PETERSON PLAN BUDGET SAVINGS
IN BILLIONS OF DOLLARS

TOTAL SPENDING CUTS	$569
TOTAL REVENUE INCREASES	+320
	=889
NEW INVESTMENT SPENDING	-101
BUDGET SAVINGS	=788
CBO BASELINE DEFICIT	-742
PETERSON PLAN BALANCE (SURPLUS)	=$46

expenditures'' as taxes, spending cuts will still outweigh tax hikes by 1.8 to 1.

Balancing the budget, of course, is not an end in itself. With that in mind, I'd like to focus attention on a couple more indicators that say a world about what my action plan, or a similar one, would do for America.

First, take national savings. From 1994 to 2004, my plan will improve our federal fiscal balance by 4.9 percent of GDP. It will also increase net federal investment by 1 percent of GDP. That's a total improvement in what we save and invest of roughly 5.9 percent of GDP, even without any possible increase in private savings we may see due to new and more positive economic incentives. In the CBO baseline projection, by contrast, ballooning budget deficits would cause a further deterioration of 3 percent of GDP in our already woefully inadequate rate of net national savings. In 1992, net national savings in the United States almost dipped below zero. Without any rise in private-sector saving above its average since the late 1980s, a business-as-usual budget scenario would push net national savings well below zero!

Then consider our national debt. Here the changes wrought by my plan are truly striking. In the CBO's baseline projection, the publicly held national debt will more than double—from $3.6 trillion to $8.2 trillion—between 1994 and 2004. As a share of GDP, it will rise from 55 to 82 percent, close to where it was just after World War II. Under President Clinton's original budget plan, it would grow to about $6.6 trillion by 2004, or about 65 percent of GDP. If we enact my plan, our publicly held national debt will rise only to a little over $4 trillion (in 1999), then start declining. As a share of GDP, it will not grow at all. Instead, after holding steady at around 55 percent through 1996, it will fall to 47 percent by 2000 and to 38 percent by 2004, close to where it was in the early 1970s.

And what about the longer term? Quite simply, my action plan spares us an economic future as catastrophic as it is unthinkable. If you put the do-nothing CBO-baseline projection on fast forward beyond the year 2004, you find that the vicious circle linking interest and entitlement cost hikes with higher deficits and still higher interest costs will begin to spiral out of control. By 2020, the projections say, net interest costs will hurtle past 12 percent of GDP—or $1.2 trillion in today's dollars—and deficits will be closing in on 20 percent of GDP. Meanwhile, the national debt will soar to over twice the size of our economy. Numbers like these make most of today's Latin American economies seem prudently managed by comparision. And by 2040? Interest costs will hit roughly 35 percent of GDP, deficits 45 percent of GDP, and the national debt 600 percent of GDP. Here we are looking at total fiscal meltdown. My plan, on the other hand, lays the foundation, if politicians and the public can stay the course, *for keeping the federal budget at or near balance throughout the next half century.* It would allow us once again to contemplate our economic future with confidence.

Few policy experts dispute the direction or the magnitude of these trends. But a projection, they remind us, is not a prediction. A projection tells us where we are heading, not necessarily where we will end up. Naturally, they're right. Yet when they simply shrug their shoulders and assume that we will sometime and somehow overhaul our federal budget, the experts sidestep all the tough questions. There are those, of course, who apparently believe that we can just raise taxes—enough to cover the entire deficit—and then keep raising them to cover the built-in growth in entitlements. But as we have seen, that would require a new Clinton-scale tax hike roughly every four years over the next half century. (Perhaps the announcement could be made as part of each new president's inaugural message to the American people!) My suggestion is different: Along with some revenue hikes, institute structural entitlement reforms whose savings are guaranteed to grow over time, and that will be sure to stop the future hemorrhage in federal benefits and interest costs. Instead of pushing liabilities into the future, we'll take our national destiny into our own hands and free up vital resources that we and our children will someday need to meet challenges and build dreams we can now only dimly imagine.

Finally, let's focus on generational equity and the moral imperative that we not harm our future. In Chapter 8, I talked about the deeply disturbing "generational accounting" measure developed by economist Larry Kotlikoff. According to Larry, if we hold ourselves harmless from benefit cuts or tax hikes and continue to pass on massive liabilities, tomorrow's Americans will have to pay 71 percent of their lifetime incomes in net taxes. I asked Larry to look at how my plan might change this number. He found that the lifetime tax rate of Americans now in their forties (for instance) would rise by only about a percentage point above its current-law level—from between 29 and 31 percent to between 30 and 32 percent. And what about the tax rate to be paid by Americans yet to be born? It would fall from 71 to 39 percent. By way of comparison, consider the results when Larry ran this same calculation to determine the impacts of President Clinton's budget plan on our generational accounts. The tax rate of future generations would also have fallen, but only to 59 percent. Is there really any doubt that we must go all the way in balancing the budget?

NOW IS ALWAYS THE RIGHT TIME

Today we often hear public figures and academic experts say that the goal of vigorous deficit reduction is commendable—but that now is not the right time to pursue it. So long as the current recovery remains "vulnerable" and threatens to dump us back into the last recession, they warn against trying to balance the budget within any foreseeable time horizon. I would like to think all these counselors of caution are arguing in good faith. Many sincerely do believe that the mid-1990s are an especially unfavorable moment to initiate bold action. On the other hand, some have a track record of offering virtually the same advice when the economy is revved up. Then, they tell us, we have to tolerate big deficits in order to make sure that we don't fall into the next recession. And whenever the business cycle is not enough, the political election cycle gives us other reasons to pause. Apparently, now is never the right time.

To give the critics their due, I won't deny that vigorous action on the deficit carries with it real but bearable risks. That is why my plan stresses gradualism. Its goal is to raise our national savings rate steeply over six years, yet at a pace no faster (as a percent of GDP per year) than what we have achieved many times before in our history without a recession. That is why my plan stresses investment through targeted budget outlays and targeted tax reforms. Lower interest rates may not be enough to keep the economy buoyant. For the first couple of years, we must use active public leverage to get investment purchases to accelerate at least as fast as consumer purchases decline. That is also why my plan pays special attention to economic incentives. If we want households to become bigger savers and businesses to become smarter investors, we must overhaul tax and benefit policies that push them in the wrong direction.

But let's be honest. However many precautions we undertake, extremists on both sides of the political spectrum—those who lead the chorus of temporizers—will never be satisfied. They will always regard large deficits as the least threatening of all evils. On the left, strident "neo-Keynesians" claim that any cuts in federal spending will sooner or later trigger a destructive economic contraction in which falling "aggregate demand" will defeat the purpose of a higher supply of savings. On the right, strident "supply-siders" claim that any raising of tax rates (even proposals to trim welfare for the well-off are considered taxes in sheep's clothing) will destroy incentives to work and save and thus, in a similar fashion, plow our economy into an indefinite recession—or worse.

Yes, each side is motivated by a different ulterior motive. The left wants to keep public spending high; the right wants to keep tax rates low. But otherwise their pleadings have much in common. Both sides argue that maximizing the size of the next year's economy must take precedence over how our savings rate might affect the size of the next decade's economy. But sides believe that short-term confidence is alone sufficient to generate growth or—among those whose minds are stuck in the Go-Go Sixties—even to keep us on track toward guaranteed prosperity. Over the last twenty years, both sides have embarrassed each other by lining up in the same do-nothing camp whenever the issue of explicit deficit reduction has come to the fore in national politics. By whipping up *economic* fear among the public, both sides provide useful cover for elected officials who dare not act out of their *political* fear that any pay-now, gain-later policy would hurt them come reelection time. Most important, both sides have emerged victorious from all of the important debates. The left gets to keep its high spending (while proclaiming "sacrifice") and the right its low taxes (while denouncing "free lunches"). Only our children, the unambiguous losers, get hung out to dry.

Hidden within this case for inaction lies a central premise that I adamantly deny. The critics begin with the obvious truism that long-term goals require short-term survival, and then jump to the choiceless imperative that we focus all our attention on ensuring immediate stimulus and bolstering "investor psychology." Thus, any discussion of long-term goals becomes pointless. I hold, on the contrary, that an absolute national commitment to a long-term goal is not only necessary to achieve long-term prosperity, but, by now, has also become necessary to create the very short-term consumer and investor confidence needed to help us out of our immediate economic predicament.

The critics make a big issue out of investor psychology, but I sometimes wonder if they understand how investors really think. Let me speak from my own personal experience in dealing with the countless executives—from small venture capitalists to Fortune 500 CEOs—whose daily business is to make investment decisions. The first thing to understand about such decisions is that they are typically part of a long-term business strategy that stretches out at least ten or twenty years into the future. Now, if I were to rank the worries most often pondered by executives in laying out business strategies, there is one I would put right at the top: their deep mistrust of government's ability to provide businesses with a reliable and consistent economic environment—and specifically, their concern about the dire consequences of endless debts, deficits, and fiscal irresponsibility.

To begin with, executives worry about how higher deficits and scarcer national savings will jack up the long-term cost of capital. But that's not all. They also worry about how government's crisis-to-crisis attempts to bandage its fiscal wounds will lead to unpredictable tax hikes, mysterious regulatory mandates, and mindless chops in the very areas of public spending (such as education or infrastructure) that really do serve the public interest. It is no accident that when U.S. business executives decide to relocate production abroad, one reason they cite frequently is the sheer uncertainty of U.S. economic policy. I believe most investors would actually prefer higher yet stable tax rates—if they knew that such rates would be part of a sustainable economic plan and a solid political consensus. What terrifies them is the prospect of endless uncertainty punctuated by makeshift expedients. Over the last twelve years, Congress has already legislated seven major changes in the tax code—most of them designed, at least in part, to raise more revenue. As we have seen, the future promises more of the same: convulsive short-term fixes on top of directionless long-term drift.

This uncertainty among investors ultimately reflects a broader uncertainty among the general public. Most Americans wonder whether we will ever regain control of our economic destiny—or if so, when. Opinion surveys show that Americans often mention "deficit spending" in response to extremely general questions about what is going wrong with our country—as though budget balancing has come to represent (as it should) a historic moral test of our national character. Both pollsters and journalists have noticed that there is a growing impatience with the ideologues on both sides of the political aisle, those who keep holding America's future hostage to their own fantasies. Maybe the real continuum in American politics today is not between left and right, but between the ideological and the pragmatic—where the most shrill and extravagant rhetoric is associated with the most irresponsible fiscal expediency and the most improvident fiscal policies.

In the end, ordinary Americans are coming to understand that there is no real choice between the long term and the short term. Even at the price of temporary discomfort, the long term must prevail.

Maybe a medical analogy will help. Imagine a patient who suffers from arteriosclerosis—a condition induced by long-term lifestyle habits (poor diet, smoking, lack of exercise) and replete with short-term dangers and discomforts (angina, palpitations, shortness of breath). He goes to see two doctors. One prescribes a treatment that focuses mostly on alleviating the short-term problem—perhaps some quick-fix surgery, but no serious emphasis on major lifestyle changes. The other doctor, focusing long-term, prescribes radical (if temporarily onerous) changes in the patient's behavior: exercise, no drinking, no smoking, new diet, regular hours, and so on. The new regimen is to be introduced as fast as possible without putting the patient in immediate danger. Medical science, to say nothing of common sense, tells us that the second doctor's advice is far more likely to prolong the patient's life, enhance his well-being, and even renew his own sense of self-respect. Structural deficits are like a chronic disease. We get the disease by abandoning long-term habits of fiscal health. The only cure is to relearn those habits—even if the price is accepting some short-term discomfort.

Take another look at the numbers described in this chapter. I believe they offer ample evidence that enacting my plan to balance the budget would vastly improve America's economic fortunes—and moral standing—as it enters the next century. Accompanied by a modest rise in private-sector savings rates, my plan would push our rate of capital formation back up to globally competitive levels. It would reignite the upward trajectory in U.S. productivity and living standards. It would replenish the investment resources of our public sector, on the principle that we will never become a competitive economy without a competitive physical, human, and intellectual infrastructure. It would rekindle America's faith in public institutions—and especially in their ability to make farsighted choices on behalf of our future. And it would do all this without an abrupt economic "crisis," without forsaking America's commitment to helping the poor and disabled, and without overlooking our promise to provide a minimum floor of protection for the elderly.

Yes, the Peterson Budget Action Plan would require modest and temporary sacrifices from middle- and upper-income Americans. But choosing to sacrifice something for the sake of the right future is what being a democratic republic is all about. No one will do it for us. We must do it ourselves. And if a sacrifice must be made, I think most Americans would prefer to make it now, voluntarily, as a means of steering toward the right future, rather than later, involuntarily, amid economic crisis and social upheaval, or even, as Paul Tsongas would say, an intergenerational war. No American wants such an outcome.

Conclusion:
Facing Up
Means Living Up

"It is often easier to fight for principles than to live up to them." So said Governor Adlai Stevenson. And he was right in a very contemporary sense: Today, the landscape in Washington is filled with the storm and fury of politicians willing to fight for the principles they espouse. At least, they appear eager for battle when it comes to giving an impassioned speech on the Senate floor, or denouncing the opposition party in a press conference, or going at it with each other on *MacNeil/ Lehrer* or *Crossfire*. But precious few of them are actually *living up* to their much-vaunted and often-flaunted principles.

As a result, we have a White House, as well as 435 congressmen and 100 senators, who all agree that the deficit *must* be cut. Indeed, the majority now loudly proclaim that we must go all the way and balance the budget. They are more than willing to fight for their "principles" as to *how* we should proceed. Then, when it gets down to the nitty-gritty of making specific real sacrifices, the job doesn't get done. Somehow in this cacophony of conflict, they just don't live up to their proclaimed goals.

This gap between words and deeds is conditioned by certain open secrets inside the beltway. There, everyone knows that the politician who is most reluctant to spell out the specifics of his own budget-balancing plan will have the best partisan bargaining position when a real plan is hammered out. Until then, it's far better politics to spout easy generalities, half-truths, and half-answers.

I even hear a few say that the resulting political gridlock reflects the strength of our principled disagreement over *how* the budget should be balanced. I have argued the opposite: that the perpetuation of gridlock reflects the weakness of our consensus about how seriously to take the welfare of the future and about whether the budget should be balanced at all. How else can we explain the endless gamesmanship, speechifying, and delay perpetrated at our children's expense? How else can we account for so many leaders who "fight for principles" without taking responsibility for institutions that manifestly fail to "live up to them"?

The Republicans proclaim, as a general principle, that they favor spending cuts and abhor tax increases. However—and it is a *big* however—the indispensable entitlement cuts they talk about are often glib generalities that avoid the specific tough questions. We hear them say, "Let's cap entitlements." But what does that mean? They add that defense has already been cut enough. On the right fringes of the Republican party, we hear one more stanza of the supply-side melody: Another tax cut and we can "grow our way" out of the problem. This, of course, is fiscal nonsense.

From the traditional Democrats, we hear the same old refrains: Slash defense, tax the rich and the fat corporations, don't touch entitlements, and (on this one, they seem to sing in unison with the conservatives), get rid of "waste, fraud, and abuse." Some in the Democratic party continue to plead for massive trillion-dollar infrastructure "investment" programs, aka pork-barrel jobs programs. Others push for a middle-class tax cut either because the middle class supposedly needs it or because they're convinced the economy needs it. This, too, is fiscal nonsense.

All of today's debate about how to allocate spending cuts and tax increases is, at bottom, the old debate about who wins and who loses. In effect, each party is saying, "I want my friends to win and yours to lose."

All these "principles" perpetuate gridlock. They are obviously flawed. We must say a resounding no to this politics of posturing and choicelessness.

· NO: Defense cuts alone are not enough.
· NO: Taxing the rich alone is not enough.
· NO: Eliminating waste, fraud, and abuse alone is not enough.
· NO: Spending cuts alone are not enough.
· NO: Tax increases alone are not enough.

The right answer to what must be done is "all of the above," and then some. We need both spending cuts *and* tax increases. We need defense cuts *and* we need to clean up waste, fraud, and abuse. We need to marry the objectives of both Republicans and Democrats, liberals and conservatives. But most of all, we need what both sides in the debate would prefer to ignore: We need the great American middle class to play the role it must in saving the American Dream for our children.

The reader who has come this far down the road with me understands by now why I place such great stress on balancing the budget and turning back the debt tide that will otherwise drown much of what is best in this great country of ours.

I have written of the *moral imperative* to defend the interests of our children and grandchildren, to rescue them from the suffocating burden of debt we are now passing on to them, and to prevent an ugly age war in our future. How can we condemn these unrepresented fiscal victims to long-run tax rates net of benefits received of 71 percent, compared with a fairer rate of 39 percent under the kind of plan I have proposed?

I have also written of the *economic imperative* to curb our gluttonous consumption habits and once again augment our national savings as a source for investment, both public and private, in machines and human beings. But not only must we invest *more*, we must invest *smarter*. If Democrats threw money at social programs in the 1960s and if Republicans threw money at defense in the 1980s, we must *not* just throw money at "investment" in the 1990s—if those "investments" are bloated educational establishments, pork-barrel public infrastructure, dubious "big science," flawed welfare programs, and the like. No, the economic imperative is to invest both *more* and *smarter* in ways that lead to new productivity, renewed vigorous growth, and a future of rising living standards.

In concluding this book, let me now turn very briefly to a third imperative—the *political imperative*. It is not just our economic system that is failing us, but our political system. Yet just as it is useless for Democrats and Republicans to blame each other, it is equally useless for the public at large simply to blame the politicians. After all, we elected them. And all the corruption, hypocrisy, demagoguery, and fundamental choicelessness we find in today's political leaders is little more than a reflection of the same qualities in our society as a whole. Yes, we need to reform the political system, and yes, we need better, more visionary, and more responsible political leaders—leaders like Warren Rudman and Paul Tsongas, who are fiscally conservative, socially compassionate, and politically courageous (and sadly, but not coincidentally, out of office).

But if we, the people, want our political system to serve us better, we, the people, must also change ourselves for the better. We ordinary citizens must begin to think long-term instead of short-term. We must invest more in protecting the interests of our children and posterity instead of hunkering down to protect our own self-interest in the here and now. We must learn once again to think of ourselves more as contributors, less as victims. And we must remember that along with our rights as citizens also come duties. For if we are all victims with many rights and few duties, who among us is it who will build a better tomorrow?

If we can close our budget deficit and triple our rate of net national savings, we will, almost by definition, have established the basis of a new politics in America. Indeed, balancing the budget to increase investment is perhaps the best single crucible in which to forge a new American politics for the twenty-first century. The process itself demands that we unite on a nonpartisan basis; that we engage in true problem solving and consensus building; that we think very deeply about fundamental questions such as the roles of government, the private sector, and the public at large in the solution; and that we once again learn to make farsighted choices and courageous tradeoffs.

The budget cannot be balanced without building a powerful coalition in favor of the general interest, long-term progress, and future generations. But once such a coalition is built, and once such a change has taken place in our political environment, America will be better able to solve many other seemingly intractable problems, from racial divisions, teenage pregnancies, and illiteracy to litigiousness and environmental degradation.

Thus, while the budget deficit is one of our worst social nightmares, it also provides a great social opportunity to begin to set things right again by saving and investing in the future. It is a "single issue" around which many important issues can be constructively approached. It is an issue that requires every American constituency to redefine its self-image and role in society. It offers the promise of a national catharsis and the transformation of our fallen American character to a renewed sense of citizenship and a longer-lasting state of grace.

The poet W. B. Yeats wrote, "Nothing can be sole or whole / That has not been rent." America has been torn apart by conflicting special interests, a have-it-all hubris, and an entitlement ethos run amok. Balancing the budget and getting our economic house in order offer us the chance to become whole again as a nation and as a people.

In his classic *Democracy in America,* Alexis de Tocqueville made this sobering observation: "The American republic will endure until the politicians find they can bribe the people with their own money." But today it's even worse than that. It's our children's money we're spending. Bonhoeffer was right: "The ultimate test of a moral society is the kind of world it leaves to its children." Look into the eyes of your children and grandchildren. You will see that we don't have a moment to waste.

PART III

A Visual Guide to America's Real Leading Indicators

America's Real
Leading Indicators

The year was 1937. America was recovering from the Great Depression. But unemployment remained high and inflation threatened to take off. Unable to cover its growing spending commitments, Congress hiked taxes. At the same time, the Fed tightened monetary policy. These untimely actions helped abort the four-year recovery then under way. Once again, the nation plunged into depression.

In the wake of this policy debacle, Secretary of the Treasury Henry Morgenthau, Jr., turned to the National Bureau of Economic Research in New York for help. The task: to compile a list of economic indicators to help forecast the timing and severity of future turns in the business cycle. Building on research already under way, Wesley Mitchell and Arthur Burns soon published their classic *Statistical Indicators of Cyclical Revivals*—the grandfather of the list of "leading, coincident, and lagging" indicators we now use to forecast recessions and recoveries and to fine-tune government fiscal and monetary policy.

Today, the ups and downs of economic indicators have become routine factors in our lives. Announced on the evening news, scrutinized by economists, and anxiously tracked by policymakers at the White House and in Congress, these indicators are by now so familiar that they often sound like some kind of doggerel: "Durable goods orders rose in September." "Unemployment insurance claims were at a two-year low in October." "The prime rate is down a quarter point since January." "The consumer expectations index is up."

Over the years, some of the indicators have changed. Monthly upticks in "inner tube production" wouldn't tell us much today. But history has proven the value of the concept. For the most part, leading indicators have led and lagging indicators have lagged throughout our ten postwar business cycles. By tracking them, we can gain some useful insights into how the economy will be doing three months, six months, or a year from now. As a result, policymakers are far better able today than in 1937 to take steps to forestall a recession or speed a recovery.

The problem with these short-term indicators, however, is that all too often they monopolize our attention. By constantly fixing our gaze on our short-term economic performance, they have discouraged us

from paying serious attention to our longer-term direction. By suggesting that cyclical demand-management is all we need to bother about,
they have led us to assume that the fundamentals would take care of
themselves. Today we find ourselves, in effect, calibrating and preparing second by second for each new ocean wave, while paying no attention to which way the tide is running hour by hour. Preoccupied by
the next few months, most government economists and statisticians
have little to say to many younger Americans who worry that the tide
may be running out on them forever.

NEEDED: A NEW SET OF LEADING INDICATORS

After two decades of stagnating living standards, it's clear that America's deepest economic problems today have little to do with the tran-
sient business cycle. They're rooted in our neglect of savings and
investment and of the other long-term economic and social inputs on
which tomorrow's prosperity ultimately depends. If we fail to change
course, our children will inherit a second-rate economy in a nation
that's become a second-rate power.

As I've argued, our fixation on the short term has become an all-
purpose excuse for our failure to accept any temporary sacrifice for
longer-term gain—for our failure once again to assert control over
our national destiny. It seems it's never the right moment in the
business cycle—or the political election cycle—for a decisive change
in course. The "leading indicators" are always a bit off. Maybe we're
just coming out of a recession. Or then again, maybe we're about to
slip into one. An exchange at a recent conference of The Concord
Coalition underscores this lack of connection between our policy
concerns and our real economic problems. Paul Volcker, former Fed
chairman, a Concord vice-chairman, and one of our more farsighted
statesmen at large, was quizzed about whether the Clinton plan
might be going too fast and too far on deficit reduction. He replied
that too much deficit reduction is something he never loses sleep
over. None of us should.

The point, of course, is not that business cycles are unimportant, or
that government need no longer concern itself with managing them.
We obviously want to know what our near-term future looks like and
what the effects of changes in fiscal and monetary policy will be. Rather,
the point is that we now also need a new set of indicators that focus our
attention on the long-term future—indicators that tell us how America
will be doing a decade or a generation from now.

What kind of indicators? Topping the list should be measures of
what America is saving and investing—not just in business plant and

equipment, but in new technologies, in public infrastructure, and in the health and education and skills of tomorrow's workforce. The list must also include a detailed accounting of the liabilities we are passing on to the future, from our official national and foreign debts to the huge hidden costs of our retirement and health-care entitlements. Above and beyond these statistics, we would want to look at indices of social cohesion—such items as divorce rates and crime rates, whose costs can't be measured in dollars and cents but that have a crucial impact on both our economic fortunes and our overall quality of life. All are measures of the fundamental economic and social inputs that over the long run are correlated with rising productivity and living standards. Only if we rivet our attention on such leading indicators will we be able to sift out what really matters from what doesn't and make political choices that truly benefit our collective future.

A BRIEF PREVIEW OF THE NEW "PETERSON SLIDE SHOW"

When I first arrived in Washington in 1971, I had yet to appreciate how myopic our economic policymaking had become. I naively expected I would be greeted by in-depth analyses of the deterioration in fundamental economic inputs that was then beginning to cloud America's future. Instead, I discovered that almost no one was really looking at that problem, let alone seeking to develop coherent solutions.

With the enthusiasm of an amateur (and the naivete of a noneconomist), I set about gathering information from every conceivable source, public and private, and then presented the results of my research as a volume of charts and tables and a color slide show. I called it "The U.S. in a Changing World Economy." The first audience for what became known as the "Peterson Slide Show" (my punster wife dubbed it "The Great American Slide") was the Council on International Economic Policy, chaired by Richard Nixon. But in the months that followed, I inflicted it on any number of willing (and sometimes even eager) groups of legislators, businessmen, labor leaders, and journalists. To my surprise, the printed version became a minor best-seller, at least by U.S. Government Printing Office standards.

That Peterson Slide Show has gone through many transformations and rebirths over the past two decades. The charts that follow are the latest. They are intended as a guide to what I would argue are America's *real* leading indicators. Though they are long-term in nature, they are among the ones I believe we should be most deeply concerned about. But this latest "slide show" is more than just a collection of statistics. It also tells a story—and takes the reader on a guided tour of where America is today, how we got here, and where we're headed.

Some colleagues initially thought that a chart presentation of this sort might be out of place in a book that is not aimed at policy experts versed in the arcane details of the federal budget and our national economic accounts. But if I had any doubts about the effective role charts can play in educating the public about the necessity of balancing the budget and reinvesting in our future, Ross Perot's masterful use of them in his 1992 "infomercials" laid those doubts to rest.

How Are We Doing?

The first section, "How Are We Doing?" begins by exploring the consequences of perhaps the most important economic development of the past two decades: the sudden end of America's postwar productivity miracle. We learn that Europe and Japan are rapidly catching up with America in per-worker output and could soon pass us. We also see that our flat productivity growth has inevitably been translated into stagnant incomes and rising poverty rates. The result is a colossal gap between what we once expected and what we now experience. Where it used to take a few decades for U.S. living standards to double, at today's pace it will take centuries.

The Fading of the American Dream

A most troubling symptom of our economic malady is the widening gap between the fortunes of the young and old. In the second section, "The Fading of the American Dream," we see that our productivity slowdown has barely touched the upward mobility of America's eldest, but has pushed the incomes of younger Americans—and especially families with children—off a cliff. Not only are today's young workers *not* on a path to exceed the incomes of their parents at the same age, they may not even *match* their living standards. Wherever we look— whether to soaring child poverty rates, to the rising tax burden on young families, or to their declining rates of homeownership—the trends all point the same way. Never has an economy bestowed so much on the old while passing over the young.

The Great Consumption Tilt

In the third section, "The Great Consumption Tilt," I shift our attention from the symptoms to the causes of America's fall from grace. We see how rates of U.S. consumption have soared and how rates of U.S. savings and investment have plummeted—compared to both our own historical record and that of our competitors abroad. Looking at other long-term inputs that are linked to improved standard-of-living outputs—infrastructure, research and development, technical personnel, patents—the trends are no more encouraging.

A disturbing subtheme of this section is the price we all must pay for our 1980s debt party. The charts reveal how—thanks to massive borrowing from abroad and from the future by every sector of our economy—we managed to make the 1980s a decade of a make-believe economic miracle without the bother of producing a real one. Along the way, we examine some key legacies of the 1980s: yawning trade deficits, runaway health-care spending, and a swollen market for domestic services in everything from strip malls to lawyering that has tilted our entire economy toward consumption in the here and now.

The Age of Deficits and Entitlements

The fourth section, "The Age of Deficits and Entitlements," turns to the central role played by federal budget policy in skewing our priorities toward present consumption. We learn how, with the deficit spigot wide open, we have added three times more to our gross national debt since 1980 than was added during all presidencies from George Washington to Jimmy Carter, how this sea of red ink extinguishes between half and two-thirds of our scarce private savings, and how almost none of this money has gone to finance new public investments. We also focus on some other unpleasant realities: The growth in entitlements (plus interest on the national debt) is the driving force behind federal spending and deficits; the lion's share of public benefits passes over the young on its way to retirement and health-care programs for the old; and in this system of skewed priorities entitlements are at least as likely to benefit the *rich* as the poor.

Shadows Falling over the Next Generation

"Shadows Falling over the Next Generation," the final section, looks at how well we are preparing our children to meet the challenges of the next century. Sadly, America ranks near the top among major industrial countries in terms of the damage that we inflict on the young (whether through family trauma, economic poverty, or neglect of their health)—and near the bottom in terms of what we invest in them (whether measured by how long they study in school or by how prepared they are for the modern workplace when the studying is over). Yet we expect them to cope with a rapidly aging society, foot the mushrooming bill for our public retirement programs, finance a national debt of staggering proportions, and pay for a health-care system whose projected costs are utterly unsustainable.

It's time we wake up to the leading indicators that really matter. Only if we remember the original promise of the American Dream—to leave behind more than we take—will we be able to restore that dream to our children. Sometimes, as the old saying goes, a picture is worth a thousand words. Take a look at these pictures and you will see why I believe a massive shift in our priorities is an urgent national cause.

CHART NOTES

A few notes may be helpful in understanding the charts.

- The "Big 7" (or G-7) nations consist of the United States, Japan, Germany, Canada, the United Kingdom, France, and Italy. Of these, the "Other Big 7 Nations" refers to the last four. Each indicator for these four is calculated as an unweighted average.
- In charts dealing only with the United States, "workers" refers to the Bureau of Economic Analysis definition of "persons engaged in production," which equals all "full-time equivalent employees" plus all self-employed persons. In international comparisons, "workers" refers to Bureau of Labor Statistics employment data for major countries.
- Gross Domestic Product (GDP) is now the standard measure of aggregate national economic activity preferred by international organizations and U.S. federal agencies. For the United States, GDP refers to all goods and services produced with labor and property located geographically within the United States, as opposed to Gross National Product (GNP), which refers to production with labor and property supplied by U.S. residents. Most of the (minor) difference between U.S. GDP and GNP reflects the difference between the product of U.S.-owned capital abroad and the product of foreign-owned capital in the United States. In both cases, Net Domestic Product or Net National Product (NDP or NNP) subtracts the depreciation of capital stock.
- The Census Bureau definition of "family" means two or more related persons living together in the same household. A "household" can also refer to unrelated persons or an individual living alone.
- The Census poverty level for the United States, which varies with the number of persons in a household and the age of its head, was originally set in 1961 at three times a household's estimated "economy food plan." Ever since, it has been raised in line with the CPI. The official poverty measure counts only reported pretax *cash* income.
- Fiscal years refer to the "budget years" of the federal government. Until 1976, a fiscal year began on July 1 of the prior calendar year. Since 1977, it has begun on October 1 of the prior calendar year.

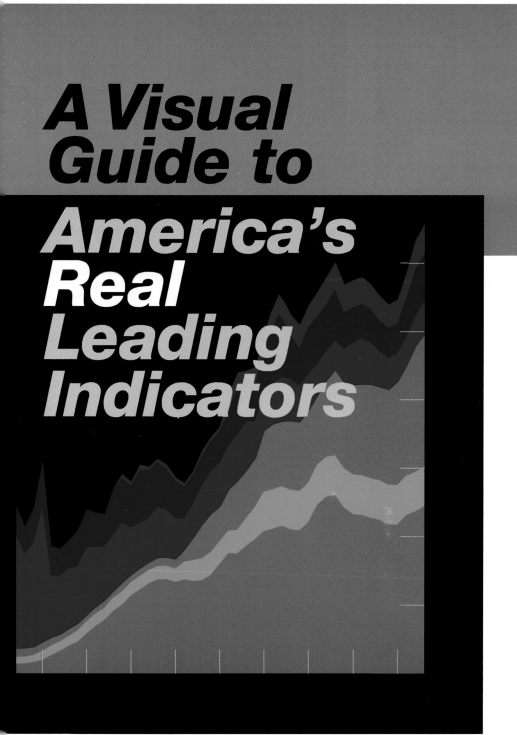

A Visual Guide to

America's Real Leading Indicators

1.
HOW ARE WE DOING?

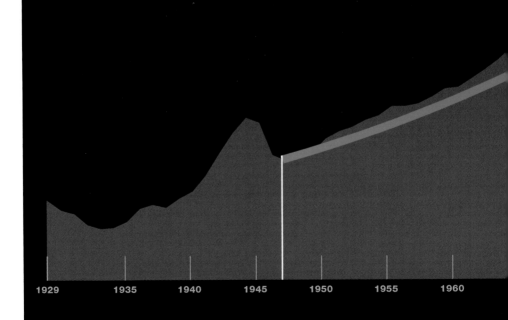

1929   1935   1940   1945   1950   1955   1960

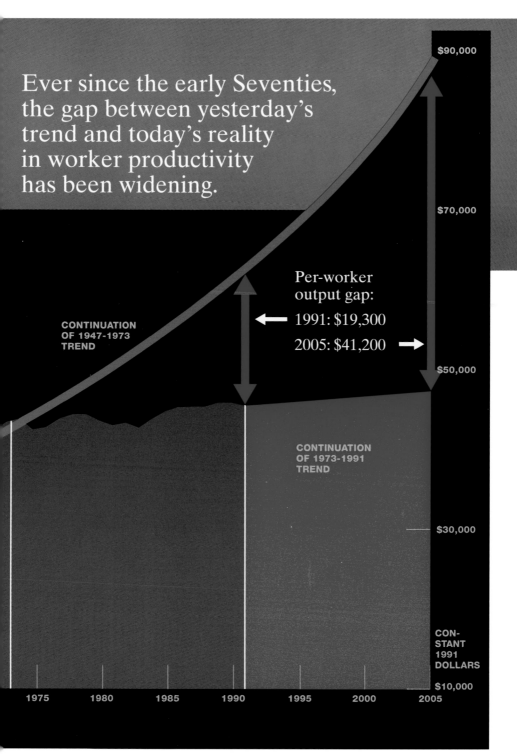

Ever since the early Seventies, the gap between yesterday's trend and today's reality in worker productivity has been widening.

$90,000

$70,000

Per-worker output gap:
1991: $19,300
2005: $41,200

CONTINUATION OF 1947-1973 TREND

$50,000

CONTINUATION OF 1973-1991 TREND

$30,000

CON-STANT 1991 DOLLARS

$10,000

1975   1980   1985   1990   1995   2000   2005

(1.1) U.S. NET DOMESTIC PRODUCT PER WORKER
IN CONSTANT 1991 DOLLARS, 1929 TO 2005
SOURCE: BEA (1993)

America is still (barely) the world's most productive economy, but other industrial countries are catching up fast, . . .

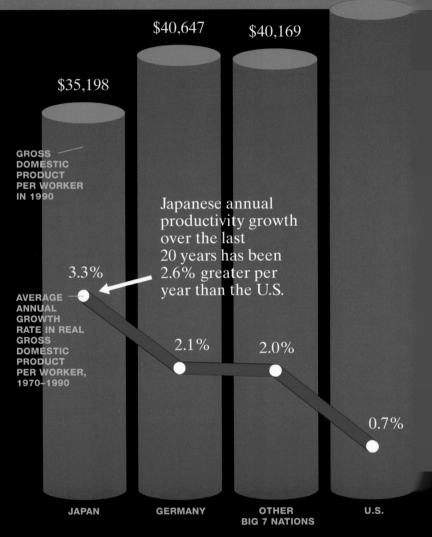

$35,198

$40,647

$40,169

$44,872

GROSS
DOMESTIC
PRODUCT
PER WORKER
IN 1990

Japanese annual productivity growth over the last 20 years has been 2.6% greater per year than the U.S.

3.3%

AVERAGE
ANNUAL
GROWTH
RATE IN REAL
GROSS
DOMESTIC
PRODUCT
PER WORKER,
1970–1990

2.1%

2.0%

0.7%

JAPAN

GERMANY

OTHER
BIG 7 NATIONS

U.S.

(1.2) GROSS DOMESTIC PRODUCT PER WORKER IN 199
IN U.S. DOLLARS
NOTE: CURRENCIES COMPARED AT PURCHASING-POWER PARITIES.
SOURCE: BLS (1992); OECD (1992)

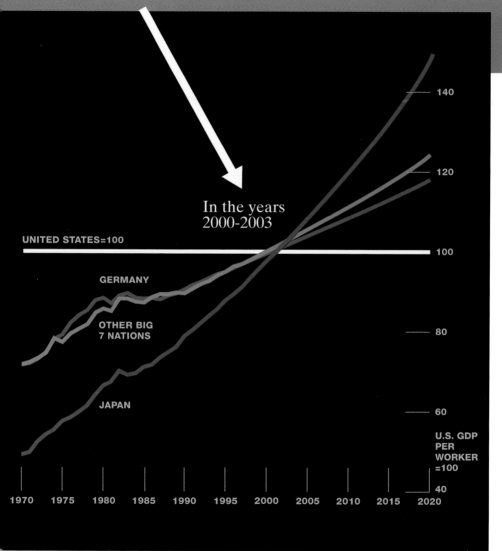

...and, if recent trends continue, Japan and Europe will soon pass us.

In the years
2000-2003

UNITED STATES=100

GERMANY

OTHER BIG
7 NATIONS

JAPAN

140

120

100

80

60

U.S. GDP
PER
WORKER
=100

40

1970 1975 1980 1985 1990 1995 2000 2005 2010 2015 2020

(1.3) GROSS DOMESTIC PRODUCT PER WORKER

U.S.= 100, 1970 TO 2020, PROJECTIONS BASED ON 1973-1990 GROWTH TRENDS

NOTE: CURRENCIES COMPARED AT PURCHASING-POWER PARITIES; PROJECTIONS CALCULATED
FROM LEAST-SQUARES REGRESSION ON 1973-90. SOURCE: BLS (1992); OECD (1992)

Inevitably,
flat productivity growth
translates into stagnating
American wages
(however wages are defined), . . .

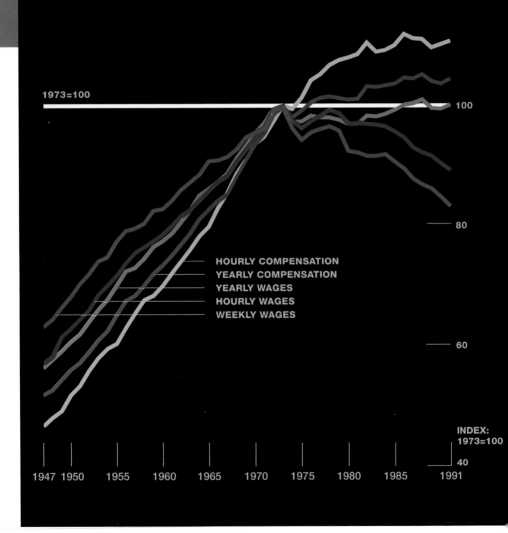

1973=100

HOURLY COMPENSATION
YEARLY COMPENSATION
YEARLY WAGES
HOURLY WAGES
WEEKLY WAGES

100

80

60

INDEX:
1973=100

40

1947 1950   1955   1960   1965   1970   1975   1980   1985   1991

**(1.4) MEASURES OF AVERAGE REAL WAGES AND
AVERAGE REAL COMPENSATION PER U.S. EMPLOYEE**

1973 = 100, 1947 TO 1991

NOTE: "WAGES" MEANS TAKE-HOME PAY; "COMPENSATION" INCLUDES ALL FRINGE BENEFITS,
SUCH AS HEALTH INSURANCE. SOURCE: BEA (1993); BLS (1993)

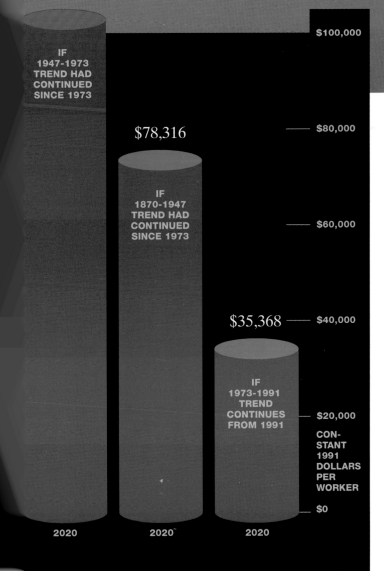

a colossal
between what
pected—and
w experience.

$103,562

$100,000

IF
1947-1973
TREND HAD
CONTINUED
SINCE 1973

$78,316 — $80,000

IF
1870-1947
TREND HAD
CONTINUED
SINCE 1973

— $60,000

$35,368 — $40,000

IF
1973-1991
TREND
CONTINUES
FROM 1991

— $20,000

CON-
STANT
1991
DOLLARS
PER
WORKER

— $0

2020   2020   2020

.S. YEARLY WORKER COMPENSATION IN 1991
2020 BASED ON PAST TRENDS IN CONSTANT 1991 DOLLARS
, BLACKMAN, AND WOLFF (1989); EAEH, "WAGES AND PRICES" (1980)

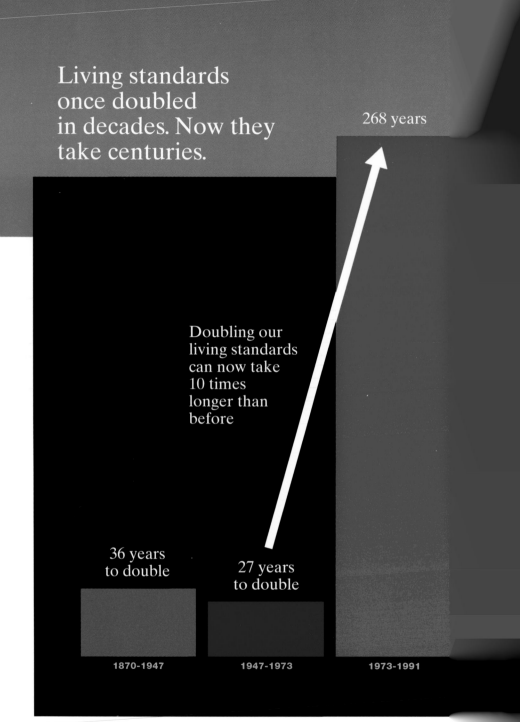

Living standards once doubled in decades. Now they take centuries.

268 years

Doubling our living standards can now take 10 times longer than before

36 years to double

27 years to double

1870-1947

1947-1973

1973-1991

(1.6) YEARS REQUIRED FOR U.S. LIVING STANDARDS TO
AT DIFFERENT ANNUAL GROWTH RATES OF REAL COMPENSATION PER WC
1870-1947, 1947-1973, 1973-1991

SOURCE: BEA (1993); BAUMOL, BLACKMAN, AND WOLFF (1989);
EAEH, "WAGES AND PRICES" (1980)

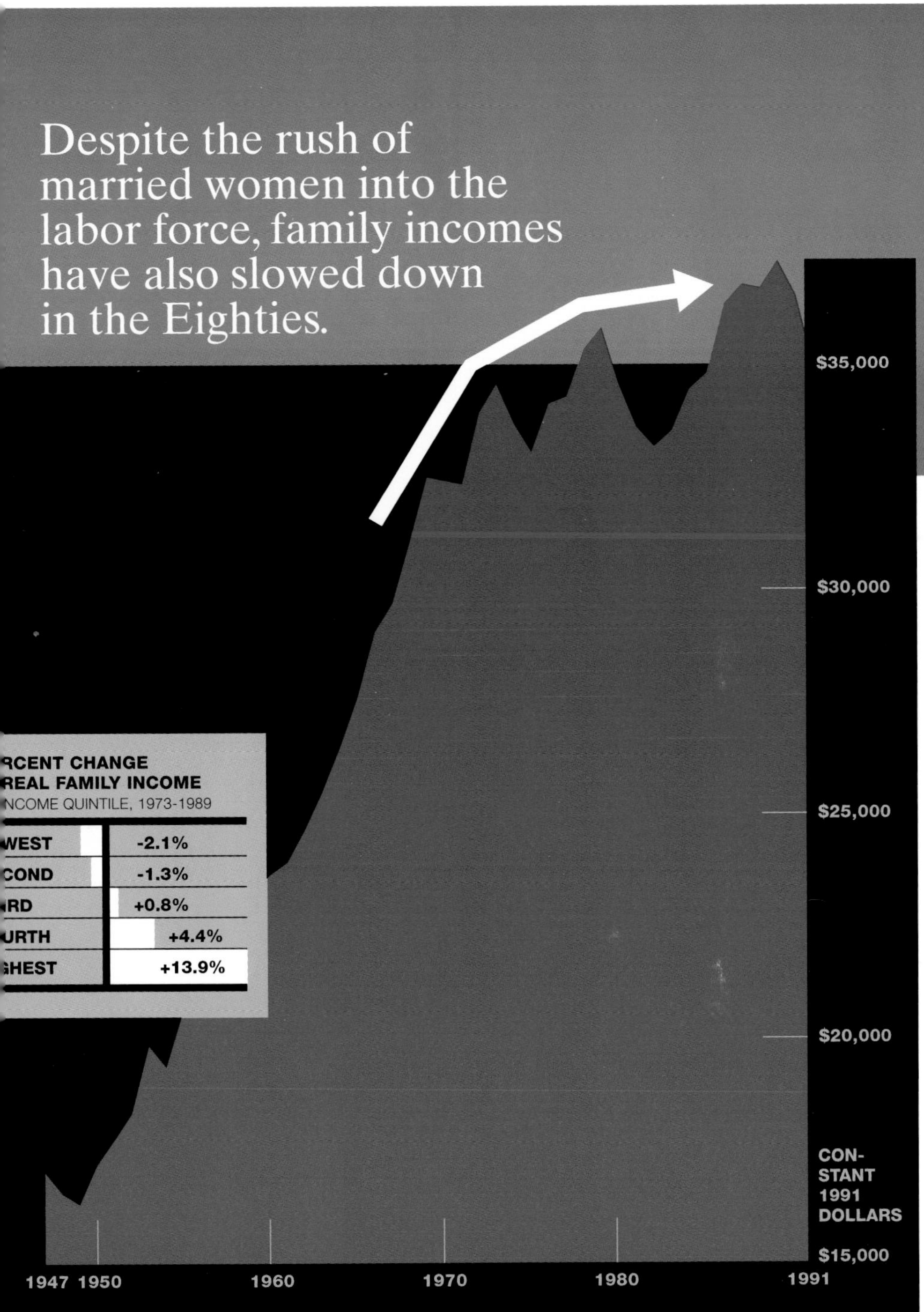

Despite the rush of married women into the labor force, family incomes have also slowed down in the Eighties.

$35,000

$30,000

RCENT CHANGE REAL FAMILY INCOME NCOME QUINTILE, 1973-1989	
WEST	-2.1%
COND	-1.3%
RD	+0.8%
URTH	+4.4%
GHEST	+13.9%

$25,000

$20,000

CON-
STANT
1991
DOLLARS

$15,000

| 1947 1950 | 1960 | 1970 | 1980 | 1991 |

(1.7) U.S. MEDIAN FAMILY INCOME
IN CONSTANT 1991 DOLLARS, 1947 TO 1991

SOURCE: CENSUS (1992); WAYS AND MEANS (1992)

With living standards no longer rising for most Americans, we are no longer "winning the war" against poverty.

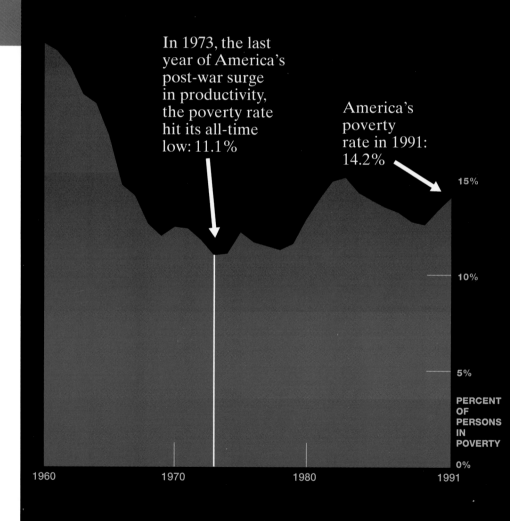

In 1973, the last year of America's post-war surge in productivity, the poverty rate hit its all-time low: 11.1%

America's poverty rate in 1991: 14.2%

15%

10%

5%

PERCENT OF PERSONS IN POVERTY

0%

1960   1970   1980   1991

(1.8) OFFICIAL U.S. POVERTY RATE
FOR ALL PERSONS, 1960 TO 1991
SOURCE: CENSUS (1992)

> As for "quality of life," the record does not bode well for our children, our future, and our sense of community.

OTHER BIG 7 NATIONS		
	UNITED STATES	

OTHER BIG 7 NATIONS	UNITED STATES	
21	53	**BIRTH RATE OF TEENAGE WOMEN,** PER 100,000, AGE 15-19, 1980-81
19	29	**PREGNANCIES ENDING IN ABORTION,** PERCENT OF ALL PREGNANCIES, 1989
38	60	**IMPACT OF ALCOHOL AND DRUG ABUSE IN THE WORKPLACE,** AS RATED BY NATION'S BUSINESS LEADERS, 1990 (SCALE: 0=LOW, 100=HIGH)
14	81	**AIDS CASES PER 100,000 PERSONS,** OFFICIALLY REPORTED, AS OF 1991
3.3	9.4	**MURDERS PER 100,000 PERSONS,** REPORTED TO POLICE, 1988-90
1.4	21.9	**MURDERS PER 100,000 MALES,** AGE 15 to 24, 1987-88
0.7	3.7	**MURDERS PER 100,000 CHILDREN,** AGE 1 TO 19, 1983-86*
13	114	**REPORTED RAPES PER 100,000 WOMEN,** AGE 15-59, 1980-85**
20	29	**REPORTED VIOLENT CRIME VICTIMS,** BY PERCENT OF POPULATION, 1989
74	426	**PRISON POPULATION PER 100,000 PERSONS,** 1988-90***
4	29	**HOUSEHOLDS WITH HANDGUNS,** BY PERCENT OF ALL HOMES, 1981-83
84	310	**NUMBER OF LAWYERS PER 100,000 PERSONS,** 1986-91***
0.5	2.6	**COST OF CIVIL LITIGATION,** AS A PERCENT OF GDP, 1986***
36	57	**PERSONS WHO SAY THAT KEEPING MONEY THEY FIND CAN ALWAYS OR SOMETIMES BE JUSTIFIED,** BY PERCENT OF POPULATION, 1981-83
2.8	5.8	**CO_2 EMISSIONS FROM ENERGY USE,** BY TONS PER CAPITA, 1988
849	1,901	**MUNICIPAL WASTE,** ANNUALLY GENERATED TONS PER CAPITA, LATE 1980s
78	50	**NATIONAL ELECTION VOTERS,** BY PERCENT OF ELIGIBLE VOTERS, 1971-88
24	11	**PAID VACATION DAYS,** AVERAGE PER YEAR, 1991

*EXCLUDING JAPAN **EXCLUDING GERMANY ***EXCLUDING CANADA

(1.9) SOCIAL INDICATORS: INTERNATIONAL COMPARISON

SOURCE: SHAPIRO (1992) AND OTHER

2.
THE FADING
OF THE
AMERICAN DREAM

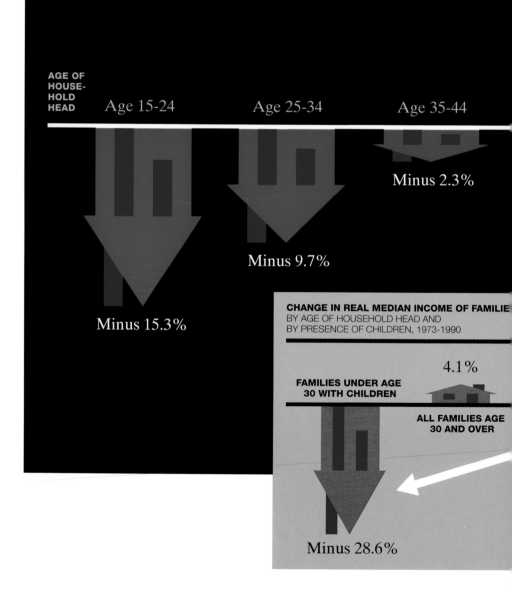

AGE OF HOUSE- HOLD HEAD	Age 15-24	Age 25-34	Age 35-44

Minus 2.3%

Minus 9.7%

Minus 15.3%

CHANGE IN REAL MEDIAN INCOME OF FAMILIES
BY AGE OF HOUSEHOLD HEAD AND
BY PRESENCE OF CHILDREN, 1973-1990

4.1%

**FAMILIES UNDER AGE
30 WITH CHILDREN**

**ALL FAMILIES AGE
30 AND OVER**

Minus 28.6%

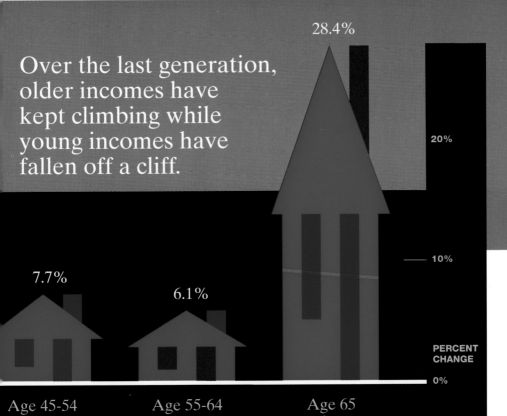

Over the last generation, older incomes have kept climbing while young incomes have fallen off a cliff.

28.4%

20%

10%

7.7%

6.1%

PERCENT
CHANGE

0%

Age 45-54

Age 55-64

Age 65
and over

The living standards
of young families with
children have been
especially hard hit

(2.1) CHANGE IN U.S. REAL MEDIAN HOUSEHOLD INCOME
BY AGE OF HOUSEHOLD HEAD, 1973 TO 1991

SOURCE: CENSUS (1992); TABULATION OF CENSUS DATA, CDF (1992)

Poverty today is nearly three times more likely to afflict the very young as the very old.

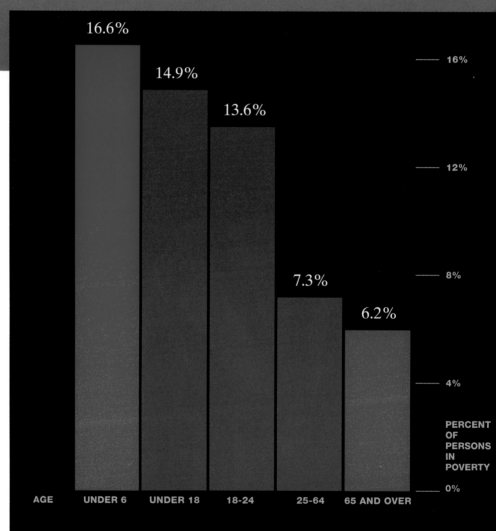

16.6%

14.9%

13.6%

7.3%

6.2%

16%

12%

8%

4%

PERCENT
OF
PERSONS
IN
POVERTY

0%

AGE   UNDER 6   UNDER 18   18-24   25-64   65 AND OVER

(2.2) U.S. TOTAL-INCOME POVERTY RATES IN 1990
BY AGE GROUP
NOTE: TOTAL-INCOME POVERTY COUNTS AS INCOME THE VALUE OF ALL NON-CASH BENEFITS,
SUCH AS HEALTH INSURANCE AND HOUSING. SOURCE: CENSUS (1991)

"Outdoing Mom and Dad": Is that an unrealistic hope for today's young adults?

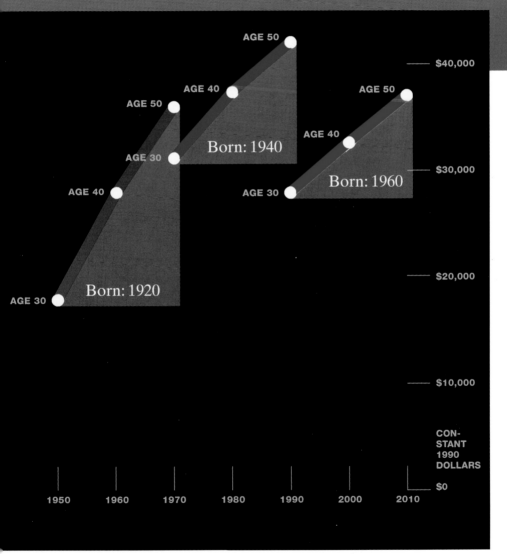

AGE 50

AGE 40

AGE 50

AGE 50

AGE 40

AGE 30

Born: 1940

AGE 40

AGE 30

Born: 1960

AGE 40

Born: 1920

AGE 30

AGE 30

$40,000

$30,000

$20,000

$10,000

CON-
STANT
1990
DOLLARS

$0

1950   1960   1970   1980   1990   2000   2010

(2.3) AVERAGE EARNINGS OF
FULL-TIME YEAR-ROUND MALE WORKERS IN U.S.

BY BIRTH YEAR, IN CONSTANT 1990 DOLLARS

NOTE: AGE 40 AND 50 PROJECTIONS FOR 1960 BIRTH YEAR ARE
AVERAGES OF OPTIMISTIC AND PESSIMISTIC SCENARIOS.

SOURCE: TABULATION OF CENSUS DATA, CED (1992); LEVY AND MICHEL (1991)

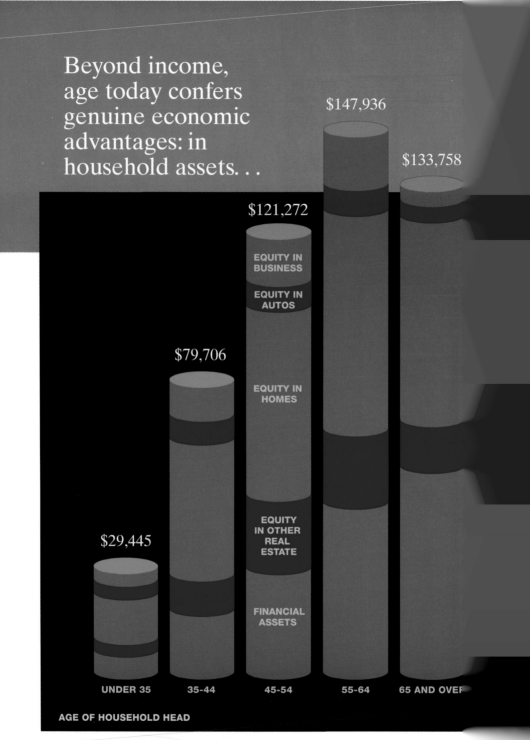

Beyond income, age today confers genuine economic advantages: in household assets. . .

$147,936

$133,758

$121,272

EQUITY IN BUSINESS

EQUITY IN AUTOS

$79,706

EQUITY IN HOMES

$29,445

EQUITY IN OTHER REAL ESTATE

FINANCIAL ASSETS

UNDER 35   35-44   45-54   55-64   65 AND OVER

AGE OF HOUSEHOLD HEAD

(2.4) AVERAGE U.S. HOUSEHOLD NET WORTH IN 1988
BY TYPE OF ASSET AND AGE OF HOUSEHOLD HEAD
SOURCE: CENSUS (1990)

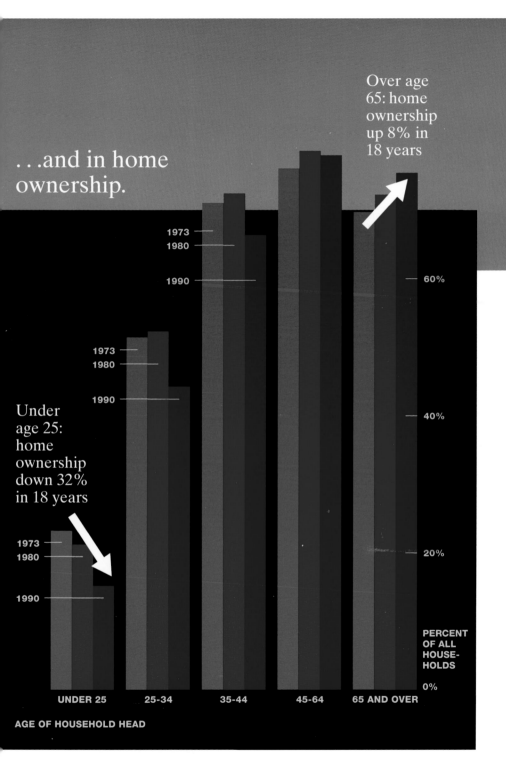

Over age 65: home ownership up 8% in 18 years

...and in home ownership.

1973
1980

1990

60%

1973
1980

1990

Under age 25: home ownership down 32% in 18 years

40%

1973
1980

1990

20%

PERCENT OF ALL HOUSE-HOLDS

0%

UNDER 25   25-34   35-44   45-64   65 AND OVER

AGE OF HOUSEHOLD HEAD

(2.5) HOME OWNERSHIP IN U.S.
AS PERCENT OF ALL HOUSEHOLDS, BY AGE OF
HOUSEHOLD HEAD, IN 1973, 1980, AND 1990
SOURCE: JCHS (1991)

Age confers
a huge advantage
in health insurance
coverage...   99.1%

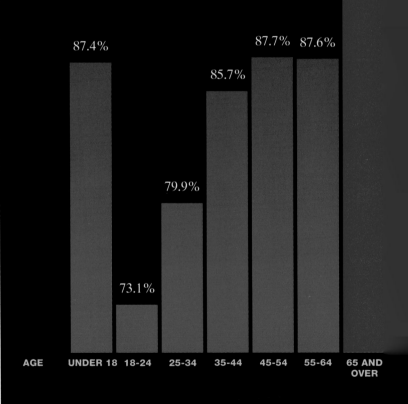

87.4%

85.7%

87.7% 87.6%

79.9%

73.1%

AGE   UNDER 18 18-24   25-34   35-44   45-54   55-64   65 AND
                                                            OVER

**(2.6) PERCENT OF PERSONS COVERED
BY HEALTH INSURANCE IN U.S.**
AT SOME TIME DURING 1991, BY AGE GROUP

SOURCE: CENSUS (1992)

$7,155 in taxes

. . .and (even) in taxes.

$6,000

Working-age
couple with
$30,000 in wage
income pays
eight times more
taxes than an —— $4,000
elderly couple
with $30,000
in retirement
income

FICA TAX

—— $2,000

INCOME TAX

$900 in taxes

INCOME TAX

TOTAL
TAX
LIABILITY
IN 1992

$0

WORKING-AGE COUPLE
WITH ONE CHILD

ELDERLY COUPLE
WITH NO CHILDREN

(2.7) TOTAL U.S. FEDERAL TAX LIABILITY IN 1992

FOR WORKING-AGE AND ELDERLY JOINT-FILING COUPLES WITH $30,000 OF INCOME

NOTE: FICA TAX INCLUDES BOTH EMPLOYER AND EMPOLYEE CONTRIBUTION.

ELDERLY HOUSEHOLD, IT IS ASSUMED, RECEIVES $12,000 IN SOCIAL SECURITY, $6,000

IN A TAXABLE PENSION, AND $6,000 IN TAXABLE INTEREST INCOME.

SOURCE: WAYS AND MEANS (1992)

3.
THE GREAT
CONSUMPTION TILT

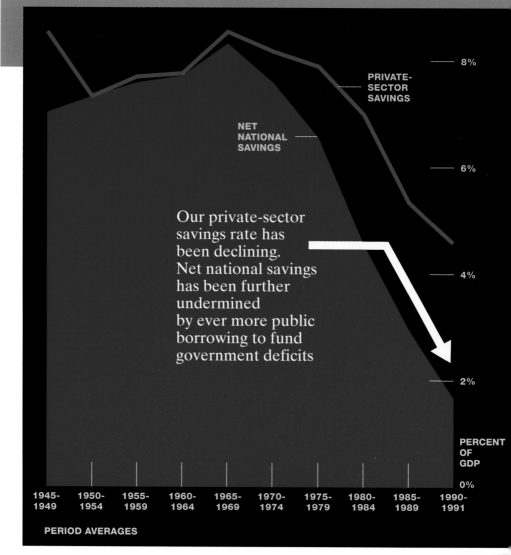

PRIVATE-
SECTOR
SAVINGS

NET
NATIONAL
SAVINGS

8%

6%

Our private-sector
savings rate has
been declining.
Net national savings
has been further
undermined
by ever more public
borrowing to fund
government deficits

4%

2%

PERCENT
OF
GDP

0%

| 1945-1949 | 1950-1954 | 1955-1959 | 1960-1964 | 1965-1969 | 1970-1974 | 1975-1979 | 1980-1984 | 1985-1989 | 1990-1991 |

PERIOD AVERAGES

(3.1) U.S. NET NATIONAL SAVINGS

AS A PERCENT OF GROSS DOMESTIC PRODUCT, PERIOD AVERAGES, 1945 TO 1991

NOTE: EXCLUDING PUBLIC-SECTOR INVESTMENT; "NET" MEANS
NET OF DEPRECIATION ON CAPITAL STOCK. SOURCE: BEA (1993)

As our rate of savings
has fallen, our rate
of personal consumption
has continued to rise.

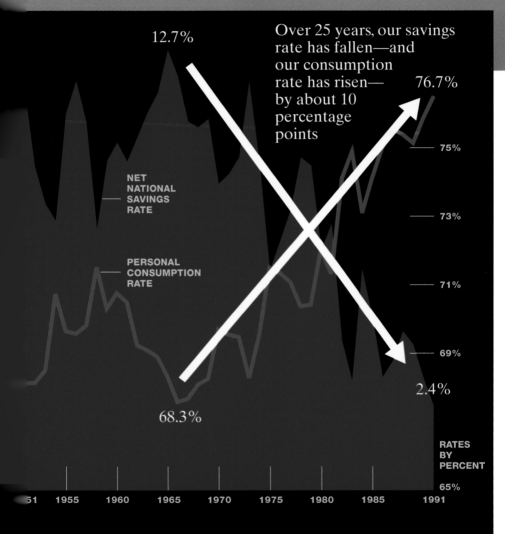

12.7%

Over 25 years, our savings
rate has fallen—and
our consumption
rate has risen—
by about 10
percentage
points

76.7%

75%

NET
NATIONAL
SAVINGS
RATE

73%

PERSONAL
CONSUMPTION
RATE

71%

69%

2.4%

68.3%

RATES
BY
PERCENT

65%

51 1955   1960   1965   1970   1975   1980   1985   1991

(3.2) **U.S. PERSONAL CONSUMPTION RATE AND
U.S. NET NATIONAL SAVINGS RATE**
AS A PERCENT OF NET NATIONAL PRODUCT, 1951 TO 1991
NOTE: NET NATIONAL PRODUCT EQUALS GROSS NATIONAL PRODUCT MINUS CAPITAL
DEPRECIATION; IT CONSISTS ENTIRELY OF PERSONAL CONSUMPTION, NET NATIONAL
SAVINGS, AND GOVERNMENT PURCHASES; SEE CHART 3.1. SOURCE: BEA (1993)

Our consumption rate ranks first among all industrial nations.

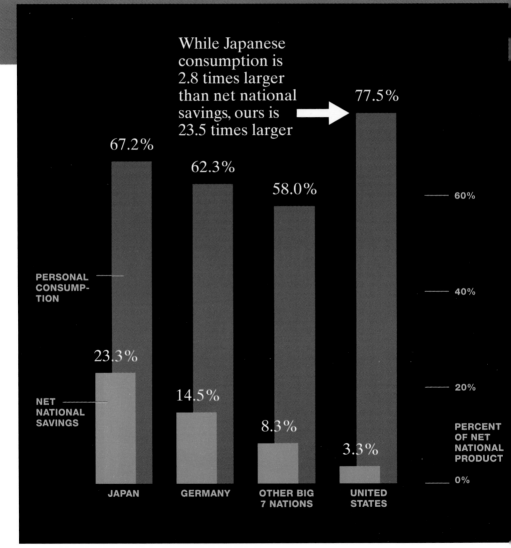

While Japanese consumption is 2.8 times larger than net national savings, ours is 23.5 times larger

77.5%

67.2%

62.3%

58.0%

PERSONAL CONSUMP- TION

60%

40%

23.3%

14.5%

8.3%

3.3%

20%

NET NATIONAL SAVINGS

PERCENT OF NET NATIONAL PRODUCT

0%

JAPAN   GERMANY   OTHER BIG 7 NATIONS   UNITED STATES

(3.3) PERSONAL CONSUMPTION AND NET NATIONAL SAVINGS

AS A PERCENT OF NET NATIONAL PRODUCT, AVERAGE OF 1988 TO 1990

NOTE: SEE CHART 3.2; NET NATIONAL SAVINGS IN THIS CHART INCLUDES PUBLIC-SECTOR INVESTMENT. SOURCE: OECD (1992)

Case study in runaway consumption: No other country spends so much on health care— with such mediocre results.

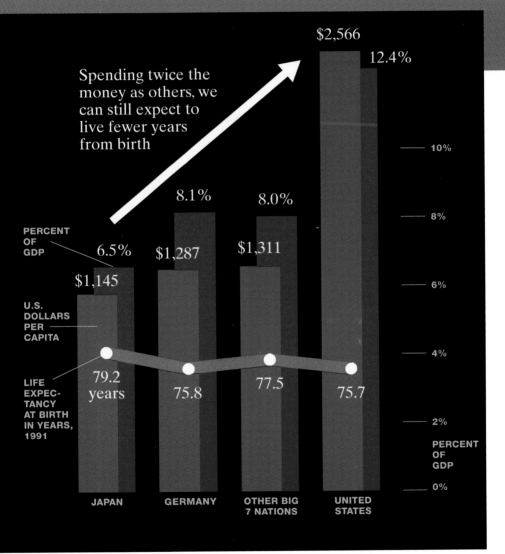

Spending twice the money as others, we can still expect to live fewer years from birth

$2,566

12.4%

8.1%

8.0%

PERCENT OF GDP

6.5%

$1,287

$1,311

$1,145

U.S. DOLLARS PER CAPITA

LIFE EXPEC-TANCY AT BIRTH IN YEARS, 1991

79.2 years

75.8

77.5

75.7

10%

8%

6%

4%

2%

PERCENT OF GDP

0%

JAPAN

GERMANY

OTHER BIG 7 NATIONS

UNITED STATES

(3.4) NATIONAL HEALTH-CARE SPENDING IN 1990

AS A PERCENT OF GDP, IN U.S. DOLLARS PER CAPITA

NOTE: OTHER CURRENCIES TRANSLATED INTO U.S. DOLLARS AT PURCHASING-POWER PARITIES.

SOURCE: OECD (1990, 1991); HCFA (1993); CENSUS (1991); WHO (1991)

By world standards, our investment behavior is poor, our savings performance is poorer, and our infrastructure record is the worst.

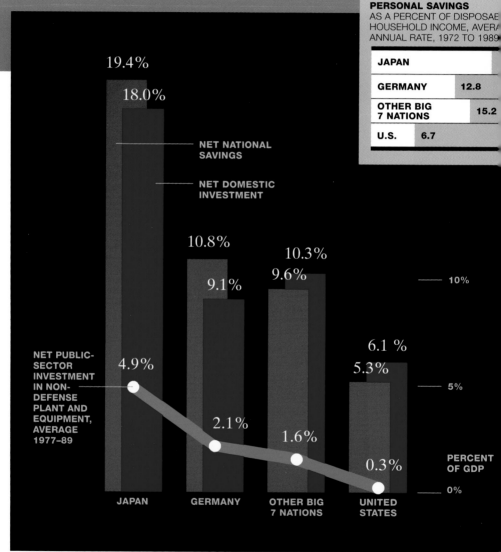

PERSONAL SAVINGS
AS A PERCENT OF DISPOSABE
HOUSEHOLD INCOME, AVERA
ANNUAL RATE, 1972 TO 1989

JAPAN	
GERMANY	12.8
OTHER BIG 7 NATIONS	15.2
U.S.	6.7

NET NATIONAL SAVINGS

NET DOMESTIC INVESTMENT

NET PUBLIC-SECTOR INVESTMENT IN NON-DEFENSE PLANT AND EQUIPMENT, AVERAGE 1977–89

19.4%
18.0%

10.8%
9.1%

10.3%
9.6%

6.1 %
5.3%

4.9%

2.1%

1.6%

0.3%

10%

5%

0%

PERCENT OF GDP

JAPAN   GERMANY   OTHER BIG 7 NATIONS   UNITED STATES

(3.5) NET NATIONAL SAVINGS AND NET DOMESTIC INVESTMENT
AS A PERCENT OF GDP, AVERAGES FOR 1973-1990
NOTE: INCLUDING PUBLIC-SECTOR INVESTMENT; PUBLIC-SECTOR INVESTMENT
EXCLUDES PUBLICLY-OWNED BUSINESSES. SOURCE: OECD (1990, 1992)

The rate at which we invest
in new ideas is also
falling behind those of our
toughest competitors.

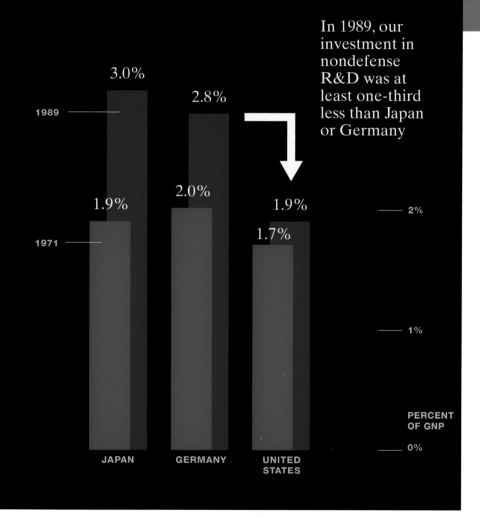

In 1989, our investment in nondefense R&D was at least one-third less than Japan or Germany

3.0%
2.8%
1989

2.0%
1.9%
1.9%
1.7%
1971

— 2%

— 1%

PERCENT OF GNP

— 0%

JAPAN   GERMANY .   UNITED STATES

**(3.6) TOTAL NONDEFENSE EXPENDITURES ON
RESEARCH AND DEVELOPMENT**
AS A SHARE OF GROSS NATIONAL PRODUCT, 1971 AND 1989
SOURCE: NSB (1991)

Japan, most notably, is racing by us in the training of new engineers, and gathering more and more U.S. patents.

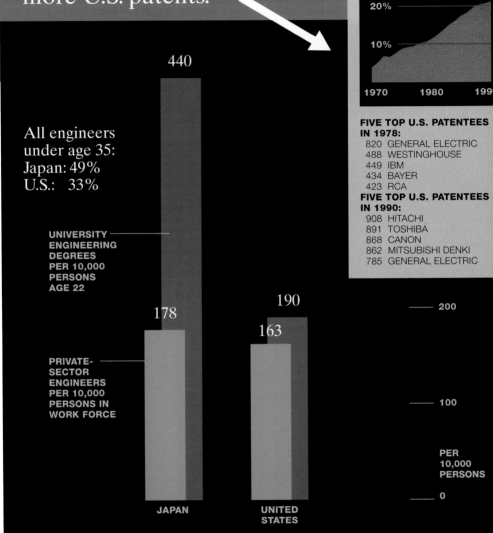

U.S. PATENTS GRANTED TO JAPANESE INVENTORS AS A PERCENT OF ALL U.S. PATENTS GRANTED, 1970–199

20%

10%

1970   1980   199

440

All engineers under age 35:
Japan: 49%
U.S.:   33%

UNIVERSITY ENGINEERING DEGREES PER 10,000 PERSONS AGE 22

178

PRIVATE-SECTOR ENGINEERS PER 10,000 PERSONS IN WORK FORCE

190

163

FIVE TOP U.S. PATENTEES IN 1978:
820 GENERAL ELECTRIC
488 WESTINGHOUSE
449 IBM
434 BAYER
423 RCA
FIVE TOP U.S. PATENTEES IN 1990:
908 HITACHI
891 TOSHIBA
868 CANON
862 MITSUBISHI DENKI
785 GENERAL ELECTRIC

200

100

PER 10,000 PERSONS

0

JAPAN

UNITED STATES

(3.7) UNIVERSITY ENGINEERING DEGREES AND PRIVATE-SECTOR ENGINEERS
JAPAN AND UNITED STATES, 1985-86
SOURCE: NSB (1989, 1991)

S. investment
ncy of the Eighties:
e ever catch up?

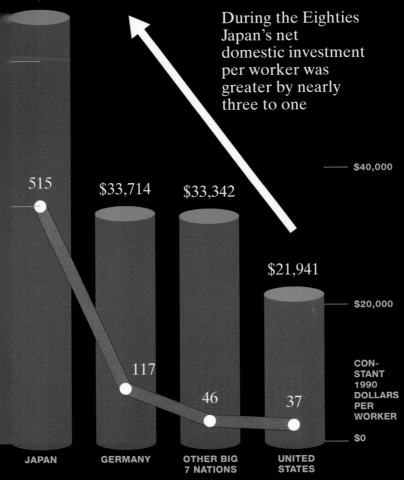

$62,366

During the Eighties
Japan's net
domestic investment
per worker was
greater by nearly
three to one

515

$33,714 $33,342

$40,000

$21,941

117

46   37

$20,000

CON-
STANT
1990
DOLLARS
PER
WORKER

$0

JAPAN   GERMANY   OTHER BIG   UNITED
                      7 NATIONS   STATES

L CUMULATIVE NET
INVESTMENT PER WORKER
ROUGH 1990, IN CONSTANT 1990 DOLLARS
S COMPARED AT YEARLY EXCHANGE RATES AND ADJUSTED FOR U.S. INFLATION;
C-SECTOR INVESTMENT. SOURCE: OECD (1992); IFR (1991)

Or must we hope to defy the strong empirical connection between investment and productivity?

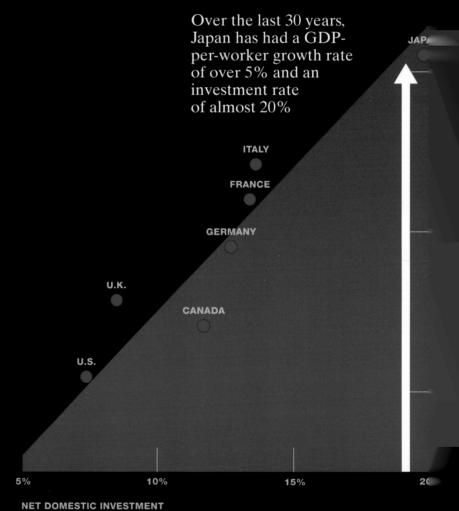

Over the last 30 years, Japan has had a GDP-per-worker growth rate of over 5% and an investment rate of almost 20%

JAPAN

ITALY

FRANCE

GERMANY

U.K.

CANADA

U.S.

5%   10%   15%   20%

NET DOMESTIC INVESTMENT AS PERCENT OF GDP

(3.9) ANNUAL GROWTH IN REAL GDP PER WORKER AND NET DOMESTIC INVESTMENT AS A PERCENT OF GDP

CORRELATION ACROSS BIG 7 NATIONS, 1960 TO 1989

NOTE: INCLUDING PUBLIC-SECTOR INVESTMENT. SOURCE: BLS (1992); OECD (1992)

America's own history,
for more than a century, is an
object lesson: Investment
and growth go hand in hand.

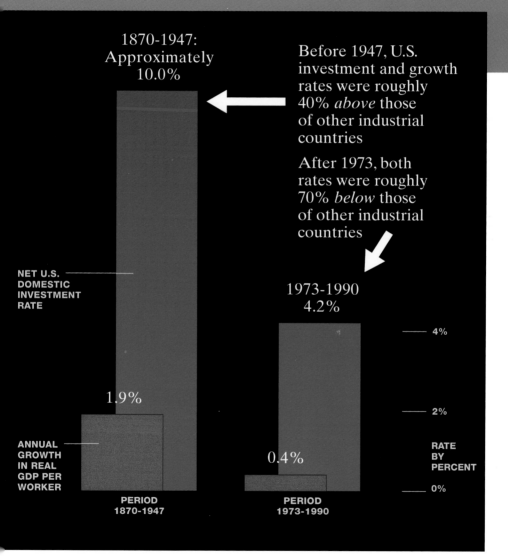

1870-1947:
Approximately
10.0%

Before 1947, U.S.
investment and growth
rates were roughly
40% *above* those
of other industrial
countries

After 1973, both
rates were roughly
70% *below* those
of other industrial
countries

1973-1990
4.2%

NET U.S.
DOMESTIC
INVESTMENT
RATE

1.9%

ANNUAL
GROWTH
IN REAL
GDP PER
WORKER

0.4%

4%

2%

RATE
BY
PERCENT

0%

PERIOD
1870-1947

PERIOD
1973-1990

**(3.10) ANNUAL GROWTH IN REAL U.S. GDP PER WORKER
AND U.S. NET DOMESTIC INVESTMENT AS A PERCENT OF GDP**
PERIODS 1870-1947 AND 1973-1990
SOURCE: BEA (1993); BAUMOL, BLACKMAN, AND WOLFF (1989); EAEH, "SAVINGS AND INVESTMENT" (1980)

In the Eighties, we
enjoyed make-believe
prosperity without
the bother of producing it...

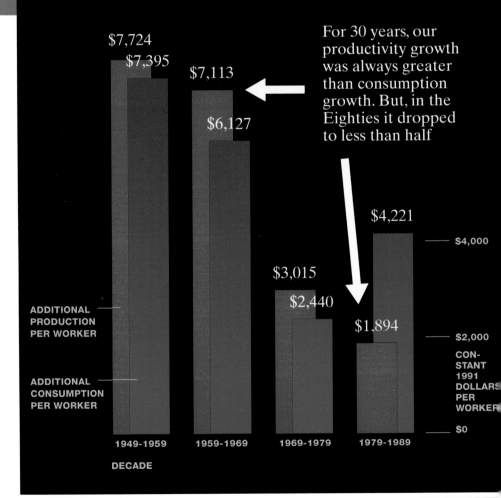

$7,724
$7,395
$7,113
$6,127

For 30 years, our
productivity growth
was always greater
than consumption
growth. But, in the
Eighties it dropped
to less than half

$4,221
— $4,000

$3,015
$2,440
$1,894
— $2,000

ADDITIONAL
PRODUCTION
PER WORKER

ADDITIONAL
CONSUMPTION
PER WORKER

CON-
STANT
1991
DOLLARS
PER
WORKER

— $0

1949-1959   1959-1969   1969-1979   1979-1989

DECADE

**(3.11) GROWTH OF U.S. NET NATIONAL PRODUCT AND
PERSONAL CONSUMPTION PER WORKER**
IN CONSTANT 1991 DOLLARS, FROM FIRST TO
LAST YEAR OF FOUR DECADES
SOURCE: BEA (1993)

...thanks to unprecedented
levels of debt incurred
by every economic sector
on our way to becoming the
world's #1 debtor nation.

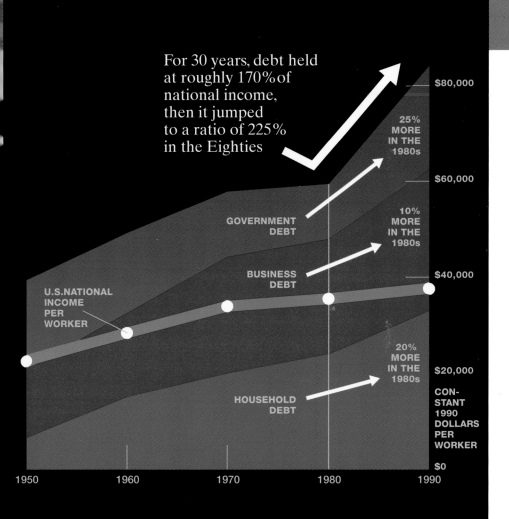

For 30 years, debt held
at roughly 170% of
national income,
then it jumped
to a ratio of 225%
in the Eighties

$80,000

25%
MORE
IN THE
1980s

$60,000

GOVERNMENT
DEBT

10%
MORE
IN THE
1980s

BUSINESS
DEBT

$40,000

U.S.NATIONAL
INCOME
PER
WORKER

20%
MORE
IN THE
1980s

$20,000

CON-
STANT
1990
DOLLARS
PER
WORKER

HOUSEHOLD
DEBT

$0

1950   1960   1970   1980   1990

**(3.12) U.S. NONFINANCIAL DEBT AND
U.S. NATIONAL INCOME PER WORKER**
IN CONSTANT 1990 DOLLARS, 1950 TO 1990
SOURCE: FED (1992); BEA (1993)

The legacy of the Eighties: a towering mountain of trade deficits, . . .

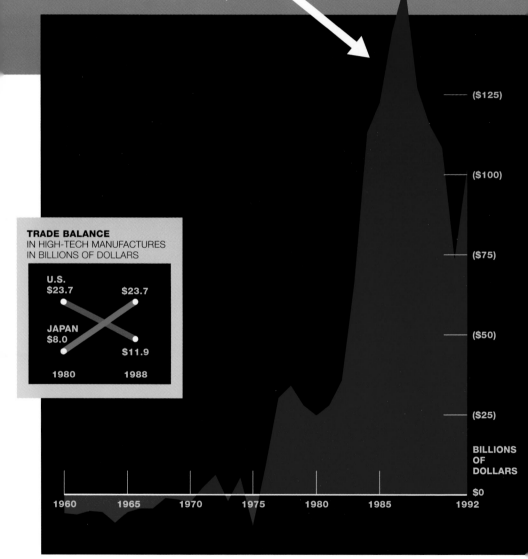

TRADE BALANCE
IN HIGH-TECH MANUFACTURES
IN BILLIONS OF DOLLARS

U.S.
$23.7 $23.7

JAPAN
$8.0
                $11.9

1980   1988

($125)

($100)

($75)

($50)

($25)

BILLIONS
OF
DOLLARS

$0

1960   1965   1970   1975   1980   1985   1992

(3.13) U.S. MERCHANDISE TRADE BALANCE
1960 TO 1992
SOURCE: CENSUS (1993); NSB (1991)

...along with a pulverized tradable goods sector and a bloated market for domestic services.

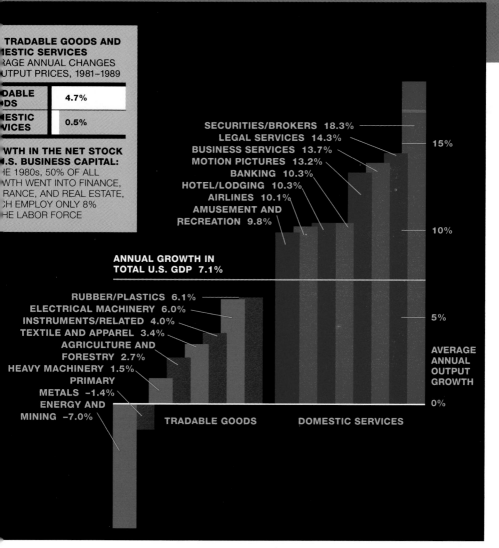

TRADABLE GOODS AND
[D]MESTIC SERVICES
[AVE]RAGE ANNUAL CHANGES
[IN O]UTPUT PRICES, 1981–1989

[TRA]DABLE [GOO]DS	4.7%
[DOM]ESTIC [SER]VICES	0.5%

[GRO]WTH IN THE NET STOCK
[OF U].S. BUSINESS CAPITAL:
[IN T]HE 1980s, 50% OF ALL
[GRO]WTH WENT INTO FINANCE,
[INSU]RANCE, AND REAL ESTATE,
[WHI]CH EMPLOY ONLY 8%
[OF T]HE LABOR FORCE

SECURITIES/BROKERS 18.3%
LEGAL SERVICES 14.3%
BUSINESS SERVICES 13.7%
MOTION PICTURES 13.2%
BANKING 10.3%
HOTEL/LODGING 10.3%
AIRLINES 10.1%
AMUSEMENT AND
RECREATION 9.8%

15%

10%

**ANNUAL GROWTH IN
TOTAL U.S. GDP 7.1%**

RUBBER/PLASTICS 6.1%
ELECTRICAL MACHINERY 6.0%
INSTRUMENTS/RELATED 4.0%
TEXTILE AND APPAREL 3.4%
AGRICULTURE AND
FORESTRY 2.7%
HEAVY MACHINERY 1.5%
PRIMARY
METALS –1.4%
ENERGY AND
MINING –7.0%

5%

AVERAGE
ANNUAL
OUTPUT
GROWTH

0%

TRADABLE GOODS

DOMESTIC SERVICES

(3.14) U.S. TRADABLE GOODS AND DOMESTIC SERVICES
BY INDUSTRY, AVERAGE ANNUAL OUTPUT GROWTH, 1981 TO 1989
SOURCE: BEA (1993)

4.

THE AGE
OF DEFICITS AND
ENTITLEMENTS

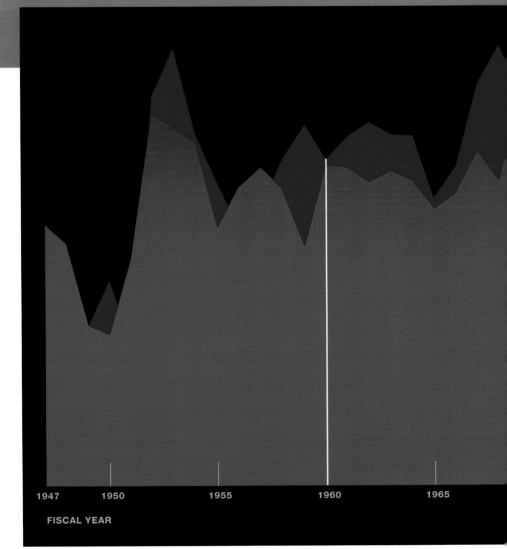

1947   1950   1955   1960   1965

FISCAL YEAR

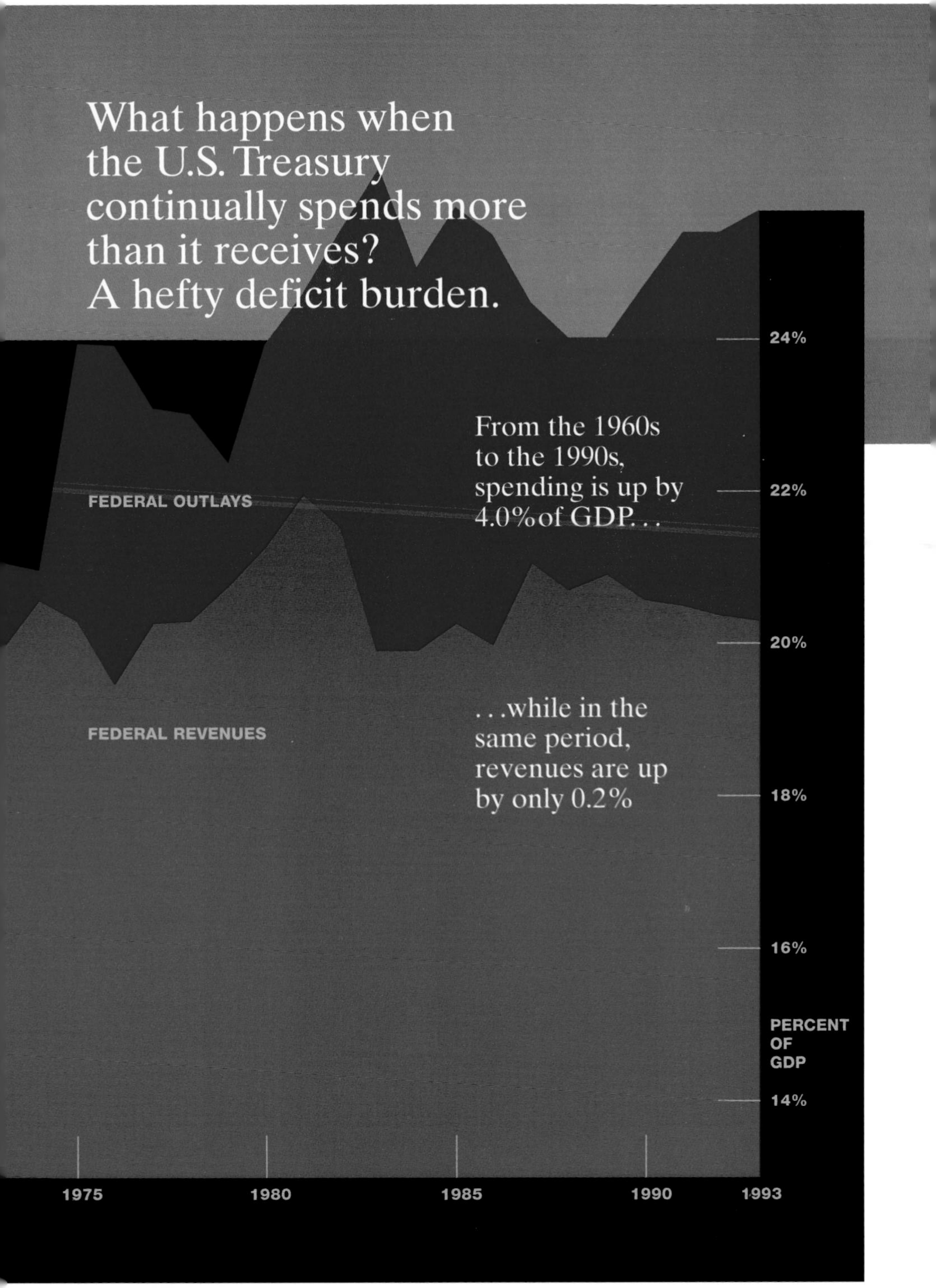

What happens when
the U.S. Treasury
continually spends more
than it receives?
A hefty deficit burden.

24%

From the 1960s
to the 1990s,
spending is up by   22%
4.0% of GDP...

FEDERAL OUTLAYS

20%

FEDERAL REVENUES

...while in the
same period,
revenues are up
by only 0.2%   18%

16%

PERCENT
OF
GDP

14%

1975   1980   1985   1990   1993

(4.1) FEDERAL OUTLAYS AND REVENUES
AS A PERCENT OF GROSS DOMESTIC PRODUCT, FISCAL YEARS 1947 TO 1993
SOURCE: OMB (1993)

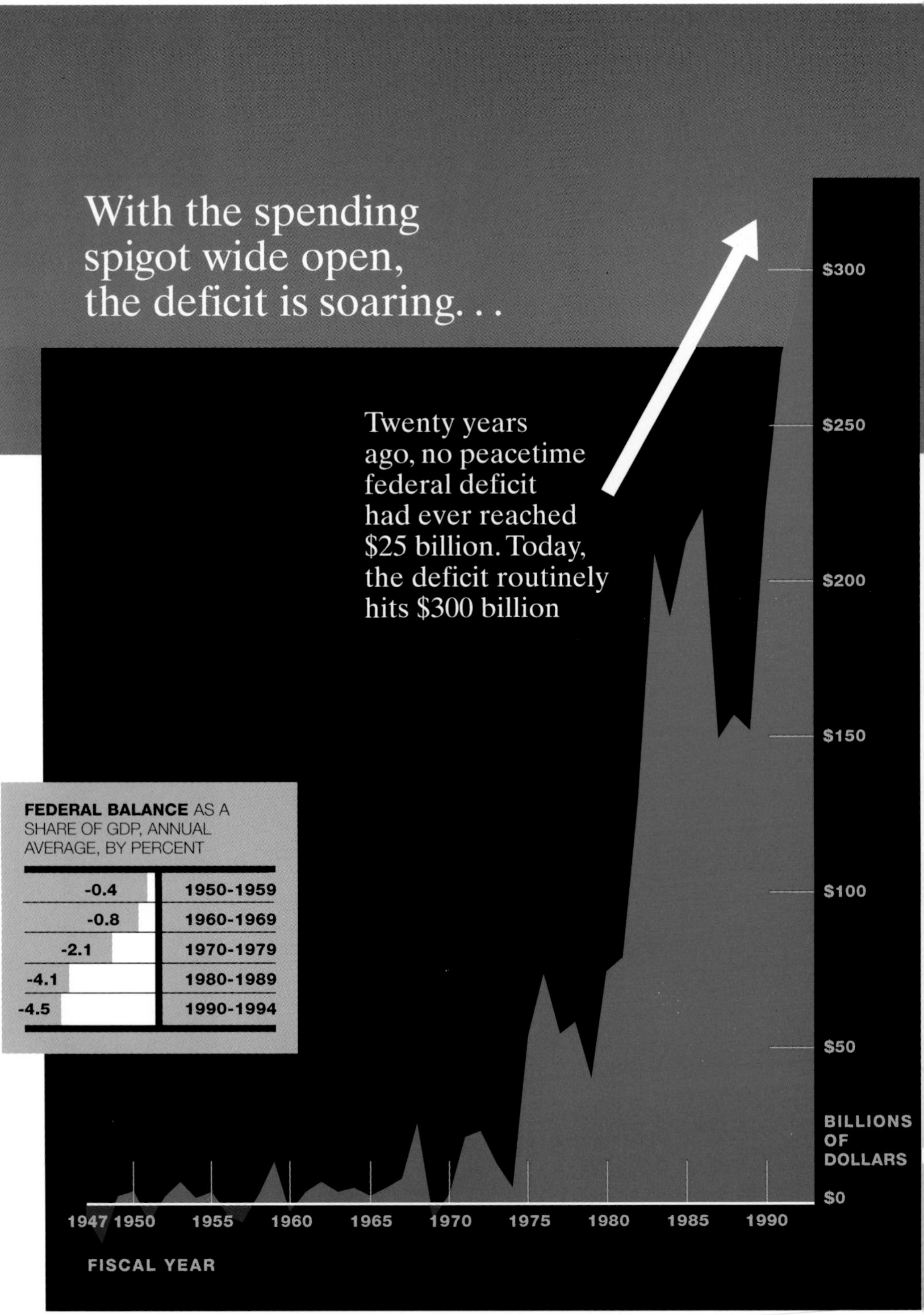

With the spending
spigot wide open,
the deficit is soaring. . .

Twenty years
ago, no peacetime
federal deficit
had ever reached
$25 billion. Today,
the deficit routinely
hits $300 billion

$300

$250

$200

$150

$100

$50

BILLIONS
OF
DOLLARS

$0

FEDERAL BALANCE AS A
SHARE OF GDP, ANNUAL
AVERAGE, BY PERCENT

-0.4	**1950-1959**
-0.8	**1960-1969**
-2.1	**1970-1979**
-4.1	**1980-1989**
-4.5	**1990-1994**

1947 1950   1955   1960   1965   1970   1975   1980   1985   1990

FISCAL YEAR

(4.2) FEDERAL DEFICITS (+) OR SURPLUSES (-)

IN BILLIONS OF DOLLARS, FISCAL YEARS 1947 TO 1993

SOURCE: OMB (1993)

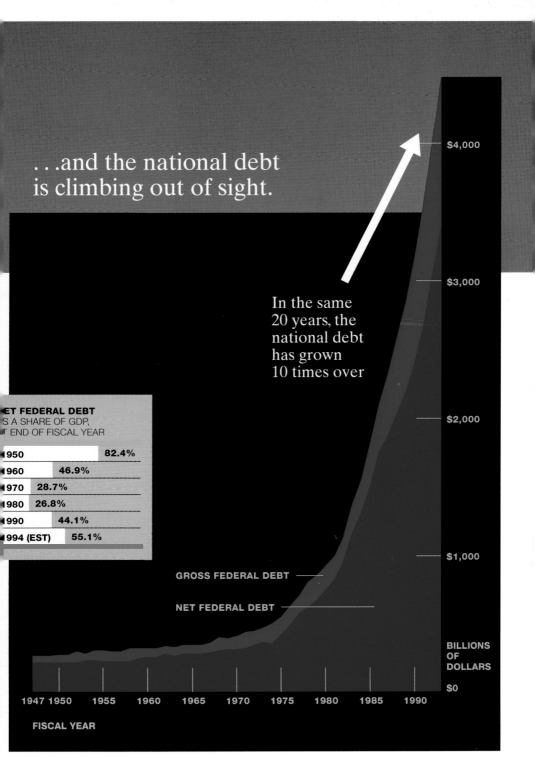

...and the national debt
is climbing out of sight.

In the same
20 years, the
national debt
has grown
10 times over

$4,000

$3,000

$2,000

$1,000

ET FEDERAL DEBT
S A SHARE OF GDP,
T END OF FISCAL YEAR

950	82.4%
960	46.9%
970	28.7%
980	26.8%
990	44.1%
994 (EST)	55.1%

GROSS FEDERAL DEBT

NET FEDERAL DEBT

BILLIONS
OF
DOLLARS

$0

1947 1950   1955   1960   1965   1970   1975   1980   1985   1990

FISCAL YEAR

(4.3) GROSS AND NET FEDERAL DEBT

IN BILLIONS OF DOLLARS, END OF FISCAL YEARS 1947 TO 1993
NOTE: "GROSS" INCLUDES TREASURY DEBT HELD BY OTHER FEDERAL AGENCIES;
"NET" INCLUDES ONLY TREASURY DEBT HELD BY THE PUBLIC. SOURCE: OMB (1993)

We have been
indulging in a profligacy
unimaginable to
our ancestors, . . .

The $3,549 billion
additional debt gathered
in the last 12 years
is more than
three-quarters
of the total

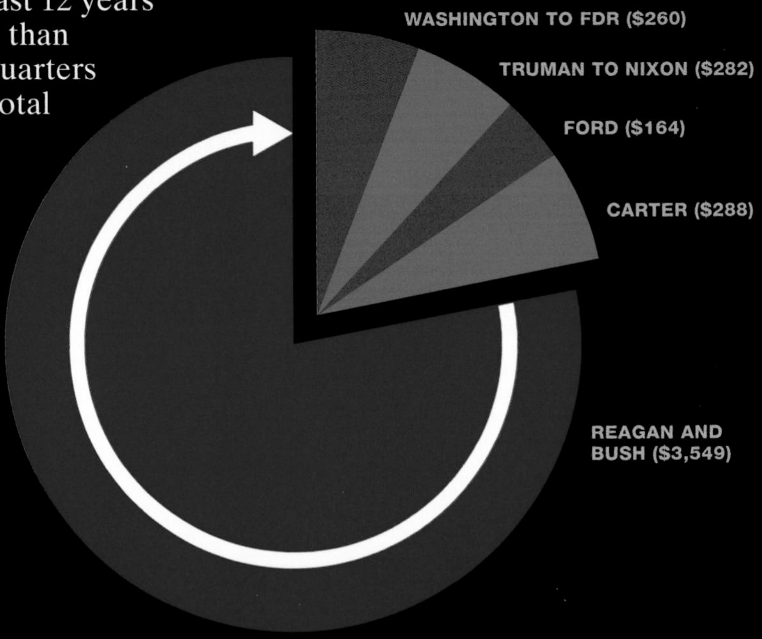

WASHINGTON TO FDR ($260)

TRUMAN TO NIXON ($282)

FORD ($164)

CARTER ($288)

REAGAN AND
BUSH ($3,549)

(4.4) CUMULATIVE GROSS FEDERAL DEBT
ADDED DURING 41 AMERICAN PRESIDENCIES, IN BILLIONS OF DOLLARS
NOTE: SEE CHART 4.3. SOURCE: OMB (1993)

...thoughtlessly using up over 70% of our scarce private savings while allotting less and less to public investment.

The federal borrowing as a share of private savings has soared from 15% to over 70% in 20 years

Over the same period, the share of the budget we devote to investment has been shrinking

NONDEFENSE INVESTMENT OUTLAYS AS A PERCENT OF ALL FEDERAL OUTLAYS

PERCENT OF NET PRIVATE-SECTOR SAVINGS

71%

63%

60%

51%

40%

28%

20%

15%

11.9%

5.2%

-1% -1% 1% 2%

0%

1950 1955 1960 1965 1970 1975 1980 1985 1990

CALENDAR-YEAR PERIOD

(4.5) FEDERAL BORROWING AS A SHARE OF NET PRIVATE SAVINGS
AVERAGE ANNUAL PERCENT PER PERIOD, 1950 TO 1991
NOTE: NEGATIVE NUMBERS INDICATE BUDGET SURPLUSES. NONDEFENSE INVESTMENT
REFERS TO GROSS FEDERAL OUTLAYS ON NONDEFENSE PLANT, EQUIPMENT, AND R&D;
BOTH DIRECT SPENDING AND GRANTS-IN-AID. SOURCE: BEA (1993); OMB (1993)

Over the last three decades,
interest and entitlements
have risen from 34 to 67 percent
of all federal spending.

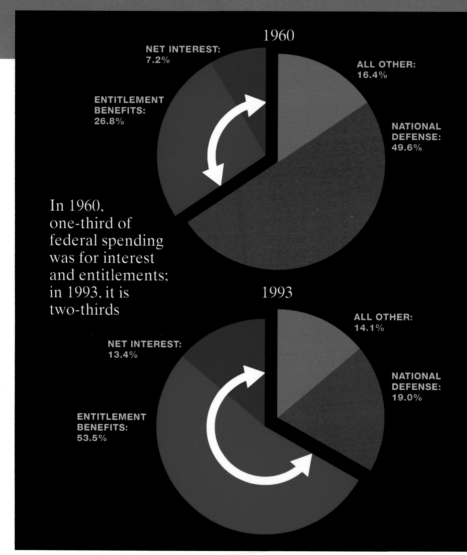

1960

NET INTEREST:
7.2%

ALL OTHER:
16.4%

ENTITLEMENT
BENEFITS:
26.8%

NATIONAL
DEFENSE:
49.6%

In 1960,
one-third of
federal spending
was for interest
and entitlements;
in 1993, it is
two-thirds

1993

ALL OTHER:
14.1%

NET INTEREST:
13.4%

NATIONAL
DEFENSE:
19.0%

ENTITLEMENT
BENEFITS:
53.5%

(4.6) FEDERAL OUTLAYS BY TYPE

AS A PERCENT OF ALL OUTLAYS, FISCAL YEARS 1960 AND 1993

NOTE: ENTITLEMENT BENEFITS INCLUDE OMB'S "PAYMENTS FOR INDIVIDUALS" PLUS FARM PRICE
SUPPORTS AND HEALTH CARE FOR MILITARY RETIREES AND THEIR DEPENDENTS.

SOURCE: OMB (1993); CBO (1993); BEA (1993)

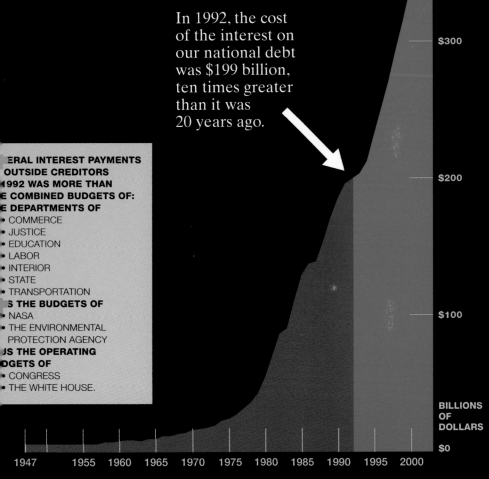

The recent surge in interest costs is the price we must pay for our widening deficit.

In 1992, the cost of the interest on our national debt was $199 billion, ten times greater than it was 20 years ago.

ERAL INTEREST PAYMENTS
OUTSIDE CREDITORS
1992 WAS MORE THAN
E COMBINED BUDGETS OF:
E DEPARTMENTS OF
• COMMERCE
• JUSTICE
• EDUCATION
• LABOR
• INTERIOR
• STATE
• TRANSPORTATION
S THE BUDGETS OF
• NASA
• THE ENVIRONMENTAL
  PROTECTION AGENCY
JS THE OPERATING
OGETS OF
• CONGRESS
• THE WHITE HOUSE.

$300

$200

$100

BILLIONS
OF
DOLLARS

$0

1947   1955   1960   1965   1970   1975   1980   1985   1990   1995   2000

FISCAL YEAR

**(4.7) ANNUAL INTEREST COST OF
THE PUBLICLY HELD NATIONAL DEBT**
IN BILLIONS OF DOLLARS: HISTORY AND
FUTURE PROJECTIONS, FISCAL YEARS 1947 TO 2003
NOTE: SEE CHART 4.3; PROJECTIONS ARE JANUARY, 1993 CBO BASELINE.
SOURCE: OMB (1993); CBO (1993)

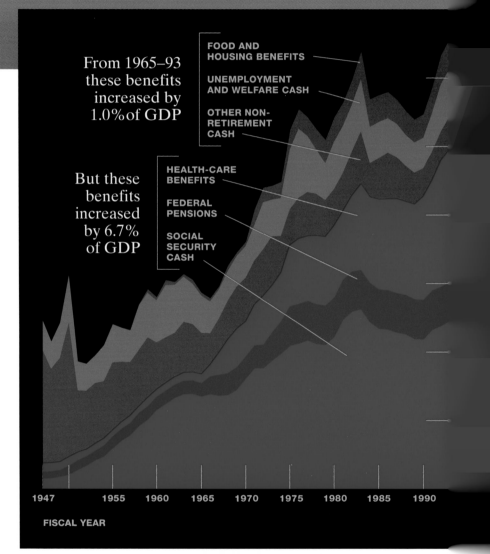

Social Security, pensions, and health-care benefits account for virtually all of the historical expansion in entitlements. . .

From 1965–93 these benefits increased by 1.0% of GDP

FOOD AND HOUSING BENEFITS

UNEMPLOYMENT AND WELFARE CASH

OTHER NON-RETIREMENT CASH

But these benefits increased by 6.7% of GDP

HEALTH-CARE BENEFITS

FEDERAL PENSIONS

SOCIAL SECURITY CASH

1947   1955   1960   1965   1970   1975   1980   1985   1990

FISCAL YEAR

(4.8) FEDERAL ENTITLEMENT OUTLAYS BY TYPE
AS A SHARE OF GDP, FISCAL YEARS 1947 TO 1993
NOTE: SEE CHART 4.6; "OTHER NONRETIREMENT CASH" INCLUDES
STUDENT AID, FARM PAYMENTS, AND VETERANS' PENSIONS.
SOURCE: OMB (1993); CBO (1993); BEA (1993)

...and today amount to
three out of every four dollars
in federal benefit outlays.

FOOD AND
HOUSING
BENEFITS:
6.9%

UNEMPLOYMENT
AND
WELFARE CASH:
10.3 %

OTHER
NONRETIRE-
MENT CASH:
7.6%

SOCIAL
SECURITY
CASH:
36.4%

FEDERAL
PENSIONS:
8.5%

HEALTH-CARE
BENEFITS:
30.4%

In 1993,
these benefits
amounted to 75.3%
of all federal entitlements

**(4.9) FEDERAL ENTITLEMENT OUTLAYS
BY TYPE IN FISCAL YEAR 1993**
AS A PERCENT OF TOTAL ENTITLEMENT OUTLAYS
NOTE: SEE CHARTS 4.6 AND 4.8. SOURCE: OMB (1993); CBO (1993); BEA (1993)

Nearly three-quarters of federal entitlements are disbursed without any regard to financial need, and only one-sixth of all entitlements serves to raise Americans out of poverty.

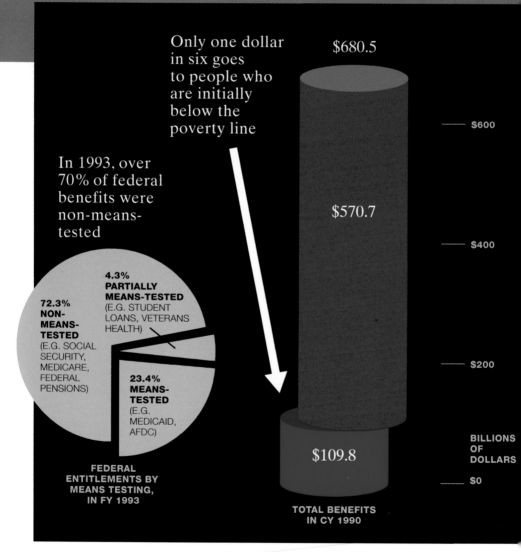

Only one dollar in six goes to people who are initially below the poverty line

$680.5

$570.7

$109.8

$600

$400

$200

$0

BILLIONS OF DOLLARS

In 1993, over 70% of federal benefits were non-means-tested

4.3% **PARTIALLY MEANS-TESTED** (E.G. STUDENT LOANS, VETERANS HEALTH)

72.3% **NON-MEANS-TESTED** (E.G. SOCIAL SECURITY, MEDICARE, FEDERAL PENSIONS)

23.4% **MEANS-TESTED** (E.G. MEDICAID, AFDC)

FEDERAL ENTITLEMENTS BY MEANS TESTING, IN FY 1993

TOTAL BENEFITS IN CY 1990

(4.10) ENTITLEMENTS AND THEIR IMPACT ON POVERTY:
COMPOSITION OF FEDERAL BENEFITS BY MEANS TESTING IN 1993
AND TOTAL PUBLIC BENEFITS GOING TO HOUSEHOLDS
ABOVE AND BELOW THE CENSUS-DEFINED POVERTY LINE IN 1990
NOTE: SEE CHART 4.6; TOTAL PUBLIC BENEFITS INCLUDE ALL BENEFITS THAT CAN BE ALLOCATED
BY INCOME OF RECIPIENT. SOURCE: OMB (1993); CBO (1993); BEA (1993); NTUF (1992)

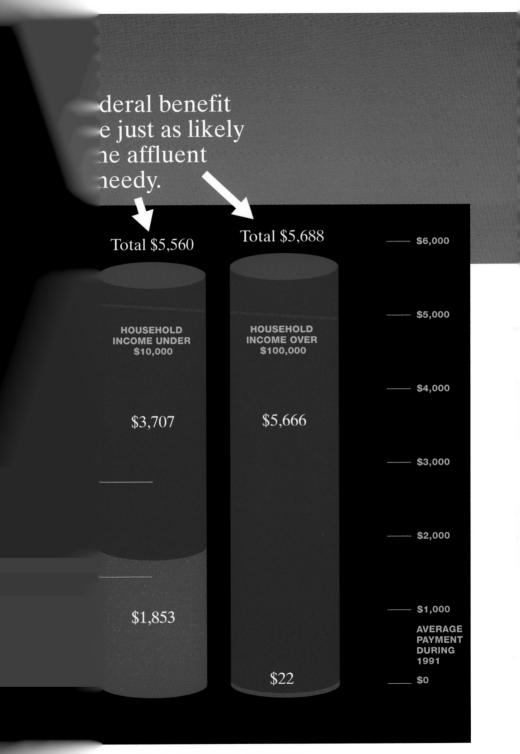

deral benefit
e just as likely
he affluent
heedy.

Total $5,560   Total $5,688   —— $6,000

                                             —— $5,000

HOUSEHOLD   HOUSEHOLD
INCOME UNDER   INCOME OVER
$10,000 $100,000

                                             —— $4,000

$3,707 $5,666

                                             —— $3,000

                                             —— $2,000

                                             —— $1,000

$1,853   AVERAGE
                                             PAYMENT
                                             DURING
                                             1991
                      $22   —— $0

FEDERAL BENEFIT OUTLAYS
MENT TO ALL HOUSEHOLDS IN TWO INCOME BRACKETS
DERAL BENEFITS THAT CAN BE ALLOCATED BY INCOME OF RECIPIENT.

Benefits to the elderly now tower 11 to 1 per capita over benefits to children...

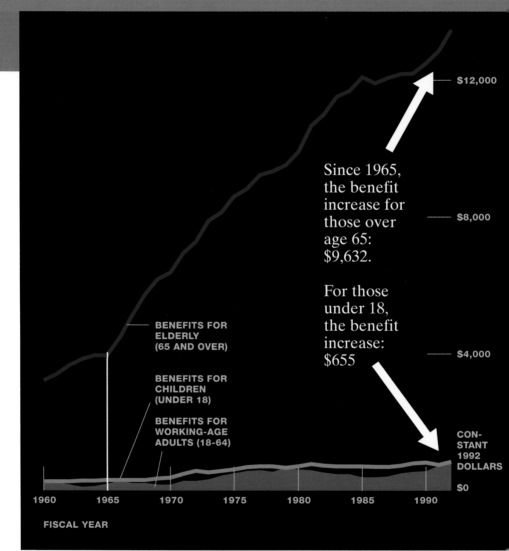

Since 1965, the benefit increase for those over age 65: $9,632.

For those under 18, the benefit increase: $655

$12,000

$8,000

$4,000

CON-
STANT
1992
DOLLARS

$0

BENEFITS FOR
ELDERLY
(65 AND OVER)

BENEFITS FOR
CHILDREN
(UNDER 18)

BENEFITS FOR
WORKING-AGE
ADULTS (18-64)

1960   1965   1970   1975   1980   1985   1990

FISCAL YEAR

(4.12) FEDERAL BENEFITS RECEIVED PER CAPITA
BY AGE GROUP IN CONSTANT 1992 DOLLARS, FISCAL YEARS 1960 TO 1992
SOURCE: NTUF (1992)

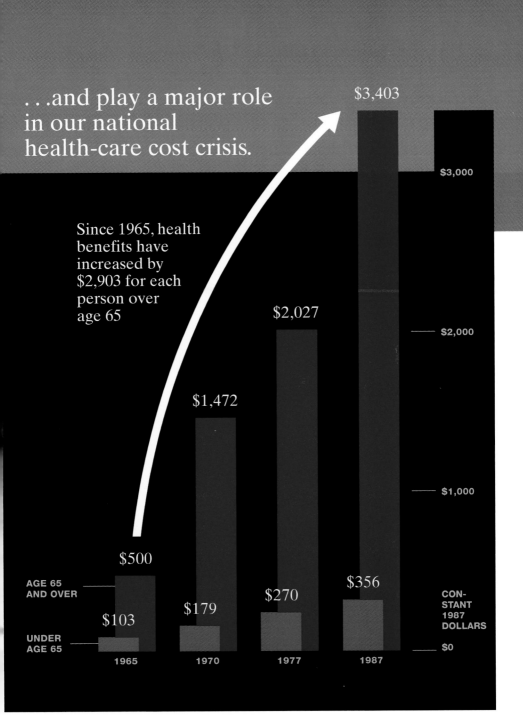

...and play a major role in our national health-care cost crisis.

Since 1965, health benefits have increased by $2,903 for each person over age 65

$3,403

$3,000

$2,027

$2,000

$1,472

$1,000

$500

AGE 65 AND OVER

$356

$270

$179

CON- STANT 1987 DOLLARS

$103

UNDER AGE 65

$0

1965   1970   1977   1987

(4.13) PUBLIC HEALTH-CARE BENEFITS RECEIVED PER CAPITA
BY AGE GROUP IN CONSTANT 1987 DOLLARS FOR SELECTED YEARS, 1965 TO 1987
NOTE: INCLUDES ALL STATE, LOCAL, AND FEDERAL HEALTH-CARE BENEFITS.
SOURCE: HCFA (1980, 1984, 1989)

The "pay back" on Social Security and Medicare far exceeds what retirees have paid in plus interest— and it's mostly tax free.

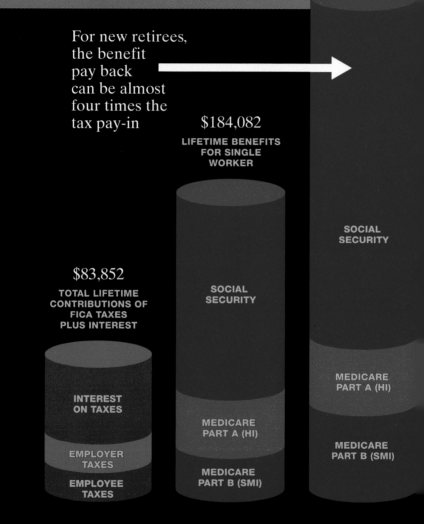

$308,328
LIFETIME BENEFITS FOR WORKER WITH NONWORKING SPOUSE

For new retirees, the benefit pay back can be almost four times the tax pay-in

$184,082
LIFETIME BENEFITS FOR SINGLE WORKER

$83,852
TOTAL LIFETIME CONTRIBUTIONS OF FICA TAXES PLUS INTEREST

INTEREST ON TAXES

EMPLOYER TAXES

EMPLOYEE TAXES

SOCIAL SECURITY

MEDICARE PART A (HI)

MEDICARE PART B (SMI)

SOCIAL SECURITY

MEDICARE PART A (HI)

MEDICARE PART B (SMI)

(4.14) BENEFIT PAY BACK ON FICA TAX CONTIBUTIONS

FOR AVERAGE-EARNING WORKER RETIRING AT AGE 65 IN 1991

NOTE: AVERAGES FOR MALES AND FEMALES; INTEREST RATE ON FICA CONTRIBUTIONS CALCULATED AT AVERAGE YIELD IN SOCIAL SECURITY TRUST FUNDS. "PRESENT VALUE" IS A STANDARD MEANS OF TRANSLATING PAST AND FUTURE DOLLARS INTO A SINGLE CURRENT MEASURE. SOURCE: WAYS AND MEANS (1992)

For today's privileged
federal pensioners, benefits
tower above even the
cushiest Fortune 500
pension packages.

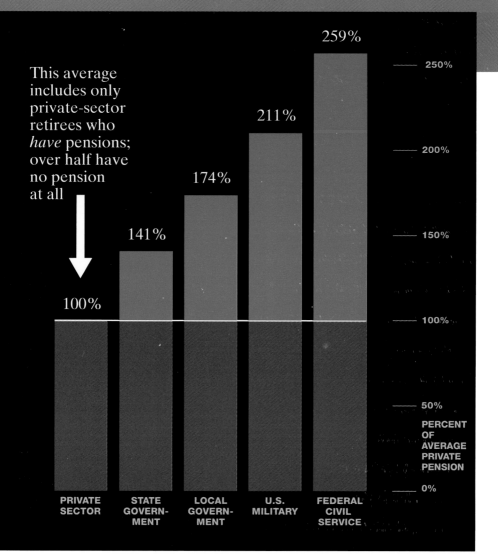

This average
includes only
private-sector
retirees who
have pensions;
over half have
no pension
at all

100%

141%

174%

211%

259%

250%

200%

150%

100%

50%

PERCENT
OF
AVERAGE
PRIVATE
PENSION

0%

PRIVATE
SECTOR

STATE
GOVERN-
MENT

LOCAL
GOVERN-
MENT

U.S.
MILITARY

FEDERAL
CIVIL
SERVICE

**(4.15) AVERAGE MONTHLY PENSION
FOR RETIRED GOVERNMENT EMPLOYEES**
AS A PERCENT OF AVERAGE FOR PRIVATE-SECTOR RETIREES, DECEMBER 1986
NOTE: THE PRIVATE-SECTOR AVERAGE DOES NOT REFLECT THE LATE AGE OF ELIGIBILITY.
COVERAGE OF PUBLIC EMPLOYEES IS VIRTUALLY UNIVERSAL, WITH ELIGIBILITY BEGINNING AT
AGE 55 FOR THE CIVIL SERVICE AND AGE 38 FOR THE MILITARY. SOURCE: CENSUS (1987)

5.
SHADOWS FALLING OVER THE NEXT GENERATION

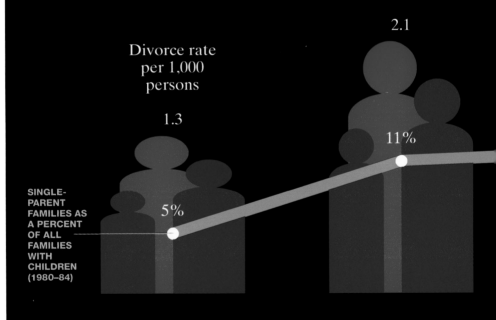

Divorce rate
per 1,000
persons

2.1

1.3

11%

5%

SINGLE-
PARENT
FAMILIES AS
A PERCENT
OF ALL
FAMILIES
WITH
CHILDREN
(1980–84)

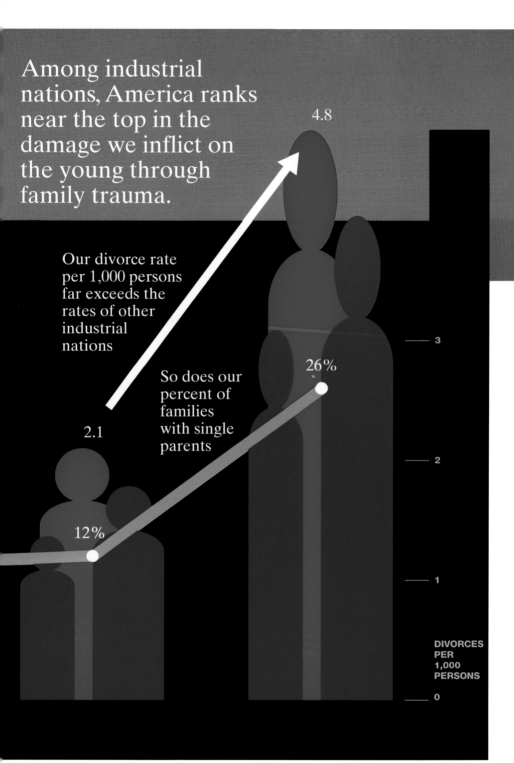

Among industrial nations, America ranks near the top in the damage we inflict on the young through family trauma.

Our divorce rate per 1,000 persons far exceeds the rates of other industrial nations

So does our percent of families with single parents

4.8

26%

2.1

12%

3

2

1

DIVORCES PER 1,000 PERSONS

0

(5.1) FAMILY INDICATORS: INTERNATIONAL COMPARISON
DIVORCES PER 1,000 PERSONS (1987-89) AND SINGLE-PARENT FAMILIES
AS A PERCENT OF ALL FAMILIES WITH CHILDREN (1980-84)
NOTE: FOR FAMILIES LED BY SINGLE PARENTS,
THE "OTHER BIG 7" AVERAGE DOES NOT INCLUDE CANADA OR ITALY.
SOURCE: SHAPIRO (1992); OECD (1990)

We also rank
at the top in
childhood poverty...

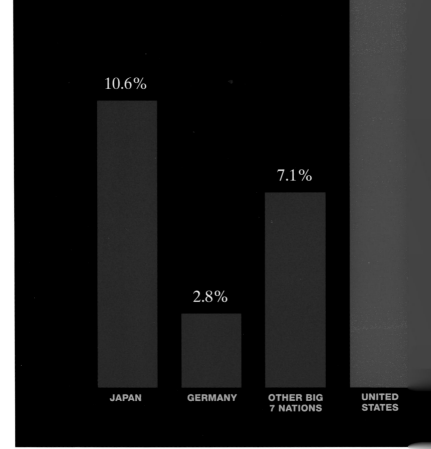

20.4%

10.6%

7.1%

2.8%

JAPAN   **GERMANY**   **OTHER BIG**   **UNITED**
                              7 NATIONS   **STATES**

(5.2) CHILDREN UNDER AGE 18 LIVING IN POVERTY
AS A PERCENT OF ALL CHILDREN UNDER AGE 18 (1980-84)
NOTE: "POVERTY" DEFINED AS LIVING IN HOUSEHOLDS WITH INCOMES BELOW 40 PERCEN
NATIONAL MEDIAN; SLIGHTLY DIFFERENT MEASURE USED FOR JAPAN; "OTHER BIG 7" AVE
DOES NOT INCLUDE ITALY. SOURCE: SMEEDING (1992); PRESTON AND KONO (1988)

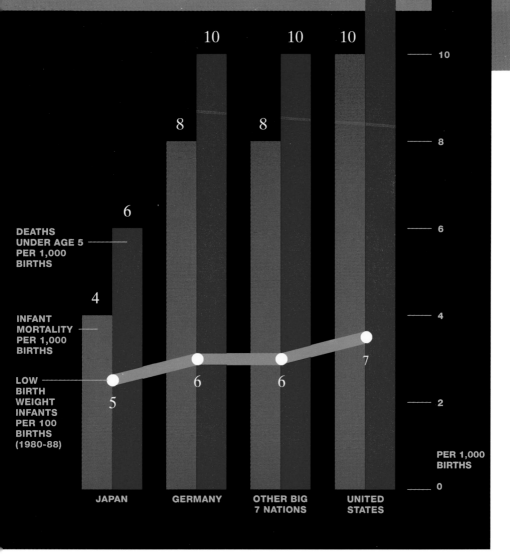

...and (despite the billions we spend on doctors) in the public and private neglect of early childhood health.

DEATHS UNDER AGE 5 PER 1,000 BIRTHS

INFANT MORTALITY PER 1,000 BIRTHS

LOW BIRTH WEIGHT INFANTS PER 100 BIRTHS (1980-88)

JAPAN   GERMANY   OTHER BIG 7 NATIONS   UNITED STATES

PER 1,000 BIRTHS

(5.3) INFANT MORTALITY AND DEATHS UNDER AGE 5

PER 1,000 BIRTHS (1989)

SOURCE: CDF (1991); UNICEF (1991)

We rank lowest in what is invested in the young— fewer days in school and less study at home, . . .

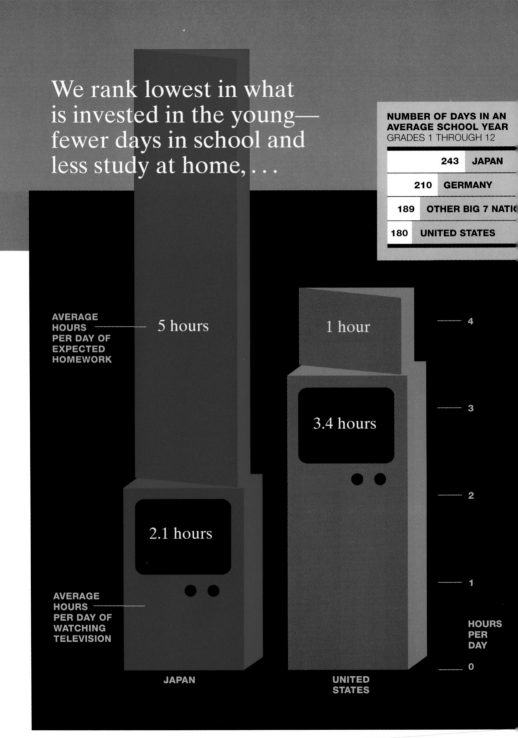

NUMBER OF DAYS IN AN AVERAGE SCHOOL YEAR GRADES 1 THROUGH 12	
243	JAPAN
210	GERMANY
189	OTHER BIG 7 NATI(
180	UNITED STATES

AVERAGE HOURS PER DAY OF EXPECTED HOMEWORK

5 hours

1 hour

3.4 hours

2.1 hours

AVERAGE HOURS PER DAY OF WATCHING TELEVISION

JAPAN

UNITED STATES

HOURS PER DAY

4

3

2

1

0

(5.4) HIGH SCHOOL STUDENTS IN JAPAN AND UNITED STATES
AVERAGE HOURS OF TV WATCHING PER DAY AND AVERAGE HOURS
OF HOMEWORK TYPICALLY ASSIGNED ON SCHOOL DAYS (1988-89)
SOURCE: NGA (1991); NCES (1991); NIELSEN (1990); WHITE (1987); KODAIRA (1990)

...which prepares
American youth
inadequately for the
modern workplace.

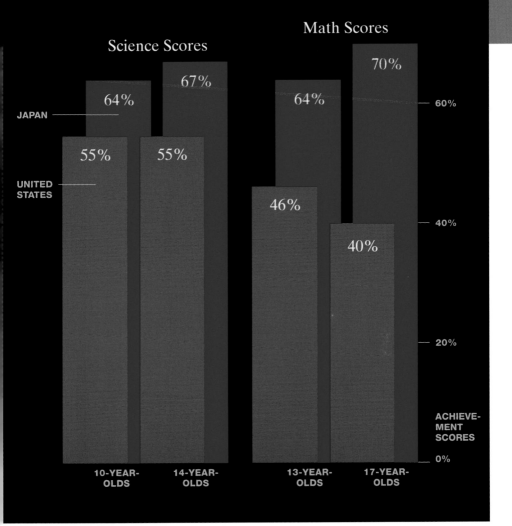

Science Scores

Math Scores

JAPAN

UNITED
STATES

67%
64%
70%
64%
55%
55%
46%
40%

60%

40%

20%

ACHIEVE-
MENT
SCORES

0%

10-YEAR-
OLDS

14-YEAR-
OLDS

13-YEAR-
OLDS

17-YEAR-
OLDS

(5.5) AVERAGE MATH AND SCIENCE ACHIEVEMENT SCORES
COMPARISON OF U.S. AND JAPANESE STUDENTS (1982-86)
NOTE: PERCENT CORRECT OR PERCENT OF MAXIMUM SCORE. SOURCE: IEA (1988); CAEP (1992)

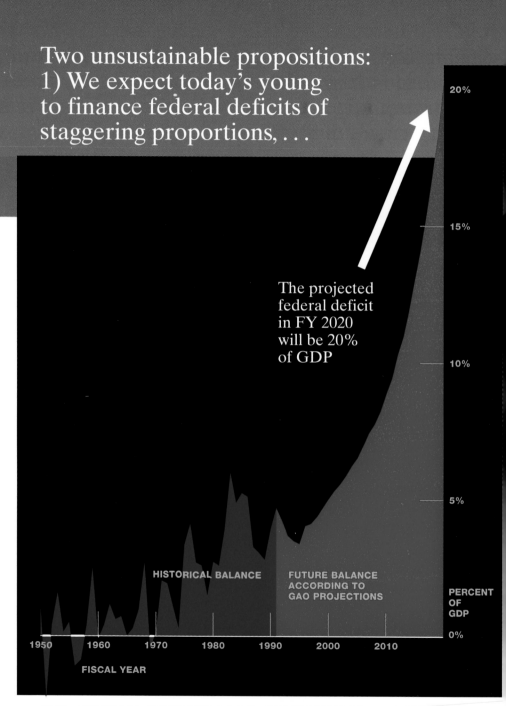

Two unsustainable propositions:
1) We expect today's young
to finance federal deficits of
staggering proportions, . . .

The projected
federal deficit
in FY 2020
will be 20%
of GDP

20%

15%

10%

5%

HISTORICAL BALANCE

FUTURE BALANCE
ACCORDING TO
GAO PROJECTIONS

PERCENT
OF
GDP

0%

1950   1960   1970   1980   1990   2000   2010

FISCAL YEAR

(5.6) FEDERAL DEFICITS (+) OR SURPLUSES (-)
AS A PERCENT OF GDP, HISTORY AND PROJECTIONS, FISCAL YEARS 1950 TO 2020
NOTE: PROJECTIONS BY THE U.S. GENERAL ACCOUNTING OFFICE; THEY ASSUME
NO CHANGE IN CURRENT POLICY. SOURCE: OMB (1993); GAO (1992)

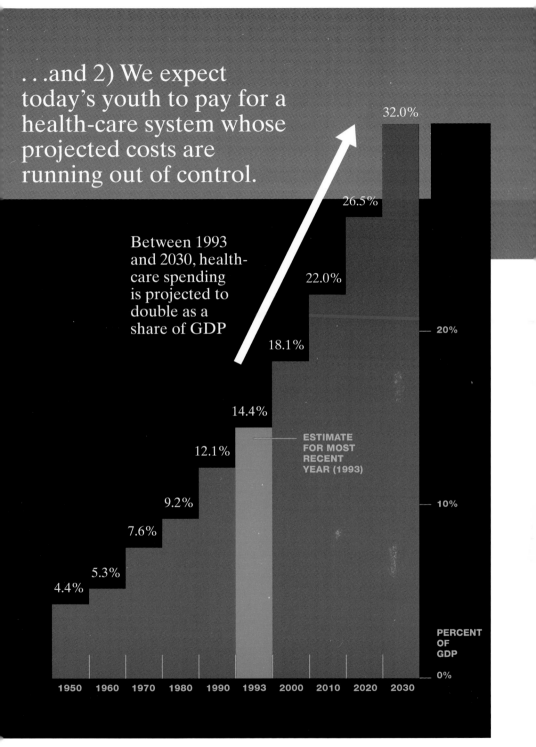

...and 2) We expect today's youth to pay for a health-care system whose projected costs are running out of control.

Between 1993 and 2030, health-care spending is projected to double as a share of GDP

32.0%

26.5%

22.0%

18.1%

14.4%

ESTIMATE FOR MOST RECENT YEAR (1993)

12.1%

9.2%

7.6%

5.3%

4.4%

20%

10%

PERCENT OF GDP

0%

1950 1960 1970 1980 1990 1993 2000 2010 2020 2030

(5.7) U.S. NATIONAL HEALTH-CARE SPENDING
AS A PERCENT OF GDP, HISTORY AND PROJECTIONS, 1950 TO 2030
NOTE: PROJECTIONS BY THE U.S. HEALTH CARE FINANCING ADMINISTRATION;
THEY ASSUME NO CHANGE IN CURRENT POLICY. SOURCE: HCFA (1993)

Later in life, we are asking today's young to cope with the extra retirement costs of longer lifespans, . . .

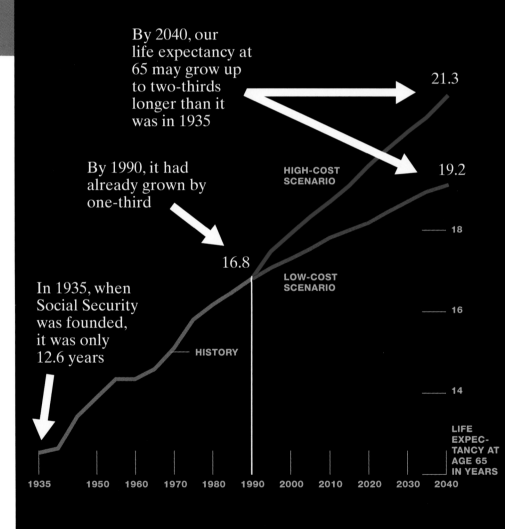

By 2040, our life expectancy at 65 may grow up to two-thirds longer than it was in 1935

21.3

19.2

By 1990, it had already grown by one-third

HIGH-COST SCENARIO

18

16.8

LOW-COST SCENARIO

In 1935, when Social Security was founded, it was only 12.6 years

HISTORY

16

14

LIFE EXPEC-TANCY AT AGE 65 IN YEARS

1935 1950 1960 1970 1980 1990 2000 2010 2020 2030 2040

(5.8) EXPECTED YEARS OF REMAINING LIFE AT AGE 65

HISTORY AND FUTURE PROJECTIONS, 1935 TO 2040

NOTE: AVERAGES FOR MALES AND FEMALES; PROJECTIONS BY THE TRUSTEES OF THE SOCIAL SECURITY AND MEDICARE TRUST FUNDS; THE "LOW-COST" SCENARIO IS THE OFFICIAL BASELINE DEMOGRAPHIC AND ECONOMIC SCENARIO "II"; THE "HIGH-COST" SCENARIO IS THE OFFICIAL SCENARIO "III"; THE PROJECTIONS ASSUME NO CHANGE IN CURRENT POLICY. SOURCE: OASDHI (1992)

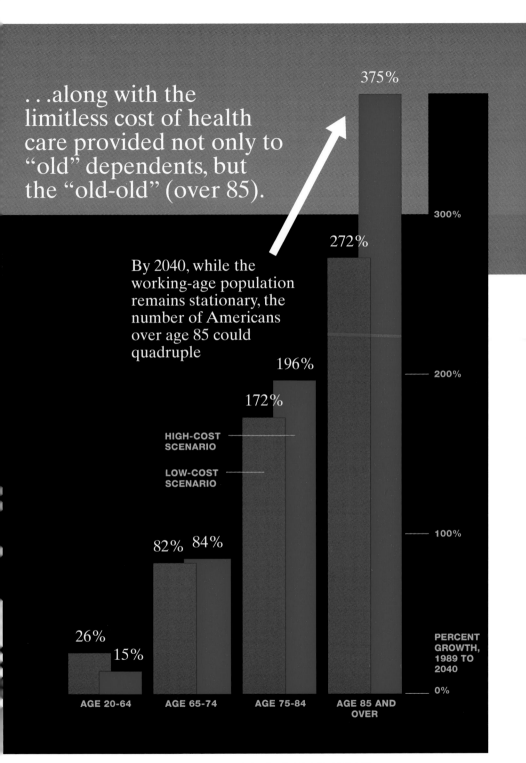

...along with the limitless cost of health care provided not only to "old" dependents, but the "old-old" (over 85).

By 2040, while the working-age population remains stationary, the number of Americans over age 85 could quadruple

HIGH-COST SCENARIO

LOW-COST SCENARIO

375%

272%

196%

172%

82% 84%

26%

15%

AGE 20-64   AGE 65-74   AGE 75-84   AGE 85 AND OVER

300%

200%

100%

PERCENT GROWTH, 1989 TO 2040

0%

(5.9) PERCENTAGE GROWTH IN U.S. POPULATION
BY AGE BRACKET, HISTORY AND PROJECTIONS, 1989 to 2040
NOTE: SEE CHART 5.8. SOURCE: OASDHI (1992)

The "aging of America": ultimately it will mean that a growing number of Social Security and Medicare recipients must be supported by each worker's paycheck, . . .

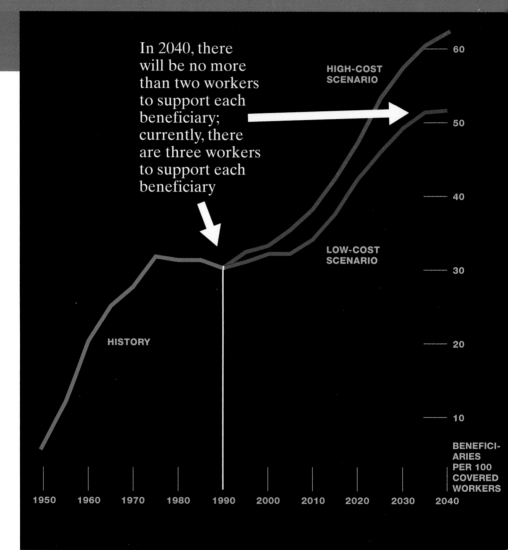

In 2040, there will be no more than two workers to support each beneficiary; currently, there are three workers to support each beneficiary

HIGH-COST SCENARIO

LOW-COST SCENARIO

HISTORY

60

50

40

30

20

10

BENEFICI-
ARIES
PER 100
COVERED
WORKERS

1950 1960 1970 1980 1990 2000 2010 2020 2030 2040

(5.10) SOCIAL SECURITY BENEFICIARIES PER 100 WORKERS
HISTORY AND PROJECTIONS, 1950 TO 2040
NOTE: SEE CHART 5.8. SOURCE: OASDHI (1992)

...and—unless current policy is reformed—it could cost future workers over half of their payroll in taxes.

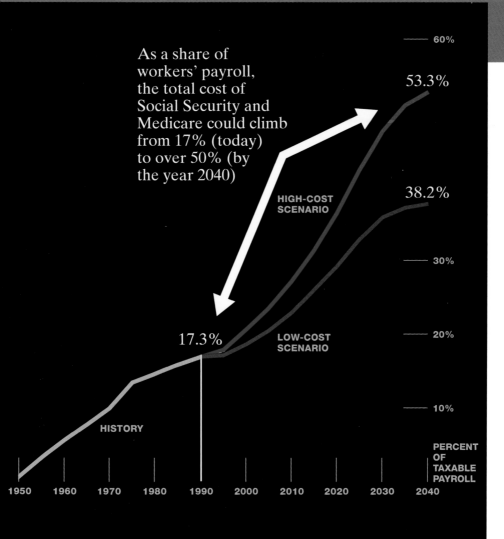

As a share of workers' payroll, the total cost of Social Security and Medicare could climb from 17% (today) to over 50% (by the year 2040)

HIGH-COST SCENARIO

LOW-COST SCENARIO

HISTORY

60%

53.3%

38.2%

30%

20%

17.3%

10%

PERCENT OF TAXABLE PAYROLL

1950 1960 1970 1980 1990 2000 2010 2020 2030 2040

(5.11) TOTAL SOCIAL SECURITY AND MEDICARE BENEFITS
AS A PERCENT OF THE TAXABLE PAYROLL OF ALL COVERED WORKERS, HISTORY AND PROJECTIONS, 1950 TO 2040
NOTE: INCLUDES BOTH PARTS "A" AND "B" OF MEDICARE; SEE CHART 5.8
SOURCE: OASDHI (1992)

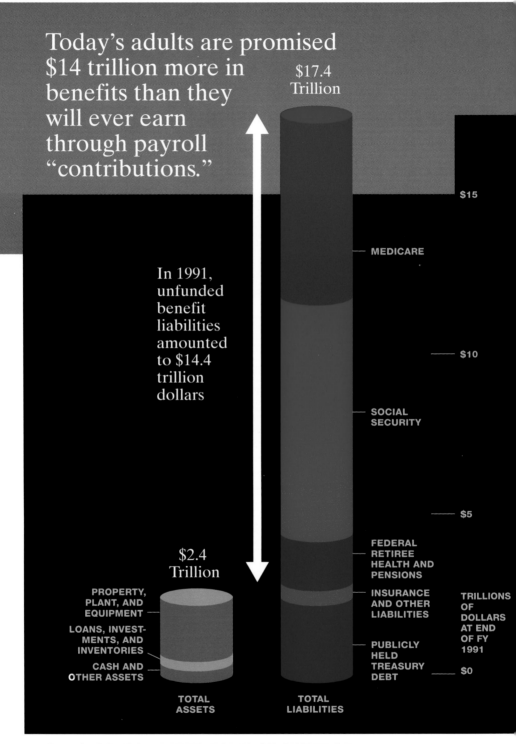

Today's adults are promised $14 trillion more in benefits than they will ever earn through payroll "contributions."

$17.4 Trillion

$15

MEDICARE

In 1991, unfunded benefit liabilities amounted to $14.4 trillion dollars

$10

SOCIAL SECURITY

$5

FEDERAL RETIREE HEALTH AND PENSIONS

$2.4 Trillion

INSURANCE AND OTHER LIABILITIES

TRILLIONS OF DOLLARS AT END OF FY 1991

PROPERTY, PLANT, AND EQUIPMENT

LOANS, INVEST-MENTS, AND INVENTORIES

CASH AND OTHER ASSETS

PUBLICLY HELD TREASURY DEBT

$0

TOTAL ASSETS

TOTAL LIABILITIES

(5.12) CONSOLIDATED BALANCE SHEET OF THE FEDERAL GOVERNMENT

TOTAL ASSETS AND LIABILITIES AT THE END OF FISCAL YEAR 1991

SOURCE: OMB (1993); ROBERTSON (1992)

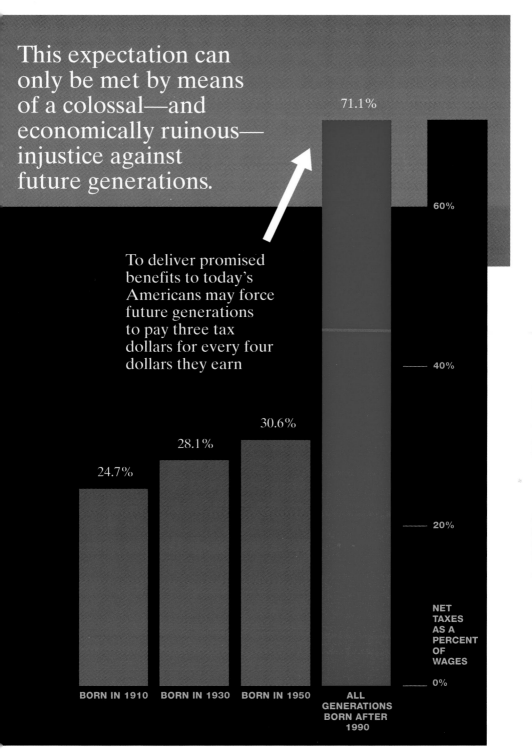

This expectation can only be met by means of a colossal—and economically ruinous—injustice against future generations.

To deliver promised benefits to today's Americans may force future generations to pay three tax dollars for every four dollars they earn

71.1%

60%

40%

30.6%

28.1%

24.7%

20%

NET TAXES AS A PERCENT OF WAGES

0%

BORN IN 1910 **BORN IN 1930** **BORN IN 1950** **ALL GENERATIONS BORN AFTER 1990**

(5.13) AVERAGE LIFETIME NET TAXES
ALL TAXES PAID LESS ALL PERSONAL BENEFITS RECEIVED,
AS A PERCENT OF WAGES, ASSUMING NO CHANGE IN
TAX OR BENEFIT POLICY FOR ANYONE BORN THROUGH 1990
NOTE: TAXES AND BENEFITS FOR ALL LEVELS OF GOVERNMENT; "WAGES" REFERS
TO ALL LABOR INCOME; EACH RATE IS EXPRESSED AS A RATIO OF
PRESENT VALUES AT BIRTH. SOURCE: OMB (1993); KOTLIKOFF (1992)

SOURCES

ABF: AMERICAN BAR FOUNDATION
BAUMOL, BLACKMAN, AND WOLFF (1989):
WILLIAM J. BAUMOL, SUE ANNE BATEY
BLACKMAN, AND EDWARD N. WOLFF,
PRODUCTIVITY AND AMERICAN LEADERSHIP
(MIT PRESS, 1989)
BEA: BUREAU OF ECONOMIC ANALYSIS,
U.S. DEPARTMENT OF COMMERCE
BG: THE BLACKSTONE GROUP
BLS: BUREAU OF LABOR STATISTICS,
U.S. DEPARTMENT OF LABOR
CAEP: CENTER FOR THE ASSESSMENT OF
EDUCATIONAL PROGRESS
CBO: CONGRESSIONAL BUDGET OFFICE,
U.S. CONGRESS
CDF: CHILDREN'S DEFENSE FUND
CED: COMMITTEE FOR ECONOMIC
DEVELOPMENT
CENSUS: BUREAU OF THE CENSUS, U.S.
DEPARTMENT OF COMMERCE
COMMERCE: U.S. DEPARTMENT OF COMMERCE
CQ: CONGRESSIONAL QUARTERLY, INC.
EAEH: GLENN PORTER (ED.), *ENCYCLOPEDIA OF
AMERICAN ECONOMIC HISTORY* (1980)
EIA: ENERGY INFORMATION ADMINISTRATION,
U.S. DEPARTMENT OF ENERGY
FED: BOARD OF GOVERNORS OF THE FEDERAL
RESERVE SYSTEM
HCFA: HEALTH CARE FINANCING
ADMINISTRATION, U.S. DEPARTMENT OF HEALTH
AND HUMAN SERVICES
IEA: INTERNATIONAL ASSOCIATION FOR THE
EVALUATION OF EDUCATIONAL ACHIEVEMENT
IFR: INTERNATIONAL FEDERATION OF ROBOTICS
JCHS: JOINT CENTER FOR HOUSING STUDIES OF
HARVARD UNIVERSITY
KODAIRA (1987): SACHIKO IMAIZUMI KODAIRA,
"TELEVISION'S ROLE IN EARLY CHILDHOOD
EDUCATION IN JAPAN" (NHK BROADCASTING
CULTURE RESEARCH INSTITUTE, 1987)
KOTLIKOFF (1992): LAURENCE J. KOTLIKOFF,
GENERATIONAL ACCOUNTING
(FREE PRESS, 1992)
LEVY AND MICHEL (1991): FRANK LEVY AND
RICHARD C. MICHEL, *THE ECONOMIC FUTURE OF
AMERICAN FAMILIES* (URBAN INSTITUTE, 1991)
NCES: NATIONAL CENTER FOR EDUCATION
STATISTICS, OFFICE OF EDUCATIONAL RESEARCH
AND IMPROVEMENT, U.S. DEPARTMENT OF
EDUCATION
NGA: NATIONAL GOVERNORS ASSOCIATIONS
NIELSEN: A.C. NIELSEN COMPANY
NSB: NATIONAL SCIENCE BOARD, U.S. NATIONAL
SCIENCE FOUNDATION
NTPA: *DIRECTORY OF NATIONAL TRADE AND
PROFESSIONAL ASSOCIATIONS* (COLUMBIA
BOOKS, 1993)
NTUF: NATIONAL TAXPAYERS UNION FOUNDATION
OASDHI: BOARDS OF TRUSTEES OF THE FEDERAL
OLD-AGE AND SURVIVORS INSURANCE AND
DISABILITY INSURANCE TRUST FUND, AND OF THE
FEDERAL HOSPITAL INSURANCE TRUST FUND
OECD: ORGANIZATION FOR ECONOMIC CO-
OPERATION AND DEVELOPMENT
OMB: OFFICE OF MANAGEMENT AND BUDGET,
EXECUTIVE OFFICE OF THE PRESIDENT
PRESTON AND KONO (1988): SAMUEL H.
PRESTON AND SHIGEMI KONO, "TRENDS IN
WELL-BEING OF CHILDREN AND THE ELDERLY
IN JAPAN," IN JOHN L. PALMER AND ISABEL V.
SAWHILL (EDS.), *THE VULNERABLE* (URBAN
INSTITUTE, 1988)
ROBERTSON (1992): A. HAEWORTH
ROBERTSON, *SOCIAL SECURITY: WHAT EVERY
TAXPAYER SHOULD KNOW* (RETIREMENT POLICY
INSTITUTE, 1992)
SHAPIRO (1992): ANDREW L. SHAPIRO, *WE'RE
NUMBER ONE* (VINTAGE, 1992)
SMEEDING (1992): TIMOTHY SMEEDING,
"WHY THE U.S. ANTIPOVERTY SYSTEM DOESN'T
WORK VERY WELL" (*CHALLENGE,* JAN-FEB 1992)
UN: UNITED NATIONS
UNICEF: UNITED NATIONS CHILDREN'S FUND
WAYS AND MEANS: COMMITTEE ON WAYS AND
MEANS, U.S. HOUSE OF REPRESENTATIVES
WHITE (1987): MERRY WHITE, *THE JAPANESE
EDUCATIONAL CHALLENGE* (MACMILLAN, 1987)
WHO: WORLD HEALTH ORGANIZATION

Budget Savings
and the Cost of Tax and
Benefit Changes
under the Peterson Budget
Action Plan:
Summary Tables

Table 1
Peterson Action Plan Savings by Budget Area[1]
(Billions of Dollars, FY 1994 - 2004)

	1994	1995	1996	1997	1998	1999	2000	2001	2002	2003	2004
TOTAL BUDGET SAVINGS	9.0	88.4	174.2	251.5	325.3	400.4	483.3	546.2	615.7	694.9	788.2
FOREIGN POLICY: TOTAL	8.3	7.5	22.4	46.2	49.8	51.4	52.5	54.3	55.6	57.5	59.5
(1) Defense Outlay Cuts	8.3	7.5	22.4	46.2	49.8	51.4	52.5	54.3	55.6	57.5	59.5
DOMESTIC DISCRETIONARY: TOTAL	0.0	(8.6)	(17.1)	(25.7)	(34.3)	(42.9)	(51.4)	(54.1)	(57.1)	(60.1)	(63.2)
(2) 10% Real Cut in Current Budget	0.0	5.6	11.3	16.9	22.6	28.2	33.8	34.8	35.7	36.7	37.6
(3) New Investment Spending	0.0	(14.2)	(28.4)	(42.6)	(56.8)	(71.1)	(85.3)	(88.9)	(92.8)	(96.7)	(100.8)
ENTITLEMENTS: TOTAL	0.4	(4.3)	18.4	42.0	77.4	114.5	155.2	178.7	206.7	239.7	280.5
Entitlements: Across the Board											
(4) Comprehensive "Affluence Test": Total	0.0	11.8	23.7	35.5	47.4	59.2	71.1	75.7	80.7	86.1	93.0
Social Security	0.0	5.6	11.1	16.7	22.2	27.8	33.3	34.9	36.4	38.1	40.9
Medicare	0.0	3.8	7.5	11.3	15.1	18.8	22.6	25.0	27.8	30.9	34.3
Federal Pensions	0.0	1.9	3.9	5.8	7.8	9.7	11.6	12.2	12.7	13.3	13.8
Other Benefits	0.0	0.6	1.2	1.8	2.3	2.9	3.5	3.6	3.7	3.8	3.9
(5) Taxation of Benefits: Total	0.0	3.7	7.5	11.6	15.9	20.5	25.4	26.7	28.2	30.0	32.8
85% of Social Security	0.0	2.5	5.0	7.8	10.7	13.7	16.9	17.6	18.4	19.1	20.5
25% of Medicare	0.0	0.6	1.3	2.0	2.8	3.8	4.9	5.3	5.8	6.2	6.8
100% of Other Benefits	0.0	0.6	1.2	1.8	2.4	3.0	3.6	3.8	4.1	4.6	5.5
(6) Expanded EITC	0.0	(5.7)	(6.0)	(6.2)	(6.5)	(6.8)	(7.0)	(7.3)	(7.7)	(8.0)	(8.3)

[1] All projected savings are relative to January 1993 CBO baseline.

Table 1 (Con't)
Peterson Action Plan Savings by Budget Area
(Billions of Dollars, FY 1994 - 2004)

	1994	1995	1996	1997	1998	1999	2000	2001	2002	2003	2004
Entitlements: Retirement											
(7) Rise in Social Security Retirement Age	0.0	2.2	4.5	6.8	9.6	12.6	16.0	20.0	24.6	29.5	35.6
(8) Federal Pension Reform	0.0	0.5	1.1	1.8	2.4	3.1	3.7	4.3	4.8	5.3	5.7
(9) Expansion of SSI to Poverty Level	0.0	(15.6)	(16.7)	(17.9)	(18.7)	(19.4)	(20.2)	(21.1)	(22.0)	(22.9)	(23.9)
(10) Repeal of Social Security Earnings Test	0.0	(5.2)	(5.1)	(5.0)	(4.9)	(4.8)	(4.7)	(4.6)	(4.5)	(4.4)	(4.4)
Entitlements: Health Care											
(11) Taxation of Employer-Paid Health Insurance	0.0	3.0	7.5	13.9	22.5	30.7	40.0	43.5	47.2	51.2	55.5
(12) Reform of SMI (Medicare, Part B)	0.0	4.7	9.5	14.2	18.9	23.7	28.4	31.4	34.8	38.6	42.8
(13) CBO Plan for Universal Health Coverage	0.0	(7.6)	(16.6)	(26.9)	(30.1)	(33.4)	(36.8)	(40.6)	(44.6)	(48.6)	(53.0)
(14) Health-Care Cost Control Program	0.0	0.6	2.2	4.8	8.7	14.3	21.8	31.9	45.1	61.5	82.0
Entitlements: Other											
(15) Limitation of Home Mortgage Tax Deduction	0.0	1.0	2.1	3.1	4.2	5.2	6.3	7.1	7.9	8.7	9.5
(16) Reduction in Farm Deficiency Payments	0.0	0.7	1.5	2.2	2.9	3.7	4.4	4.6	4.8	5.0	5.2
(17) Expansion of User Fees	0.4	1.4	3.1	4.1	5.0	5.9	6.8	7.1	7.4	7.7	8.1

Table 1 (Con't)
Peterson Action Plan Savings by Budget Area
(Billions of Dollars, FY 1994 - 2004)

	1994	1995	1996	1997	1998	1999	2000	2001	2002	2003	2004
GENERAL REVENUES: TOTAL	0.0	84.3	126.1	144.4	162.8	178.9	194.9	204.2	212.7	221.1	229.9
General Revenues: Higher Rates/New Taxes											
(18) Higher Marginal Tax Rates: Total	0.0	27.9	29.3	30.7	32.0	33.3	34.7	36.1	37.7	39.3	41.0
Individual Income Tax Rates	0.0	22.6	23.8	24.9	26.0	27.1	28.2	29.3	30.7	31.9	33.3
Corporate Tax Rates	0.0	5.2	5.5	5.7	6.0	6.3	6.5	6.8	7.1	7.4	7.7
(19) 5% Consumption Tax	0.0	53.6	84.2	90.6	97.2	101.3	105.3	109.7	114.6	119.4	124.5
(20) 50 Cents per Gallon Gasoline Tax	0.0	7.9	15.8	23.7	31.6	39.4	47.3	50.7	52.9	55.1	57.5
(21) Higher Federal "Sin" Taxes: Total	0.0	3.6	7.2	10.8	14.4	18.1	21.7	22.5	23.2	23.9	24.6
Excise Tax on Cigarettes	0.0	2.1	4.1	6.2	8.2	10.3	12.3	12.7	13.0	13.4	13.7
Excise Tax on Alcohol	0.0	0.8	1.7	2.5	3.4	4.2	5.1	5.4	5.6	5.7	5.9
50% Business Meals & Entertainment	0.0	0.7	1.4	2.1	2.8	3.5	4.2	4.4	4.6	4.8	5.0
General Revenues: Investment Incentives											
(22) Permanent R&D Tax Credit	0.0	(4.6)	(4.8)	(5.0)	(5.2)	(5.5)	(5.7)	(5.9)	(6.2)	(6.4)	(6.7)
(23) Worker Training Incentives	0.0	(5.1)	(5.5)	(6.1)	(6.7)	(6.9)	(7.2)	(7.5)	(7.8)	(8.2)	(8.5)
(24) Indexation of Capital Gains	0.0	1.0	0.0	(0.2)	(0.5)	(0.8)	(1.1)	(1.4)	(1.7)	(2.1)	(2.4)
NET INTEREST SAVINGS	0.3	9.5	24.4	44.5	69.5	98.5	132.0	163.1	197.8	236.7	281.5

Table 2
Federal Spending as a Share of GDP by Budget Area
(CBO Baseline and Peterson Action Plan Budgets, FY 1994, 2000, 2004)

	1994		2000		2004	
	Baseline	Action Plan	Baseline	Action Plan	Baseline	Action Plan
TOTAL OUTLAYS	23.1%	22.9%	24.1%	21.4%	26.0%	21.3%
Foreign Policy	4.7%	4.6%	4.0%	3.4%	3.8%	3.2%
Defense Discretionary	4.4%	4.3%	3.7%	3.1%	3.5%	2.9%
International Discretionary	0.3%	0.3%	0.3%	0.3%	0.3%	0.3%
Domestic Discretionary[1]	3.6%	3.6%	3.2%	3.8%	3.0%	3.6%
Mandatory Spending	12.5%	12.5%	14.0%	12.9%	15.5%	13.6%
Social Security	4.9%	4.9%	4.9%	4.5%	5.0%	4.4%
Medicare	2.6%	2.6%	3.7%	2.8%	4.8%	3.3%
Medicaid	1.4%	1.4%	2.1%	2.4%	2.6%	2.7%
Federal Pensions	1.1%	1.1%	1.1%	1.0%	1.2%	1.0%
All Other	2.5%	2.5%	2.1%	2.2%	2.0%	2.1%
All Other	-1.0%	-1.0%	-1.1%	-1.1%	-1.1%	-1.1%
Net Interest	3.2%	3.2%	4.0%	2.4%	4.7%	2.0%
TOTAL REVENUES	18.7%	18.7%	18.7%	21.8%	18.6%	21.8%
SURPLUS/DEFICIT	-4.4%	-4.3%	-5.4%	0.3%	-7.4%	0.5%
DEBT HELD BY PUBLIC	55.5%	55.4%	67.2%	46.9%	81.6%	38.1%

[1] Action Plan projection includes 1% of GDP in new investment spending.

Table 3
The Cost to Families
of Fully Phased-in Tax and Benefit Changes[1]
in the Peterson Action Plan
by Income Group
(At 1993 Income Level)

Income Group	Total Tax and Benefit Changes ($ Million)	Average Change per Family ($ Actual)	Tax and Benefit Changes as a Percent of Total Family Income	Percentage of Plan Savings Borne by Income Group	Percentage of Families in Income Group
**** - $10,000	($16,199)[2]	($734)[2]	-25.6%[2]	-8.3%[2]	19.9%
$10,000 - $20,000	$3,246	$231	1.5%	1.7%	12.7%
$20,000 - $30,000	$21,640	$1,278	5.1%	11.0%	15.3%
$30,000 - $40,000	$26,005	$1,817	5.2%	13.3%	12.9%
$40,000 - $50,000	$26,421	$2,278	5.1%	13.5%	10.4%
$50,000 - $75,000	$50,554	$2,776	4.5%	25.8%	16.4%
$75,000 - $100,000	$27,015	$3,723	4.2%	13.8%	6.5%
$100,000 - $200,000	$30,336	$5,608	4.1%	15.5%	4.9%
$200,000 & Over	$27,103	$23,294	4.7%	13.8%	1.0%
Total	$196,121	$1,766	4.1%	100.0%	100.0%

[1] Includes all changes that could be modeled; see technical note on following page.
[2] Negative numbers [- or ( )] mean a gain in net benefits.

TECHNICAL NOTE

The tax and benefit changes summarized in Table 3[1] include computer simulations of the following components of the Peterson Action Plan: (1) the affluence test (Social Security, Medicare, and federal pensions only); (2) benefit taxation (85 percent of Social Security and 25 percent of the insurance value of Medicare remaining after the affluence test); (3) the expanded Earned Income Tax Credit; (4) taxation of employer-paid health insurance in excess of the plan's caps for family and individual coverage; (5) the cap on the home-mortgage interest deduction at $20,000 for couples and $12,000 for individuals; (6) President Clinton's proposed higher marginal tax rates, including the 36 percent top marginal rate and the 10 percent surcharge on taxable income in excess of $250,000; (7) the 5 percent federal retail sales tax (exempting food, housing, and education); (8) the 50-cents-per-gallon gasoline tax; and (9) the increase in the federal cigarette excise tax to $1 per pack and the increase in alcohol excise taxes to $16 per proof gallon. Estimates of the plan's SSI and Medicaid benefit increases were added to the simulation results.

Income is adjusted gross income (as defined by the Internal Revenue Code), less business losses, plus: tax-exempt interest; the nontaxable portion of Social Security benefits; the insurance value of Medicare; employer contributions for health and life insurance plans; the employer portion of Social Security payroll taxes; and tax preferences subject to the alternative minimum tax.

---

[1] Prepared by Pete Davis from computer simulations run by The Policy Economics Group, KPMG Peat Marwick, Washington, D.C.

Index

Clinton, Bill (*cont.*)
first State of the Union address of,
20
as forsaking good economics for
good politics, 37–40
on gasoline taxes, 163
on health-care costs, 23–24, 116,
117–18, 144–145, 282
marginal income tax proposal of,
32, 291–92
Miyazawa meeting with, 194
next steps of, toward balancing
the budget, 258–59
rich used as scapegoat for budget
problems by, 30, 32, 36–37
Clinton, Hillary Rodham, 24, 117,
157
Clinton administration:
COLA reform and, 90
defense budget of, 206
Earned Income Tax Credit under,
254
foreign vs. economic policy focus
of, 197
investment agenda of, 23, 255
National Economic Council of,
189–90, 202
tax hikes and, 20–21, 32, 250–51,
291–92, 294–95
tax revenue projections of, 291–92
Clinton budget, 21–24
consumption relabeled as investment in, 23
defense cuts in, 267–68
expectations about, 21–22
honesty of, 256
"investment" concept in, 23
middle class as defined in, 26, 30
Social Security taxation in,
276–77
tax avoidance and revenue projections of, 32, 291–92
Clinton economic policy:
balanced budgets lacking in,
37–39
release of, 20
timing of spending cuts in, 22
trap in, 36–40
Clintonomics, 21
Cohen, Wilbur, 78

COLAs (cost-of-living adjustments),
82–85
cap on, 89
cutting of, 280
"diet," 252, 272–73
freezes of, 272–73
special interest groups and reform
of, 90
Cold War:
economic policy in, 188–90
economic war vs., 60–61
instability in Middle East and,
167–68
military spending and, 97
peace dividends of, 84*n*, 267
see also post-Cold War era
college enrollment, in post-World
War II period, 51
commercial television, 75
Committee for a Responsible Federal Budget, 142
Committee for Economic Development (CED), 58, 148, 200, 271
Committee on Economic Security,
258
commodity price supports, federal,
26, 112, 113, 289–90
Community Health Purchasing Alliances, 146
competitiveness, monitoring of, 188–
189, 317
Competitiveness Policy Council
(CPC), 54
Concord Coalition, 38, 242, 257,
316
on "affluence test" methodology,
274*n*
purpose of, 40–43
Congress, U.S.:
on Clinton budget "investments,"
23
mixed incentives of, 43
publicly paid staffers in, 80
Congressional Budget Office, 38,
105, 118, 285
baseline deficit projections of, 22,
261–62, 265–66, 271–72, 300–
303
congressional districts, political patronage to, 23

406